# THE
# SECRET WAR
# WITH IRAN

The 30-Year Clandestine Struggle Against
the World's Most Dangerous Terrorist Power

## Ronen Bergman

Translated by Ronnie Hope

FREE PRESS
New York   London   Toronto   Sydney

FREE PRESS
A Division of Simon & Schuster, Inc.
1230 Avenue of the Americas
New York, NY 10020

First Free Press hardcover edition September 2008

FREE PRESS and colophon are trademarks of Simon & Schuster, Inc.

For information about special discounts for bulk purchases,
please contact Simon & Schuster Special Sales at 1-800-456-6798
or business@simonandschuster.com

DESIGNED BY ERICH HOBBING

Manufactured in the United States of America

1   3   5   7   9   10   8   6   4   2

Library of Congress Cataloging-in-Publication Data
Bergman, Ronen.
The secret war with Iran: the 30-year clandestine struggle against the world's
most dangerous terrorist power / Ronen Bergman.
p.  cm.
1. Iran—Foreign relations—20th century.   2. Iran—Foreign relations—21st century.
3. Iran—Military relations.   I. Title.
DS274.B47  2008
955.05'4—dc22
2008013640

ISBN-13: 978-1-4165-5839-2
ISBN-10:     1-4165-5839-X

*For my father,*
*Shmuel Bergman:*
*He sets the standards*
*for kindness, honesty, and devotion.*

# CONTENTS

PART IV

THE SECOND COMING OF HIZBALLAH

237

PART V

THE FIRST SHI'ITE BOMB

299

# PREFACE

George W. Bush famously described Iran as part of the "axis of evil," while Iranian leaders regularly refer to the United States as the "Great Satan." But presidential rhetoric in Washington and Tehran aside, the Iranian clerical regime (and not the Iranian People) is unquestionably an enemy of the United States. Consider: Iran has chemical weapons and an active nuclear weapons program. It is a sponsor of international terrorism. It is dedicated to spreading a brand of Islamic revolution that is virulently anti-Western. In short, many of the concerns that were cited—and disputed—as grounds for invading Iraq are indisputably true of Iran.

True, Iran has not launched full-scale invasions against its neighbors, as Saddam Hussein did against both Iran and Kuwait. Instead, it has been skillful in conducting its military adventures so as to avoid the wrath of the West. For the past twenty years Iran has masterfully used Hizballah as a proxy, maintaining a veneer of deniability. It has sponsored terrorists, working closely with al-Qaeda prior to 9/11, after which point it became expedient to maintain some distance from that network. And while the world had become obsessed with Osama bin Laden and his lieutenants, it forgot that the most dangerous of all terrorists before the advent of al-Qaeda, a Lebanese Shi'ite by the name of Imad Moughniyeh, who was responsible for the death and kidnapping of the biggest number of Americans until 9/11, was alive and well and a frequent welcome visitor to Tehran, until he was blown up by a car bomb in Damascus early in 2008.

The Iranian threat is a top priority of the U.S. defense and foreign policy establishment. This threat has appeared particularly urgent ever since Western intelligence agencies—the CIA and the Mossad, as well as MI6, the French DGSE, and the German intelligence service—suddenly realized in 2002 that despite their concerted and often coordinated efforts to track the development of Iran's nuclear program, and

their overall assessment that Iran's nuclear ambitions were being successfully contained, the Iranians had been able to fool them. Their nuclear
program has advanced to the point where production of an Iranian
nuclear bomb is now probably no more than a few years away.

This unsettling discovery raises a fundamental question: What exactly
are Iran's nuclear ambitions? When the day dawns—as it may well soon
do—and Iran is in possession of a nuclear bomb, what will it use it for?
According to a CNN/USA Today/Gallup Poll from 2006, over 80 percent of Americans believe that Iran would supply nuclear weapons to
terrorists to be used against the United States. Many in the U.S. defense
establishment agree. Indeed, the Pentagon and the CIA, in close cooperation with Israel's Mossad and the Israeli air force, are drawing up plans
to deliver a knockout blow to Iran's nuclear installations before any
weapons are produced. However, it is also possible—some would say
probable—that the main purpose for which Iran wants nuclear weapons
is to deter the United States from doing to Iran what it has done to
Saddam Hussein.

What is clear today is that any decision to strike Iran from a
distance—much less invade it—can only be made against the background of the bitter experience in Iraq. America went to war against one
man, Saddam, and defeated him, only to become mired in the quicksand
of the complex and intractable tribal and religious conflicts of an entire
country. If there is one thing that everyone agrees on, it is that drawing lessons from the military imbroglio in Iraq is imperative. And the
most important of these lessons is that there is no substitute for high-
quality intelligence. Know thy enemy, both his strengths and his weaknesses. Even if the startling and disputed announcement in the U.S.
National Intelligence Estimates in 2007 that Iran had halted its nuclear
weapons project in 2003 was correct, it is clear to all that Iran could easily pick up where it left off, using the enriched uranium that it admits it
is producing.

The problem is that after three decades of trying to meet the Iranian
challenge with a variety of strategies—covert negotiations, arms deals,
critical dialogue, containment, direct political confrontation, and indirect action against its proxies—we still do not understand Iran. We do
not know what its leaders want to do, and we do not know how to stop
them from doing it.

Or, at least, we do not know enough. The West, most notably the

United States and Israel, has maintained for three decades an effort to gather, analyze, share, and act upon covert intelligence on Iran. This book follows the drama of this secret intelligence struggle against Iran. At its heart are the two most concerned countries: Israel and the United States. Both have played a complex role, each trying to compensate for the other's disadvantages, as they cooperate in intelligence gathering and in operations. There have been many failures, and some successes, too. This book brings these fascinating and sobering stories to light, in order to contribute to the understanding of a regime that is a far greater danger to the West than Saddam Hussein's Iraq ever was.

The story ventures along the secret paths inside the intelligence communities of both countries, while describing in detail many Mossad operations. The United States relies on Israel's intelligence agencies for much of its Middle Eastern intelligence collection. Israeli successes are immediately shared with the United States and Israeli failure means American blindness. In many instances, Israel and its battles have served as testing grounds for American weapons and for combat tactics developed in the United States.

This book is based on thousands of documents, and some three hundred interviews with pertinent people in twenty countries, the names of two hundred of whom appear in the Bibliography. Unless cited specifically in the text, all interviews quoted were conducted by the author. A detailed survey of Iran's part in international terror requires the use of intelligence material gathered by Israel, the United States, France, the United Kingdom, and Germany. Research on such a subject is highly complex. Many sources are necessarily anonymous. Disinformation and simple errors have often crept into journalists' reports on Iran. I have made every attempt to verify and cross-check the information here, yet it is not always possible to be certain of every detail; intelligence sources have their own agendas. Whenever accounts differ, I have tried to say so.

Ultimately, however, an abundance of corroborated testimonies and independent sources leaves no room for doubt as to the general trends: Iran consistently supports terrorist operations against a wide and ambitious variety of targets. And Iran is consistently trying to acquire nuclear weapons.

Here, then, is a view of the greatest security challenge the United States is facing.

# PART I

# GREEN STORM RISING

# CHAPTER 1

# The Twilight
# of the Iranian Monarchy

At least one immediate lesson was learned from the catastrophe that befell the CIA in Tehran with the collapse of the rule of the Shah: Shred your secret documents both vertically and horizontally.

On November 4, 1979, nine months after Ayatollah Ruhollah Khomeini overthrew the Iranian monarchy, a group of students decided to stage a demonstration in front of the U.S. Embassy in Tehran. The angry crowd soon found that they could enter through the gate without resistance. They poured into the compound and seized dozens of embassy staff: the start of America's worst hostage crisis, which lasted 444 days, and helped destroy the presidency of Jimmy Carter. Among the protestors was one particularly militant young man by the name of Mahmoud Ahmadinejad. Some of the American diplomats would later testify that he was one of their jailers and maltreated them in a particularly brutal way.

The hostage takers, who called themselves "Muslim student followers of Imam's line," discovered a treasure trove of intelligence inside the embassy.

Just over a year earlier, as tension in Iran began to mount, the CIA's representatives in Tehran had decided to ship a large part of their classified documents out of the country, just in case. The documents were packed into crates and flown to the United States—only to be returned to the embassy two months later. The staff found it too difficult to work without an archive, and besides, in an emergency, the classified material could always be shredded.

As the student revolutionaries entered the embassy grounds, CIA station personnel began urgently feeding the secret papers into shredding machines. Most of the material was shredded into thin strips. The stu-

dents, some of whom were soon to be among the founders of the intelligence services of the Islamic Republic, found only a small number of
documents intact. But the CIA had not taken into account the determination of the revolutionaries.

Some 250 female students were given a painstaking job. First they
combed the embassy compound garbage bins and retrieved the shreds.
Then they set about sorting them and putting them back together. The
task took two years of meticulous labor. Today, as a consequence of
their success, high-security shredders use spiral-toothed blades which
leave only tiny scraps that crumble in one's hands.

The students had recovered a treasure trove of top-secret information
on all the aspects of Iranian-American relations. The reconstructions of
those documents were released in book form in limited editions. Some
were even put on sale in bookshops in Europe.

By June 1985, sixty-one volumes of selected documents had been
published. They provided priceless insights into the intelligence methods and diplomatic activity used by the United States and Israel in
Iran.

They were also highly embarrassing to the old Iranian regime. The
CIA's five thousand paid informers encompassed government officials
and officers in the military of all ranks, including at senior levels. The
restored documents led to purges by the Revolutionary Guards of the
bureaucracy, the media, and the armed forces, and to executions of top
personages who had collaborated with the CIA. They revealed the extent
to which the United States was involved in Iran's internal affairs, with the
connivance of the Shah, who owed his hold on power to American
intelligence.

In 1953, the Shah was forced to go into exile, after the liberal Mohammad Mossadegh practically took over the government. In August of the
same year, Naamtallah Nasiri, a young captain in the Iranian army,
approached Mossadegh and in an act of great courage, handed him a
letter of dismissal signed by the Shah. Mossadegh was surprised and a little amused. He did not know that behind Nasiri and the Shah stood a
powerful conspiracy, with both the CIA and the British MI6 as partners.
The two agencies initiated "Operation Ajax," which called for "sponta-
neous" mass protests in Iran and a number of clandestine actions that
eventually led to the triumphant return of the Shah. (In 2000, U.S. secretary of state Madeleine Albright officially apologized for America's

role.) Nasiri later became a general and headed the much-feared SAVAK, the Shah's secret police.

The reconstructed documents also reveal the extent to which the CIA's analysts failed to grasp the danger of the Shah's overthrow. One of the documents was an evaluation sent by the CIA to Jimmy Carter's White House in August 1978, which argued there was no chance that the Shah would be toppled in the near future, despite the increased rioting. A few weeks later, the National Intelligence Estimate came out, containing a prediction that the Shah's rule would last another ten years.

Admiral Stansfield Turner, CIA director from 1977 to 1981, said in a press interview later, "We did not understand who Khomeini was and the support his movement had. We were just plain asleep."

The strips of shredded documents also demonstrated the extent of CIA knowledge of Israel's intelligence activities, and detailed the intimate relations between the Israelis and the Shah's regime. For example, they described a secret meeting between Major General Ezer Weizman, the renowned former commander of the Israel air force who had been appointed minister of defense in the government of Menachem Begin in 1977, and Lieutenant General Hassan Toufanian, Iranian deputy minister of war and armaments. Toufanian was a CIA informant who supplied the agency with the meeting's protocol. It offered clear evidence that Israel had developed, manufactured, and intended to sell to Iran long-range ballistic missiles capable of carrying nuclear warheads under the code name of "Operation Tzor."

Reuven Merhav, head of the Mossad station in Iran at the time, explains that the Shah wanted to work with Israel more than ever after the election of Jimmy Carter in 1976. "Carter began asking questions about human rights, including everything that was going on in Iran," recalls Merhav. "The Iranians were scared that the gates would close in America and Western Europe, and were looking for alternative sources of supply" for their weapons needs.

Israel and Iran planned to build a tremendous military co-production line, the biggest Israel had partnered in until then. There were a total of six projects. Israel was to supply the know-how and Iran the money and test sites. At the end of the process, the Iranians were supposed to be able to produce the weapons systems themselves. The largest project concerned Israeli-made ballistic surface-to-surface missiles with a range of 700 kilometers. As one senior Israeli military source at the center of the relations with Iran explains, "The Shah wanted Iran to become a regional power, and to be a regional power, he needed a mighty army. He needed a fleet of Boeing 747s to fly his generals, his ministers, and himself around, so he bought no fewer than twelve. He needed to host international conferences, so he built guesthouses with golden bathrooms; and he needed missiles. I know that he was also thinking of nuclear weapons."

The deal called for Israel to supply Iran with its Jericho missile, which is based on an old French design. Though Israeli censorship doesn't allow publication of specifics about the Jericho, according to non-Israeli media, it can carry a nuclear warhead, and according to the authoritative *Jane's Defense Information* publications, three squadrons of Jericho missiles at the Israeli air force base known as "Wing 2," located near a village called Zacharia, southwest of Jerusalem, are in fact armed with nuclear warheads. In addition to the Jericho missiles, the projects included plants for the manufacture of 120mm mortars and artillery pieces; the development of a modern sea-to-sea missile called *Perah* (Hebrew for "Flower") with a range of 200 kilometers; and a warplane originally called the "Lion," later the "Young Lion" or *Lavi*.

A very senior source in the Israeli Ministry of Defense reveals that the weapons deal with Iran was fraudulent. With each of the six joint projects, the Israelis planned to deceive the Iranians by providing them only an outdated version of the weapon in question, while using Iranian money to build a new generation for Israel's exclusive use.

The details of the various deals were worked out at a series of meetings, mostly between the Israeli ambassador to the Shah's regime, Uri Lubrani, and General Toufanian. The latter was very close to the Shah and was in charge of all military purchases abroad, as well as local weapons development and manufacture. Yaakov Shapiro, the Defense Ministry official in charge of coordinating the negotiations with Iran from 1975 to 1978, recalls: "In Iran they treated us like kings. We did business with them on a stunning scale. Without the ties with Iran, we would not have had the money to develop weaponry that is today in the front line of the defense of the State of Israel."

After witnessing a missile test at a secret base south of Tel Aviv and the destruction of a target far out to sea, a highly impressed General Toufanian persuaded the Shah to proceed with the deal with Israel. The agreement was conditional on each side setting up straw companies in

Switzerland, owned in turn by companies registered in the Virgin Islands. The deals would be signed between the companies without a word about the governments involved, and the papers were worded in such a way that if they were ever discovered, their true nature would not be discernible.

Yet the efforts made by the Shah's army to disguise these projects were exposed even before the U.S. Embassy was occupied. General Mohammad Antazemi, who reported to Toufanian and knew of the deals, wanted to save his skin once the Ayatollah Khomeini took power. After hiding out for a few days, he turned himself in, requesting immunity in exchange for the documents about the Swiss straw companies. He took members of the Revolutionary Guards to a secret apartment in Tehran where he had hidden copies of hundreds of reports and of the correspondence between Israel and Iran. His thanks were that he was strenuously interrogated and then executed by a firing squad in one of the city's squares.

The surprising success of Khomeini's revolution put a stop to Israel's plans to arm Iran. Indeed, if Khomeini had not taken power as early as he did, he might have taken over a country armed with long-range missiles capable of carrying nuclear warheads and with a range that covered large areas of Europe and all of Israel, as well as a jet fighter that was supposed to be the best in the world.

The Israeli relationship with Iran changed radically in 1979, as did America's. The revolutionary regime had turned the country's two most useful allies into its greatest enemies. Unfortunately, neither enemy knew much about the new man in charge in Tehran.

Sayyid Ruhollah Khomeini was many things. He was far from the simple conservative many in the West thought him to be. A closer look at his doctrines reveals that the man who preached for a return to "pure Islam" was in fact a revolutionary (or a cynic, depending on which way you look at it), who reshaped Shi'ite Islam to suit himself and his lust for power, not hesitating to bend in accordance with the demands of a changing reality.

The Shi'ite faith was born out of a deep feeling of deprivation and grievance. The Shi'ites claim that the legal heir to the Prophet Mohammad was his son-in-law and cousin, Ali Ibn Abu Talib, and that all subsequent rule over Muslim believers should have been in the hands of his descendants. *Shi'a* is an abbreviation of the phrase "the faction of Ali." The Sunnis, by contrast, claim that Mohammad died without appointing an heir. Ali did rule for a few years, from 656 to 661, but they were years of constant internal strife. Finally, he was murdered, whereupon the Umayyad dynasty took over and ruled from 661 to 750. To this day, the Shi'ites see that as a criminal and despicable usurpation, and the reign of the first three caliphs as an arbitrary confiscation of the Prophet's inheritance. The Shi'a were born as victims of injustice.

In the dominant Shi'a tradition, there are, in effect, two kinds of people. The first is the superior few, generally no more than a dozen, who are entitled to issue religious directives independently, dictating to their followers. They are chosen in accordance with their knowledge and seniority by Shi'ite institutions, the most important of which are in the holy city of Qom in Iran.

All others are the "imitators," who must choose one of the ayatollahs and obey his rulings.

For centuries, the greatest weakness in the Shi'ite establishment was the divisions and personal rivalries between the different ayatollahs. Only rarely did one of them rise above the others and manage to unite a large-scale following. Khomeini was the first in hundreds of years who succeeded in uniting almost the entire Shi'ite faith under his leadership.

Khomeini bore the hereditary title *Sayyid*, meaning "Lord," used only by descendants of the Prophet Mohammad.

Since the first imam, Ali, rule over the Shi'a had passed from father to son. In 874, after the murder of the eleventh imam, al-Hassan al-Askari, his son, then a small child, is said to have gone into a cave at Samarra, some 100 kilometers north of Baghdad, and has never been seen since. The Shi'ites believe that when the day comes, the hidden imam will be revealed again, as the *Mahdi*, or messiah.

Khomeini belonged to the Mussawis, descendants of the seventh imam, Mussa ibn Jaafer. After seizing power and declaring the Islamic Republic, Khomeini appointed other *sayyids* from the same clan to most key positions, including the presidency, the head of the Supreme Court, the deputy speaker of the Majlis or Parliament, and dozens of ministers, deputy ministers, district governors, ambassadors, legislators, and directors of state-owned companies.

Sayyid Ahmad, Khomeini's grandfather, settled in the city of Khomein in around 1840, and set up his own small religious school. He was considered a peerless Islamic scholar. Six months after his son Ruhollah was born, in 1902, Mustafa (Ahmad's son) was murdered. The fact that he was stabbed six times and his son was only six months old rendered the child a *bad kadam,* or a child born under an evil sign, destined to bring only disaster on himself and his family. The repulsion with which the family and neighbors viewed the boy was so powerful that his mother sent him to a distant aunt, who undertook to bring him up until he turned sixteen.

As a young man in his family's hometown of Khomein, the future revolutionary became a well-known preacher, acutely expert in the intricacies of the faith, but lacking in charismatic oratory. For many years he professed, at least outwardly, the conservative teachings of the Shi'a, by which religious sages do not rule themselves but only advise the king. In 1962, however, Khomeini underwent a dramatic change: After a period of seclusion, he emerged from his bedchamber convinced that he had been visited by the Archangel Gabriel, God's special messenger, who had told him that Allah had chosen him for great things.

From that moment on, the ayatollah's conduct was completely different. For one thing, he began to speak simply, abandoning his hitherto complex, profound style, so that more people would understand him. His new vocabulary was limited to some two thousand words. By sheer repetition of certain phrases they took on the nature of magical incantations. Second, he began to portray the world as a clash between good and evil. The evil must be uprooted and destroyed, a duty that had to be performed by the good, who were both judges and executioners. His followers among the poor found this persuasive.

Finally, in order to prepare himself for the role that he now desired, Khomeini shook off the basic separation of civil and religious authority that had always prevailed in the Muslim empires, and declared there was no longer a need for a king advised by religious sages. The government should be in the hands of the sages themselves. Not only was monarchical rule no longer acceptable, but so was any regime that was not headed by a religious authority. The presidents of Egypt and Syria and the kings of Jordan and Saudi Arabia were all heretics, whose rule was illegitimate.

Khomeini's ideology, advocating a return to "pure Islam untouched by foreign influences," constituted a great innovation for the Shi'a. And his next great innovation drastically changed the way the Shi'ites interpreted their defining historical event, the battle of Karbala, in 680.

When Hussein, the son of the Imam Ali, tried to reclaim rule over Islam for his family, he and seventy of his followers were killed in the battle. The anniversary is marked in the Ashura ceremonies, where the participants cut themselves until the blood flows. The Iranians had mourned the death of Hussein for some fourteen hundred years, seeing it as a great tragedy. Khomeini told them that Hussein had died in honor, and that death should be sanctified, whereas life was something to have reservations about. "You must pray to Allah that he grant you the honor of dying for the sanctification of his name," he preached.

Khomeini's attitude to the issue of martyrdom was meant to prepare the ground for his assumption of power. He explained to his supporters that the highest sanction in the hands of the state was the power to execute its citizens. Take this sanction away, by changing death to a desired reward, and the state became powerless.

Khomeini's next step was to shatter the most important traditional custom of Shi'ite theology. He allowed the believers, even encouraged them, to call him "Imam." This title had been reserved by the Iranian Shi'ites for Ali and the eleven leaders who came after him. Until the inevitable return of the missing thirteenth imam at some unpredictable time, no religious sage had had the right to use the title. Without stating it explicitly, Khomeini was creating the impression that he *was* the missing imam, who had returned as a messiah, or *Mahdi*.

In 1963, a short time after formulating his new doctrine, Khomeini launched an open campaign against the Shah from Qom, Iran's holiest city. He was swiftly arrested. Not long after, mass rioting broke out in the capital and other cities. Many were killed with the battle cry "Long live Khomeini!" on their lips. After a year in prison, he was released and placed under house arrest in Tehran before he was allowed to return to Qom, where he resumed his incitement against the regime. Khomeini now focused his attacks on the law that gave U.S. military personnel diplomatic immunity in Iran. He was arrested again and sent into exile in Turkey. From there he went to the Shi'ite holy city of Najaf in Iraq. The lessons that he taught there attracted more and more students, and during the 1970s he became, from afar, one of the most powerful of the Shah's opponents. This physically weak, stern-featured seventy-seven-year-old, after a brief sojourn as an exile in Paris from September 1978, returned to his homeland on February 1, 1979. He was received by millions at Tehran's airport, and without any weapons, defeated the sixth strongest army in the world.

In his comprehensive biography of Khomeini, *The Spirit of Allah*, the European-based Iranian writer Amir Taheri describes an audiocassette he obtained in the autumn of 1977 ostensibly of a sermon delivered by the cleric. To him it sounded like a forgery by the SAVAK, the Shah's secret police, aiming to present Khomeini in a grotesque and ludicrous light. The sermon dealt mainly with a purported conspiracy between the Shah and "the Jews and the believers in the Cross," first to degrade and then to destroy Islam in Iran. The Shah, continued the preacher, had plotted to force Muslims to accept the laws and government of the foreign enemies of Islam, and had even commissioned a portrait of the Imam Ali, the fourth caliph, in which "the champion of the believers" is depicted with blue eyes and a blond beard, as if to hint that one of the most important founding figures of Islam was actually a European Christian.

Taheri was convinced that the tape was the work of an actor, imitating Khomeini, for how could Khomeini himself have ignored the real economic and political problems of Iran, resorting instead to such a direct appeal to the lowest fanatical impulses prevalent amongst the ignorant masses? He maintained that the Shah's secret service was trying to make Khomeini out to be a base character, who exploited people's lowest impulses to incite them against the monarch, and that the ayatollah could not be so shallow.

But the recording is in fact authentic. With this cassette and many similar ones, Khomeini explained to his listeners how they were not only being denied the right to a decent life in this world, but as silent witnesses to "the crimes of the Shah against the Prophet and his descendants," they were even at risk of losing the world to come. The Shah tried to teach "the little people" how to live, and he failed. Khomeini had now appeared to teach them how to die. He succeeded.

According to the Mossad's estimate, by the end of 1978, over 600,000 cassettes containing recordings of Khomeini's sermons had been distributed in Iran. Each one was listened to in secret by groups of ten or more Iranians, so that at least 6 million Iranians out of a population of 48 million had been exposed to the fanatical preacher by the late 1970s. They heard him saying things like, "The despised shah, that Jewish spy, the

American snake, whose head must be crushed with a stone," or, "The shah says that he is giving the people freedom. Listen to me, you puffed-up toad! Who are you, to grant liberty? It is Allah who grants liberty; it is the law that grants liberty, it is Islam that grants liberty, it is the constitution that grants liberty. What do you mean when you say you have granted us liberty? What gives you the ability to grant anything at all? Who do you think you are?"

It was on the strength of these tapes that Khomeini founded the first theocratic regime in modern times, in the fifteenth most populous country in the world. He defeated the mighty defense establishment that the Shah had built up, and he inherited the largest arsenal of modern weapons in the Middle East. He also inherited foreign currency reserves of over $30 billion, and an oil industry that brought in revenues of $120 million per day.

The distribution of the Khomeini cassettes was observed, of course, by the watchful eyes of the SAVAK. The organization's heads asked the Shah for permission to raid Khomeini's distribution centers—but it was refused. By this time, President Jimmy Carter was pressuring the ailing Shah about civil rights, and the Shah did not dare to limit freedom of expression in Iran in such a manner. The cassettes became legitimate merchandise in large retail chains. Khomeini soon dared to make his sermons even harsher and more outspoken. Another propaganda tool serving Khomeini was none other than the Persian-language broadcasts of the British Broadcasting Corporation. The channel gave him a platform. His regular broadcasts made him the unchallenged leader of the Iranian revolutionary movement. "Our movement," he said in one of them, "is still like a tender sapling that needs the blood of martyrs to make it grow and become a tall tree."

The BBC was not the only body to fall captive to Khomeini's spell on the eve of his revolution. The elderly cleric realized that he would never be able to take power without the help of certain opposition groups, some of which were ideologically opposed to him. With the Shah as their common enemy, however, he entered into pacts with all of the rivals of the monarchy, playing down the vast differences among them. The Shi'ites have a name for this technique: *khode*, which means tricking someone into misjudging his position. Khomeini himself boasted in 1984 in an interview that he had employed *khode* in order to deceive "the enemies of Islam."

Khomeini managed to gather together the moderate left, including both Communists and liberals, all of whom were confirmed secularists. These movements, mainly the Communist Toudeh Party, had all been crushed under the iron boot of the Shah's secret service, despite his lip service to human rights and freedom of expression. They saw Khomeini as the harbinger of freedom, either turning a blind eye to the fanatical aspects of his preachings or seeing them as an attempt to win over the masses.

As for the opposition movement closest to his ideology, the *Mujahideen Khalq*, he promised the group a share of power when he got his hands on it. It was a promise he would fail to keep.

During his Iraqi exile, and then in France, Khomeini had sharpened two other concepts for use in his psychological warfare: *tanfia*, which means removing the enemy's sting; and *takiya*, or concealing your true opinions from people when in a hostile environment. This blatantly cunning style of leadership, which Khomeini openly boasted of after taking over the reins of power, would have a significant impact on the conduct of the government of Iran after he died, and on the conduct of Shi'ites all over the world, but especially that of Hizballah.

The return of the exiled Khomeini as the leader of the first Islamic revolution in modern history was an enormous, unprecedented setback to the joint interests and combined efforts of the Americans and the Israelis in the Middle East.

One cannot grasp the magnitude of the blow that the revolution dealt to the defense establishments of America and Israel and their intelligence agencies, as well as the hostility that the new regime felt toward those countries, without a brief description of the clandestine aspects of those relationships.

From day one of its founding, Israel aimed to forge regional alliances with forces that were hostile to its own enemies, mainly the Arab states, on the principle that "the enemy of my enemy is my friend." The founder of the Mossad, Reuven Shiloah, termed this effort the "Peripheral Alliance Strategy"—a reference to the establishment of contacts, mostly clandestine, with countries located in the "outer belt" that borders Israel's neighboring enemies on the other side—Iran, Turkey, and Ethiopia—and with underground movements of minorities having shared interests.

Another cornerstone of Israel's foreign policy was the attempt to forge itself into a strategic and intelligence asset to the United States. Israel was eager to demonstrate that despite its diminutive size and lack of natural resources, it could succeed where the Americans could not. Israel sought to position itself as the final frontier protecting the West from the spread of communism into Asia and Africa. Issar Harel, the legendary Mossad director, said in his last interview, given for this book, that he wanted his organization to operate as "the long arm of the United States" in these arenas.

In the mid- and late 1950s Reuven Shiloah, then adviser to the foreign minister and envoy to the United States, forged a special relationship between the Israeli and American intelligence communities. He made the Asian and African initiative one of his top priorities and used his contacts in the State Department and the CIA to convince the United States of the importance of an Israeli presence on those continents. This was also one of the topics discussed between him and James Jesus Angleton, the CIA's head of counterespionage, and probably the most powerful and loyal ally of Israel within the agency, past or present. As early as 1960, CIA director Allen Dulles was quoted as saying that Israel was now the only ally in the Middle East on which the CIA could rely.

The Peripheral Alliance Strategy was given the code name *Klil* (Hebrew for "Perfection"). Within its framework, a cooperation agreement was signed in August 1958 between the Mossad and its Turkish counterpart, MIT (*Milli Istihbarat Teskilati* or National Intelligence Organization). Later, through the efforts of Shiloah, it was joined by the Iranian SAVAK, the Persian acronym for the Royal Organization for Security and Intelligence. The tripartite agreement was named "Trident" (Mossad called it "Ultra-Watt").

Immediately afterwards, Prime Minister David Ben-Gurion sent a personal letter to President Eisenhower, in which he explained: "With the goal of erecting a high dam to stem the Nasserite-Soviet tidal wave, we have begun tightening our links with several states on the outside perimeter of the Middle East. . . . Our goal is to organize a group of countries, not necessarily an official alliance, that would be able to resist Soviet expansion by proxy, such as [Gamal Abdul] Nasser [of Egypt]."

The Trident agreement called for periodic meetings between the heads of the intelligence bodies of the three states, with a different country serving as host each time. Israel considered this an unprecedented strategic achievement, having positioned itself as the central axis between two Muslim countries in a military-intelligence pact. In regional disputes that arose between Turkey and Iran, Trident served as a platform and Israel as arbitrator. Harel even ordered the construction of a special luxury installation near the Mossad Academy, north of Tel Aviv, in order to host these meetings and other secret guests.

"At the time," observed a former top Mossad official who was involved in planning the *Klil* meetings, "all the heads of intelligence in Turkey, Iran, and Ethiopia had a direct link to the boss, whether it was the Shah or the Turkish prime minister or [emperor] Haile Selassie. Through Klil, it was possible to pass messages and ideas directly to the ruler. It gave us a double orgasm, and with the inclusion of Ethiopia, a triple orgasm."

The Khomeini revolution was not a total surprise to everyone, as the episode recounted below will reveal. On March 13, 1978, a flight not listed in the register of the Iranian Civil Aviation Authority landed on the island of Kish, off the coast of southern Iran. There were only two passengers on board the large executive jet, which was painted white, with no markings. A ghost flight.

A platoon of heavily armed soldiers awaited the plane, with a large black limousine and men in civilian clothes standing by. The two passengers got off, shook hands warmly with the civilians, and disappeared into the black Mercedes. The soldiers mounted jeeps and two motorcycles and the convoy set off.

On the plane were Israeli ambassador Uri Lubrani and Mossad Tehran station chief Reuven Merhav, now on their way to a secret meeting with His Imperial Majesty Mohammad Reza Cyrus Pahlavi Shah. "On the way, we immediately saw that all the terrible rumors we had heard about Kish were all true," Merhav recalls. Kish was the spot where the Shah had decided to build his own European-style holiday resort. It soon became his favorite residence, the location of his headquarters for most of the year, as well as the place where the egregious corruption of Iran's royal family and leadership reached its peak.

Lubrani and Merhav had come to lay before the Shah a secret, revolutionary plan. Some people in Israel at that time were capable of looking ahead, beyond the horizon. The Mossad and the Foreign Ministry feared that the Shi'ites in Lebanon were increasingly becoming captives of extremist Islamist ideology. A young and fanatical preacher by the name of Mohammad Hussein Fadlallah, who would later become the spiritual compass for Hizballah, was already reaping great success among them. The Israelis believed that massive aid to this population, along the lines of the assistance Israel was already giving the Christians in Lebanon by rebuilding the wrecked infrastructure in the south—assistance in the export of commodities and in other economic matters—could prevent that process of radicalization. Lubrani and Merhav, with the blessing of the CIA station in Tehran, had come to Kish to try to persuade the Shah to finance the project.

Only Lubrani was granted an audience. He left the magnificent gilt-decorated chamber in a somber mood. "The Shah is detached from reality, living in a world of his own, almost delusional," he told Merhav. "He is surrounded by sycophants who don't tell him the truth about the situation in the country." The Israelis didn't know that by then, cancer was spreading through the body of the doomed monarch.

While Lubrani was with the Shah, Merhav had some meetings of his own, with top Iranian intelligence officials, and he took a trip around the island. "It was the playground for all the top people," says Merhav. "There were scheduled flights there and back, but anyone wanting to buy a ticket had to get an okay from the SAVAK. Evidence of the astonishing corruption was everywhere. The two of us, Uri and I, were very negatively impressed by the hedonistic atmosphere, the extravagance. There was a special landing strip for a Concorde that flew there from Paris every two weeks, loaded with special delicacies. There were boutiques with the latest in French fashions. Next to the palace there were small holiday apartments that ministers and senior officials bought for hundreds of thousands of dollars, just to be close to His Majesty. And there was no shortage of prostitutes from France. In short, everything that money could buy."

On the way back, the two Israelis discussed what they had seen and heard, and agreed that the regime was teetering, that something very bad was about to happen. Then they fell silent, each one with his own thoughts about the implications for the sensitive and important relationship between the fragile regime and Israel. Lubrani thought about the secret gigantic arms deals, while Merhav mulled over the future of "Ultra-Watt," as the Mossad intelligence alliance with Iran was code-named.

Soon after their visit, the two men transmitted a grave warning to the Israeli security establishment: the rule of the Shah was crumbling. The unlikely coalition established between secular and religious opponents of his regime, along with the flagrant corruption and the monarch's detachment from reality, were leading to the imminent demise of the Pahlavi dynasty.

Their reports were the topic of a special meeting held at the Mossad headquarters in Tel Aviv, with representatives of the Foreign Ministry, to decide whether the Israeli intelligence community should adopt their assessment, and what to do about the situation. Most of the participants felt that the reports were a reflection of the subjective impressions of people in the field who were too close to the events, too swayed by their acquaintance with the figures involved, and, most important, too affected by what they had seen during a single visit to Kish. Iran was strong, the group concluded; the Shah's regime was established on the bayonets of the army and the interrogation cellars of the SAVAK, and would last for many more years. Nevertheless, one of those present said, "We can't keep this to ourselves. We have to inform Gardenia."

"Gardenia" was the code name used by the Israelis for the U.S. Central Intelligence Agency. The United States and Iran maintained the closest of relationships, many aspects of which were kept secret. The depth and intimacy of these ties cannot be exaggerated. The United States saw in Iran and Israel its most important strongholds in its endeavors to prevent the Soviet Union from expanding into Asia and the Middle East.

The Mossad's Tevel department, the organization's liaison with other intelligence agencies, translated Merhav's report from Hebrew into English, and officials brought it to a meeting with the CIA's station heads in the U.S. Embassy in Tel Aviv. When they presented the major points, they noticed raised American eyebrows, a politer version of the blunter responses that the report had evoked from the Israelis themselves.

The report was forwarded to Washington, where the CIA's experts on Iran and their State Department counterparts discounted it. The sixth biggest army in the world, equipped with the best of American armaments plus a huge, powerful, and very aggressive secret service, was being threatened by precisely whom—a fanatical preacher with a few whimsical followers? What exactly was he capable of doing? The CIA had thousands of informants in Iran at that time, far more than Lubrani and Merhav had, but the agency was nonetheless completely blind to what was happening in the country.

Two months later, Eliezer Tsafrir arrived in Tehran to replace Merhav as head of the Mossad station. After a brief overlapping period, Merhav handed over to Tsafrir the keys to his official car and to the comfortable residence that the Iranians had put at the disposal of the chief Israeli spy in their country.

"You've got the keys now," Merhav said gloomily, "but I'm afraid I'm handing over more than just a flat and a car. I'm worried that this friend of ours will soon be an enemy, that our intimate intelligence partner will become one of our main adversaries, and that he'll give us a very hard time. I'm giving you Iran with a time fuse."

Khomeini made all the right moves. The Shah, however, made mistakes. His son, Reza Cyrus Pahlavi, is perhaps the best person to explain his downfall:

> My father, in a way, was a gambler who lost in the biggest wager of his life. He thought he would be able to educate the public to undergo many changes and make it adjust to the modern era. All of this was happening during the Cold War, in a society in which 70 percent of its members didn't know how to read or write. The pace of progress in Iran was such that it made the social fabric very fragile.
>
> Father never saw how the ignorant rural population fell victim to Khomeini's manipulation. Those people had religious feelings but they were also very naïve, easily tempted, and confused—which is what Khomeini wanted—between modernization and Westernization. They were convinced that the steps father was taking were anti-religious.
>
> My father made another mistake when he failed to understand the Communists, who were being encouraged by Moscow to undermine the relations between Iran and the United States. The leftists thought they'd topple the government and that Khomeini would retire to Qom to teach Islam, and leave the government to them. They were wrong of course. Khomeini came and killed or expelled them all.

During the second half of the 1970s, Khomeini's propaganda began bearing fruit. The small demonstrations in the provincial cities reached Tehran and the number of participants rose steadily, from tens to hundreds to thousands. As the demonstrations swelled, the weakness of the police became increasingly evident. As Brigadier General Yitzhak Segev, an Israeli military attaché in Tehran at that time, explains: "The Iranians on the government side were fools. There's no other way to put it. Their faith in the Shah and his strength was blind, not to say drugged, and fed on the faith of the Shah himself, who used to boast that he had already known eight American presidents, all of whom were gone, while he was still there. Unlike earlier occasions, when orders were given to open fire, this time the Shah hesitated, because of his serious illness and also because of Carter's threats that he would not go through with the sale of F-18 aircraft if the Shah continued violating human rights."

One day in August 1978, Iranian air force commander General Amir Hossein Rabiei summoned Segev to a secret meeting in Tehran. "I want to ask something personal of you," Rabiei said, as Segev recalls. " 'Bring General [Moshe] Dayan here. The Shah admires him very much. Somebody has to tell him what's going on in the streets.' I told him, 'But General, it is you who always tells me that every time you wait for an audience with the Shah, you sit in the first chair of twelve, because he respects you so much. Why don't you tell him?' Rabiei looked at me in surprise and with a little contempt. 'That's correct, but he sits on an elevated throne and looks down on us and all we can say is, "Yes, sir, yes, sir." And all the time he is crying or laughing alternately, and saying, "Have pity on my people." ' "

Moshe Dayan was foreign minister at the time, but was still thought of mainly as a general by the Iranians. He flew in urgently on a commercial flight, wearing a wig, a hat, and sunglasses to hide his trademark eyepatch. As Segev recounts: "Before the meeting with the Shah, Geizi Tsafrir [who had replaced Merhav as head of the Mossad station] took Dayan to meet General Nasiri [the head of SAVAK]. Dayan said to him, 'Listen, Nasiri, I hear from my people that you have problems here and the regime is tottering.' Nasiri smiled and said, 'My dear general, I don't know what your people report to you, but we are in full control of the situation. There is no need to discuss that marginal subject. I wish to speak to you about the topic that really bothers His Majesty, the war between Ethiopia and Somalia.' Dayan tried again later in the conversation to get back to the internal situation, but Nasiri smiled again and said, 'But General Dayan, I have assured you that we are in full control.' Dayan turned to me and whispered in Hebrew, 'He's completely senile, this is a waste of time.' The meeting with the Shah himself produced the same result."

In January 1978, a flyer concocted by the SAVAK, highly insulting to Khomeini, was distributed in Tehran in the name of a new independent organization. In August, the SAVAK's forgery was exposed and this new provocation sparked a wave of protests, starting in Qom and spreading to Tabriz and several other cities. Security forces shot at the crowds, but still showed some restraint and refrained from using all of their firepower to quell the rioting; nevertheless, hundreds were killed.

Two weeks later, in early September, an Iraqi Airlines plane on an unscheduled flight landed at Tehran's Meharabad Airport, carrying only one passenger, Barazan al-Takriti, the half brother of the ruler of Iraq, Saddam Hussein. He was the head of Saddam's secret police, who had come with a message to the Shah: You must treat the rioters with an iron fist, and Iraq will come to your aid if you need us. Al-Takriti hinted to the Shah that it would be no problem to have Khomeini eliminated in Najaf, Iraq—where Khomeini had been living since 1966. The Shah now made the mistake that would cost him his throne. Instead of accepting the tacit offer, he requested that Iraq *deport* Khomeini. Al-Takriti acquiesced, and France agreed to take the exile in.

As Merhav explains, "The Shah never understood that it was precisely in Iraq that Khomeini was still under some kind of supervision, and in any case stuck in a hole far from the media's spotlights. The Shah gave him, on a silver platter, all of the world's media."

At the request of Khomeini's followers, France also agreed to have a number of telephone and telex lines installed in the post office near the ayatollah's new home, linked directly to Iran. For the first time in sixteen years, Khomeini was able to maintain almost hourly contact with his field commander in Tehran, Ayatollah Murtaza Mutahhari. A local recording studio cancelled all of its other dealings in order to produce thousands of cassettes of the ayatollah's daily broadcasts and interviews, for shipment to Tehran. Khomeini's broadcasts now reached Iran almost immediately. Journalists from all over the world waited on line outside his home to film and to interview the holy man.

The French government, practicing high-level realpolitik, believed that a Khomeini government would be beneficial, helping to steer military and civilian contracts to France. President Valéry Giscard d'Estaing even began trying to persuade the Shah's Western allies not to prolong his reign. Hundreds of thousands of Iranians were marching in Tehran's streets every day. Brigadier General Segev describes the scene vividly:

"Have you ever heard a million people shouting together? It's scary and awesome at the same time. By this time we [the Israeli staff in Tehran] were already worried about being attacked, and we went into the streets wearing only revolutionary Persian clothes. We joined the demonstrations in order to report home on what was happening. The demonstrations were organized in an exemplary and orderly fashion. The protestors had flowers ready, and when they met soldiers, they would approach them with a smile and stick flowers into the barrels of their rifles."

Between October 1, 1978, and January 31, 1979, the day before Khomeini's return to Tehran, more than 100,000 well-heeled people fled the country. They took with them some $15 billion. This exodus, and the export of almost 10 percent of the country's foreign currency reserves, was a vote of no confidence in the Shah's regime on the part of his most natural supporters.

By November 1978, the country was almost totally paralyzed. Its main services, commerce, and the oil industry nearly stopped functioning. The Shah had lost his grip on the population and it was unclear whether the armed services were still with him. Khomeini had begun to set up an alternative administration by issuing decrees and appointing delegations to supervise their implementation. Ali Akbar Hashemi Rafsanjani was dispatched to the oil fields as his representative. On December 22, the heads of the Israeli delegation in Tehran gathered for a difficult meeting in the home of Mossad station chief Geizi Tsafrir, to discuss the possibility of having to evacuate the entire Israeli community in the city. Meanwhile, Israel began evacuating women and children and the experts of the Tzor program, the arms deals signed between Israel and Iran in 1977, who took all the blueprints for the weapons systems with them.

When Ayatollah Khomeini took power, he immediately broke off all ties between Iran and Israel. The Israelis were extremely nervous as to whether the Iranians would move to claim the return of the immense advances that had been paid for the Tzor project and for which nothing had been provided. When the amounts that Israel owed Iran became clear to Khomeini's regime, the Iranians decided to sue for $5 billion. The debt was made up of three components: oil supplied by Iran but not paid for; weapons that were paid for but never supplied; and the amounts paid in advance for the six parts of Operation Tzor, which never came to fruition. International arbitration on the matter has been going on since

1983 in Geneva and Paris. The basic Israeli claim in the arbitration is: we signed the deals with the Shah, who was replaced in an illegal process by a regime that we do not acknowledge. Bring back the Shah and we will pay you back your money.

By January 1979, Iran would descend into full-scale chaos, and the Israelis and Iranian Jews left behind would be in serious danger.

CHAPTER 2

# Death to the Infidels

On January 1, 1979, Erwin Muller, a former Gestapo officer and member of the Spider network that smuggled top Nazis out of Germany after World War II, sat beside the gates of two magnificent animal cages, now open and empty, and wept. Brigadier General Yitzhak Segev, the Israeli military attaché in Tehran, stood next to him and tried to find words to console him. "In the hallucinatory situation that we were all in, with the mobs flooding the streets with holy fury, this was a particularly hallucinatory comic interlude," Segev recalls. Khomeini's mobs were taking control in Iran. The royal family was on the run—and not all of their royal pets could survive.

Four years earlier, the director of Israel's National Parks Authority, General Avraham Yaffeh, had had the idea of recreating herds of the animals that had roamed the country in biblical times, among them the fallow deer. Such animals, he discovered, could be found in Iran. At around the same time, the brother of the Shah, Prince Abdul Reza, a pampered member of the royal family, came on a visit to Israel. His major occupation was hunting. The walls of his palaces were full of stuffed trophies. He told his hosts that he had heard that in the Negev Desert there was an ibex with a horn span 1.5 meters wide, three centimeters more than the world record. Yaffeh seized the opportunity and made a deal: Israel would allow him to hunt an ibex in exchange for a pair of fallow deer.

The minister of agriculture issued a special hunting license. The ibex was located and steered to an appropriate site, where the prince was allowed to fire a fatal bullet. The royal taxidermist who had accompanied Abdul Reza immediately injected embalming substances to ensure the carcass's preservation. The grateful prince promptly issued a permit for the export of a pair of fallow deer from Iran. For budgetary reasons, the Israeli Parks Authority left the matter in abeyance until the last minute. On November 28, 1978, as rioting in Iran approached a crescendo and the government's grip weakened, the Parks Authority sent a crew to Tehran. With vehicles and security provided by Segev, they travelled to a nature preserve on the shore of the Caspian Sea, picked up two pairs of fallow deer (the royal family had generously broadened the original permit for one pair), and returned to Tehran, where they hoped to lodge the animals in the local zoo until a flight to Israel could be arranged. But the director of the zoo, Erwin Muller, flatly refused. As Segev recalls, "We applied some pressure on the embassy security officer and we put the beasts into a corral that we fenced off in the embassy yard."

Then another problem cropped up. It turned out that in order to fly the animals out, a special permit was required, and Muller was the only person competent to issue it. "We asked him, and to our surprise he agreed," says Segev. "And we soon understood the reason for his generosity. He would grant the permit only if we agreed that the royal tiger and lion be included in the shipment. The Shah kept the animals in cages in his palace grounds, under Muller's care, but as the riots spread they were moved to the zoo. Muller was frightened that like the other symbols of the monarchy, they would fall victim to the angry mobs, and he wanted them shipped to Holland. I had no choice, and I agreed."

After another round of heavy pressure, this time applied to El Al Airline managers in Tehran, and a flood of phone calls from Israel, space was allocated on the next flight out for the four deer and the lion and tiger, at the expense of some Jewish passengers and the cargo of carpets they wanted to ship out. On January 1, 1979, Segev arrived at the zoo in a convoy of vehicles, to pick up the two big cats. He found Muller there, crying. "It turned out we were a couple of hours too late. Thousands of demonstrators had broken into the zoo and slaughtered both of the big cats. Muller was distraught with grief."

Segev sped off to the airport. The deer were loaded onto the plane and flown to Israel. They were eventually turned loose in a nature preserve near Haifa, on Mount Carmel. Ten years later, a forest fire swept through the area, destroying much of the preserve's flora and fauna, but the fallow deer and their numerous offspring bunched together in a small clearing (around a modest monument that had been erected by Carmella and Yitzhak Segev, in memory of their son Sharon, who fell in the line of duty in the IDF's Armored Corps). They survived the blaze. Today there are 650 fallow deer in Israel, all of them descendants of the two couples brought out of Iran.

• • •

The differing fates of the cats and the deer mirrored the two possibilities facing many foreigners in Iran at the time of the revolution. As the turmoil swelled and the United States maintained its pressure on Tehran not to violate human rights, the Iranian top brass played with the idea of carrying out a military coup, but couldn't decide how and where to begin. As Segev recalls, "All of the senior officers were waiting for the visit of the deputy commander in chief of American Forces in Europe, General Robert E. Huyser, who came on January 8, 1979, a week before the Shah's departure. They wanted to hear from him only one thing—that if they took over the government, the United States would prevent a Russian invasion of Iran. That is all. They could have handled everything else by themselves, eight hundred thousand troops, eight hundred generals."

The United States, however, wanted to keep the regime the way it was. The administration believed that a coup attempt would be the worst move the army could make. Huyser came to Tehran in order to *thwart* any attempt at a putsch by the generals. All he would say was that President Carter had sent him to ensure a democratic Iran. He succeeded in sewing discord among the generals and causing enough disputes and confusion to frustrate plans for a coup, and the minute he left Tehran, ties between some of the generals and the revolting mullahs tightened. The chief of staff, General Abbas Gharabaghi, and many senior SAVAK officials, saw which way the wind was blowing and took steps to ensure their futures by going over to the revolutionaries.

On January 16, the Shah—ailing and debilitated—decided that without American backing, he had best pack up and leave. He took a box with a few clods of Iranian soil, and with his wife Farah Diba and a handful of aides flew to Egypt, where he was welcomed as a head of state by his friend, President Anwar al-Sadat. Many Iranians sincerely believed that the Shah would return once again, as in 1953, with still greater power, backed by the CIA and British intelligence. Some generals, who still regarded him as their commander in chief, tried to contact him in Egypt, but they were told that his imperial majesty, the king of kings, was on a private visit and that all matters should be referred in his absence to the council of regents. Air Force commander General Rabiei was determined to shoot down any aircraft carrying Khomeini to Iran, but insisted that the Shah approve this idea before he issued orders. Since he never managed to speak personally to the monarch, he had to cancel the plan.

Though many generals did not know what to do, Khomeini had few doubts. He intentionally cultivated the image of a strongman. One of the first orders he gave to his personal representative in Tehran, Ayatollah Mutahhari, shortly before his arrival, was that only approved photographs of himself should be printed and displayed in public. He especially opposed the distribution of two photographs that had been plastered all over the city—one showing him wearing spectacles, which he feared could be construed as a sign of weakness, and the other showing him smiling kindly. Islamic tradition states clearly that the Prophet Mohammad never smiled and that he dismissed those who smiled as superficial and morally dubious. Within days, all of the objectionable portraits had been taken down and replaced with new ones, in which the imam's thick eyebrows were highlighted, suggesting angry determination.

On February 1, Khomeini loyalists took over Tehran's Meharabad international airport. The ayatollah landed there in a chartered Air France jumbo jet and was greeted by triumphant rejoicing such as Iran had never before witnessed.

Avraham Geffen,* an Iranian Jew who was to play many clandestine roles in the long war with Iran, was working at that time in the El Al office in Tehran. He was one of the local Jews who provided logistical help to the Israeli Embassy and the offices of the Jewish Agency (a body that organizes immigration to Israel). He would soon try to help secure the escape of Israeli government personnel.

"On the day that Khomeini arrived," Geffen recalls, "I was called urgently to the airport, whose administrators were still functioning, more or less, and from their point of view I was the El Al representative. They brought welding tools and broke into the safe in the El Al office at the airport. The company owed them money, and they were honest. They took in cash what was coming to them, and they gave me the rest to transfer to Israel via banks abroad.

"When Khomeini's plane arrived, everyone went out to welcome the ayatollah. I was standing twenty meters away from him, and hundreds of guards were separating him from the excited crowds. All of Iran's streets were strewn with flowers on that day. When the plane landed, state TV played the anthem of the Shah's regime. The reaction was not long in coming, and the Revolutionary Guards occupied the network building."

---

* A pseudonym, as the Mossad banned publication of his real name in this book.

Brigadier General Segev recalls the confusion among the old guard. "A week before Khomeini arrived, I met Generals Rabiei and [army aviation chief Manucher] Khosrodad. I asked them if they were intending to do anything. Raviei asked me, 'Segev, do you think we're going to sit and do nothing? Khomeini is going to land here. We'll take him with his entourage from the airport to Kish Island and kill them all.' On the strength of that meeting, I advised [Foreign Minister] Dayan to leave the embassy's senior staff where they were. We evacuated fifteen hundred Israelis, but I hoped that things would work out in the end and I wanted to keep a foothold intact. I was afraid that if we abandoned the embassy entirely, we wouldn't be able to come back."

When Khomeini returned, Segev, like Geffen, stood amid the welcoming crowds. "We saw the mass of humanity flooding the airport," Segev recalls, "and then I saw my friend General Rabiei arriving in his personal helicopter, in order to fly Khomeini away himself. He thought that that's how he would get himself immunity." Needless to say, it wasn't to the island of Kish that the commander of the Imperial Air Force piloted the revolutionary leader.

Khomeini turned down a proposed series of visits to the universities that had been hotbeds of the revolution so as not to share the glory with the partners in his triumph, and headed instead for the Tehran cemetery, where he made a fiery speech. "Islam has been moribund for almost fourteen hundred years; we have returned it to life with the blood of our youth. . . . Very soon we will liberate Jerusalem and pray there." As for the government of Shahpour Bakhtiar, who had been appointed prime minister by the Shah before he left, Khomeini dismissed it with one short sharp statement: "I will break their teeth."

On February 11, that government crumpled; Bakhtiar admitted he had lost control and fled the country disguised as an Air France steward. His government was replaced by one headed by Mehdi Bazargan, a Khomeini supporter whom the imam decided to make use of in the interim period after the revolution. Khomeini did not want to be too closely associated with the purges to come.

There were thirty-four Israelis stranded in Tehran when the revolution broke out, including office and security personnel of the embassy, Mossad and military, the Jewish Agency, and El Al. They hid out in three apartments. Avraham Geffen and another Iranian Jew carried messages between the apartments and brought food and drink. They also brought the ambassador, Yosef Harmelin, and his staff fresh news from the corridors of power, which they acquired through old connections and substantial bribes. Amazingly, the international telephone exchange was still working and they were in contact with Israel.

The embassy itself had hardly been functioning since the Shah left. Only the security officer and a few other workers were there, and Iranian army tanks stood outside. Other remaining staffers were in hiding. Most of the embassy's secret documents had been flown to Israel in November 1978, preventing a preview of what was to happen at the U.S. Embassy ten months later. On the morning of February 10, one Israeli, Zadok Ofir, hiding in an apartment with several others, began making a traditional Jewish *chulent* stew for lunch. While it was cooking, Harmelin and Segev decided to go and see what was happening at the embassy. They were stunned to find that the tanks had gone. Segev returned to the apartment and put a call through to chief of staff Gharabaghi, who had already made his secret deal with Khomeini and was one of the few top officers to survive the purges that started soon afterward. He told Segev that the army had decided to adopt a neutral position and therefore all forces had been ordered to return to their bases. The conclusion was that the embassy was now at the mercy of the revolutionaries. Rumors reached Segev that a mob was marching on the airport, and he made a call and ordered the one remaining El Al jumbo jet to take off immediately.

Three hours later, Avraham Geffen joined one of the demonstrations, carrying a picture of Khomeini and chanting slogans against the Shah. "Suddenly I saw someone go onto the platform and begin to incite the thousands of people there against America and Israel, ranting about all the things that should be done to them. The bottom line of his speech was a call to march to the Israeli Embassy not far from there. The huge crowd, perhaps ten thousand people, cheered in agreement. I dashed to my car and I told the local El Al branch chief to step on the gas. We made for the embassy, but got stuck in a traffic jam on the way. It looked as if all of Tehran had taken to the streets. I got out of the car and ran like a rocket, faster than I ever thought I could, toward the embassy.

"The Iranian guard unit wasn't there anymore and the Israeli security guard let me in. Inside, I found a few guards and embassy staffers going about their business as if nothing was happening. I started screaming at them, trying to understand what exactly they were doing there while the mob was approaching. At first, they never quite believed that such a thing could be happening in Tehran. They didn't want to leave the embassy, which was very dear to them. I yelled that they were crazy, and if they didn't run away quickly, the mob would come and kill them all. In the end I persuaded them and they immediately set fire to some boxes of secret material that they had prepared for destruction. Everyone piled into a few cars and left through the back gate of the embassy. A few minutes later, the mob arrived. They couldn't break down the gate, so they climbed over the fence. Very soon they had conquered the embassy."

Segev also wanted to get back to the embassy, but couldn't get through the mob. He watched the proceedings from a distance. "There were a quarter of a million people there, I estimated, protesting in front of the embassy, and pushing against the fences."

Geffen recalls what happened next: "I went back a few hours later, like an interested onlooker. I speak and look like a native and no one suspected me. I arrived just in time for a speech by Yasser Arafat from a balcony before a tumultuous, inflamed crowd in the embassy courtyard. He asked the Revolutionary Guards to hang the PLO flag over the embassy, where the Israeli flag had been, and he said the building would now be the Palestinian Embassy. The Iranians agreed, of course."

The crowd looted everything that could be moved. Some of them got hold of a gigantic Persian carpet that had once graced the floor of the ambassador of Nazi Germany in Tehran. After World War II, the Jews of Tehran had purchased the carpet and in the 1960s donated it to the Israeli Embassy.

For the staffers in 1979, the escape from the embassy was only the start of their drama. From the embassy, Segev drove to the General Staff Headquarters to protest against the embassy takeover. When he got there, he found that it too had been taken over. He called General Rabiei on the phone and asked for a plane to fly the remaining Israelis out, but was told the airport was already under the control of Ayatollah Mohammad Beheshti, someone to be avoided at all costs. General Khosrodad told Segev that he would be able to get him out, but as for the rest, he could only say he was really sorry.

Segev remembers it vividly:

We went back home. We were hiding in my apartment, which was known to be the residence of the military attaché. I ordered an immediate evacuation. But Zadok said, "Come on, Itzik [diminutive of Yitzhak], I've spent hours on this *chulent*." I thought about it for a while and I decided, fuck them. We'll eat this stew whether Khomeini likes it or not. We sat down to eat, and put a sentry by the window. In the middle of the meal, the sentry reported that a Revolutionary Guards jeep had pulled up outside and armed men had entered the building. We drew our pistols and waited for them next to the door. We were tense. We decided to kill them off, something like Samson when he said, "Let me die with the Philistines." We looked through the peephole and saw them coming up the stairs, passing by our door, and going up the stairs to the third floor. It turned out that they had come to pick up a senior revolutionary commander, who had been a top army officer and had defected. He was a good friend and had even taken part in meetings in my apartment. To his credit, although he knew who lived under him, he never turned us in.

The revolutionaries departed with my neighbor, and we went back to the *chulent*. Two minutes later, there was a knock on the door. The landlord had arrived with a huge basket full of towels. He was sure that they'd killed us and he'd come to clean up. Instead of corpses, he found us chomping our stew, and he stood there frozen in shock.

Years later, in June 2007, at a historical forum near Tel Aviv assembled as part of the research for this book, old enemies met, as new friends, to reconstruct the events of January 1979. Among them were Segev and Hani al-Hassan, the PLO's first ambassador to Iran, who had directed the revolution's intelligence efforts and commanded the imam's bodyguards during the days immediately following Khomeini's return.

Al-Hassan recalled with a grin: "We knew that General Segev was in Tehran and running for his life. We did everything to try and trap him. We wanted to swap him for Palestinian prisoners in Israeli jails." Segev responded, in turn, that "Hani al-Hassan was at that time one of the targets on the hit list of Israeli intelligence."

Today, the two bitter enemies have founded the Sons of Abraham Association, dedicated to peace. Al-Hassan says he regrets that the Palestine Liberation Organization was one of the few allies that Khomeini had in the Arab world before the revolution. It trained the core of the Revolutionary Guards at its bases in Lebanon, and assisted with funds, guidance, and equipment. When Khomeini flew into Iran, he summoned Yasser Arafat and requested as much help as he could provide in the formation of the new regime.

Arafat flew into Tehran on February 5, with al-Hassan and a large crew of the PLO's best-trained commandos, Force 17, Arafat's personal bodyguards, whom he turned over to protect Khomeini. Al-Hassan explains that among the documents that had been neither removed nor burned at the embassy was a list of the names of all the Mossad agents in Iraq. Arafat ordered that the document be delivered immediately to Saddam Hussein. Among his other duties, al-Hassan was the PLO's liaison with the Iraqi ruler, who was very fond of him. Despite Arafat's explicit order, however, al-Hassan evaded handing over the list. "I didn't know if it was genuine, or just a Mossad attempt to spread disinformation. I knew one thing—Saddam never took chances with things like this. The minute he got the list he would have all the people on it rounded up, tortured, and eventually murdered. I didn't want to have it on my conscience."

Meanwhile, life in Iran became more dangerous for many people, not just the remaining Israelis. Khomeini's people began hunting down members of the opposition. At first, violence was used only against the Shah's senior personnel. Khomeini ordered the execution of several senior officers in order to nip in the bud any remnant notions of a coup by the old imperial army. Mock trials were arranged. Among the first victims were General Nasiri, for years the commander of the mighty SAVAK, and General Khosrodad. The task of presiding over a show trial was offered to a number of mullahs, but they politely rejected the historical opportunity. In the end, the imam instructed Ayatollah Khalkhali to do the job. Khalkhali acted with dispatch, turning a classroom into a courtroom, where he sentenced five generals to death. The generals were taken to the roof of the school building and blindfolded. In photographs of the event, signs of torture are clearly visible on their bodies. Next, many other leaders of the military and the defense establishment were executed. Some of them were "killed" three times—by shooting, hanging, and drowning. Others were shown more respect: they were seated on carpets from their native districts and shot in the head.

"Altogether, I formed strong and friendly ties with sixty senior members of the regime in Iran," says Segev. "To my great regret, in the days after Khomeini's return I was forced to see fifty of them killed, on television or with my own eyes. My name was explicitly mentioned in some of the verdicts. One of them was the man from the airport administration who had helped me get approval for the takeoff of the El Al jumbo jet. I don't regret our relations with Iran, they were a strategic asset, but to have all of these things on my conscience was very hard in those days."

Ultimately, the twelve Israelis who had taken refuge in Segev's apartment on February 10 decided to leave. The group began wandering from one Jewish home to another, and in each home the frightened residents hinted gently that their presence was not wanted.

Once, to obtain vegetables, Segev went to the market. He didn't know that buyers were expected to bargain with vendors, because his wife had always done the family's marketing, so he attracted attention. A local commander armed with a Kalashnikov AK-47 began asking questions. "I took him aside, and told him I was from the PLO and represented it in Iran. All of a sudden it turned out that he spoke Arabic, and knew quite a lot about the PLO. Luckily, a few weeks earlier, Military Intelligence had sent out a background review, so I could show him that I knew what I was talking about. His eyes lit up, and he took me back to the stall and told them enthusiastically that I represented the only body that supported the revolution and ordered them to give me everything free. Years later, I told this story to Arafat, and he said dryly, 'You bastard. I see that your Palestinian identity saved your life.'"

"One morning," says Geffen, "I woke up before everyone else in our hiding place in an apartment in Eisenhower Street. I looked out of the window and I saw that the game was up. The building was surrounded by heavily armed soldiers and jeeps mounted with heavy machine guns. We were sure they were there for us. After a brief parley, I went downstairs, like an inquisitive resident of the building, and started speaking to one of the soldiers, standing at the ready next to a machine gun. 'What's going on?' I asked. 'Who are you looking for?' It turned out that the Revolutionary Guards intelligence suspected there was a CIA agent living in the building. But they had already broken into the apartment and found it empty and would be leaving shortly. I agreed with him, at the top of my voice, that all of the American and Israeli agents must be wiped out, and the sooner the better. I was so relieved that they hadn't come for us that I launched into a long speech of praise for Ayatollah Ruhollah Khomeini. Later I even put together some light refreshments for the soldiers."

Eventually, it was arranged in a meeting between Minister of Defense Weizman and CIA representatives in Tel Aviv that the Israelis would fly out with a group of Americans in two Pan Am planes that were due to land in Tehran in mid-February. At the airport there was a six-hour wait, as tensions were high. Finally, after hours on the plane and repeated passport checks, one plane took off. The Israelis, who had gone through so much in the previous weeks, asked the pilot not to report that there were Israelis on board until they were clear of Iranian airspace because they feared they could still be forced to land. It was only when they landed in Frankfurt and saw the El Al plane that would take them on to Israel that they knew they were safe.

By the end of 1979, some thirteen thousand Iranian officers had resigned or been dismissed, including all with the rank of brigadier or higher. Of some eighty senior generals who had served as the top command under the Shah, at least seventy were executed, along with two hundred other commanders.

The revolution had no definitive plans, either economic or social, or even political. Khomeini had no idea of how to rule the country he had just taken over, which was so vast and so wealthy, but also so full of problems. He bestowed more and more tracts of land on the groups of mullahs who were his power base, but he had no understanding at all of banking, oil economics, industry, or social services. Whenever he encountered a problem in any of these spheres, which until then had been handled in accordance with the Shah's Western ideas, he would say that it was all "a web of intrigue woven by the Jews," and repeat the most significant slogan that he had coined during his long years of exile in Iraq: "Islam is the solution."

As a substitute for an agenda, the Khomeini revolution turned to mass murder, and purity laws. Women had to cover up. A series of bans on music, contraceptives, alcohol, and card and dice games were imposed.

The Revolutionary Guards, which were set up soon after Khomeini's return to Iran under the name "The Revolutionary Organization of the Masses of the Islamic Republic," became the regime's main instrument for holding the country in a steel grip. The Guards protected the regime and enforced its orders and laws at home; they also tried to export revolution abroad. When Iraq invaded the country in 1980, the Revolutionary Guards even took over command of the armed forces.

In parallel, Khomeini began to act against his most committed allies.

The Mujahideen Khalq movement,* which was also known as the Iranian Freedom Fighters, had been fighting the Shah since 1965, at first non-violently. In the 1970s, the leaders of the movement began to believe that only violent action could bring about the end of the monarchy. Their attacks started in outlying areas of the cities and remote provinces, but they later began operating in the center of the country as well. In response, the Shah pitted the SAVAK against them and had several members executed.

The Mujahideen, religious extremists who in some senses were to the right of Khomeini on the political spectrum, had joined Khomeini's movement, but they soon realized that the revolution that was unfolding before their eyes was hardly the kind of victory they had hoped for. They were excluded from power, and soon became the chief opposition to Khomeini. At first the group organized peaceful protests, then demonstrations, and finally a series of quite successful violent actions against Khomeini power centers. The peak came on June 28, 1981, when a powerful bomb went off in the headquarters of the Islamic Republican Party in southern Tehran, killing Ayatollah Mohammad Beheshti, second in command to Khomeini, and over seventy others leaders, including ten ministers and deputy ministers, as well as Mohammad "Ayatollah Ringo" Montazeri, a senior military commander who got his nickname because of his love of firearms.

Hashemi Rafsanjani, a future two-term president, was saved from certain death by leaving the meeting of the party leadership minutes before the blast. The deaths of strongman Beheshti and so many other key personages threw Tehran into chaos, and for some hours it looked as if the Islamic regime was on its last legs. But Khomeini once more succeeded in closing ranks, calling on the nation to stand firm and be even more prepared for sacrifice.

Khomeini acted harshly and decisively. His followers chased down the Mujahideen's members, and the revolutionary courts had them executed in droves. A wave of executions began that continued for a year without interruption. On one day, September 19, 1981, 149 people, mostly aged sixteen to twenty-five, were shot to death in Tehran's Evin Prison, including thirty-two women. By the end of the year, those sentenced to death numbered 6,000.

* Unrelated to the Afghani Mujahideen movement.

The revolutionary regime had also begun a crackdown on the Jews of Iran.

Signs of anti-Semitism had begun appearing in the Islamist struggle against the Shah in the middle of 1978. Shi'ite clerics incited believers against the Jews. Leaflets were distributed calling for revenge against the Jews for "the crimes of international Zionism, and for their plundering the resources of the state and consistent support for Israel, the enemy of the Arabs and of Islam." Leaders of the Jewish community received threatening letters, wealthy merchants were called upon to get out of the country, and slogans like "Death to the Jews" were daubed on synagogue walls. In September 1978, a Jewish student was murdered in the city of Mashad, and in Hamadan an attempt was made to blow up the community's building. Anti-Semitic publications such as *The Protocols of the Elders of Zion*, with a commentary by Nazi propaganda chief Joseph Goebbels, were translated into Farsi and disseminated throughout the country. Ayatollah Yahya Noori called openly for attacks on the Jews. The merchants of Tehran's Grand Bazaar boycotted their Jewish colleagues and bought nothing from them; word was that they would soon be able to take it all for free when the Jews were wiped out.

The seeds of anti-Semitism planted before the revolution took root and grew into one of the perennial and most prominent themes of declarations by the leaders of Iran, who sometimes mixed their attacks on Zionism and calls to destroy Israel, vicious enough in themselves, with the slogans of classical European Jew hatred and sweeping generalized attacks on Jews everywhere. The new regime made life difficult for the population in general, but their attitude to the Jews was particularly hostile. Khomeini's militias patrolling the streets easily found excuses to make targets of the homes and businesses of Jews even before they evolved into the Revolutionary Guards. Moreover, Khomeini ordered the cessation of free emigration for Iranians, as the wealthy ones who had failed to leave before the Shah did now tried to do. The regime demanded that anyone wanting to emigrate must receive permission from the authorities and would be allowed to take only a minimal amount of money and valuables.

The assessment in the Mossad was that immediately after the impending revolution, chaos would reign in Iran; and indeed, in the years 1979–81, in a complex and clandestine operation code-named *Shulhan Arukh* or "Laid Table," the Mossad exploited the turmoil to rescue some

40,000 Jews out of a total of 100,000. It used any and all means to do so. This operation was executed by *Bitzur,* the Mossad's section that deals with diasporic Jewish communities in danger.

Central to the operation was Avraham Geffen. After the Israeli Embassy personnel departed, Geffen, who had worked as a kind of all-purpose messenger for El Al and the Jewish Agency (which was in charge of the immigration of Jews to Israel before the revolution), was the only person left in Tehran who could handle the loose ends that they had left behind. In the post-revolutionary chaos, he was overlooked by the militants, and so survived.

Geffen was brought into the operation some weeks after the revolution, when he received a call from David Shofet, the son of the head of the Tehran Jewish community, Rabbi Yedidya Shofet, saying, "Come and meet a friend." The "friend" was a Mossad agent, who put Geffen in charge of the Iranian end.

The hundreds of Jews who joined the operation were divided into groups and briefed on the escape process. The toughest cases were those who did not have passports, and families with a son of age for the military. Using one of the community's rabbis, the Mossad set up a document forgery industry in Tehran. Passports were provided for those who lacked them, and draft-age men were given birth certificates making them a year or two younger. Groups of Jews flew out on three to seven regular commercial flights a week leaving Iran for Europe, under Geffen's supervision.

The operation went on for months without being disturbed. The revolutionary regime, not yet fully established, still lacked the skilled personnel to keep a close eye on goings-on at the airport. But luck was not always on Geffen's side.

"One Saturday, a large group of emigrants was due to leave," he recounts. "Two families lost their way and never reached the airport. Their plane was a scheduled flight to Athens. There were also regular passengers on it, who of course wanted to leave on time. I gave out some bribes to the right people and managed to get the departure delayed. We waited a whole hour for the two families, but they didn't show. Meanwhile, the regular passengers understood that I had some status at the airport, and they came to complain to me. The Jews also gathered around me and there we stood, in the middle of the terminal, waiting for the latecomers."

Geffen didn't realize that an official of the regime was watching the situation unfold, and he ordered Geffen arrested, as well as all the Jews who had been on the flight.

"They grilled me for hours," Geffen recalls, "for the time being without beatings, but very harshly and with a lot of threats. A fat officer of Khomeini's 'morality police' managed to find out who I was and my past links with El Al. He demanded that I tell him everything I knew about that airline that 'sucked the blood of the Muslim world,' in his words. He reminded me that when the entire airport was on strike against the Shah's regime, only El Al carried on working and even brought a full team of workers from Israel, including people to clean toilet bowls and basins.

"I had an arrangement with my father-in-law, that if I did not contact him at a certain hour every day, he should go to my apartment and clean out everything connected to Israel. [Geffen couldn't ask his wife to do it, as she was unaware of his activities, for her own safety.] Luckily, he did what we had arranged. Soldiers came and conducted a thorough search a few hours later."

Geffen was taken to the prison on Shimran Street where he was subjected to severe daily questioning, beaten, and starved. "They accused me of sending Jews to training camps in Israel. But luckily for me, they were not at all convinced that I was really from the Mossad. As far as the outside world was concerned, I had simply vanished. Jews who managed to leave Iran brought the news to the Mossad people in Israel, who got very agitated. One of the immigrants even took the trouble of calling my wife in Israel [she had left Tehran a few months earlier] and telling her I was dead."

Geffen was lucky in the end. "One day, in the middle of an interrogation session, I saw an angel, a real angel in the form of a senior officer who had once worked at the airport. Before the revolution, we used to sit and chat for hours about all kinds of things. Once I even helped him when he had a money problem. The officer took my interrogator aside for a short talk, and came back to me. You must understand that at that period, proper governmental institutions had not yet been formed in Iran, just groups of fanatics grabbing chunks of power for themselves. The group that was in charge of my prison wanted money to release me—a lot of money. The officer spoke to my father-in law, who organized a campaign to raise the amount from the community. With the help of some very rich Jews, who knew what I had been doing, they managed to collect $150,000 ransom, and I was released."

Afraid to go home, in case he might be kidnapped by some other group that wasn't bound by the deal, Geffen hid out in the homes of friends, each night in a different house. His connection with the Iranian officer became a regular business relationship. The officer had been appointed to a senior post in the new regime's embryonic secret service, and had access to all the leaders of the government and to the prisons. Jewish families, through Geffen, gave him large amounts of money to get their relatives out of prison or even in some cases to have death sentences commuted.

In April 1980, Geffen left Iran; but after a brief period of working and training in Israel, he was asked to return. "I replied that I would go unwillingly, as if I'd been drugged, for the sake of the sacred cause." On September 22, 1980, war broke out between Iran and Iraq. The Tehran authorities feared a mass flight of eligible draftees, and control over people flying out of the country was tightened. In December, Geffen got in touch with the well-connected officer. "He cursed me. He told me I was a fool and that he did not intend to collaborate with me this time. I told him to wait for me at Tehran airport. I brought with me four giant bottles of Johnny Walker that the Mossad had given me. That broke the ice. I found that the situation in Iran had deteriorated since I left. The authorities were squeezing the Jews and everyone, really everyone, was demanding bigger bribes. Everywhere, in the synagogues, on the streets, people would come up to me and grab my shirt and ask me to get them out of Iran."

Geffen spent another half-year in Iran until the operation was thwarted when the air routes that the Jews had been using were totally blocked. Bitzur searched for alternatives. Disjointed reports reaching the Mossad indicated that some Iranian Jews had managed independently to establish contact with smugglers in the country's border zones. The Mossad joined this effort, and coordinated illicit border crossings in a complex, perilous operation that cost the lives of not a few of the emigrants. Some of the routes passed through mountainous terrain and steep gorges that took a heavy toll through exhaustion and fatal falls.

More than once, buses full of Jews were apprehended on their way to the border. They were usually allowed to go on, in exchange for payment of a fine. The smugglers, however, were sentenced to long terms in Iranian jails.

Avraham Geffen served in the Mossad for a few more years before he retired in the mid-1980s and opened a small minimarket in Tel Aviv. The Mossad, he says, did not assist him and his family in resettling in Israel.

In 2008, there were still between 20,000 and 30,000 Jews in Iran. They are harassed by the authorities and their freedom of worship is limited. In public, they are subject to Islamic laws, such as the obligation for women to wear the veil. They live in constant fear.

CHAPTER 3

# Operation Seashell:
# How Israel Secretly Armed Iran

Saddam Hussein had watched the chaos in neighboring Iran intently. He knew Iran had lost its American and Israeli patrons, of course. And he was not unaware of the effects on the Iranian armed forces of the massive purges of the senior officer corps and of the fact that the flow of arms promised to the Shah's regime had been blocked, either by the exporting countries or by Khomeini himself, who was interested in weakening the army as much as possible. Saddam had made himself president of Iraq in July 1979, although he had been running the country long before that. He had perceived a chance to pounce on a large, oil-rich neighbor, and to put a stop to talk of the export of Khomeini's revolution to his own country, which had a suppressed Shi'ite majority.

At first, Saddam had worked at trying to undermine the stability of the new regime from the inside. He initiated a broad plan to "liberate" part of Khuzestan, a city in western Iran, and to install a new Iranian government there under the patronage of the exiled Shah. The attempted rebellion was set for July 10, 1980, but the plan was discovered by Khomeini's intelligence and crushed with great brutality. Most of the 250 conspirators who were arrested were executed. After several such attempts, Saddam gave up on the idea of subversion and decided to take a more direct path.

On September 22, 1980, Iraqi forces marched into Iran. Saddam aimed to conquer vast swathes of territory containing particularly rich oil fields. He also wanted to retake control of three islands in the Gulf, as well as shipping rights in the Shat al-Arab waterway, which he had been forced to cede in 1975. More generally, he believed a war would bolster his popularity.

Saddam had a large, well-trained army at his disposal, which had been armed by the West as a counter to Soviet penetration of the Persian Gulf region. The Iranian army was weak, and missing most of its officer corps, and the Iraqi columns advanced almost without meeting any opposition, conquering city after city and oil field after oil field. The way seemed clear for Iraq to occupy all of Iran, and the Khomeini regime was hanging by a hair.

But Saddam Hussein had not taken into account the devotion and fanaticism of the followers of the imam—nor the potential for Israel to intervene clandestinely on the side of the Islamic Republic of Iran.

## JULY 24, 1981: A REMOTE ARMENIAN MOUNTAINSIDE

A huge, scorched black crater gaped at the rescue team, which immediately understood there was no one left for them to rescue. All they could do was extricate the remains of eight unidentifiable bodies. The aircraft that had been carrying them had been loaded so full of munitions and fuel that when it exploded in the air and crashed into a mountainside, there was almost nothing left of it or its crew.

Media reports said that the plane had lost its way and entered Soviet airspace over Azerbaijan. One of the Soviet air force jets sent to intercept it was said to have mistakenly collided with it, causing the crash. The truth is much more sinister, and shadowy.

The Argentinean ambassador in Moscow at the time, Leopoldo Bravo, was with the rescue team. Authorities had informed him that an aircraft belonging to the Argentinean cargo airline TAR had penetrated Soviet airspace and collided with another plane. The embassy ran a quick check which revealed that, in fact, a Canadair jet belonging to the company had vanished from radar screens near the Soviet-Turkish border on July 18. But the ambassador had not been able to figure out why an Argentine plane was in that area and what cargo it was carrying. Inquiries in Argentina had turned up nothing.

In fact, the plane's mission was well known at the time among a close circle in Israeli intelligence, and certain arms dealers. The aircraft was ferrying Israeli arms to Khomeini's regime, in secret, to assist in Iran's war with Iraq.

Saddam Hussein's invasion was only ten months old. The war would last for eight years, and cost over a million lives, but at the time it seemed likely that Saddam's superior forces would soon be parading through Tehran. The newly purged Iranian military was dominated by the Revolutionary Guards, and Khomeini needed immediate replacements for the trained soldiers he had purged or lost from the Shah's army.

Among the problems the Iranian forces had no answer for were minefields that had been sown by the Iraqis between the front lines of the two armies. At first, the Revolutionary Guards tried driving herds of donkeys or other animals over the mined areas to clear a path for the troops. But as soon as the first beast was blown up, the others abandoned the mission and refused to advance to their certain deaths. However, another solution was in the offing.

The imam grasped that the war held a powerful attraction for Iran's teenagers, who constituted a majority of the population. He issued a religious edict permitting boys older than twelve to volunteer for front-line forces, without securing the permission of their parents or guardians. Most of those who volunteered were inducted into a new popular militia called the *Basij*. A quarter of a century later, this militia would serve as the central force that secured the election of Mahmoud Ahmadinejad as president of Iran. These volunteers became the protégés of the imam, who promised them a place in Paradise if they died on the battlefield. Khomeini did not invent this idea. Falling in battle during *jihad*, including self-sacrifice on the field of combat, is an exalted precept in Shi'a, opening the gates of heaven for those who do so. But Khomeini was the first to elevate the concept of martyrdom into a central, systemic means of circumventing the Islamic ban on suicide.

Tens of thousands of boys and men, wearing scarlet headbands bearing the words "Long Live Khomeini," streamed to the war zone. Many carried plastic "keys to heaven," made in Taiwan. They cleared minefields by running across them, as human testers. They attacked and destroyed Iraqi tanks, employing kamikaze methods. Each one wrote a will before going into combat, with the help of special scribes who were sent to the front for this purpose. Most of these testaments were letters addressed to the imam or to "Dear Mom."

In *The Spirit of Allah*, the Iranian journalist Amir Taheri quotes one of these testaments: "How miserable, how dismal, how ignorant I was for all of the 14 years of my unfortunate life that passed me by without my knowing Allah. The Imam has opened my eyes . . . How sweet, sweet, sweet, is death. It is like a blessing that Allah has bestowed upon his favorites."

Khomeini had solved his manpower problem, but he still badly needed weapons and supplies. Iran's stockpiles were running low. During the Shah's regime, Israel and America had kept Iran well armed; but now, following the seizure of the U.S. Embassy and the subsequent hostage crisis, America had declared a general boycott of Iran, and demanded that its allies do the same.

Not everyone complied with the U.S. demands. The French, for one, weren't averse to bending the embargo. One French firm, apparently under the protection of a high official in French intelligence, signed a contract with a British firm to supply engines for Scorpion light tanks to Iran. On the bills of lading they claimed the engines were bound for Jordan, although the Jordanian army had no Scorpion tanks. They also approached the Israel Defense Ministry's representative in Paris, offering to act as intermediary for sales of Israeli supplies.

Amazingly, Israel responded. Khomeini's regime openly endorsed the destruction of Israel, yet there were enough people in Israel who thought they should sell arms to him, in secret, for the operation code-named "Seashell" to be born. It puts the later Iran-contra scandal to shame.

There were four main reasons why Operation Seashell went forward. First, Israel could not come to terms with the military, intelligence, and diplomatic losses that it had sustained with the disruption of relations with Iran after the revolution. Arms exports would at least give it a foothold in Tehran. In Israel's defense establishment, the lesson had been learned from many cases over the years that swiftly supplying weaponry and military know-how to a totalitarian state will bring the supplier as close as possible to the rulers, because the weapons are their means of holding on to power.

Second, it was hoped that the infusion of weaponry would intensify the Iran-Iraq War and lead to the mutual destruction or, at least weakening, of two enemies.

Third, Israeli officials feared a victorious Saddam Hussein. Finally, more than anything else, the weapons industry wanted to make money. As one Israeli Defense Ministry official, a key figure in Operation Seashell, recalls: "I do not remember even one discussion about the ethics of the matter. All that interested us was to sell, sell, sell more and more Israeli weapons, and let them kill each other with them."

Iran's appeal for arms came through various front companies. The Zurich-based Center for Logistic Support Corporation wrote to SIBAT, the arm of the Israeli Defense Ministry that deals with defense exports, in January 1981. The letter explained that

> The continuing war between Iran and Iraq has created an immediate requirement for a continuous and organized supply of spare parts and weapons to back up the current needs of the Iranian Defense forces.
>
> As a result of the Iranians' initiative, we are in the process of establishing a center for Logistic Support in Europe (CLS) which will serve the Iranian requirements in the aerospace and defense fields. This organization is directly connected to the Iranian Ministry of War who would like to use them in its reorganization procedures for future purchases from the Western World.

The company's support center was located on the sixth floor of NIOC House, 4 Victoria Street, London, a building belonging to the National Iranian Oil Company, which also housed the Iranian-British Chamber of Commerce.

All of the Iranian requests for help through various channels landed in the Kirya, the precinct in Tel Aviv that houses the Defense Ministry and the headquarters of the Israel Defense Forces (IDF).

The first deal was carried out through one shrewd Iranian arms dealer via French intermediaries. The dealer bought 250 tires for Phantom jet fighters, along with communications equipment, 106mm recoilless guns, mortars, and ammunition, all from Israel. He paid $2 million up front. The goods were shipped via Lisbon. It turned out, however, that he was bilking his Iranian customers. He charged them $56 million, and promptly disappeared.

But this scam did not shut the pipeline down; and orders from Iran kept on coming. SIBAT's head, Zvi Reuter, approached the Israeli technology and arms company Elul, owned and managed by a man named David Kolitz, to examine the possibility of using it as a conduit for arms sales to Iran. Kolitz, who had done business in Iran under the Shah selling agricultural equipment, agreed to participate. In the old days he had sold automated chicken coops. Now, he would sell guns and materiel.

One of the main players in Operation Seashell was a Portuguese arms dealer by the name of George Piniol. He arrived in Israel in early 1980 on a visit coordinated by SIBAT, bearing letters of credit worth tens of millions of dollars. He had already established a front company called

Koffer Holdings Ltd., registered on Jersey in the Channel Islands, as a cover. His first deal was relatively modest: 150 M-40 antitank guns and 24,000 shells for each gun. Piniol used bank checks to pay for them. He had a very detailed shopping list, presumably dictated by Iran: spare parts for tank and aircraft engines; shells for 106mm recoilless rifles and for 130mm, 203mm, and 175mm guns; and TOW vehicle-mounted launchers and missiles. He was equipped with any number of fake certifications stating that the end user for his acquisitions was a company in Peru.

Elul's sales staff soon realized that everything the Iranians wanted—a total of 360 tons of spare parts and ammunition—was available in the warehouses of Israel Military Industries (IMI) and Israel Aircraft Industries (IAI), or at the Israel Defense Forces stockpiles. It was decided to gather all the consignments from all the different sources for each shipment in one large central hangar at the IAI's Ben Gurion International Airport headquarters, placed under heavy guard. The hangar would be emptied and restocked many times, as the flood of Israeli arms to Iran continued.

The Iranians wanted the goods yesterday, and shipment by sea was out of the question. Secrecy demanded that a complex airlift operation be devised, carried out entirely at night in unmarked aircraft to ensure that neither Israel nor Iran would be associated with it. Piniol managed to get officials of the Argentinean airline Transporte Aereo Rioplatense (TAR), some of them based in Miami, to assign an aircraft to the operation and ignore the fraudulent bills of lading, in exchange for nearly $300,000. The plane could carry only 20 tons at a time, so eighteen flights were required. The value of the entire deal was $75 million, paid by Iran.

In a letter to the IMI, Elul pledged that "in the event of any mishap connected to the transportation and delivery of the goods to the buyers, we will, to the best of our ability, take all necessary measures to ensure that there will be no publication of information that could link in any way at all the deal with IMI or the State of Israel."

To finalize the operation, a meeting was held at IAI headquarters on July 15, 1981, to discuss what the "top-secret" minutes of the meeting described as "The order of the Elul company in the matter of Seashell." The Defense Ministry's director of security, Haim Karmon, approved "the transportation of the items ordered, including ammunition, by air

shipment [and] insisted that on the cargo manifests on each flight neither
the nature of the goods nor their production source be specified, apart
from mention of the place of loading . . . the terminology used in the
letters of credit would be 'pipes, cylinders, and spare parts.' " Following
that meeting, Elul deputy CEO Dan Kav wrote a detailed letter in English to Raphael Peled of Israel's Bank Leumi, with clear instructions for
handling the transfer of funds and how to refrain from using the name of
Israel or revealing the true nature of the arms shipments on any documents. The deals were carefully constructed to look utterly innocent. The
"pipes, cylinders, and spare parts" were officially addressed to a German
company.

To this day, David Kolitz, owner of Elul, denies the whole thing,
insisting that "Elul does not trade in arms, has never exported weapons
and/or ammunition to Iran at any time and has never served as a 'front'
for such government activities, if there were any such activities."

> Question: But your signature appears on the documents from Elul that
> deal with the trade with Iran and your name appears as a participant in
> all of the meetings on the subject.
> Kolitz: I am not saying that you are a liar and I am not saying that you are
> insane. Despite the documents that you have mentioned and despite
> my signature, I repeat my earlier response.

The Iranian impresario behind Operation Seashell was a man whose
name crops up frequently in the secret wars between Iran, Israel, and the
West: Dr. Sadeq Tabatabai, a distant relative of Khomeini and one of his
confidants in sensitive matters. It was he who ordered the Iranian purchasing agents to contact Piniol. On April 7, 1981, Tabatabai wrote to
Koffer Holdings, Piniol's straw company in Jersey, and made clear that
Iran would be the end user of the goods to be supplied. He identified
himself as a representative of the "Defense Council" of the revolution,
the leading body in Iran's security and intelligence system, one of the
most important administrative bodies in the country.

To a large extent, Tabatabai owed his successful career to Israel. For his
role in arranging the arms shipments from Israel, he gained much prestige, and Khomeini made sure he was promoted. He would become
deputy interior minister and a top Iranian representative in Lebanon,
where he was among the founders of Hizballah. He was in charge of arms

shipments from Iran to the militia. Following instructions from Tehran, it was Tabatabai who would later push for the abduction of two Israeli soldiers by Hizballah that led to the war in the summer of 2006.

The Israelis worked out a list of simple code names and numbers for the ingredients of the operation. A Shafrir air-to-air missile, for example, was "1," a Howitzer gun "2," a mini-Uzi submachine gun "8," and the destination of Iran "11." The plane carrying the goods was code-named "Britannia." A problem arose at the planning stage: IAI and Defense Ministry officials didn't want foreign pilots to enter their secure space at the airport, but Israeli pilots weren't keen on flying to Iran. The solution: a stopover in Cyprus. Pilots of Israel's Arkia Airline were used on the first leg, from Tel Aviv to Larnaca, Cyprus, and were replaced by crews recruited by Piniol from South Africa and other countries for the flight to Iran.

This system worked smoothly eight times. Every few nights, the TAR plane took off, loaded to the roof with huge amounts of arms and ammunition. After the stopover and second leg, it was unloaded secretly at a military airport near Tehran, before flying back to Israel. It was on the ninth flight that the plane disappeared off the radar screens over Armenia.

The mystery of the plane's crash on that remote Armenian mountainside remains unsolved to this day. A combined Mossad–Defense Ministry investigation concluded that all signs indicated the Soviet Union was responsible. One view is that the aircraft penetrated Soviet airspace in error, and was shot down. A second is that the Russians had learned of the arms shipments to Iran and viewed them as an extension of America's long arm in the Middle East, and so they intentionally intervened. Yet another hypothesis, for which no serious foundation exists, was that a very prominent American media figure who was visiting Israel at the time heard about the operation and found it so objectionable that he leaked its details so that the Iraqis got wind of it, and it was they who shot the plane down.

Yet the crash and the loss of the crew did not stop Operation Seashell. Piniol, the Elul company, and the Israeli defense establishment were too determined. There were still large amounts of materiel in the IAI hangar and Iran was planning a major counteroffensive, for which it needed massive amounts of weaponry. Ten days after the crash, Piniol turned up in Israel and tripled his orders. He had managed to set up a link between

Israel's Red Sea port of Eilat and the Iranian port at Bandar Abbas. Israel's Energy Ministry helped organize this route in the belief that it would be possible to get oil in exchange for the arms shipments. Oil was not forthcoming, but a great deal of money changed hands as a large number of shipments, comprising hundreds of tons of arms and ammunition, ensued by sea. (One of the machine guns sold to Iran at that time would be used by Hizballah twenty-five years later to kill Israeli troops in the July 12, 2006, incident that led to Israel's most recent war in Lebanon.)

Piniol's deals were not the only ones in Operation Seashell. There were other channels through which Israeli arms, ammunition, and parts were reaching Iran. With that equipment, Iran succeeded in turning the tide of the war.

The Revolutionary Guards relaxed their control of Iran's military, and the old professional officer corps reasserted itself. The army chief of staff, General Kassam Ali Zaher-Nijad, proved to be a skilled military leader. Under his command, with the help of the Israeli arms, Iran launched a successful counteroffensive in early October 1981 to break the Iraqi siege of Abadan, a key oil city. Subsequently Iran retook almost all of the land conquered by Iraq, including twelve cities and more than a thousand villages. In July 1982, Iranian forces invaded Iraqi territory for the first time.

With the outbreak of the Iran-Iraq War, the Israelis faced a classic conundrum in foreign policy: If two of your enemies are fighting each other, whom should you help? It can be hard to sit on the sidelines, rooting for a draw, and it is somewhat understandable that key Israelis feared a total victory by Saddam Hussein. But Iran would soon start using the arms Israel had shipped to it on Israel itself, and on Western targets.

PART II

# THE HIDDEN WAR
# IN THE MIDDLE EAST

CHAPTER 4

# Dangerous Games:
# The Lebanon War and the Birth
# of Hizballah

In retrospect, it is hard to believe that Israel and the West failed to foresee the birth of Hizballah. For one thing, Shi'ite Iran and the Shi'ites in Lebanon had long been linked. Even before Khomeini, the Shah had ascribed great importance to the Shi'ite population in Lebanon. In many ways, the Shah's regional policy as far as neighboring countries were concerned (with the obvious exception of Israel) was imitated by Khomeini, who merely changed the ideology behind it.

In 1971, Khomeini met a cleric who made a deep impression on his thinking: Mussa al-Sadr, whose niece had married Khomeini's son, Ahmad. Al-Sadr was a native of the city of Qom, the holiest city in Iran and the second holiest to the world Shi'ite community. It was here that Khomeini had developed his principal doctrines and the leaders of the revolution, and here that the Shi'ite leaders of Lebanon were educated. He had close links to the Shah, and with the Shah's blessing had travelled to Lebanon to set up a Shi'ite charitable organization, with the help of the SAVAK, the Shah's secret service. Soon al-Sadr became the leader of the Shi'ites of Lebanon. He crowned himself, just as Khomeini did, "imam," a title that connotes leadership of the entire Shi'ite community and implies divine properties.

It was al-Sadr who in 1975 set up *Amal* ("Hope"), an umbrella organization that addressed all aspects of life in the Shi'ite community. His religious authority was strong, but he played a dangerous game politically. He was trusted by the Shah, and enjoyed the generous assistance of the Shah's secret police. In turn he supplied the Shah's emissaries with a comprehensive picture of the situation in Lebanon, and no less important, of what was happening in the Arab capitals, where the leaders treated him as a welcome guest on his frequent visits. He established links with the CIA station in Beirut, too, and gave the agency much valuable information about the Soviet and East German presence in Syria and Lebanon.

In August 1978, al-Sadr vanished during a visit to Libya. His disappearance was the most important defining moment for the Shi'ites of Lebanon. Nobody knows what happened to him. Plenty of suspects had motives: the Libyan ruler, Muammar al-Gaddafi, was al-Sadr's host at the time of his disappearance and would not have been happy that he was working with the CIA. The Shah's regime might have wanted to pay him back for his support of the Islamic revolutionaries. The Khomeini camps were aware of al-Sadr's ties to the Shah and might have wanted to get rid of a rival. Finally—and this was the Mossad's assumption at the time—Yasser Arafat was unhappy that al-Sadr was trying to block his growing influence in Lebanon. Al-Sadr's disappearance will likely remain a mystery, one of many in the complicated yet crucial history of modern Lebanon.

With al-Sadr gone, his deputy Sheikh Mohammad Hussein Fadlallah became the supreme Shi'ite spiritual authority in Lebanon. The Iranian crisis and Khomeini's triumph were just months away.

Before the Iranian revolution, the notion of an Islamic state had been a remote ideal; all of a sudden, in 1979, the men who had spent their years in the study halls of Qom and Najaf were the masters of Iran. Eager to win the goodwill of Islamic Iran, the senior Shi'ite clerics of Lebanon soon officially declared their loyalty to the Imam Khomeini.

Officials of the revolutionary regime then began visiting Lebanon. First to arrive was Dr. Sadeq Tabatabai, then the deputy head of the defense council (who in the 1980s would be in charge of the Iranian side in the secret arms deals between Tehran and Israel). He was enthusiastically welcomed by the Shi'ites and their leaders in May 1979. He also met with Yasser Arafat and other Palestinian leaders, visiting southern Lebanon and wearing the combat uniform of the Amal militia, packing a pistol.

Lebanon's importance to the Iranians, beyond concern for the Shi'ite population and the desire to export the revolution, was magnified by another factor. Because of the country's multi-communal and politically heterogeneous makeup, and the weakness of its central government and its vulnerability to outside influence, the country was seen as something of a test model for everything happening in the Arab world, a preliminary small-scale simulation of the Great Game in which the various Arab forces were vying for hegemony in the Middle East. At the end of 1980, for example, Beirut became an arena for clashes between pro-Iraqi Lebanese elements—supported by the CIA—and pro-Iranians, with the embassies of the two countries waging their own version of the war then raging on the border between their countries, carrying out assassinations and bombings. In November 1980, the Shi'ite leader Fadlallah's car was raked by machine-gun fire from a passing car. A bullet hit his turban, but he was not hurt. In the following two years, there were more attempts on his life, and Fadlallah surrounded himself with bodyguards. One of them was an unknown man called Imad Moughniyeh. On December 15, 1980, the Iraqi embassy in Beirut was blown up by a car bomb, apparently at Fadlallah's orders, killing the ambassador and many of the staff members. Iraq, which was totally exposed and in a difficult, inferior position in Lebanon, accepted the loss of its influence there.

After the failed assassination bid against Fadlallah in 1980, the speaker of the Iranian Parliament, Ali Akbar Hashemi Rafsanjani, paid a personal visit to Fadlallah's home as a gesture of appreciation to the cleric. His name still meant very little in the Western world, but Iranian emissaries understood the importance of elite imams like Fadlallah, and they displayed increasing eagerness to harness his persuasive abilities to their revolutionary wagon.

Khomeini had been developing ties with Lebanon for some time, as well as with the Palestinians. In the 1970s, Khomeini's two sons, Mustafa and Ahmad, had paid frequent visits to the country, where they underwent political and military training, first in Amal camps in the south and later in Fatah bases near Beirut. Ahmad was registered as an honorary member of Fatah (the main faction of the PLO), and he joined Yasser Arafat's fighters in several operations against the Christians and against Israel in Lebanon and on the border. During his official visits to Iraq, Arafat had called upon Khomeini at least twice while he was still in Najaf, the Shi'ite holy city where the Iranian cleric spent thirteen years between 1965 and 1978. At these meetings it was decided that a number of Iranian supporters of Khomeini would undergo military training at Fatah bases in Lebanon.

By 1977, when the rumblings of the Islamic revolution had begun to

be heard in Iran, more than seven hundred Khomeini loyalists had graduated from Amal and Fatah training courses in Lebanon. It was from
among these men that the heads of the terror apparatuses of the Revolutionary Guards and the Ministry of Intelligence—VEVAK—would be
selected.

In November 1979, one of the first Iranian graduates of Lebanese terror camps, Mohammad Montazeri (nicknamed "Ayatollah Ringo" for his
show-off pistol draws and itchy trigger finger), took part in a PLO solidarity conference in Lisbon. There, he declared that he would recruit
100,000 Iranian volunteers to fight for the Palestinians against Israel.

He planned to begin by raising a force of 10,000 that would be flown
to South Lebanon, "the volcanic center of the Middle East and the only
place where fighting against Israel is going on."

Less than a year after the revolution, in late December 1979, the first
batch of four hundred Iranian volunteers turned up in Damascus, without prior notification, and declared their intention of going to Lebanon
to establish a Shi'ite movement. Gripped by revolutionary fervor, they
chanted slogans like, "Today Iran, tomorrow Palestine." Much to their
surprise, Syrian president Hafez al-Assad locked them up in a Palestinian
refugee camp and then sent them back to Iran. As for their leader,
Mohammad Montazeri, who had managed to sneak across the border to
Beirut, al-Assad ordered that he be caught and eliminated. Montazeri
eventually escaped, just barely, thanks to a phone call (intercepted by
Israeli intelligence) to Assad from Khomeini, who pleaded for him to be
spared. All of Iran's efforts to infect Syria with its Islamic ardor failed.
Assad was a secular dictator, and he knew that an extremist movement
could spiral out of his control and turn on his regime. Assad changed his
attitude, however, the day after Israel's invasion of Lebanon in 1982.

Civil war had broken out in Lebanon in 1975, with all of the various
denominations and factions in that multi-faceted country taking one side
or another. The main antagonists were the Maronite Christians, determined to retain their hegemony, and the forces of Yasser Arafat's Palestine
Liberation Organization, which had taken refuge in Lebanon after being
driven out of Jordan in 1970 and were now behaving as if the country
belonged to them. Other Muslim and Druze elements wanted to change
the constitution that ensured Christian domination, in order to get a
fairer, more proportionate share of the power. The Shi'ites under the leadership of al-Sadr, and before the founding of Hizballah, tended in the

earlier years of the war to adopt a more compromising, neutral stand. Some observers believe that an additional element was involved in the outbreak and the prolonging of the war, namely a "Third Force" consisting of mercenaries hired by Libya and Iraq. The war lasted for fourteen years, and it cost some 150,000 lives, with 200,000 people injured and another 17,500 defined as missing, presumed dead.

In the years 1976–78, Arafat exploited the vacuum prevalent in Lebanon to make another move that would prove to be of very great historical import: He instructed his personnel to host Khomeini's adherents in their training camps, when the Iranian cleric was still in exile from his country and unknown in the West, and to give them advanced training in various aspects of warfare. Thus, the nucleus of the Revolutionary Guards and the intelligence apparatuses of the Islamic Republic were formed.

Syria's involvement in Lebanon steadily expanded during the war—four hundred Syrian soldiers were posted there in April 1976, and in the coming months tens of thousands more were sent in to prop up the government—until it was virtually ruling the country. Syrian president Hafez Assad exploited the request for help from his Lebanese counterpart Suleiman Franjiyeh to dispatch more and more units. Syria had weighty interests in Lebanon: Most of its imports came through Lebanese ports, and the possibility of an Israeli takeover of the south of the country was seen as a strategic threat.

Also, President Assad had always believed in the idea of a "Greater Syria" which included Lebanon and parts of Israel. Apart from the political benefits Syria's domination of Lebanon provided, it also bore financial profits. Syrian officers imposed "taxes" on goods passing through the country, which was one of the main marine gateways to the Arab world. Syria also took over the lucrative drug trade that flowed from the growing fields in Lebanon to the rest of the Middle East and from there to the world.

On June 6, 1982, Prime Minister Menachem Begin ordered the IDF to launch what the government called in public "The Operation for the Peace of Galilee," which in secret military papers was known as "Operation Great Pines." It was based on the concept that emerged from the clandestine connection that existed from 1975 on between heads of the Mossad and the Lebanese Phalange (the strongest Maronite Christian group) in the Beirut area. The reason for the invasion was the presence of PLO forces in southern Lebanon, on the border with Israel, and their Katyusha rockets which they used to bombard communities in northern Israel. Begin declared publicly that the aim of the war was to advance "only 40 kilometers" beyond the border, precisely the range of the rockets, in order to remove the threat. But the army's real plan, hidden to some extent even from Begin himself, was different. Defense minister Ariel Sharon instructed the Israel Defense Forces to be ready to expel the PLO forces and the Syrians from the entire country. Especially bothersome to Israel were advance Soviet-made antiaircraft missiles that the Syrians had deployed in Lebanon. In order to carry out the plan, Sharon had forged a secret pact with the Maronite Christians in Beirut.

There were some top officials in the Mossad, among them Reuven Merhav, then in charge of the Middle East section of the foreign relations division, who warned that the Christians were hoodwinking the Israelis, using them to solve their own problems with the PLO and Syria. These warnings were ignored. Through the Mossad, close ties were forged between Begin's hawkish defense minister and the Phalangists. It was Sharon who conceived of the war plan, behind which lay the idea of a comprehensive change in the Middle East: Israel would conquer southern Lebanon, join up with the Maronites in Beirut, and kick the PLO and the Syrians out. The leader of the Christian Phalange Party, Bashir Jemayel, would be installed as the ruler of Lebanon. Then—Sharon hoped—the expelled Palestinians would take over Jordan, set up their state there replacing King Hussein's Hashemite monarchy, and give up their dream of establishing it in the West Bank.

Although Israel's border with Lebanon had been quiet for a year, on June 6, 1982, the "Great Pines Project" was activated. The official pretext for launching the war was the shooting three days before of the Israeli ambassador in London, Shlomo Argov, by a terrorist belonging to the Abu Nidal gang, an extremist Palestinian terror group which had split off from the PLO and even killed some of its members. At one of the meetings where going to war was discussed, a senior MI officer pointed out to Israeli chief of staff Rafael Eitan that the Abu Nidal group regarded Arafat as an enemy, and had nothing to do with Lebanon. Eitan replied: "Abu Nidal, Abu Shmidal, they're all PLO."

Despite the role of his organization in developing the project, Mossad director Yitzhak Hofi had warned of the dangers of becoming entangled in Lebanon. And the historical roulette game set in motion by Sharon, chief of staff Eitan, and their fellow believers did in fact end up in an entanglement far beyond anything that had been envisaged.

Although the war was first received with some understanding by the rest of the world, when it became clear that its aims were fundamentally different from those declared by Prime Minister Begin, Israel was subjected to unprecedented international criticism. Even President Ronald Reagan was infuriated that he had not been consulted or even informed. The continuing expansion of the fighting and the concomitant civilian casualties did nothing to ease the criticism. Moreover, whereas in the beginning the Israeli tanks were welcomed by the Lebanese, who believed the Israelis would throw out the hated Palestinians, it soon became clear that they were no more than another army of conquerors. The Israelis soon became the targets of a number of guerrilla forces, encouraged by the Syrians, who of course wanted to do all they could to harm the Israelis.

The PLO forces commanded by Arafat retreated into Beirut, where they were besieged and bombarded by Israeli tanks and artillery. Mossad agents made sure that the commander of the Christian forces, Bashir Jemayel, was elected president, but Syrian intelligence put paid to the Israeli plan by blowing him up at a meeting at the Phalange headquarters in Beirut. The Phalange response was to massacre hundreds of Palestinians in the Sabra and Shattila refugee camps in southern Beirut. Israel was not an active partner in this atrocity, but its forces also did nothing to prevent or stop it. Later, the Syrians managed to have the peace agreement between the Lebanese and Israeli governments annulled, thereby wiping out whatever political achievements had been racked up by Israel in the war.

The expulsion of the PLO from Lebanon—trumpeted by Sharon as a major achievement, with some justification—led to the outbreak of the First Palestinian Intifada in the occupied territories in 1987. Most important, the foundation had been laid for the establishment in Lebanon of Iran's long arm of terror and dissemination of its Islamic Revolution. After the expulsion, Iran hastily moved to fill the subsequent vacuum by setting up an effective Shi'ite guerrilla militia.

When the welcoming handfuls of rice that Shi'ite villagers in South Lebanon had scattered over the invading Israeli forces turned into a hail of grenades and roadside bombs, the Israeli deputy prime minister,

Simcha Ehrlich, complained, "They never told us that there were Shi'ites there." This sums up the true state of affairs: An ignorant Israeli government that never knew there were Shi'ites in Lebanon who constituted the largest section of Lebanon's population, or what Shi'ites were, for that matter. Israel's intelligence agency was dominated by messianic types who had seen what they wanted to see. The prime minister, who had become infirm, was detached from reality, and the defense minister, as an Israeli court later found, had misled the nation and the government into believing that the "Peace of Galilee" campaign would stop 40 kilometers into Lebanon, after clearing Palestinian terrorists out of the border area, and would make no move against the Syrian forces. The Israeli air force had shot down some one hundred Syrian planes and also destroyed all of the advanced antiaircraft missile batteries that the Soviet Union had supplied. (Israel's losses in aircraft were zero.)

For the United States, this confrontation was tremendously important (just as the performance of the Israeli air force was in the 2006 Lebanon War, but for opposite reasons). In this war, Israel used American-made aircraft equipped with new, highly accurate American armaments, plus additional weapons and instruments made in Israel or developed jointly by the two countries, which were therefore tested in real combat conditions against the Soviet bloc's most advanced planes and antiaircraft measures that had been supplied to Syria. After the air war, top U.S. Air Force officers travelled to Israel and received assessments of the American arms data that made them very happy. The Pentagon subsequently changed its analysis of the potential outcome of any full-scale aerial confrontation with the Soviets.

To Syrian president Assad, Israel's invasion was very nearly an act of war upon Syria itself. He had not only seen his army dealt a severe blow, but his most precious military asset, the air force that he himself once commanded, had been destroyed. He grasped that he would not be able in the near future to confront Israel in classical combat. However, the damage to his ego led him to take three main steps: He stopped allocating money to the Syrian army, rehabilitating the air force instead; he set up a long-range missile corps, equipped with chemical warheads to counter Israel's nuclear weaponry; and he launched and attempted to establish a high-level guerrilla force in Lebanon to strike at the unwieldly Israeli military machine at its vulnerable points.

An extremist terrorist organization sponsored by Iran suddenly seemed like a useful ally. As long as it focused on Israel, and ignored "infidel" Arab regimes, why not?

A high-level Iranian military delegation arrived in Damascus in early July 1982 to discuss how Iran could help. Among its members were the minister of defense, Mohammad Salimi; the commander of land forces, Colonel Sayed Shirazi; and the commander of the Revolutionary Guard, Mohsen Rezai, who was accompanied by his close aide, Ali Reza Askari, a functionary in the Revolutionary Guard's intelligence. They were joined by the Iranian ambassador to Syria. Rezai stated that the delegation was there "to study the problem [in Lebanon] and to implement the principles of the true jihad and to teach the Zionists a lesson." During the visit, a military agreement was signed in which Syria granted what it had refused three years previously: material support for Iran's revolution-export network. Khomeini and the secular Baath socialist Assad were odd allies, but they had common enemies: Israel and the United States. Syria had become convinced Iran could be of assistance, and for its part, revolutionary; Iran was raring to assume what Khomeini had called "a forward strategic position which makes proximity to Jerusalem possible."

Shortly after that visit, a unit called the Mohammad Rasulallah Forces, consisting of three thousand men, arrived in Damascus, then moved on to Beirut, from where it dispersed to a number of training camps across Lebanon. It was commanded by Mohsen Rafiqdoost, a graduate of the Palestinian training camps in Lebanon in the 1970s, now a minister for the Revolutionary Guards in the Iranian government. He wanted to mount a full-scale attack on Israel, but he judged that to be premature, as the Syrians and the Palestinians were not prepared for war. The main part of his force returned to Iran. Nonetheless, some five hundred Iranian volunteers remained behind. The Syrians gave them a camp at Zabadani, near the Syrian border in the Bekaa Valley.

Iran and its cohorts in Lebanon were faced with a choice: Who should command this new force? Amal, whose name is an Arabic acronym for the for Lebanese Resistance Battalions, a Shi'ite organization set up by the imam Mussa al-Sadr after the outbreak of the civil war and enthusiastically backed by Iran in the late 1970s and early '80s? Or someone else? Amal's leader, Nabih Berri, was feuding with his deputy, Abbas Mussawi, over the question of alliances with Christians. Al-Sadr and Berri wanted to work with them in the hope that they would succeed in forging a coalition that would hold the Sunni forces in Lebanon at bay. Mussawi did not. Iran backed Mussawi—and that's how Hizballah was born in mid-1983, taking the public face of a new political party.

Sheikh Mohammad Fadlallah, the key Lebanese leader of the Shi'ites, would have preferred strengthening Amal, but eventually he gave in to Iran's pressure and gave his implicit agreement to the fateful decision to establish a new party. He himself chose to remain outside Hizballah because he anticipated that its formation would split Lebanon's Shi'ite community and he aspired to secure support from both sides of the rift.

From the beginning, Hizballah's goal was to replace the existing regime in Lebanon with an Islamic leadership. This task to make Hizballah powerful enough to fulfill this goal was assigned to the Revolutionary Guards. The numbers of those joining Hizballah rose steadily. A later party leader, Hassan Nasrallah, claims that two thousand young people joined the movement in its early days, including most Shi'ite clerics from the Bekaa Valley in eastern Lebanon and Beirut.

Hizballah was an Iranian organization from day one, managed by the Revolutionary Guards and VEVAK, the Ministry of Intelligence. Iran funneled money to it, and helped Hizballah seize a training camp from the Lebanese army. In early September 1983, the Sheikh Abdullah camp was the army's main base in the Baalbek area. Hizballah's religious leaders, Mussawi, Hassan Nasrallah, and Mohammad Yazbeq headed a mass procession to the base and held Friday prayers there. They advised the commander and his men "to put themselves at the disposal of the nation and to refuse orders given by the White House and Tel Aviv." The commander and his men evacuated the base. The new owners hung a sign on the gate that revealed their goals: "The liberation of the Sheikh Abdullah base by the masses of Hizballah is the first step toward freedom from the Phalange." The base was renamed after the Imam Ali and became the headquarters of the Revolutionary Guard in Lebanon and of the Hizballah militia. The Revolutionary Guards trained Hizballah recruits under the direction of Ali Reza Askari, who spent most of his time in Iran but sent instructors in all spheres of combat, sabotage, and terror to Lebanon. Sheikh Abbas al-Mussawi, who participated in one of the courses, later remarked that "without the patronage that the Revolutionary Guards extended to the young Muslims at the time of the Israeli invasion, they would have reached the borderline of fatal despair. The presence of the Revolutionary Guards at that time was the only spot of light. People began learning the principles of the Islamic revolution and to mobilize in the correct way against the Israeli enemy and against global imperialism." In 1985, Ali Reza Askari would be appointed commander of the al-Quds force, the arm of the Revolutionary Guards responsible for exporting the Islamic Revolution, including the training of non-Iranian forces, mainly Hizballah, and would move to Lebanon. Along with the other two most prominent leaders of Hizballah—Hassan Nasrallah and Imad Moughniyeh—he deserves central credit for converting Hizballah into a military organization of significant capability.

Hizballah, which means "the party of God," didn't just want an Islamic regime in Lebanon. Ultimately, it wanted a worldwide Islamic state, centered on Iran, with Khomeini as its ruler. Later, it would become more nationalist, but in the 1980s the Imam Khomeini was perceived as both its political and its religious leader. The aims of Hizballah (or its embryonic name, "The Organization of the Oppressed on Earth") were predictable: the ejection of foreign forces, primarily those of Israel, the United States, and France; the final eradication of the Jewish State; the liberation of Jerusalem; and the subjection of the Lebanese Christians to Islamic law.

The Iranians wanted, and in the historical perpective they were very successful, to set up a guerrilla movement in Lebanon that would be everything that the complacent, overfed, corrupt PLO, penetrated fairly easily by Israeli intelligence, was not: a lean, tough, well-trained fight machine whose personnel could not be persuaded with cash to give up information about their brothers, and which would have the capabilities of commando units in the best armies in the world. In brief, Iran intended to establish a terror organization in Lebanon, the likes of which the world had not yet seen.

Fadlallah wasn't completely on board with all this. He was at pains to depict himself as a pragmatist and a Lebanese patriot. He assured the Christians that he had no intention of imposing an Islamic state by force, and he objected to the demands voiced by Iranian emissaries to topple the Lebanese regime. The Lebanese nation, he asserted, had the right to determine its own fate. He wanted to be the Khomeini of Lebanon, rather than a subject of Khomeini himself.

Still, he and Hizballah could agree on some things: A state sitting on land that was holy to the Muslims could not be ruled by infidels, and therefore everything possible must be done to wipe the political entity named Israel, and run by Jews, off the map. Another target they set for themselves was the foreign forces deployed in Lebanon.

In 1983, in the wake of Israel's invasion, the UN formed the Multinational Force (MNF) to oversee the withdrawal of the PLO from Lebanon, and then to help maintain stability and peace there.

American Marines and French paratroops formed the core of the MNF. Its purpose was to bring peace to Lebanon and to end the bloody civil war that had been raging there since 1975. Under the protection of the MNF, the PLO did leave Beirut. Yet Hizballah remained, and stared at the foreign fighters living in barracks with murder in its eyes.

CHAPTER 5

# The Poor Man's Smart Bomb: The Reinvention of Suicide Bombing

"Dubbie and I were preparing to leave the building, and then it blew up. I remember a giant ball of flames and then the blast. Or was it the blast first and then the flames? All the walls flew outward. We fell from the fifth floor almost to the ground, without being able to hold on to anything, because we were just dropping through the air. A metal fridge that was in our room fell against a chair, and my head was in the space between them. Thanks to that chair, I wasn't crushed to death. I lay there with my face down, unable to move, with almost my whole body except my head covered by tremendously heavy stones and walls."

Even years after the event, Aharon "Roni" Halevy, today a driving teacher from Tiberias but at the time an investigator for the IDF Military Police CID (Criminal Investigation Division), shudders when he remembers what happened at seven o'clock on the morning of November 11, 1982. "Dubbie" is Dov Eichenwald, CEO of the Yedioth Ahronoth publishing house, one of Israel's biggest publishers, who was on reserve duty in Lebanon at the time. Halevy continues:

"Klein and Zada, two other CID investigators, were pleading for help in feeble voices, and I yelled to the rescue teams to save them first, because they had no air and could hardly breathe. I stretched my arm out to Zada and told him to reply to me by squeezing my hand if he could hear me, because I wanted to keep him awake until the rescuers reached him. After a while, the squeezing stopped, and I understood that he was no longer alive. I tried to pass an oxygen pipe that had been pushed through the ruins by a doctor to my other friend, Itzik Levi. I placed the nozzle close to his face, so he could try to get some air from it. But it didn't help. They both died.

"It was only around noon that they got Dubbie out. He was on top of

63

me, and I was still stuck underneath. There was a doctor, Dr. Linn, who knew I was there but couldn't find a way to reach me. He decided that the only way to get me out was to amputate both my legs. He thought that if they didn't get me out quickly, I'd die of exhaustion. I heard the conversation between him and the rescuer clearly, and I demanded that they give up on the idea. I said that I would rather stay there, in one piece. I was frightened that they would take the liberty of cutting off my legs without my permission, and I began yelling as loud as I could that they must not do it. Then, one of the rescuers thought of removing the chair that was holding the fridge up in order to get to me, and at the last moment, with my last drop of strength, I managed to explain to him that the chair was my guardian angel. Eventually, at around five in the afternoon, they managed to get to me through a tunnel through the rubble and to pull me out. I had serious wounds to my head, legs, and arms, as well as internal injuries to my liver and kidneys."

The death toll was unbearable, a tragic number of Israeli victims which set a record that has never been broken: seventy-five soldiers, border policemen, and Shin Bet operatives were killed that morning, as well as twenty-seven Lebanese. The seven-story building that housed the military government in Tyre was reduced to a pile of rubble. Only twenty-four of the people inside survived.

It is now clear that the explosion in Lebanon in November 1982, the first one on this scale in that country, was one of the hinge events in the tragic history of suicide bombing worldwide: it was the bomb that spawned a movement. Yet astonishingly, Israel covered up the fact that it was an attack, and to this day makes the claim that it was an accident. At the time, the IDF appointed an internal inquiry committee to find out what had happened. Ignoring a stack of evidence to the contrary, it determined that "a malfunction in the building's cooking gas cylinders" had caused the explosion. The case then went to the IDF's CID, whose long, secret, and thoroughgoing probe came up with a different conclusion. They found three eyewitnesses who had seen a Peugeot car racing right into the building at a crazy speed.

Two of the witnesses were Lebanese who had been seared by the wave of heat from the blast. They had talked to the doctor who treated them in the Tyre hospital immediately afterward, and the doctor confirmed their statements to the investigators. The Military Police investigators found the engine of a Peugeot buried under the wreckage of the building. They identified it by its serial number as having been acquired in Lebanon and confirmed that it was not in the IDF's use. They also found a leg that did not belong to any of the bodies of the victims. A reconstruction of the blast supported the hypothesis that it had been caused by a car bomb. Yet the IDF buried the CID report deep in a safe. The Shin Bet, which lost most of its operational personnel in South Lebanon in the bombing, also ignored the CID findings. To this day it denies knowledge of the report's existence.

The research for this book turned up an affidavit by a Shin Bet man who served in an operational capacity in Lebanon, and later reached a very high position in the organization. In his statement, he said that after the blast in Tyre, he had received a detailed intelligence report containing a full description of the preparations for the suicide bombing, and of all the Hizballah links to the attack. According to the affidavit, the Shin Bet command ordered the report to be pigeon-holed and not discussed again.

Officers in Unit 504 of Military Intelligence, the "HUMINT" group that runs agents and interrogates enemy prisoners, deny to this day that information had reached them before and after the blast indicating that members of the Shi'ite organization "The Oppressed of the Earth" (Hizballah's early name) were responsible. Yet their unit did, in fact, learn that the car bomb used in the attack was assembled in a garage in Beirut belonging to one of the organization's members.

At the Mossad, no one paid any attention to reports of a memorial service attended by senior Hizballah officials at the tiny village of Dir Qanoun al-Nahr, near Baalbek in Lebanon, where a small monument had been erected in memory of the suicide driver of the Peugeot, one Ahmad Qassir. The reports said that a certificate honoring Qassir had reached his family home from the Commander of the Islamic Nation, none other than Ayatollah Ruhollah Khomeini. The certificate bore a portrait of the Imam, and the emblem of the Islamic Republic where Ahmad Qassir's deed was greatly praised.

Despite all of this clear evidence, to this day Israeli intelligence claims that there was no intelligence failure, that there was not even a terror attack, just a problem with gas cylinders. It is possible to see in the papering-over of the Tyre disaster an analogy for Israel's apparent determination to ignore the true significance of Hizballah itself. The Israeli intelligence community has often downplayed Shi'ite terror, pretending that it is at most a transient nuisance. The same was true for the CIA and the West in general, from 1982 until the attacks on the United States of 9/11.

Judge Yitzhak Dar of Haifa District Court was a member of the team that probed the case, and helped write the report that the intelligence community claims doesn't exist. "This thing has been burning inside me for many years," he says. "What especially disturbs me and infuriates me is that despite the conclusions that we in the CID reached, everybody wanted to believe that it was negligence about gas cylinders, and not a terror attack. Thus, they wasted a very valuable year of preparations for the next attack, one which could have been prevented with a little awareness of the potential for the use of car bombs. We didn't prepare, and we were hit with the second Tyre disaster."

Hizballah, and its Iranian sponsors, followed up the Tyre car bombing with a quick succession of similar strikes. On November 4, 1983, exactly a week before the first anniversary of the Tyre disaster, Nakad Sarbukh, an Israeli Border Policeman who was guarding an army base in the same city, saw a suspicious pickup truck speeding in the direction of the base. "He was racing like mad," Sarbukh said later. "I knew straightaway that his intentions weren't kosher." He opened fire at the vehicle, spraying it with 130 bullets, but failed to stop it. The suicide driver smashed into the base, and detonated the 500-kilo bomb he was carrying. The building housing the Shin Bet's operations on the base crumpled, and surrounding buildings and tents were also damaged. Twenty-eight Israelis, mostly Shin Bet operatives and border policemen, were killed, as well as thirty-two Lebanese prisoners who were in detention at the base. Many others were wounded.

Working together, American and Israeli intelligence soon established who was responsible: the Islamic Jihad, which claimed responsibility, was in fact the military arm of Hizballah. Heading the organization was a man who until then had been unknown to Mossad and the CIA: Imad Moughniyeh. He is the Hizballah equivalent of Osama bin Laden, with one difference—Osama was still out there in 2008, but Moughniyeh was found and dispatched by a car bomb in Damascus in January 2008.

"In another time, another place or another nation, Imad Moughniyeh would have been a start-up entrepreneur," says "the Major," as David Barkai was known to his Lebanese contacts and enemies. During the late

1980s and early 1990s, Major Barkai was commander of the large base maintained in the north of Israel by Unit 504 of Israeli Military Intelligence. He was in charge of the Moughniyeh file, among others, and offered this assessment of Moughniyeh before the Damascus hit: "His is one of the most creative and brilliant minds I have ever come across. He is a man with deep understanding, an excellent technical grasp and leadership ability. Unfortunately, a mixture of personal and geopolitical circumstances led him to channel his outstanding talents into the path of blood and destruction and to make him into such a dangerous enemy."

Many intelligence operatives in many countries studied the figure known as "the Iranian Jackal." Barkai, his staff, and their successors devoted innumerable hours to Moughniyeh in a riveting, cunning, and cruel battle of wits. For years, Israelis as well as the Americans were incapable of putting a stop to the Jackal's inspired and bloody activities; he was an elusive bomber. At any given time, there were conflicting reports among Western intelligence agencies about his whereabouts and activities. In London, a source connected to British intelligence admitted shamefacedly in 2001 that despite the great interest that the United Kingdom had in "Mr." Moughniyeh, they hadn't the faintest idea where he was or what he might be planning. In the United States, Moughniyeh was on the FBI's Most Wanted List for twenty-one years. On July 12, 2006, Moughniyeh managed to spark the latest war between Israel and Hizballah, when he orchestrated the kidnapping of two Israeli soldiers, Ehud Goldwasser and Eldad Regev. He was an invaluable proxy warrior for the Iranians.

According to a highly classified assessment paper composed by Israeli Military Intelligence in 1996, "Iran uses terror against Israel rarely and rationally, out of an awareness of the grave diplomatic damage which it could cause itself if its role were to be exposed." Accordingly, Iran usually refrains from carrying out attacks directly, and its involvement usually follows an indirect course." That "indirect course," says the report, went through Imad Moughniyeh.

Moughniyeh was born December 7, 1962, in the village of Tayr Dibba in southern Lebanon, the oldest of three sons and a daughter. His parents, Amina and Mahmoud Jawad, had married a year before. His father was an observant Shi'ite who died in 1979, one of the only members of the family to die a natural death. According to Israeli intelligence files,

Moughniyeh spent most of his childhood in Bir al-Abed, one of the Shi'ite slums in southern Beirut into which many Palestinians had crowded after fleeing from Jordan when King Hussein cracked down on the Palestine Liberation Organization in September 1970.

In the late 1970s, after dropping out of high school, Moughniyeh joined Yasser Arafat's Fatah movement, and underwent guerrilla training. Later, he joined Force 17, Fatah's elite security unit, and became a body-guard for Arafat's deputy, Salah Khalaf (aka Abu Iyad). In 1982, when the PLO was about to leave Beirut for Tunis as a result of Ariel Sharon's invasion, many of its Shi'ite members, including Moughniyeh and his two brothers, Fouad and Jihad, decided to remain in Lebanon. In 1983, at the height of the wave of his suicide bombings against American, French, and Israeli targets in Lebanon, Moughniyeh found the time to wed his cousin, Saada Badr al-Din. Their daughter Fatima was born on August 2, 1984, and their son Mustafa on January 7, 1987.

Although during that period his way of life had been totally secular, Moughniyeh and his brothers joined al Dawa, one of the small extrem-ist Shi'ite groups that were later drawn together into Hizballah. Mough-niyeh began to be more observant of some Islamic precepts and, according to some reports, stopped seeing women other than his wife, at least in public. Yet even much later, his high rank notwithstanding, he was not considered a very pious Shi'ite. In a phone conversation recorded by Israeli intelligence in 1999, Sheikh Naim Qassem said about Moughniyeh: "He's no great saint when it comes to religion, but his glorious military achievements make up for that and assure him a place in Paradise."

Unlike other young Hizballah leaders, Moughniyeh was neither a Muslim religious authority nor a wielder of political influence. Instead, he was simply the man of action and the brains behind the organization's most daring operations. In its early days, Hizballah was sorely in need of someone like him.

David Barkai, who was one of Israel's top experts on Moughniyeh dur-ing the 1980s, has a keen understanding of the special capabilities Moughniyeh brought to Hizballah. Barkai came to Unit 504 in the early 1980s after serving as a soldier in a crack commando unit, as an instructor in the army's officers' course, and as an officer in the air force's rescue unit. He holds bachelor and master's degrees in Oriental studies from the Sorbonne, as well as a black belt in Judo. In 1986, he was appointed commander of the Unit 504 base, responsible for running agents in most of Lebanon and Syria. Soon after that, he received a special citation for identifying a terrorist in the course of a pursuit operation, engaging him in hand-to-hand combat, and killing him. "You must remember," Barkai recalls, "that in 1982 and 1983, Hizballah was a movement that represented itself as an authentic ideological product, whose members travelled to Iran mainly to study religion, however banal that might sound. In many spheres, they had no operational capability at all, and it was into that vacuum that Iran's Revolutionary Guards entered. Imad Moughniyeh, who had by then acquired a great deal of operational skills and know-how as a contractor for the execution of terrorist actions, was the right man in the right place for them."

In his comprehensive PhD dissertation on Hizballah, Brigadier General Shimon Shapira, a former senior Military Intelligence officer and military secretary to Prime Minister Benjamin Netanyahu, describes the family of the arch terrorist as possessing very high status amongst the Shi'ites of Lebanon. One of its heads, Sheikh Mohammad Moughniyeh, was considered one of the most prominent religious authorities in Lebanon in the early 1970s.

Barkai explains, "The Moughniyeh family was already notorious in Lebanon. This clan, together with others with well-known names like Hamadi, Miqdad, and Mussawi, were the product of circumstances which made it possible for fanatical people with highly borderline personalities to act out their wildest fantasies. In a normal state, you can't keep three hundred kilos of RDX explosives and two hundred AK-47 assault rifles in your home. With the Moughniyehs and the other families, that sort of thing was the everyday norm."

Moughniyeh's first assignment in Hizballah was as head bodyguard for its spiritual leader, Sheikh Mohammad Hussein Fadlallah, who, despite friction with Tehran, was the unchallenged supreme Shi'ite authority in Lebanon. Hizballah was run by a body known as the Shura Council, which comprised at first seven, then nine, and then twelve members. The majority were clerics, the others men with military training. Hizballah did not have a leader of its own in Lebanon. Officially, its leader was Ayatollah Khomeini. The organization's founding constitution provides for decisions to be taken by majority vote; and when agreement could not be reached, for the matter to be referred to the imam.

Khomeini's representative in the council in Lebanon was Hojat

al-Islam Ali Akbar Mohtashemi-Pour, one of his closest associates, who
was appointed Iran's ambassador to Syria in 1982. He was chosen by
Khomeini to head the council and to be responsible, as Iran's representative, for the molding of Hizballah and its leadership. Mohtashemi-Pour's
influence exceeded that of any other Iranian ambassador. He controlled
a budget of tens of millions of dollars a month, and was driven by a sense
of mission and unrestrained ambition.

In March 1983, four months after the Tyre bombing, a meeting was
held in Ambassador Mohtashemi-Pour's office in Damascus that
included leaders of Hizballah, with Moughniyeh representing Fadlallah,
as well as Syrian intelligence agents, and Mohtashemi-Pour himself.
Given the success of the Tyre attack, they decided on a series of similar
attacks targeting first the Americans and then the French, with the aim
of driving the UN-backed forces out of the country. The Syrians were to
supply Hizballah with key information about the security protection of
these targets. Imad Moughniyeh sensed that this was his chance to make
a move and seize a central position in the organization, and he said that
he would take responsibility for everything, if the money and the means
were provided.

His deeds were as good as his words. Two weeks after that meeting in
Damascus, a unit commanded by Moughniyeh attacked a U.S. Marine
patrol with hand grenades, killing two Americans. But that was no more
than a trial run.

"We believe that the future has surprises in store," said Fadlallah in an
article published in mid-1983. "The jihad is bitter and harsh, it will
spring from inside, through effort, patience and sacrifice, and the spirit
of readiness for martyrdom."

Fadlallah and Moughniyeh may well deserve credit as the founders of
modern suicide bombing. In the Iran-Iraq War, the Imam Khomeini had
granted permission to his young soldiers to charge forward to certain
death against the invading Iraqi forces. But the Hizballah leader
upgraded this ruling, to allow intentional, direct suicide. Of course, the
technique is ancient. In the Bible, the eyeless Samson declared, "Let me
die with the Philistines" (Judges 16:30) when he brought the house
down in Gaza. During various historical periods Muslim fighters have
used suicide tactics. According to legend, the *hashishiyun*, a fanatical
Islamic sect that built fortresses near the shores of the Caspian Sea in the
eleventh and twelfth centuries, drugged young men and persuaded them

to go on missions of murder from which they would not return alive. They were called *fedayun*, "redeemers." The English word "assassin" is derived from the name of the sect. The Japanese in World War II made use of kamikaze pilots, who crashed their aircraft into American ships. In Peru in the 1980s, the Shining Path terrorists sent members on suicide missions. But Moughniyeh and Hizballah perfected the practice into an art form.

Two attacks were required to drive the Americans out of Lebanon. According to a Mossad investigation, carried out with the help of Israeli Military Intelligence at the request of the CIA, the truck bomb for the first hit was prepared in a region under Syrian control in the Lebanese Bekaa Valley. It was brought secretly, through Syrian roadblocks, to Beirut. When the truck accelerated past a guard station and struck the American Embassy in the Lebanese capital on April 18, 1983, the entire front section of the seven-story building was destroyed. Sixty-three of the embassy's personnel were killed, including almost the entire staff of the local CIA station, as well as Robert C. Ames, the organization's Near East Bureau chief, who happened to be visiting.

Although the attack was a painful blow to America's prestige, it failed to persuade the Reagan administration to get out of Lebanon. So, six months later, Moughniyeh raised the bar. Early in the morning of October 23, two trucks loaded with huge amounts of explosives were detonated almost simultaneously, one at the headquarters of the U.S. Marines near the Beirut airport, and the other at the base of the French paratroop regiment, a little more than a kilometer away. The truck that smashed into the Marine barracks was carrying some 5,400 kilograms of TNT and gas cylinders. It exploded at 6:20 a.m., totally destroying the building and causing the deaths of 241 Marines. The explosion at the French base a few seconds later killed fifty-eight paratroopers. According to several sources, Moughniyeh was sitting on the roof of a high-rise building, watching through a telescope.

Before the attacks, the U.S. National Security Agency had monitored messages cabled from the Iranian Foreign Ministry to the Iranian Embassy in Damascus, in which Tehran requested that a large-scale attack be mounted against the Americans. To finance the operation, the sum of $25,000 was transferred to that embassy. The NSA also picked up phone calls from the Revolutionary Guards in Baalbek requesting a green light for the attacks from the embassy in Damascus. These intercepted messages, however, offered no information about the planned time of implementation, the exact target, or the nature of the operation.

Robert Baer, a longtime CIA operative, says that the CIA has concrete evidence that Yasser Arafat was involved in the planning of the three 1983 Beirut attacks. This information, Baer says, was never published because of the agency's desire to maintain a working relationship with the PLO.

A few days after the double truck bombings, the intelligence service of the Lebanese right-wing Christian Phalange Party released a report that Fadlallah had blessed the two suicide bombers before they embarked on their missions. Fadlallah promptly denied that he had told anyone "to go and blow himself up," but confirmed that "the Muslims believe that when in the course of a struggle you make yourself into a human bomb, it is the same as someone who is fighting with a rifle. There is no difference between someone who dies with a gun in his hand and someone who blows himself up." He announced publicly that his refraining from issuing a *fatwa* approving the latest actions did not mean that his reservations about the bombings applied to all circumstances.

The attacks succeeded beyond Hizballah's wildest hopes. The Multi-National Force was dismantled, and the foreign troops returned to their home countries. It had taken Moughniyeh just seven months to achieve the goal set at the meeting in Damascus in March. Ultimately, the withdrawal of the MNF together with the earlier evacuation of the PLO forces from Beirut enabled Hizballah to become the dominant military and political force in Lebanon. Former bodyguard Moughniyeh had become the leading figure in the military arm of Hizballah, known as the Islamic Jihad.

The CIA made a couple of attempts at retaliation. A few months after the blast at the Marine barracks, a booby-trapped Quran sent to Mohtashemi-Pour blew up in his face as he opened the package. He was badly wounded and lost some fingers, but he survived, returned to his nefarious activities, and became a key figure in the formation of Hizballah, and later in the Iranian attempts to export their revolution to other countries. In 1985, Moughniyeh's younger brother, Jihad, was among the eighty Lebanese killed on March 8, in the explosion of a car bomb that was aimed at Sheikh Fadlallah (Jihad had succeeded Imad as Fadlallah's chief bodyguard). Most of the casualties were worshippers at the mosque where Fadlallah prayed and preached. Fadlallah himself was not hurt.

Several organizations claimed responsibility, but Hizballah accused the CIA, and over the years, evidence has accumulated to back up that claim. Four months before the car bombing, in a November 14, 1984, order, President Ronald Reagan had rescinded Executive Order 12333, in which he had ruled in 1981 that "No person employed by or acting on behalf of the United States Government shall engage in, or conspire to engage in, assassination."

Various media reports claimed the CIA had received $300,000 from Saudi Arabia to finance the job, and the money had been transferred to Elie Hobeika, the commander of the Phalange Maronite Christian militia. The national security adviser at the time, Robert McFarlane, hinted that the perpetrators of the attack had indeed received assistance in the past from U.S. intelligence units, but that they were "rogue operative[s]" acting without CIA approval. Officially, the Americans never supplied Israel with any reports on the attack, apart from a very general survey of its consequences, including photographs taken at the scene right after the blast.

In unofficial talks, CIA agents in Tel Aviv confessed all. They told their Mossad counterparts that they had intentionally not approached Hobeika and his people, because they suspected (correctly) that they were too closely connected to their targets. Instead, the CIA recruited three Christians from Tripoli who worked in Beirut, had in the past served in the Phalange, and had also been CIA informants. They had acquired expertise in preparing bombs thanks to Israeli training of the Phalange. Now, the CIA gave them the required equipment and explosives and $100,000 to carry out the attack. The remaining preparations were left to the bombers. They packed the dynamite into an untraceable second-hand car that they parked next to the target, and they detonated the explosion with a remote control device, after ascertaining that Fadlallah was at the site.

The CIA did see to it that none of its people was directly involved, ensuring deniability at a later stage. The pictures were taken by one of the three Phalangists, positioned on a nearby roof.

Neither of these attempts harmed or curbed Moughniyeh. In the wake of the phenomenal success of the three suicide truck bomb attacks he had planned, moreover, that modus operandi became the method of choice for Islamic terror. The concept of suicide took a prominent place in the philosophy of the leaders of both Hizballah and Iran. Many observers believe that one of the greatest successes logged by radical Shi'ite Islam was to persuade their Sunni counterparts to adopt suicide bombing. Throughout the 1990s, both Palestinian terrorist groups and al-Qaeda and similar organizations, all of whom had received training from Hizballah (as well as lectures by Moughniyeh), made this their preferred modus operandi. Years later, Khomeini's successor, Ali Khamenei, even praised the sacrificial actions of Palestinian terrorists: "The height of the Palestinian resistance is manifested in the martyrdom operations carried out by the Palestinian youngsters, because of whom the enemy is panic-stricken." He added, "The actions of martyrdom and self-sacrifice for the sake of national and religious interests constitute the height of the honor, the courage, and the glory of the nation."

In the light of the Iranian Shi'ite religious rulings in favor of the suicide missions, and the successes in Lebanon, Sunni religious authorities were also called upon to grant permission for self-sacrifice in the name of Islam. The argument as to the legitimacy and justifiability of suicide attacks had been decided. On March 6, 1995, Sheikh Ahmad Yassin, the leader of the Palestinian Sunni Muslim fundamentalist movement Hamas, ruled that in any case where the suicide bomber had obtained the blessing of a qualified sheikh, his death was to be seen as not personally motivated; he was a *shahid*, a martyr, who had fallen in holy war, *jihad*.

Shin Bet refers to suicide bombers as the "poor man's smart bomb." They are very effective smart bombs, alas. No effective way of combating suicide terrorism has been found, and suicide bombing has had a decisive influence over political processes around the world. Attempts to profile suicide bombers are doomed to failure—the bombers come in all sorts, from poor to wealthy, illiterate to educated. In short, with Moughniyeh's leadership, the age of modern terror took a devastating turn in the early 1980s.

Israel, in particular, was desperate to do something about this.

On December 12, 1983, a group of Moughniyeh's counterparts blew up the American Embassy in Kuwait. The same group also struck at the French Embassy; an expatriate residential compound; the main oil refinery; and the control tower at Kuwait's international airport. Five people were killed and eighty-six injured in these attacks. Seventeen men were arrested and tried for their roles in them. Moughniyeh was apparently not involved, but his brother-in-law and close friend, Mustafa Badr al-Din, was one of seven condemned to death (but never actually executed) for their parts in the attacks. Another was Hassan Mussawi, the cousin of Abbas Mussawi, the Hizballah leader who was killed a decade later by rockets fired from an Israeli helicopter. The trial of the Kuwait Seven, and their sentences, would have disastrous results.

# CHAPTER 6

# The Drugged Octopus
# and the Rise of Hizballah

"Here, look at my hands," sighed the man who for years served in the Mossad unit responsible for running spies in Lebanon, indicating a number with his fingers. "That's it, that's the lot, that's how many quality agents the entire Israeli intelligence community mustered inside Hizballah and the Iranian intelligence presence in Lebanon in the last twenty-four years. And that's a very generous estimate."

One day, in fifty years' time if at all, when the most secret files of the Israeli intelligence community are made public, historians will no doubt be amazed at the meagerness of Israel's penetration of its mortal enemy, Hizballah. The vaunted Israeli intelligence officers with reputations akin to James Bond's will come to look more like a set of bumbling Inspector Clouseaus. Israeli intelligence's failure to penetrate and secure information on Hizbollah in the 1980s and 1990s has been one of its worst shortcomings.

From 1982 until 2000, Israel and Hizballah clashed nearly every hour of every day in Lebanon. Of the 2,000-odd engagements between the guerrilla group and the Israeli army in 1998 alone, Hizballah initiated 1,920—96 percent. Israel pulled out of Lebanon altogether in May 2000. Even after that, it remained on the defensive and most of the clashes with Hizballah, the majority along the border fence, were initiated by the militia. The price for the almost total lack of intelligence information about Hizballah's activities was paid constantly by Israeli troops, with their lives.

In contrast to the PLO of the pre-1982 era, which was hated by the local population, Hizballah enjoyed and enjoys enormous support in the Shi'ite villages of South Lebanon as well as in the Syrian and Lebanese armies. Its fighters are seen as the vanguard of resistance to Israel, and not as terrorists, making it all the more difficult for Israel to insert or acquire agents within its ranks.

Colonel Yitzhak Tidhar has had more experience of the struggle against Hizballah, and has more expertise on the subject, than most others. He began his army service in an elite combat unit, and then served for thirty years in intelligence, mostly controlling agents in Lebanon and Syria. He was responsible for the overall collection of information and operations in the search for POWs and MIAs, and then served as the deputy to the officer in charge of operations in Lebanon and Syria. Tidhar says for the record what most of his colleagues will say only confidentially: "Regrettably, apart from a few isolated specific successes, Israeli intelligence has suffered a painful failure against Hizballah and Iran in Lebanon."

The first reason for this failure, says Tidhar, was the order of priorities of Israeli intelligence. "There were always more important matters—the struggle against the Palestinians in the occupied territories, or Syria, which for years was regarded as the most serious of Israel's enemies. As long as we were confronting the issue of mainly Palestinian terrorism in Lebanon, the results of this low prioritization were hard to discern, but as time went by and the power of the Shi'ites encroached on that of the Palestinians, the pit just widened and deepened."

Low priority, but high confusion. Until the end of the 1980s, eight separate Israeli intelligence units operated in Lebanon, not only with an absolute lack of coordination, but often in bitter rivalry. The group included the Shin Bet; the Mossad; MI's Unit 504; the army's Lebanon Liaison Unit (which worked with the South Lebanon Army, Israel's proxy militia in the area); the SLA's own security and intelligence unit; the Military Police Intelligence Unit; the Israeli police's Lebanon Border Unit; and *Yahalom* (Hebrew for "Diamond"), a separate police intelligence unit. In the mid-1990s, as if the situation weren't enough of a mess, the newly established antiterror unit of the National Security Council joined the crowd. "It was like a drugged octopus," said a Shin Bet man.

Until the 1982 war, Israel's army had been responsible for gathering intelligence in Lebanon, spearheaded by Unit 504. After the invasion, however, Prime Minister Begin instructed the head of the Shin Bet, Avraham Shalom, to deploy in the army's wake and assist in interdiction of terror attacks. The Shin Bet had since 1967 acquired much experience in combating Palestinian terrorism in the West Bank and Gaza, and it was the Palestinians who were Israel's perceived enemy in Lebanon. Moshe Arens, who took over from Ariel Sharon as minister of defense in the Begin government in February 1983, described the situation in Lebanon as "total intelligence chaos." He set up a unit in his ministry to coordinate the various branches operating there. He appointed Uri Lubrani to head it, a position he was still holding in 2008. Unfortunately, Lubrani's many years of efforts to construct a rational system of intelligence gathering have been met by constant fighting on the part of the rival organizations, the kind of infighting that Israelis call "the wars of the Jews."

In the first few months after the Lebanon War began, relations between the Shin Bet and Unit 504 were amicable; but the longer the occupation of Lebanon continued, the more those relations deteriorated. Unit 504 complained that the Shin Bet was using overly aggressive methods against the local population, sowing seeds of Shi'ite hostility to Israel. Even some Shin Bet officials have their regrets today. Gideon Ezra, who headed the organization's operations in Lebanon and later served as a cabinet minister in a number of governments, most recently in the unlikely post of minister for the environment in the cabinet formed by Ehud Olmert in 2006, explains: "We decided to settle accounts with the Shi'ites for their connections with Fatah. We sort of forgot that the Shi'ites had not done it out of their own free will, but were threatened and pressured in various ways. Those aggressive, anti-Shi'ite actions were unnecessary."

David Kubi arrived in Lebanon at the start of the war to serve briefly as the Shin Bet's intelligence coordinator in Sidon and the Palestinian refugee camps in the vicinity. In 1984, he became commander of the Sidon sector. He laments what happened at that time. "In the beginning, we enjoyed a supportive attitude on the part of the bulk of the Shi'ites in the area, including members of Amal. More than once they approached us at their own initiative to inform us about Palestinian terrorists. But the longer our stay in Lebanon drew out, [the more] the majority of the Shi'ites began to hate us. I felt this especially on my return in 1984, when I understood from them that the prolonged occupation was significantly impinging on the fabric of their daily lives, having to pass through innumerable roadblocks and other humiliations.

Throughout the southern region, we witnessed the beginnings of the popular resistance movement."

Kubi experienced the change directly, on the first day of his second stint in Lebanon, on April 21, 1984. He joined a team going to meet a Shi'ite informant, only to be ambushed at the entrance to the village of Anakun, east of Sidon. "It was a well-planned ambush, and we got out of it only by a miracle and because of the poor marksmanship of the Hizballah men, who fired two RPG grenades at my vehicles and missed. The automatic fire was more accurate and penetrated the car, missing me by a few centimeters."

In 1985, the Israelis decided to set up a central body, run by the Shin Bet with Unit 504 participation, to take responsibility for thwarting terror operations against Israeli troops in Lebanon. Named OS, the acronym of the Hebrew for "Collection and Interdiction," the organization was commanded by a man named Haim Borro. It lasted only two years, breaking up amidst bitter recriminations. Borro recalls the spat: "We reached the stage where we announced that if we [Shin Bet] don't function alone, we pack up and go home."

After that, Shin Bet personnel began to accuse Unit 504 of filing false reports and of corrupt conduct. They claimed that 504 officers were smuggling electrical appliances and other goods from Lebanon into Israel. One Shin Bet operative told of being invited to a party given by a South Lebanese collaborator for his 504 controllers, and some local friends. It turned out to be a full-fledged orgy. Captain Jean-Pierre Elraz of Unit 504, for one, was later convicted of smuggling. He was also arrested on charges of murdering one of his agents, but not enough evidence was found to indict him. A psychiatric opinion submitted in his trial for smuggling described him as "possessing psychotic narcissistic personality traits . . . a distorted conscience, with a constant need to live out his delusions of grandeur." After serving his five-year term for smuggling, Elraz was discharged from the army. In May 2001, he was charged with far more serious crimes: the murder of the security officer of a kibbutz, as well as the stealing of dozens of rifles and other materiel from the kibbutz armory and selling it to terrorist organizations that used it to kill Israelis. He was convicted and sentenced to life plus twenty years. Elraz is an extreme example of misbehavior among Military Intelligence officers, but according to Shin Bet's accusations, he was not the only problem.

Meanwhile, in the early to mid-1980s, Hizballah's strength dramatically increased. Israel's top agent in Syria and Lebanon, known to the heads of the intelligence community as "Dugman" (Hebrew for "Male Model"), delivered dozens of reports on the organization, until he relocated in 1985. In an interview in 2006, he expressed disappointment that his reports were not taken seriously: "I and my network documented Hizballah's activities in the cities and villages and we brought photographs of the command centers in Beirut. I had a car with cameras fitted to both front doors and I used to travel up and down around the Dahya, the region where they had begun to set up their headquarters, taking pictures of what was going on there. I also drove around the Imam Ali camp of the Iranian Revolutionary Guards in the Bekaa, and the Iranian Embassy, to take photos. One of the people working for me documented a training compound they set up near Baalbek. Although we warned the Israelis about what was happening in Lebanon, I had the feeling that they weren't really listening to me."

In 1986, the head of Military Intelligence, Major General Amnon Lipkin-Shahak, held a meeting of all the officers who were running agents in Lebanon. "We are being battered by Hizballah," he told them, "but we know nothing about them. Iran is behind them, and giving them training, financing, and advanced technology. We don't have any agents inside. They are compartmentalized and their messages are securely coded. I am instructing you to treat the recruitment of agents in Hizballah as a top priority and to do everything possible to penetrate it."

Subsequent efforts bore some fruit. The most successful operation of all concerned a source code-named "Hypnosis," who was recruited two years earlier and after the meeting with Shahak became Israel's most valuable source in Lebanon. The information that he produced helped foil many attacks against Israeli troops, including a plan to blow up a sewage tanker truck full of explosives next to the Fatma crossing on the Israel-Lebanon border. Information from Hypnosis also prevented an attack on the American ambassador to Lebanon and the political officer at the embassy in 1988. Hizballah had planned to explode a powerful bomb next to their convoy on the way to a visit to Sidon, but Hypnosis warned of the attack. A report was conveyed to Unit 504, which passed it to the CIA station in Tel Aviv, which informed Langley, and from there the word was passed to the embassy in Beirut and the visit was cancelled.

Lebanese army sappers dismantled the bomb, and the protection of the embassy staff was strengthened.

The Israelis hoped that Hypnosis would help them penetrate Iran. Says a senior intelligence operative: "If it wasn't for 'the wars of the Jews' in Israeli intelligence that wrecked the whole thing, we could have gotten a lot more information out of the operation that could have served us well for many years." Once again, Unit 504 presented a problem. In February 1988, Colonel Yakov (Kobi) Frumer became the commander of 504. Major Barkai of Unit 504 is still bitter about it. "The man didn't understand anything about intelligence. He gave us operational orders that anyone who had any experience in running agents knew were silly and endangered people's lives. It was impossible to argue with him. He sent agents on dangerous and superfluous missions, thereby causing agents to be exposed, and in some cases eliminated."

Frumer fired most of 504's field officers. Their forced departure stopped in one fell swoop the work of key agents in Syria and Lebanon, practically eliminating the backbone of Israel's intelligence operation in Lebanon. The links with whatever contacts they had in Hizballah, chiefly through the Hypnosis operation, were severed. Operations for the planting of new agents in the organization were never carried out, and Israeli intelligence became blind once again in Lebanon.

Coordination between the army and the intelligence branches was also deeply flawed. On January 13, 1987, an infantry unit unknowingly shot dead a top agent, ironically code-named "Clumsy," as he approached the border fence in order to deliver an urgent warning about an impending terror attack, which in fact did occur that night. No one had briefed the infantry unit on guard of the possibility that agents might appear and of the signs that they would use to identify themselves. There was no inquiry after the incident.

In another incident on April 26, 1988, in a combined initiative of Hizballah and the Palestinian Popular Front, a guerrilla unit infiltrated Israeli territory in the eastern sector of the Lebanese border, near Mount Hermon, and killed an Israeli infantry battalion commander and a tracker. A pursuit operation was launched, and in accordance with standing orders, which call for a 504 "special duties officer" to take part in all such actions, David Barkai joined it. The idea was that if a guerrilla is caught, he can be interrogated on the spot for information on his base or other targets, and planes can then be called in to bomb them.

The next day, another two gunmen entered Israeli territory in the same sector. Again a pursuit was launched and again Barkai, together with another special duties officer, Captain Doron, joined the pursuing force. In the course of the chase, information reached them with the names of the two fleeing terrorists. As they advanced with the search team, Barkai and Doron called out to the gunmen on bullhorns and urged them to surrender. As Barkai recalls, what happened next was a debacle: "There were helicopters above that were searching. I was running with the forward command group that was controlling the pursuit. Doron was a couple of dozen meters ahead of me. The helicopters reported that they had located the terrorists in a wadi. We ran like crazy and called on them to surrender. We began sliding down the slope of the wadi and we could see them from above. I had a great feeling. The fact that we could call them by their names made it more likely that they would surrender. I thought we would be able to question them and get a lot of information that we could make immediate use of.

"As we slid down the side of the wadi, we called out that they were surrounded and that we promised not to harm them if they surrendered. They got up, one after the other, threw down their weapons and their flak jackets, and raised their hands. Our force lined up facing them, ten to twenty meters away. We acted according to orders. We told them to remove their jackets and to lie on their backs on the ground. But they never managed to carry out that order. Someone yelled, 'Kill them.' An infantryman opened fire and right away everyone joined in and sprayed them with bullets, riddling their bodies. Doron and I yelled out, 'Cease fire, cease fire,' but no one obeyed. Something very grave had occurred. Prisoners had been shot, and in addition we had lost important intelligence information."

Another intelligence officer who witnessed the killings says, "It was like a shooting range. What really shocked me was the indifference with which everyone, including the officers, accepted what had happened. As if it was nothing."

Barkai and Doron wrote a detailed report on the incident, including the killing of the terrorists. Colonel Frumer distributed it to other units, but Barkai and Doron were surprised to see that it had been edited. Barkai recalls, "In the final report, the whole part about the killing of the terrorists had been left out, and the rest had been rewritten to make it sound as if they had been killed during an exchange of fire. Frumer's clerk told me that he had taken out that part because 'it wasn't relevant.' "

Beyond the lack of coordination between the fighting echelon and the intelligence services, the main problems remained in the sphere of coordination between the services themselves. A Mossad official stated that "At no stage did the prime minister put all the heads of all the organizations into one room and tell them they were not leaving until they decide how to work together and cooperate in order to beat the Hizballah." In the intelligence community, there were people who argued that Hizballah's terror was a strategic threat, which could have a fundamental impact on the larger Middle Eastern situation, but the decision-making echelon paid them no heed. In Jerusalem's eyes, Lebanon was a nuisance, not a real danger.

Major (Res.) Ehud Eiran served in Lebanon in a combat role and is now doing research on Israel's counterinsurgency operations there, as a fellow at Harvard University's Kennedy School of Government. Eiran asserts that for most of the time Israel's goal was to simply secure its northern border area, rather than to confront the "asymmetric" challenge posed by Hizballah's guerrilla fighters. Only toward the mid-1990s did Israel change its approach, when doing so was too late.

At the end of 1989, due to the sorry state of Unit 504, it was decided to bolster the involvement of the Shin Bet in Lebanon. That's when the Shin Bet set up Mabat, the security apparatus of the South Lebanon Army. They dreamed of a network of intelligence coordinators who would help prevent terrorist actions against the SLA and Israeli forces. But the results were far short of that dream. Mabat personnel could be spotted a mile off. Each one carried a short-barrel M-16 rifle with grenade thrower attached, loaded and hanging diagonally across the body. On their belts were two mobile phones, one each for the Lebanese and Israeli communications networks. To all this equipment the secret operatives added a pistol or two, grenades, and a whole lot of ammunition. Wherever possible, preferably in front of cameras, they would strike heroic poses and put on particularly ferocious faces. The Mabat personnel never fulfilled most of the hopes that had been pinned on them. "We never knew if we should believe them, these SLA-niks," says one Israeli agent. "The results that they produced were very scanty."

The American intelligence community was extremely worried about

Israeli intelligence's poor performance. In March 1990, at one of the periodic meetings that the director of the Mossad holds with his CIA counterpart, Shabtai Shavit heard disconcerting criticism from CIA director William H. Webster. The information coming from Israel about Hizballah and the reports that Israel conveyed to Washington about its activities against the organization had created the impression that Israel had a serious problem on its hands, Shavit was told.

Right under the nose of the Israeli intelligence community, and with the close guidance and accompaniment of Iran, Hizballah slowly but steadily improved its fighting capability. In one well-organized attack on a joint IDF-SLA fortress in May 1992, the militia's meticulous planning was evident. The guerrillas had clearly carried out days of reconnaissance patrols along the ridge overlooking the fortress. They mined the approach roads to block reinforcements, and launched a two-pronged offensive from opposite directions, precisely timed, with covering fire.

The Hizballah guerrillas conquered the position and managed to hold it briefly, flying their yellow flag from its flagpole. More important, they videotaped the whole operation and broadcast it on their TV station, a major propaganda coup.

More and more attacks like this one occurred as the 1990s progressed. Israeli forces continued to occupy a broad swath across southern Lebanon, presenting many targets. Generally, under the IDF's heavy fire, plus air support, the militiamen failed to succeed in conquering those positions. And when they did manage it, they couldn't hold them. Yet the psychological effect of these operations, and the toll taken in the lives of Israeli soldiers, were devastating. The Israelis had to invest more and more resources in force protection, and the Israeli public began to question whether the military presence in Lebanon, whose whole aim was to protect the civilian communities in the north of the country against Hizballah fire, was worth the cost.

Far from the Israel-controlled security zone, Hizballah constructed a model of an IDF fortified position. Men practiced storming it, over and over, for many long days. They preferred raiding positions that were jointly manned by the IDF and the SLA. When they attacked, they used two hundred to three hundred men, usually greatly outnumbering the units manning the positions. The attackers often did not even try to occupy the positions. Nonetheless, a steady stream of lightning raids caused many SLA men to defect to Hizballah, and made it difficult for the SLA to recruit replacements.

At the same time, Hizballah was secretly building up and diversifying its arsenal. In March 1993, two Sagger missiles were fired at an SLA patrol. These wire-guided Russian antitank weapons had reached the militia six months earlier, via ship, from Iran. Later, one of them penetrated an Israeli Merkava tank's armor, which is supposed to be the strongest in the world. (Luckily for the crew, it failed to explode.) Three weeks after that, in an assault on an SLA position, Hizballah used Saggers against fortifications rather than tanks, killing three men. The attacks all came as surprises. After the last operation, senior Hizballah cleric Subhi Tufeili declared: "We've got Saggers and we will still show the Zionists how we'll blow them up." Israeli intelligence had not known about the missiles until they were first used against Israeli forces.

Israel's gravest lack—the one that brought all other problems in its wake—was its shortage of human intelligence. For many years, Israel had been able to rely on information from Arab informants and collaborators. Its intelligence units, primarily the Mossad, were considered true masters of HUMINT, penetrating Arab states and organizations at will. American intelligence, whose technology was superb but whose HUMINT was weak, relied on Israel for a steady supply of intelligence to fill in its own gaps. Yet Hizballah remained largely impenetrable.

Asked why it was so difficult to recruit spies from the ranks of Hizballah, Colonel Tidhar explained: "It's easy to recruit a man without a national identity, and for many years there was no such identity in Lebanon, especially among the Shi'ites, who always felt rejected and screwed. Suddenly, Hizballah provides them with a religious and communal home. Suddenly, they have a framework to identify with, to straighten their backs. For people like this it is much more difficult to betray their community."

The conduct of Shi'ite prisoners under questioning—whether by Israelis, who were restricted from 1999 on by a High Court ruling against torture, or by SLA interrogators, who used brutal methods—was also very different from that of Palestinians. Their ability to withstand physical pressure was matched by their profound grasp of Israel's methods. A Military Intelligence officer relates what happened once when, together with a Mossad operative, he questioned a Hizballah prisoner:

"He was remarkably intelligent and well informed. Although we were both in civilian clothes, he got the picture from our questions and said: 'You're from MI and you're from the Mossad, and you are both trying to recruit me.' "

While Israeli intelligence was demonstrating its impotence, Hizballah was moving ahead toward its main goal: the foundation of a Shi'ite Islamic state in Lebanon. Each year, Iran increased its contribution to Hizballah and to the many social and educational institutions it operated. By 1987, Iran's annual funding reached a total of $100 million, small change for the oil-rich state, but a great deal of money in Lebanese terms. Through Hizballah, Iran wanted to create alternative social machinery to that of the Lebanese government, covering all aspects of life from education and culture to health, welfare, economics, and even a military force.

Hizballah's success enabled the Shi'ites to stand tall in Lebanon. To an oppressed and wretched majority, living in a divided country full of conflicts, Hizballah gave its Shi'ite followers a reason to be proud, and a compass pointing to good and evil.

Iran's financial support was channeled into Lebanon through a number of Iranian agencies, which functioned independently from the central government in Tehran. One of these quasi-governmental foundations, the Imam Khomeini Relief Committee, opened its first branch in Lebanon early in 1983. By 1990, it was granting monthly allowances to 2,500 families, and more than 7,500 families had received aid for medical treatment. "Without the Iranian assistance, it would have taken [Lebanon's] Muslim believers fifty years to reach their present situation," said Sheikh Ali Yassin, a Hizballah cleric.

Hizballah was developing into a powerful political force in Lebanon. When that country's civil war was quieted by the Taif agreement, signed in the Saudi Arabian town of that name in October 1989, all sides except Hizballah were forced to disarm. The Taif agreement and the relative quiet that it brought to Lebanon led Iran to change Hizballah's political tactics, from its intentional alienation from the central government to a new willingness to join in, including participation in elections.

Syria did try to act as a check on Iran's influence with Hizballah. Syrian president Hafez al-Assad placed severe restrictions on the freedom of action of the Revolutionary Guards in Lebanon, and rejected Iran's demand to set up a command structure to control Hizballah directly.

Syria was interested in limiting but not eliminating the Iranian presence in Lebanon. Damascus chose not to deal directly with Hizballah matters, so as not to be identified too closely with the organization (this changed in 2002, with a decision by Assad Jr.). On the other hand, it wanted the organization to obey whenever Syria gave it orders to stop shooting at Israel, and not to be totally beyond Syria's control. But Iran remained the primary sponsor of the group.

Hizballah's leaders, from the organization's very beginnings, and in line with Iranian propaganda tactics, have made maximal use of mass media ever since the summer of 1984, when the movement's weekly bulletin, *Al-Ahad*, first appeared. Since then it has come out every Friday. In 1985, Iran sent some old Radio Tehran transmitters to Lebanon, and trial broadcasts began of Sawt al-Mustazafin (the Voice of the Oppressed), Hizballah's radio station. In 1992, its television station, Al Manar, was set up. Since 1996, the organization has had an official Web site (/http://www.hizbollah.tv) that includes up-to-date information on its activities and the utterances of its leaders, with video clips and photographs.

Although it enforces strict field security, Hizballah has never tried to hide its military wing. On the contrary, since the summer of 1985, it has staged processions and parades. The first one started off from the religious school in Baalbek, accompanied by the band of the the scouts of the imam al-Mahdi. A year later, in the summer of 1986, when the parade was repeated, there were reports of five thousand Hizballah fighters marching through Baalbek. Prominent among the speakers was the representative of the Iranian Revolutionary Guards.

To supplement Iran's cash infusions, over the years Hizballah became involved in several kinds of illegal activity. Skimming the profits of drug deals is by far the most lucrative of them. Both opium poppies and cannabis are grown in Lebanon.

A report produced in November 1992 by U.S. Representative (now Senator) Charles E. Schumer, then chairman of the House Judiciary Subcommittee on Crime and Criminal Justice, showed that some 20 percent of the heroin consumed in the United States originated in Lebanon at the time.

Lebanon's Bekaa Valley used to be the country's breadbasket. Until the Syrians arrived in 1976, the farmers grew wheat, vegetables, and grapes in this strip of fertile land 30 kilometers wide and 110 kilometers long. Yet within ten years, beginning in the early 1980s, the percentage of land devoted to cultivating drug plants rose from 10 percent to 90 percent or more. The Syrian presence also altered the nature of drug growth in Lebanon, from a preponderance of cannabis, from which hashish and marijuana are derived, to opium poppies, the source of heroin. The Schumer Report estimated that there were thirty to forty laboratories producing drugs locally, mostly in areas under Hizballah's control.

As Hizballah's domination of events in Lebanon grew, so did its involvement in the drug trade. There's no indication that the militia's men use drugs themselves, or benefit personally from the profits of the traffic. Hizballah, like Hamas and other fundamentalist Islamic organizations, seems devoid of personal corruption. Most of its members are loyal to its principles and ideology, and few are out for material gain. But as an organization, Hizballah apparently has no qualms about profiting from the drug business. The Schumer Report estimated that it raked in at least $10 million a year from taxes.

Israeli intelligence data shows that the volume of the Bekaa's drug cultivation and production has varied over the years since the Schumer Report. From 1995 to 1998, the quantities shrank to a certain extent, because of the desire of Syria and Lebanon to give the impression that they were joining in the U.S.-led war on drugs. After 1998, cannabis cultivation began rising again, as a result of the country's economic crisis and the needs of the locals. Furthermore, shifts in crop levels were sometimes offset by increases in laboratory production, especially of heroin and cocaine, using raw materials imported from abroad. The profits to be made from these hard drugs are larger, and it is harder for the international community to monitor production. The Israeli police seize a large quantity of drugs smuggled in from Lebanon every year, estimated at only a tenth of the total of some 10 tons cultivated annually.

Hizballah has also been involved in criminal activity apart from the drug business. It collects a tithe from Lebanese involved in the commerce in luxury automobiles and other goods stolen in Europe that are brought to the Bekaa or "resold" to their owners for large sums of money. There were several reports in Europe toward the end of the 1990s saying that Hizballah members were collaborating with European and international criminals in the transfer of stolen cars to Lebanon by sea, en route to other Middle Eastern countries to be sold.

In November 2001, the Spanish police reported the arrest of criminals connected with Hizballah who had committed large-scale fraud connected with vacation apartments in the Caribbean, including forgery, extortion, money laundering, and other offenses.

In the late 1970s and up to 1985, the Mossad and other agencies maintained a constant and intensive pursuit of a Syrian arms dealer and banker, Monzer al-Kassar, who operated from the Spanish resort town of Marbella. The arms shipped by al-Kassar were key to the success of Hizballah in its early years, when the links with the Iranians and their arms stores were not altogether reliable. Agents of Caesarea, the Mossad's special operations unit, were on his tracks, and time after time, the Israelis debated eliminating him. His Mossad file reveals that al-Kassar, who was very close to the Syrian leadership, was deeply involved in other crimes in Lebanon as well, and in money laundering. He had intimate ties with Hizballah and its agents abroad. In June 2007, Spain arrested al-Kassar on behalf of the U.S. government, and on June 13, 2008, he was extradited from Spain to face federal charges at the Southern District Federal Court in New York City. He has been charged with conspiracy to provide material support or resources to a foreign terrorist organization, conspiracy to kill U.S. citizens, conspiracy to kill officers and employees of the U.S., conspiracy to acquire and use antiaircraft missiles, and money laundering.

The money Hizballah has brought in through such activities has contributed to its rise as a major terrorist force. Hizballah's moneymaking, and even its harassment of Israeli forces in the occupied zone of Lebanon, pale in comparison to its acts of terrorism. With Iranian guidance, Hizballah has played an important role in inspiring the wider rise of terror.

# CHAPTER 7

# The Meat Market:
# How Iran and Hizballah Perfected
# the Art of Hostage Taking

"It's the realization that hurts most," he recalls. "The realization that it is actually happening to you, that you too are becoming another figure in the statistics of hostage taking, that until they take the stinking blindfold off your eyes, until you get out of it, many long months will go by. It took two days from the moment that they put the muzzle of a Kalashnikov to my temple and pushed me onto the floor of the Volvo before I realized that this was a story that wouldn't end too quickly."

The French journalist Roger Auque spent a full year as a prisoner of Hizballah after his capture in Beirut in January 1987, most of it either blindfolded or in absolute darkness. He had been a reporter covering other kidnappings, and he later became a mediator involved in a long series of games connected to the Lebanese hostage takings. In between, he learned about that brutal business as one of its victims.

Auque arrived in Lebanon in 1982, a twenty-six-year-old freelance journalist aiming to make a name for himself by covering the hottest spot on the earth. "Those were crazy years," he recalls. "We could get up in the morning, travel to the south or to the Bekaa to cover an attack or a bombing, return to Beirut, have fun with the girls at the pool, and file our stories to Paris in the evening."

Within a short period, Auque's considerable courage had helped him become the Beirut correspondent of several French and Canadian networks and newspapers. His audacity came to the fore in 1985, when a Hizballah gang hijacked a Jordanian airliner and threatened to blow it up on the Beirut Airport runway unless a relative of Imad Moughniyeh, Mustafa Badr al-Din, who was being held in Kuwait for a series of terror attacks, was released along with his gang members. Auque took a camera, walked up to the plane, and asked the hijackers if he could come up the gangway and interview them. After a brief consultation, they decided not to shoot him—or so they told him—and to grant him his request. Thus Auque became the first and last journalist ever to interview Moughniyeh. As he recalls, "It was over very quickly, perhaps ten minutes. It was very clear who was giving the orders on the plane. This may sound banal, but Moughniyeh looked like an ordinary man, not someone you would turn your head to look at in the street. Not tall, a little plumpish. Very decisive, charismatic to a certain degree."

In the end, the Jordanian plane was blown up, but only after its passengers were released. The hijackers slipped away and disappeared into Beirut, without achieving their demands.

Auque filed one of his first reports from Beirut shortly after arriving there, on June 20, 1982. That was the date that the embryonic Hizballah kidnapped a foreign citizen for the first time. He was David S. Dodge, an American and the president of the American University of Beirut. Dodge was held for a year before being released. No reasons for his abduction or release were given at the time. A former Mossad official now says that in exchange for letting him go, the kidnappers secured an American promise, through French mediators, that the United States would not work against the establishment of a new Shi'ite organization in Lebanon. If this official is to be believed, Hizballah was born with its own act of original sin—and the United States was its enabler.

Mohtashemi-Pour soon gave Moughniyeh an order: Start using hostage taking as a weapon. Hizballah employed it sparingly until Imad's brother-in-law Mustafa Badr al-Din was arrested along with sixteen cohorts in Kuwait, for the attack they had perpetrated against the U.S. Embassy and other targets there on December 12, 1983. Badr al-Din and seven others were sentenced to death. This is one way in which the trial of the Kuwait Seven led to repercussions. Suddenly, the fight was personal for Moughniyeh. He issued more and more orders for abductions of foreigners in order to try to secure the release of his beloved brother-in-law.

The kidnappings also served Iran and Hizballah's political purposes. First, they focused world attention on the Shi'ite organization and its cause; second, they caused the departure of many foreign citizens from Lebanon, one of Hizballah's cherished goals. As Auque explains, Iran was behind it all. "From the moment the abductions began, it was clear that it was not only a matter of pragmatic steps by Hizballah to get its members freed in other countries. First of all, everybody understood that there were Iranian hands at work here. The commanders of my jailers told me themselves that the orders to kidnap me came from Iran. The goals were much broader and they were part of the protests against and the hatred for the West."

Auque was seized on January 13, 1987, as part of an unprecedented wave of abductions by Hizballah. "With hindsight, there were clear prior indications," he recalls. "Friends of mine in Walid Junblatt's Druze militia warned me I was in danger. There were also phone calls to my home, with silence on the other end. But at the time, I thought it was more likely a girl who was angry with me than Hizballah militiamen checking if I was at home.

"On January 13, two days after my birthday, I went out at nine a.m. My driver and another journalist were waiting for me outside the building. Only when I was right outside and had locked my door did I see that two Volvos were blocking the way to the road. Ten people carrying Kalashnikovs [AK-47 assault rifles] got out of them. They pushed me into a car, tied me up, shoved me onto the floor, covered my eyes, and set off on a mad drive into Beirut."

The kidnappers were Druze, working as freelance contractors for Hizballah. Their bosses in Tehran were annoyed that the French government was playing host to the leadership of the Mujahideen Khalq, the main opposition to the Tehran regime. Iran had repeatedly demanded, unsuccessfully, that they be thrown out. Now, in exchange for freeing Auque, the kidnappers demanded a cash ransom, the closing of the Mujahideen Khalq headquarters in Paris, and French pressure on Kuwait to release Mustafa Badr al-Din and his gang.

For the first month, Auque was held in a cellar in West Beirut. "That was the most horrible time. I had only a candle and a mattress. When the guards were in the room, my eyes were blindfolded. There was no day and no night. Tiny amounts of food, and terrible solitude. I fluctuated between hope and despair. From time to time one of the guards would come in, cock his weapon, and fire at the wall next to me. A kind of a game. Sometimes they would all come in and say they had decided to execute me."

Later, Auque was moved to an apartment with blacked-out windows in a Beirut high-rise building. Once, he tried to escape, but was caught at the last moment by his captors: "They had left the key in the lock. I pushed my shirt through the space under the door, and with a toothbrush I pushed the key out and onto the shirt. I remember the moment that they caught me as the most frightening of my entire incarceration. They weighed shooting me. There were other hostages in the same building. Out of fear that the thing had been exposed, we were all moved to different places the next day." Auque was next put in an apartment in a Palestinian neighborhood. This time a heavy iron chain was attached to his ankle, to stop him from trying to escape again.

After a year in captivity, and despite strenuous efforts by France's foreign intelligence service, the Direction Générale de la Securité Extérieure, or DGSE, Hizballah achieved several of its goals. Some Iranian prisoners (but not Badr al-Din) were released. France agreed to expel the Mujahideen Khalq command from Paris. A certain sum of money changed hands. Only then was Auque freed, together with another Frenchman, a photographer, and flown to Paris in a special plane sent by the president of France. "No, I am not angry," he says now. "True, I lost a year of my life, but at least, unlike some other hostages, I am still alive, with a wife and children. That year also helped me to find God and to get to know myself far better. What's more, they aren't worth my anger. We're speaking of a gang of barbarians, fools and lunatics. On the day of my release, the guards asked me if I would ever forgive them. I replied that forgiveness from me wasn't their problem. When they came before Allah, he would punish them. I told them that seizing hostages is the weapon of cowards, not of the brave. They really didn't like this reply."

Between late 1982 and June 1986, the peak period for Hizballah's hostage operations, ninety-six foreign citizens were abducted in Lebanon. That number does not include Syrian civilians and soldiers, Israeli soldiers, Lebanese Jews, Palestinians, or UN soldiers—that is, parties more directly involved in the Lebanese civil war. Thirteen of the ninety-six were murdered. Hizballah was responsible for fifty-one of the kidnappings. Eight were carried out by the Amal, the more established and more moderate Shi'ite party and militia, and the others by various groups, including Palestinian ones.

In the first wave, Hizballah captured four Americans, a Frenchman, two Kuwaitis, and a Saudi, to back up its demand to secure the release of its men in Kuwait. In the second wave, between December 1984 and July 1985, a greater number of abductions of citizens of various nations were perpetrated. During this period, Hizballah seized five Americans, five Frenchmen, three Britons, a Swiss, and a Kuwaiti. In 1985, kidnapping as a tactic spread to other organizations. A Dutch citizen was kidnapped by the mysterious Revenge Party; a Frenchman was taken hostage by the Abu Nidal group; and unidentified groups snatched three Swiss, two Britons, an Italian, an Irishman, and a Canadian.

In the meantime, the conflict between Hizballah and Kuwait sharpened. After the Kuwaiti royal family once again refused to release its Hizballah prisoners, a Shi'ite suicide bomber crashed into the convoy of the leader of Kuwait himself, Emir Jaber al-Sabah, in Kuwait City on May 25, 1985. Two bodyguards were killed.

Moughniyeh decided to try to exert new pressure on the French in the hope that they would be able to persuade the Kuwaitis to free his brother-in-law. In March 1985, he kidnapped two French diplomats, a researcher and a journalist, in Beirut. When the British clergyman Terry Waite came to see him in 1987 in a bid to negotiate their release, Moughniyeh simply added him to the list of hostages. Waite was freed only five years later, after undergoing severe hardship in captivity.

A third wave of hostage taking occurred between February and May 1986, and was directed almost exclusively against France. Eight French citizens were seized, among them four members of a television crew. Hizballah refrained from taking American hostages between June 1985 and September 1986. This "truce" was part of the deal for the sale of arms by the United States to Iran later made infamous in the Iran-contra scandal. Yet the truce didn't last. In September and October 1986, after two American hostages were released, Hizballah renewed its campaign, abducting Frank Reed, the director of the Lebanese International School; Joseph Cicippio, an American University accountant; and Edward Austin Tracy, a writer.

The international community paid closest attention to the ninety-six of its own who were victimized by Hizballah in the 1980s. Yet local Jews fared far worse. Between March 1985 and August 1986, twelve Jews were abducted in Lebanon, including a leader of the community, Yitzhak Sasson, and several prominent members. Most of the kidnappings happened in West Beirut, where the remnants of Lebanon's Jewish community lived. All of them were carried out by Hizballah, using its alias, the

Oppressed of the Earth. The organization demanded the release of its members who were incarcerated in the al-Khiam jail in South Lebanon in exchange for freeing the Jews. Shortly after Prime Minister Yitzhak Shamir declared that Israel would not deal with terrorists, the twelve men were all murdered. Hizballah claimed that the Jews were killed as revenge for Israeli air raids on Shi'ite villages in southern Lebanon and the Bekaa.

Like other terrorist organizations, Hizballah justified its use of hostages by stressing the imbalance between the power of the imperialist world and that of the "oppressed nations." As a religious organization, however, Hizballah also had to find a justification for kidnapping innocent people that seemed to comport with Islamic law. The hostages were often represented as spies and agents of Western countries. Nonetheless, intelligence gathered by Israel and the United States indicates that a dispute arose over the religious grounds for the hostage taking. Imam Fadlallah contended that there were no grounds for it. Yet orders to seize victims continued to come from Tehran, ostensibly in the name of the Ayatollah Khomeini. Fadlallah was overruled and the seeds of his future rift with Hizballah were sown.

Giandomenico Picco was an aide to UN Secretary-General Javier Perez de Cuellar who handled negotiations for Western hostages in the late 1980s and early 1990s. Through a series of mediators, Picco managed to establish a connection with someone who was introduced to him as the person responsible for Hizballah's hostages. As he describes it, "After they searched me thoroughly, they would blindfold me and drive me into Beirut at a crazy speed. We would change cars several times and I think that my escorts were also changed. At the end, I'd find myself in an apartment, each time a different one, with one or two men, wearing ski masks. One man who was present at each meeting called himself Abdullah. The Israeli intelligence told me afterwards that it was Imad Moughniyeh. He had a quiet voice, monotonous and authoritative. He always conducted the negotiations with great self-confidence and it seemed to me, at least this is what he said, that he trusted me and my credibility."

Picco was very impressed by the shrewdness and caution with which his interlocutor handled the negotiations. Moughniyeh was always the first to leave the meetings. The guards kept Picco in his chair until "Abdullah" had gone. As he left, Abdullah/Moughniyeh would whisk his mask off in one quick movement and wave good-bye, then walk quickly away with his back to Picco.

For years, the Israelis could not fathom the hierarchical arrangements between Hizballah's various components and Syria and Iran. Some sources say that the picture is still unclear today. Where, for example, did Moughniyeh himself fit in? There was a prolonged debate in the intelligence community over whether he was a member of Hizballah, or directly subordinate to Iranian intelligence. And if he belonged to the Iranians, who in Iran was his controller? A former Mossad official says that attempts to determine the answers to these questions failed, time after time, when information turned up that overturned basic presumptions. Hizballah and Moughniyeh simply refused to behave according to Israeli assessments.

David Barkai explains why it was so hard to be certain of anything when it came to Moughniyeh: "While in the early 1980s we had only hints about Moughniyeh, as time went by we detected clear fingerprints of his in attacks against us and against Western targets. His name became synonymous with Hizballah's activities in Lebanon and abroad. He used to move around with a whole batch of fake papers and present himself in innumerable names and titles. All the time he was spreading rumors and disinformation amongst his own people, so that if, God forbid, one of them was working with us, he would feed us 'noise' and not valid information.

"Living in perpetual flight made Moughniyeh into a true paranoid, who didn't trust a soul. He began changing his circle of close associates frequently, including his bodyguards. There were several cases when one of them simply disappeared and we understood that they too, like many other Lebanese, had become part of the foundations of some new building in Beirut. On the other hand, beside this great caution, Moughniyeh also displayed a great degree of brinkmanship. He never hesitated, and in my opinion even enjoyed, taking part in operations himself. There were times when he would spend two or even four days in Tyre or Sidon [Lebanon], with the whole facade of the armored Mercedes and the Land Rovers full of guards in front and behind. In the Lebanon of those days, this had an enormous impact. Lebanese that I spoke to would shiver when they mentioned the name of Imad Moughniyeh."

Barkai speaks of Moughniyeh with a great deal of respect: "Moughniyeh brought the 'technology of terror' to the highest level of skill, verging on artistry. He knew how to utilize the very latest electronic gadgets in his operations. He recruited students at Beirut University who had previously been members of the Lebanese Communist Party (which had excelled in its attacks against us) in order to plan very audacious and sophisticated operations. Moughniyeh preferred students of electronics or mechanical engineering. After the breakup of the Communist Party these people were looking for an organization that would be radical enough for them. Imad Moughniyeh was the right man.

"People who knew him described him as a highly charismatic man, but also very impulsive. His reactions were unpredictable. We are speaking about an artist of disguise and dissimulation. He was careful not to look like an Iranian or a Shi'ite, and instructed his people to do the same. Clearly, with a meter-long beard you can't get into Germany or France or Britain."

In a Lebanese reality in which very few rules or codes of honor had survived, Moughniyeh managed to break even these. One of his most audacious operations during the hostage-taking era disregarded the gentleman's agreement that one does not harm the other side's intelligence operatives. On March 9, 1984, Unit 504 of Israeli Military Intelligence received an encrypted signal from an important agent in Hizballah, codenamed "Hypnosis," requesting an urgent meeting. This source was so important to Israeli intelligence that he was not given a radio or any kind of transmitting device, for fear that it may lead to his being caught. Another agent of the unit would pass by a certain house in Beirut every day. If a large clay pot was on the balcony, it was a sign that Hypnosis wanted a meeting with his controllers.

Because in order to reach the meeting place, the agent usually had to leave the headquarters where he worked and pass several Hizballah roadblocks at each of which he could be searched, the Israelis instructed him to take great care not to get caught carrying any document that could incriminate him. Hypnosis had access to such material, even memos in Moughniyeh's handwriting. He used to fold them up, place them in a condom, and swallow them. When he reached the meeting place, he would do what was necessary to produce the paper and show it to his controllers. Unpleasant, but essential if he wanted to stay alive. On March 10, after receiving his message the Israelis, among them David Barkai, picked him up at one of the crossings between northern Lebanon, which was controlled by the Syrians, the Lebanese army, and Hizballah, and the south, which was under Israeli occupation. Barkai relates: "He was as pale as a ghost. After his visit to the bathroom, he showed us the memo from Moughniyeh to a Hizballah squad that had been training for months for an abduction operation. They were instructed to be ready to carry out their mission in the next few days. Their target, it said, was 'a senior American intelligence officer.'

"I thanked Hypnosis, and ran to the BMW, the kind of vehicle we often used because they were common in Lebanon and we didn't want to attract attention. I drove like mad to our base inside Israel and stood next to the encryption clerk and dictated the message for our HQ in Tel Aviv."

There ensued a great debate, with ego the major element at play, over who should inform the Americans—the army or the Mossad. Eventually, it was decided that the Mossad should do it.

On March 16, 1984, the Hizballah squad acted on Moughniyeh's orders and kidnapped Colonel William Buckley, head of the CIA station in Beirut and one of the few American experts left in the region after the embassy bombing.

Barkai: "I understood that the Mossad pooh-poohed our information, as it did so often with the material we passed on, and never bothered to pass it on to the CIA. When we heard of the abduction, we were beside ourselves with anger and frustrations. It would have been so easy to prevent it. Hypnosis proved himself, but we, with our war against ourselves, caused a great tragedy." CIA director William Casey was so determined and desperate to secure Buckley's release that he supported the Iran-contra scheme to supply Iran with American and Israeli weapons. But even that didn't help. Buckley died under torture, ordered by Moughniyeh. Moughniyeh apparently even administered some of the torture himself.

On October 4, 1985, Islamic Jihad, a Hizballah surrogate organization, announced that it had executed Buckley but it was only in 1991 that his remains were found in a plastic sack on the side of the road to the Beirut airport. His body was returned to the United States on December 28, 1991, and he was buried in Arlington National Cemetery with full military honors.

On September 30, 1985, four staffers of Soviet institutions in Beirut were snatched. They included the Soviet Embassy physician, Dr. Niko-lay Swirsky; a consular department official, Arkady Katakov; the attaché

Oleg Spirin; and an engineer from the Soviet trade mission, Valery Mirikov. The latter two were actually KGB agents working under cover. The Russians were captured in two pairs by special Hizballah teams commanded by Moughniyeh. One pair had to abandon its vehicle right outside the embassy, and Katakov was wounded during the abduction. His condition worsened until finally he was killed after a few days. KGB Beirut station head Yuri Perfilyev claims that reports later reached Russian intelligence proving that it was Moughniyeh who put a bullet in Katakov's head. In an interview, Perfilyev sums up his impressions of Moughniyeh: "This was a daring and base man, who was prepared to do anything despicable in order to harm the countries and organizations whom he was fighting against."

This particular operation was not a simple Hizballah one. In a message to the media, the kidnappers identified themselves as members of an organization known as the Forces of Khaled ibn Walid. The KGB immediately identified this as one of Hizballah's front groups. The Russians also believed that Palestinians were working with Hizballah on their operation. The group's demands, however, went beyond typical Hizballah claims, including that Moscow agree to put pressure on Syria, then a loyal Soviet ally, to cease military operations against Palestinian forces in the North Lebanese city of Tripoli. According to Perfilyev, this demand was voiced to the hostages themselves.

As the crisis deepened, the kidnappers threatened to attack the Soviet Embassy. Perfilyev went to meet the Lebanese spiritual leader, Sheikh Fadlallah, under tight security, in a secret shelter in the southern suburbs of Beirut. "Fadlallah made a good impression on me: from his appearance, his way of speaking, it was clear that he was no terrorist, that he was a cleric, a commentator on the Quran who had written over forty books. He told me he did not know who had kidnapped our people. We said we were certain it was the act of one of the extremist Islamic groups, and we asked him to appeal to his followers at Friday prayers and to tell them that the Soviet Union, then a superpower, had never stood against an Arab population and had always supported the Arabs in their struggles, and that therefore a terrorist action against Soviet citizens was not logical."

Fadlallah expressed dismay and offered to help, although he said that he did not know how. They had a further meeting on October 28, at which Perfilyev allowed himself an "improvisation" that he had not cleared in advance with Moscow. He spoke of the tragedy that the kidnapping had brought to the families of the hostages, and darkly suggested that that tragedy would be dwarfed if a Soviet missile "would fall by chance, purely by chance, on the holy city of Qom in Iran, close to the Soviet border."

The ex-KGB officer chuckles today when he remembers the threat. "Apparently it had some effect."

The three surviving Soviet hostages were initially held in a Hizballah detention facility in Beirut. On October 13, they were transferred to a nearby apartment, which, judging by the sounds of aircraft that they heard, was close to the airport. In adjoining rooms they could hear other foreign hostages speaking English. They managed to catch a glimpse of two captives, who appeared to be bearded, middle-aged Europeans. The Soviet hostages said they wanted to organize an escape attempt, in which they intended to let the "Westerners" take part, but before they could carry it out they were transferred yet again, to the Bekaa Valley.

With diplomacy failing to achieve any results, the GRU, the Red Army's intelligence branch, stepped in. They identified the clan of one of the kidnappers, and snatched two members. They dumped the body of one outside his family home, his throat slashed and his amputated penis in his mouth. A note attached to the body warned that if the Russians were not released, the second captive would receive similar treatment. It worked. The three living hostages were released, after thirty days in captivity, in what the captors called "a goodwill gesture." There were no further such attempts against Russian citizens.

Moughniyeh's rapid rise to the stature of the world's most wanted man, in the era prior to Osama bin Laden, was not only due to truck bombs and small-scale hostage taking. He also perfected the art of large-scale hostage taking, building on the airplane hijackings of the 1970s by Palestinian groups. In addition to the Jordanian airliner taken soon after Roger Auque had his interview with Moughniyeh, Hizballah also grabbed two Kuwaiti planes. In one case, in December 1984, four Lebanese Shi'ites, acting on orders from Moughniyeh, hijacked a Kuwait Airways plane on its way from Dubai to Karachi. They forced the pilot to land in Tehran, where they killed two American government employees who were among the passengers. The leader of the hijackers, Abu

Haider Mussawi, was given political asylum in Iran, where he is still living today.

On June 14, 1985, Moughniyeh conceived and planned the hijacking of TWA Flight 847 between Athens and Rome, diverting it to Beirut. The minute it landed in Beirut, he boarded the plane to encourage the hijackers and to convey their demands to the negotiators standing on the runway. The FBI later discovered his fingerprints in the toilet at the back of the plane.

Shortly after the hijack was reported, Haim Nativ, the Israeli intelligence community's man in Athens, arrived at the airport to see what he could find out about the perpetrators and to determine if there were Israelis among the 152 passengers. Athens Airport was considered one of the most dangerous in the world, and the Greek law enforcement and counterterror system one of the world's weakest. With the help of a few bottles of whiskey, Nativ soon had the passenger lists and the ticket stubs. Checks and cross-checks revealed who the hijackers were and where they had booked their flights. Nativ noticed that one of the tickets booked at the same travel agency had not been used and concluded that its holder, Ali Atwa, had not managed to board the plane and might still be somewhere in the airport. Nativ persuaded the airport police to page Atwa on the public address system, saying there was an important call waiting for him. He fell into the trap and was arrested immediately.

The hijackers took the plane to Algiers and back to Beirut, three times. At the first Beirut stop, nineteen passengers were released in exchange for fuel. At the next Algiers stop, twenty more were let go. The hijackers were demanding the release of some eight hundred Lebanese prisoners in Israel's hands, as well as international condemnation of Israel's military presence in South Lebanon and condemnations of America's activities in the Middle East.

As the plane flew and landed, flew and landed, the negotiations became more and more tense. Flight attendant Uli Derickson rose to the occasion heroically. Her German made it possible to communicate with the hijackers, who knew only a few words of English, and her composure and courage saved the lives of many passengers. She managed to prevent the hijackers from separating those with Jewish-sounding names, and she even paid with her own personal credit card for fuel when the Algerian authorities refused to refuel the plane on one of its stops there.

On the second landing in Beirut the hijackers identified one of the passengers as a U.S. Navy diver, by the name of Robert Stethem. They beat him severely, shot him in the head, killing him, and tossed his body onto the runway. They were then joined on the plane by twelve additional masked men.

Moughniyeh, wearing a mask, held a press conference. At his side, according to American intelligence, was Hassan Badr al-Din, Mustafa's brother.

On Saturday, June 15, the plane returned to Algiers, and sixty-five hostages were released. The next day, it returned to Beirut for good. Eight Greek hostages, including the popular singer Demis Roussos, were released in exchange for Ali Atwa. There were forty hostages left. One more of them was allowed to go because of a heart condition. Nabih Berri, the Amal leader who was a minister in the Lebanese government at the time, took the remainder under his protection and finally secured their release on June 30, seventeen days after the hijacking. They were taken by land to Damascus and flown from there in a U.S. Air Force plane to West Germany. The Syrians, who had taken part in the efforts to end the affair, and who did not really like the high-profile media attention it was getting, demanded that the release take place on their soil, hoping to obtain some credit.

About a month later, Israel freed some sixty Shi'ite prisoners from its jails, claiming that it had nothing to do with the release of the TWA hostages. This was not strictly accurate. The American government had obtained in advance Israel's agreement to let the Shi'ites out, in order to get the whole incident wrapped up. An Israeli Military Intelligence report summing it all up said that although the hijackers got less than they had demanded, even Moughniyeh, who was under heavy Syrian pressure, had understood that prolonging the crisis would not work to his advantage. He wanted something to show for the operation, to allow him to climb down, and the Israelis provided it.

The three hijackers who were identified—Moughniyeh, Atwa, and Hassan Badr al-Din—were indicted in a U.S. District Court in 1985, and placed on the FBI's Most Wanted List. Moughniyeh is now dead; the other two have never been caught. Another one of the hijackers, a friend of Moughniyeh's named Mohammad Ali Hamadi, was arrested in Frankfurt in 1987, when he was caught trying to smuggle explosives into Germany. He was put on trial for that crime as well as his role in the murder of Robert Stethem, and sentenced to life imprisonment. In 2005, he was pardoned and released. This was normal procedure for Arab terrorists caught by the Germans. They simply didn't want to keep these hot potatoes in their jails for too long, as it was an invitation for abductions of and attacks on their citizens abroad.

On February 14, 2006, the United States submitted a formal demand to Lebanon for the extradition of Hamadi, for his part in the slaying of Stethem. Lebanon never even bothered to reply.

The hijacking and the killing were not only a heinous crime and a provocation to the West, but also a blunt challenge to the leadership of Fadlallah, who had absolutely ruled out the use of such methods. In response, he said that the operation's "many negative aspects" outweighed its benefits. "We must not get carried away by this method. Today you hijack, and tomorrow you are yourself the victim of a hijack." But Fadlallah's preaching fell on deaf ears as far as the hijackers were concerned. They were acting on orders from Tehran. As Fadlallah was forced to concede. "I came up against a blank wall, because there is a mysterious force that is behind these actions," he wrote in an article published in *Middle East Insight* in 1986 called "Islam and Violence."

The airplane hijackings continued. On April 5, 1988, Hassan Badr al-Din and several other Lebanese Shi'ites took over a Kuwait Airways Boeing 747 on a flight from Bangkok to Kuwait and forced the pilot to fly it to Mashad, in northwestern Iran, where Moughniyeh was waiting. Later it was flown to Larnaca in Cyprus, where two passengers were shot and their bodies dumped on the runway. Samir Abu Gazala, the PLO's ambassador to Cyprus, who conducted negotiations with the hijackers, described them as "very professional," adding that "the leader never showed himself." The hijackers yet again demanded the release of the Hizballah prisoners in Kuwait, but again the Kuwaiti government refused. Eventually, the hijackers took the plane to Algeria, and vanished. According to Israeli intelligence sources, they were flown by an Algerian air force plane to Damascus. They reappeared in Beirut some weeks later.

Thanks to such operations—many of which succeeded in wringing concessions from the West, and all of which were terrifying and newsworthy—Moughniyeh became the top target of Mossad, the CIA, and other intelligence agencies. Israeli Signals Intelligence tracked him for a while, but by 1988, Israeli Military Intelligence's SIGINT Division, Unit 8200, discovered that he had slipped away from their coverage. His voice was no longer heard on the communications networks. The unit understood that Moughniyeh was familiar with technology that made it possible to identify a person through the unique "signature" of their voice, and that he was taking care not to speak himself, always letting his driver, or some other aide, speak for him.

In that same year, 1988, Moughniyeh was almost arrested during a stopover at Charles de Gaulle Airport in Paris. He was en route from Lebanon to Sudan for meetings with Iranian intelligence officials and mujahideen veterans from Afghanistan. The CIA had supplied the French with the details of the fake passport Moughniyeh was using. Nevertheless, and despite a positive identification made by the Americans at the airport, the French never detained him, claiming that "he had managed to slip away." U.S. intelligence never credited this excuse for a moment, believing that the French had let him get away on purpose, for fear of the fate of French hostages in Beirut.

The CIA was stunned; but Mossad wasn't surprised. As David Barkai, who was raised in a French-speaking home and graduated from the Sorbonne, explains: "The French were the champions at this kind of thing. After they snatched some Frenchmen in Lebanon, the French Foreign Ministry bought peace through quiet agreements with Hizballah. I know of at least two cases where they closed their eyes to blatant terrorist activity, just so that their interests would not be harmed."

Perhaps the most famous of all Hizballah's hostages from the 1980s was Terry Anderson. A senior correspondent for the Associated Press, he was snatched from his car at gunpoint on March 16, 1985, and held for almost seven years before being freed in December 1991. His life was shattered. He wrote a book about the experience, and spoke to the media, but the obscene length of time of his captivity had the cruel side effect that the public had largely lost interest in his case by the time he was finally let go. Indeed, when he later sued the government of Iran under a new 1996 statute that allowed citizens to claim damages from foreign countries who support terrorism, and details of his kidnapping emerged in court, nobody was listening and the trial was only barely covered in the media. The court nonetheless found Iran guilty of kidnapping and awarded Anderson and his family $341 million in compensatory damages. The Iranians never paid, of course.

The story of his ordeal is chilling. He was abducted after a Saturday morning tennis game, and shoved onto the floor of the kidnappers' car. "I am huddled under this blanket with a man's feet on my back and a gun poking in my neck, and I hear one of the abductors say, 'Don't worry, it's political,' in English. And I thought, that was not reassuring because, you know, it would be okay if they wanted some money, but if it was political, I was in deep trouble."

He was moved from one hiding place to another many times, and held blindfolded, with his legs shackled. His captors threatened to kill him if he tried to remove the blindfold. They gave him only bread and water, and an occasional piece of cheese. In one particular location he was imprisoned in a dark and filthy cell, with only a mattress, a bottle of water, and another bottle for urine. There were other hostages there, and they all suffered from diarrhea. They were chained to the floor, and had to defecate close to where they spent all their time. Anderson estimated that he and his fellow hostages were moved twenty-five times. Each time they were tied and gagged with packing tape, with only their nostrils left uncovered. They were squeezed into narrow spaces under truck seats, and driven for hours, inhaling the vehicles' exhaust fumes. On each such trip they feared that they were being taken to be executed.

Like all the other hostages, Anderson suffered from intermittent spells of depression that lasted weeks. He was told nothing about what was going on in the world, and given only minimal information about his family. He was allowed to see a few television broadcasts in which his family appealed for his release. In the last year and a half of his captivity, his fellow hostages were released one or two at a time. He had been told from the outset that he would be the last to be freed, and it was true. On the day of his release, he was driven after dark, blindfolded, to a rendezvous with Syrian soldiers. They drove him to Damascus, where he was finally reunited with his wife, Madeleine. They had not seen each other for 2,454 days. He also met his daughter, Sulome Theresa, for the first time. Madeleine had been thirty-five years old and in her seventh month of pregnancy when he was kidnapped. She testified in court that when he never came home that day, she had prayed "that Terry had had an accident, anything, just not kidnapped."

Terry, Madeleine, and Sulome all testified on the difficulties of adapting to life together after their reunion in December 1991. Ultimately, Anderson said, they needed five years before they could function again as a relatively normal family. He revealed that the psychological damage that he sustained was far worse than he had initially thought. Intimate communication with his family took place only very slowly. Madeleine was scared of this man who seemed so different from the husband she hadn't seen for seven years, and after having been both mother and father to Sulome for six years, she found it difficult to adapt to playing only the mother's role.

One of the witnesses at the trial was retired Ambassador Robert Oakley, who had served in Beirut and went on to become director of the State Department Office of Terrorism. The court judgment notes that Oakley "positively identified the Iranian Ministry of Information and Security as responsible for causing the seizure of the hostages in Lebanon by Hezbollah." He testified that one hostage was released in exchange for the delivery of Hawk missiles to Tehran.

Judge Thomas P. Jackson found that "The evidence is conclusive that Terry Anderson was kidnapped—and imprisoned under deplorable, inhumane conditions—by agents of the Islamic Republic of Iran, known by many names but most commonly as Hezbollah."

The amounts awarded in this and other similar cases have often been enormous, but collecting them is another matter. Not only does Iran not bother to answer any pleas, but successive White House administrations from Bill Clinton's to George W. Bush's have blocked efforts to collect on the judgments from Iranian assets in the United States, for fear of retaliation. Among the other petitioners who have won large amounts is Stephen M. Flatow of New Jersey, who in 1998 won a $247.5 million judgment against Iran for sponsoring a 1995 bombing in Israel that killed his daughter, Alisa.

In another case that reached the courts, U.S. Federal Judge Colleen Kollar-Kotelly ruled on October 10, 2000, that Iran was behind the kidnap and murder of U.S. Marine Colonel William R. Higgins. She awarded his widow and daughter $353 million.

In an interview for this book, the widow, Robin Higgins, said: "I would gladly give up all of that money if I could only see the man who kidnapped and murdered my husband standing in an American court and paying for his deeds. This trial was not about money, but about giving my husband the honor that he deserves, in court. To this day, twelve years after he was kidnapped, no one has been punished for the crime. But at last Rick Higgins has had his day in court, and he has won."

One witness at the Higgins hearing was Colonel David Hurley, who from 1985 to 1988 served as the naval attaché at the U.S. Embassy in Beirut. He testified about Hizballah's expertise in the hostage game, explaining that its hostages were moved frequently. "Hizballah, or their surrogates who were keeping the hostages . . . became very concerned . . . —I guess maybe they watched too many Rambo movies— that we would locate them and mount an effort to release them." Hurley said the captors maintained "highly professional" communications security, "even admirable, in a military sense . . . despite the relatively young age, despite the lack of formal military training," making it very difficult to intercept information about the hostages' whereabouts.

"I think sometimes, early on in the eighties," Hurley continued, "we tended to denigrate the capabilities of groups like this. Later, I think we began to respect their abilities a little bit more and we realized we were facing a little more formidable foe than we had anticipated. . . . It was the consensus of the intelligence community that [their] training came from Iran."

The Syrian government was furious over the kidnapping of Colonel Higgins, the court was told. Syrian president Hafez al-Assad thought it was inappropriate to harm someone serving on a United Nations mission. So the Syrian forces in Lebanon, together with units of the Amal militia, launched a large-scale search for the missing officer. The incident caused a severe rift in relations between Syria and Iran, and an internecine war between the two Shi'ite factions, Amal and Hizballah.

Sixteen months after the Higgins abduction, on July 28, 1989, an Israeli commando force kidnapped Sheikh Abdul-Karim Obeid, a prominent local Hizballah clerical leader, from his home in South Lebanon. This was an ultimately unsuccessful attempt to create a bargaining chip for use in negotiations for the release of a missing Israeli navigator named Ron Arad. In an immediate response, Hizballah threatened that if Obeid were not released forthwith, Higgins would be executed. Israeli intelligence was certain Hizballah was bluffing and wouldn't dare to carry out the threat. Israel rejected the demand and said it would hold Obeid until Arad was freed. The next day, Hizballah released a blurred videotape showing Higgins dangling by his neck from a rope.

Christine Higgins, William's daughter from an earlier marriage, saw the footage by chance, together with friends at a summer camp. They were watching TV when a news flash was screened and they saw her father hanging.

This blood-curdling snuff film shook the American public, and led to much criticism of Israel's conduct. Israeli Military Intelligence, however, didn't take Hizballah's tale at face value. They examined the broadcast at the highly sophisticated lab at their surveillance department. They isolated certain frames and enlarged and enhanced them considerably, revealing Higgins to be wearing what were obviously winter clothes, something hardly likely in the heat and humidity of a Beirut July. They concluded that he was murdered very soon after his abduction.

His body was recovered only on December 23, 1991, when it was dumped on a Beirut street. Pathologists who examined the remains determined that Higgins had died a long time earlier, and that Hizballah had kept the body for use when the occasion arose. The U.S. armed forces Medical Examiner, Dr. Richard Cole Froede, maintained that the real cause of death had apparently been a stab to the neck.

The kidnapping and slaying of Higgins had far-reaching repercussions within Lebanon and between Syria and Iran. Before the Higgins abduction, tensions had already mounted between Hizballah and Amal. After he was snatched, they exploded into a civil war (*fitna*, in Shi'ite parlance). Higgins had been taken after meeting Amal leaders in Tyre. Hizballah claimed he was a spy for the CIA. The fact that the operation was carried out straight after a meeting with Amal officials, in an area controlled by that organization, with utter disregard for the traditional Arab obligation to be hospitable and to protect guests, led the Amal militia to charge Hizballah strongholds in fury, in a futile search for the officer.

In April 1988, vicious battles erupted between the two Shi'ite factions. Fighting spread rapidly to Beirut, and continued with varying intensity for more than two years, costing the lives of more than a thousand Shi'ites. Every issue of the weeklies of both movements carried photographs of the bullet-riddled bodies of the dead. Imad Moughniyeh's men played an important part in the fighting against Amal. Though considered better-quality fighters, they also sustained many casualties in the internecine warfare.

The civil war was a thorn in the side of the Syrians. They saw it as potential evidence of their lack of control over Lebanon. Moreover, it diverted Hizballah from its main enemy, Israel. To the Iranians, however, the battle was important as the Syrian regime was traitorous to Islam, like all non-extreme Muslim governments. Moughniyeh's loyalties were to

Iran, and he began to run wild in operations against Amal. General Ghazi Kanaan, head of Syrian intelligence in Lebanon, began regarding Moughniyeh as a problem, and by some accounts he was forced to flee to Tehran, together with his deputy, Ibrahim Akil.

British MI6 believes a slightly different story: that Moughniyeh was not so much driven out as that he chose to leave of his own accord. This version has him incensed that the Syrians had not given enough support to Hizballah in their confrontation with Amal. He was also angry to a lesser degree with the Iranians, and decided to take a kind of sabbatical at their expense.

Whatever the case, the fact is that with Moughniyeh's departure and the continuing civil war, there was a big drop in Hizballah's operations against Israel and the West. But they would make a comeback soon enough.

# CHAPTER 8

# The Hungarian Octagon:
# The Hidden Side of Iran-Contra

"So, it's direct."

"Yes, very direct."

"And who else is involved in it on your side?"

"No one. I did the whole operation independently and personally, without anyone else, without meetings, without anything, because this time we've learned our lesson from the last time." [Laughter]

"And who's responsible for it from your side?"

"The prime minister."

"Himself?"

"Yes. I want to convey two messages: One, I want you to rest assured that I am responsible for it one hundred percent, and not like in the past. This time I'm in a better situation. You'll see it for yourself in the report that you'll get in the next few days. That's one thing. The second thing is that I have solved the problem of the two suitcases of yours in exchange for things that you have got."

"Can you really handle both our suitcases and their suitcases?"

"Of course yes, certainly."

"You understand that the situation now is not as it was in the past. There are not only suspicions, but there is also great fear, mostly from their side, of trying to do something like this again. From the political aspect, it's very hard for them, especially now, this is the situation in this region. But there is a possibility of flexibility, if we show them and tell them or if they see through us a sign that there is access, a way of getting to the suitcases."

Even after over twenty years, and despite the static and interference caused by the damage that the passage of time has done to the audiotape, which has not been played since then—and is being disclosed here for the first time—the excitement and the eagerness for action, for involvement in a great operation, for effecting a major strategic change are evident in one of the two voices. In the other, the cunning and slickness stand out. The conversation was between two men from different sides of the Mediterranean Sea, who for a period of time had the world as their playground, world leaders as their puppets, and one of the juiciest scandals in recent American political history on their hands.

The first speaker, the one who wants to know if the other really has access to "our suitcases" and theirs, is Amiram Nir, the Israeli prime minister's counterterror adviser and the initiator of the second and decisive stage of the Iran-contra affair. The other man, whom Nir calls by the nickname "Manoochy," is Manucher Ghorbanifar, an Iranian arms dealer and swindler who bamboozled the United States and Israel, and then betrayed them.

The phone conversation took place on December 10, 1986, three months *after* the Iran-contra arms-for-hostages scandal had burst into public attention. Nir was at his home in Ramat Gan, and Ghorbanifar at a hotel in Paris. Nir taped the call without telling Ghorbanifar. "Suitcases" is the code word for the American and Israeli hostages in Lebanon. Even then, three months into the scandal—after the vast damage that it had caused was already evident, and a heavy shadow had been cast over Ghorbanifar for leaking it—those involved were still eager to push forward with the scheme. When the Iranian called Nir in December, he managed to get things going again, as if nothing had happened. Iran, Ghorbanifar said, was still interested in helping to free the hostages, and this time without getting anything in return, as a gesture of goodwill toward the American administration, no less. Israel and the United States, who had repeatedly allowed the Iranians and their agents to mislead them, were almost ready to play with the deception.

The Iran-contra affair proved to be yet another case of the Iranians and their allies pulling the wool over the eyes of the Israelis and the Americans. It cost many senior officials their jobs, and some even their lives.

Despite everything that has been written about Irangate, there is a great deal that remains hidden. The affair was thoroughly investigated by a commission appointed by President Reagan and headed by former Senator John Tower, and also by independent counsel Lawrence Walsh. Investigations were also held in Israel, but they were only partial or limited to certain aspects of the affair. Most of their evidence and conclusions remained classified. The Israeli role remains largely undisclosed, including that of Amiram Nir.

One of the key issues in the 1988 American elections, in which George H. W. Bush finally won the presidency, was how much he had known about the Iran-contra affair. What was not disclosed was that Nir had briefed Bush about the operation when the vice president was on a visit to Israel. Indeed, Nir could have incriminated the incoming president. The fact that Nir was killed in a mysterious chartered airplane crash in Mexico in December 1988 has given rise to numerous conspiracy theories.

During the fifteen ensuing years, a systematic series of burglaries occurred in the homes and offices of people and organizations connected to the affair, including the home of Nir's widow. The only objects stolen were documents connected to the scandal. A source familiar with the details says that the burglars, who executed the break-ins in a highly professional manner and were never caught, were looking for the documents that made up the file dubbed "The Hungarian Octagon." They never found it.

The code name referred to an even more difficult version of the Rubik's Cube, the popular puzzle invented by the Hungarian poet and architecture professor Erno Rubik. The file contained some of the most important documentation of the Iran-contra affair, which together can be rearranged to fill in a picture of sorts, much like a Rubik's Cube. Along with many documents and notes and diary entries penned by Nir, which detail every step and every development in the operation, the file contains audiotape cassettes that Nir recorded secretly. The Mossad provided Nir with a miniature tape recorder with an ultrasensitive microphone in the form of a button, with which he recorded many conversations. The file also contains photographs taken by another operative, with a camera disguised as a cigarette lighter.

To this day it is not clear if Amiram Nir was murdered, and if he was, by whom. What is clear is that the most important document in the Hungarian Octagon file proves unequivocally that George H. W. Bush surely knew about all the illegal goings-on. Overall, the file offers an authoritative and documented view of the Israeli side of the operation, and demonstrates that the affair was even more scandalous than it is usually thought to have been.

• • •

In early post-revolutionary Iran, a struggle emerged between two schools of thought among the revolutionaries. The first thought that the national interests of the country should matter most, while the second saw the Iranian revolution as merely the initial step toward the establishment of a pan-Islamic state. The latter school sought to export the revolution first and foremost.

The struggle between these approaches resulted in the development of two separate, parallel political and security systems in the country, oriented toward the state and the revolution, respectively. The first was led by Hojat al-Islam Ali Akbar Hashemi Rafsanjani, who parlayed his role under Khomeini as head of the Majlis, the Iranian legislature, into a position of power and influence in the Islamic Republic. In addition, Khomeini gave him a number of other tasks in the 1980s, the most important of which was to serve as the supreme leader's representative in the Supreme Security Council, the most powerful body in the land.

Rafsanjani was elected president in 1989, after running against Ayatollah Hossein Montazeri. Khomeini had made Montazeri responsible for spreading the revolution to other Muslim states, and in 1985 he had declared Montazeri his successor. The more that Montazeri and his staff occupied themselves with forming ties with subversive Islamic movements, from Afghanistan to North Africa, and the deeper Iran's involvement in Lebanon became, the more the tension between the two parallel systems came to the fore. The clash was partly a matter of ideology, partly of ego.

The hardships occasioned by the war with Iraq and their effect on the internal situation in Iran led Rafsanjani and his followers to the conclusion that in order to maintain the Iranian state it was necessary to dampen the revolutionary ardor and to adapt it to reality. In 1983, Rafsanjani began urging that Iran should adopt a more pragmatic foreign policy that would enable it to enlist support for its war against Iraq in the West, and more important, to obtain Western arms.

In 1984, elements in Iran sent out signals to the Reagan administration indicating that Tehran wished to improve relations between the two countries, but these overtures fell on deaf ears in Washington. As an alternative, Iran approached Israel through two go-betweens, Manucher Ghorbanifar, the Iranian arms dealer who was close to Rafsanjani, and Adnan Khashoggi, a Saudi billionaire in the same line of business, who had maintained secret contacts with Israel. The Iranians wanted Israel to sell them arms and to mediate between them and the Americans. Israel, incidentally, was aware that as early as 1981 Ghorbanifar had tried to establish contact with the Americans, but had been marked by the CIA as an untrustworthy individual. The two arms dealers, who had obvious financial motives, established contact with Israel and explained that aid from America would bolster the moderate elements inside Iran, stimulate a more positive attitude to America, and lead to the release of the American hostages.

The contacts reached their peak, still behind America's back, when Ghorbanifar arrived in Israel, using a Greek passport, one of the many that he possessed, accompanied by his colleague and helper, Cyrus Hashemi. They closed a deal, code-named "Cosmos," for a $50 million sale of combat equipment to Iran. Aside from the profit, Israel had political motives as well—the desire for a link to moderate elements in Iran—but in sum, those involved on the Israeli side admit that the chief motive was financial. After much of the materiel had already been loaded onto a ship in Eilat, however, Ghorbanifar called to say that the deal was off. His bosses in Iran had had second thoughts, he said, and wanted to postpone it. They were in any case interested in different types of weaponry, especially antitank missiles.

It was at this stage, well into the Reagan presidency, that the Americans began taking an interest. They were motivated by the wave of abductions of American civilians and officeholders in Lebanon. The administration was also frustrated by the ban that the Congress had imposed on giving support to anti-Communist groups in Central and South America, a cause close to the heart of the hawkish Republican administration.

The Americans envisaged acting on a number of tracks. One was through a company set up in the United States in late 1982, called GeoMiliTech Consultants Corporation, or GMT. This straw company was in fact a cover for American intelligence efforts to subvert the Iranian regime from the inside and to encourage what the administration termed "moderate" elements, as well as to foster anti-Soviet forces in South and Central America, especially in Ecuador, Peru, and Nicaragua.

Among those groups were the Nicaraguan rebels known as the contras, who were violently opposed to the democratically elected Sandinista government. Although the Nicaraguan elections had been recognized as fair by several European governments, the U.S. administration insisted that the results had been faked, and accused the Sandinistas of being backed by Cuba and the Soviet Union, and of supporting Communist rebels trying to overthrow the pro-American government in neighbouring El Salvador. The CIA trained the contras and acquired weapons for them, with the assistance of GMT, which had offices in Miami through which planes were chartered and monies transferred. The arms were flown to the contras by an airline connected to the CIA. (It was on one of this airline's planes that Amiram Nir later took his last trip, or so some of the Israelis involved were told.)

Top officials in the U.S. administration and intelligence had perceived that they could make use of Israel in these dealings to solve a number of burning American foreign policy problems in one fell swoop. By transferring to Israel surplus NATO materiel from Europe to replace the Israeli arms that were to be sold to the Iranians at prices substantially higher than their true market value, they could use the proceeds to finance the contras. At the same time they would be improving relations with Iran and getting the hostages in Lebanon freed.

GMT personnel arrived in Israel and held meetings with senior figures, including a visit to Defense Minister Ariel Sharon's farm in the Negev. They rented space in Asia House, a prestigious Tel Aviv office block, and ran their business from there. An agreement, revealed here for the first time, was signed between GMT and Israel on the way the deals would be implemented and how the profits and commissions would be divided. For GMT, the signatory was the president of the company, a former beauty queen and airline stewardess and conservative talk show hostess by the name of Barbara Studley, while a number of top officers and officials signed for Israel.

Managers of the company wrote to CIA director William Casey, giving details of the quadrilateral deal between the United States, Israel, Iran, and the contras, and outlining the way the money would be channeled through secret bank accounts in Switzerland.

In the summer of 1985, the Israeli government gave the deal the green light, after it had been approved by Prime Minister Shimon Peres, Foreign Minister Yitzhak Shamir, and Defense Minister Yitzhak Rabin. It was decided not to involve the Mossad and to leave the implementation to unofficial middlemen involved in the arms trade. Off-stage, pulling the strings, was the director general of the Foreign Ministry,

David Kimche, a former deputy director of the Mossad. This man of many shadowy deeds still felt the burning insult of having been thrown out of the Mossad when he thought he should have been appointed director. He began to initiate secret operations, bypassing Mossad. He maintained secret links with Iran as well as with several African countries that did not have diplomatic relations with Israel, in the spheres of military and intelligence affairs, an area usually handled by the Mossad.

Initially, at the negotiating table were the Israeli military attaché in Tehran before the revolution, Yaakov Nimrodi, who had become a wealthy businessman, and Al Schwimmer, a former U.S. Air Force flight engineer who had founded Israel Aircraft Industries in 1950, after devoting several prior years to stealing airplanes and weapons and smuggling them into Israel to secure its newly won independence. He was convicted in 1949 in the United States for these actions, which were in violation of the U.S. embargo on shipping arms to the Middle East. In 2000, he would be pardoned by President Clinton, on his last day in the White House. Ben-Gurion once called Schwimmer the most valuable contribution America had made to Israel.

David Kimche travelled to Washington, where he received confirmation from National Security Council head Robert McFarlane that President Reagan and Secretary of State George Shultz were in on the scheme. That set the ball rolling, with Ghorbanifar representing the Iranians and Khashoggi laying out the cash.

The first shipment, in August 1985, consisted of 504 TOW antitank missiles, taken from Israeli stockpiles. The next contained eighteen Hawk antiaircraft missiles, which later turned out to have been faulty after one of them exploded on an Iranian launcher. Altogether, the Iranians had the feeling that the Israelis were trying to hoodwink them. Time and again they received consignments of missiles whose use-by date had expired, or which simply nose-dived off the launchers. To this day, there is an open argument in Israel as to who gave the order to load junk missiles onto the Iran-bound cargo planes.

In exchange for the weapons it shipped to Iran, Israel received supplies from the United States. And the United States received its own benefits. On September 14, 1985, Hizballah released the American Benjamin Weir, a Presbyterian missionary who had been held hostage in Beirut for sixteen months. Yet when the Americans waited for the release of more hostages, as provided for in the deal, nothing happened. A month later, the Islamic Jihad (Imad Moughniyeh's terrorist apparatus) announced that William Buckley, the head of the CIA station in Beirut, who was kidnapped on March 16, 1984, had been executed.

One of the papers in the Hungarian Octagon file, marked "Top secret, sensitive, eyes only. Chronology, the Iranian Operation," was a memorandum to Peres in which Nir summarized the interests of the sides. Nir wrote:

> The American interest: Basically the Americans are interested in opening channels for contacts with Iranian factors who are already in, or have good prospects for reaching, positions of power in Iran, because of Iran's strategic importance and before possible changes in its path and its leadership. Separately, the White House has a commitment to try and secure the release of the hostages in the hands of extremist Shi'ite organizations in Lebanon. At a certain stage, the Americans were ready for the opening of a "dialogue of gestures" with the supply of American weapons by Israel proving the "seriousness of intent" of the United States to Iran, and the release of the American hostages in Lebanon, through Iranian influence, proving the seriousness of Iran's intentions to the Americans. All this would be a prelude to the opening of a political and strategic dialogue.

"The Israeli interest," noted Nir,

> is to assist the Americans to achieve their two goals: the building of a strategic bridge with Iran and the release of the hostages in Lebanon, against the background of the overall relationship between the United States and Israel, the strategic partnership and the friendship, as well as the American aid to Israel in various spheres. If it is possible to act in the Iranian channel for the release of the kidnapped Jews [a reference to the twelve Lebanese Jews abducted by Hizballah, all of whom were later murdered] held by extremist Shi'ite organizations in Lebanon, it should be done.

The Americans did not exactly trust the Israeli representatives. Casey asked the attorney general, Edwin Meese, in writing, to maintain "electronic surveillance" over "two Iranian agents" due to arrive in Washington for negotiations on the release of American hostages. He named the two Iranian agents as "Mr. Asgari" (a pseudonym for Ghorbanifar) and

Yaakov Nimrodi. In the document, a copy of which is in the Hungarian Octagon file, no reason is given for considering Nimrodi an intelligence target or for defining him as an Iranian agent.

In retrospect, it turned out that under the overall umbrella of concern for the hostages, innumerable other undisclosed deals were carried out between the United States, Israel, and Iran. Iran needed weapons for its war with Iraq. Israel was already helping to provide some of them, but Iran's hunger was insatiable. There were arms transactions involving hundreds of missiles of dozens of different types, fire control systems, artillery pieces, machine guns, and ammunition. One person involved in these deals recalled: "We all knew that the Americans, that is to say the Republicans who were involved in it, were doing something that was very, very illegal from their side. It can be said without any equivocation that the 500–600 tons of ammunition that we shipped to Iran, not including the weapons and other equipment like night-vision instruments for tanks and navigation systems for aircraft, helped them a great deal in the war against Iraq, perhaps even decisively. Generally speaking, there were very few Israeli companies who had anything to sell to Iran and were not selling. The entire government-owned military industry and the privately owned military industries were involved in it, very deeply."

Perusal of the internal documents of the Israeli side of the Iran-contra affair reveals that it was not only the United States that supplied arms to the Central American underground armies within the framework of the deal. Israel did so also. Israeli representatives flew to Spain and Portugal, and from there to Latin America. They sold heavy and light machine guns, various kinds of bombs, and shells of a number of calibers, all in large quantities. They worked through a straw company in Portugal called SOPROFINA. Amiram Nir always claimed that Israel was not involved in any way at all in the supply of weapons to the contras. He wholeheartedly believed that to be true. Yet even Nir, the man who drove the venture, was unaware of everything that was happening under its wings.

For example, both the Latin Americans and the Iranians needed ammunition for their Russian-made artillery, mainly 130mm shells. At first, there was a plan to begin producing the shells in Israel, but then a firm was found in Austria, named Hittenberger, which was prepared to undertake the project. Hittenberger executives asked for blueprints for the shells and for a sample, which was taken from Israel's stores. Since the Mossad was kept out of the loop, the usual channels for handling such requests were unavailable. One of the Israelis involved simply joined the crew of an El Al flight to Austria, with the Israeli president, Ephraim Katzir, aboard. The crew member brought with him a bag containing a live shell, supplied by Israel Military Industries. On June 17, 1984, a representative of the Austrian company came to Schwechat Airport in Vienna and took delivery of the sample shell.

One of the channels for supplying Iran went through a certain European state (whose name is still withheld by Israeli Military Intelligence censorship). An arms dealer with good connections in Tehran purchased large quantities of materiel in Israel, including weapons, night-vision binoculars, electronic fences, and more, and flew it all to Iran. Several companies that dealt with the extraction of gunpowder and dynamite from mines and grenades also exported the products to Iran, via intermediate points.

In December 1985, Peres, Shamir, and Rabin became dissatisfied with Schwimmer and Nimrodi. The two were replaced by Nir, who was then still counterterrorism adviser to Peres. Nir's friends argue that Peres made the decision because the prime minister felt he was losing control over the operation, and that he could not rely on two private businessmen. Nir was the natural replacement, both because he was very close to Peres and because he had established a good relationship with Peres's defense minister and sworn rival, Yitzhak Rabin. Furthermore, he was on good terms with the officials responsible for Iran and counterterror in the National Security Council. Nir's opposite number in the United States was Colonel Oliver North, an official of the National Security Council. Nimrodi fought the decision, arguing that Nir had undermined him and worked against him, but the arguments fell on deaf ears.

Nir had made his mark when he provided Oliver North with highly sensitive information from Israeli Military Intelligence about the seizure of the Italian cruise ship *Achille Lauro* by terrorists on October 7, 1985. The hijackers, members of the Palestine Liberation Front (PLF), shot an elderly Jewish American passenger named Leon Klinghoffer, and threw him into the sea with his wheelchair while he was still alive.

On October 10, after the ship had docked at Port Said and the four terrorists had been promised safe conduct, Israeli Military Intelligence picked up a message from the commander of the PLF, Abu al-Abbas, to the four men. Nir conveyed its contents to Colonel North. Soon there-after, U.S. Air Force fighters intercepted an Egyptian airliner carrying the terrorists to Tunis, forcing it to land at a NATO base in Sicily. The men were arrested and put on trial by Italy. Nir received a citation from the White House for his role.

Nir, who had married the socialite heiress to a newspaper fortune, was charismatic, very clever, and very shrewd. Above all, he was hungry for action. When he was put in charge of the arms deal with Iran, he defined its goals in a memorandum to Peres: "A way must be found to bridge the gap between the Americans (who were demanding the release of hostages before the delivery of arms or the opening of a dialogue) and the Irani-ans (who wanted the exact opposite). The risks of supplying a large amount of materiel before the hostages are free must be minimized, so that any deceit will not be worthwhile. The secrecy of the operation must be secured, in order to reduce the probability of disclosure which is liable to occur with the release of the hostages."

He went on to describe how the operation would work: "It will be arranged with the Iranians in advance how much materiel will be sup-plied for the release of the hostages (including the Jews) and before the opening of the strategic-diplomatic dialogue. An added bonus will be offered for the release of the hostages—the simultaneous release of 39 Shi'ites imprisoned by the South Lebanon Army [the pro-Israel militia run by the IDF] in al-Khiam jail."

Nir ordered that several of these prisoners who were due for release be kept in detention so that their value as bargaining chips would not be lost. He wanted Iran to view the Shi'ite release as a sweetener, something that the Iranians could use to sway Hizballah, which in turn could use it to explain "their decision" to release their Western hostages. For the United States and Israel, the sweetener was necessary in order to enable them to supply the international media with "a logical reason for the release of the hostages without it trying to dig deep and find out the real reason."

Nir wrote: "Accordingly, the story of the release of the al-Khiam pris-oners has been prepared, taking into account the use of Terry Waite, the envoy of the archbishop of Canterbury, to act in this matter and attract media attention. The 'advance' shipment of materiel, which will be agreed upon, will be transported by Israel and taken from its stores, and on its own responsibility, without any American approach or request." In this way, if Israel were to be exposed during the delivery, it would take all the blame.

At the next stage, according to Nir's original plan, "after the release of some hostages, and as speedily as possible, direct contact would be established between Iranian government factors and American and Israeli government factors in order to start building an agenda for the strategic-diplomatic dialogue. The Iranians would give, or renew, their undertaking that from the beginning of the operation there will be no more hostage taking or attacks on American citizens in Lebanon, and that no harm will be done to the rest of the American and Jewish hostages."

It was a lot to hope for. On December 30, 1985, Nir met with Ghorbanifar and Nimrodi in London, to take over the Israeli side of the operation. The various stages for the shipment of 3,500 TOW anti-tank missiles and the release of the al-Khiam prisoners in exchange for the release of the American and Jewish hostages were decided with Khashoggi. After all this, a meeting was planned between high-ranking Iranians and Americans, to set the agenda for the dialogue.

Ghorbanifar said that he would get Tehran's final approval of the details within two or three days. Nir flew to Washington, and on January 2, 1986, he presented the new plan to national security adviser John Poindexter and to Oliver North. Beforehand, he tried to establish whether the Americans had alternative methods for the release of their hostages, apart from the Iranian operation. According to the minutes of the meeting, kept by Nir, Poindexter and North surveyed the different efforts, and agreed that none of them appeared to have a chance of success.

Poindexter said that the operation had not worked so far because it had been run in a manner that was neither serious nor credible. The only justification for the supply of arms, he said, was a strategic one, and the Iran-contra efforts to date were anything but strategic. He believed that all the meetings with the Iranians ended up in petty quarrels about the times and prices of arms deliveries and never yielded any progress on the important strategic issues such as hostages, improved relations with Iran, and provision of intelligence information on the Soviet Union, which had been the original reasons for the United States having become involved in the first place.

Nir then presented the "improved" plan, stressing four aspects:

". . . the separation of the United States from the supply of arms to Iran; the bringing forward of the direct link with elements in the Iranian regime on the strategic aspect . . . the stepping up the security of the operation prevention of leaks, and the 'attractiveness for the Iranians by inserting the cover story' of the freeing of the al-Khiam prisoners."

By the strength of his personality, Nir managed to persuade the Americans to stick with the operation, and to take the path proposed by Ghorbanifar, despite the fact that he had already been declared a liar and a con man by the CIA. On January 8, North informed Nir that following a discussion between all the concerned factors, the president had given the go-ahead. He added that President Reagan wanted to reassure Israel that if a crisis broke out in the Middle East, all of the missiles that Israel had supplied to Iran would be replaced within eighteen hours.

Two weeks later, on January 22, a meeting was held in London attended by North, Nir, Ghorbanifar, and General Richard Secord, who—North explained to Nir—would run a front organization, with no apparent links to the United States, and would handle the financial, operational, and logistical aspects of Iran-contra. The purpose of the meeting was to go over the components of the agreement and to make sure that they were all clear and known to both sides. At this meeting, Nir understood from North that it had been agreed with Ghorbanifar in Washington that military intelligence about Iraq and the USSR would also be supplied to Iran, and that samples of it would be handed over at the time of the delivery of the first one thousand missiles.

North asked Nir to be the liaison with Ghorbanifar, mainly in order to ensure American separation from the deal, in case it were to be exposed. North also asked Nir to give Ghorbanifar the account number that he would receive from Secord, so that the Iranian would not be able to claim, in the event of exposure, that he had transferred money to an account whose number he had been given by the Americans. Nir agreed. At the end of the meeting, General Secord gave him the number of an account in a Swiss bank, and Nir handed it to Ghorbanifar. Other financial transactions in the venture were conducted through another straw company that had been set up under the name SEEPEE—South East European Purchasing and Export Establishment—at the Lichtenstein Landesbank in Vaduz.

After stalling for a while, Ghorbanifar deposited $10 million in the Swiss bank account. In exchange, on February 16, one thousand missiles were flown into Israel, transferred to an El Al cargo plane whose markings had been painted over, and flown on by an American crew to Tehran.

On February 18, two Israeli soldiers were abducted by a Hizballah ambush in Lebanon (they would later be murdered). The reason for the kidnapping, according to some of the parties involved, was apparently to spur the Israelis to supply more weapons to Iran. It was these two men who were from then on called "our suitcases" by the Israelis in phone calls. After several more delays, on February 25 a meeting took place in Paris between North, Nir (who was presented as an American and carried a fake American passport), a high-ranking CIA official, and Mohsen Kangarlu, an aide to the Iranian prime minister.

In a written report to Peres, Nir was enthusiastic:

The meeting was rather dramatic, in the terms of that phase. For the first time since the revolution in Iran stabilized (or a little later), fairly senior representatives of the governments of the United States and of Iran were meeting. The Iranian side at first showed apprehension and suspicion, and it took a few hours until the atmosphere thawed somewhat. A large part of the conversation centered on the relations between the two countries in the past and in the future. The hostage issue was mentioned as an obstacle that must be removed from the path, and as humanitarian aid that Iran was prepared to extend as a gesture. The subject of Iran's military needs also came up. The senior Iranian official stated explicitly that Iran was ready to work hand-in-hand with the United States to solve the problem of international terrorism. Parallel to this talk, meetings also commenced between Iranian intelligence personnel and the American intelligence team, with the participation of a CIA representative and Secord, where American military intelligence and surveys of the Soviet threat were conveyed to the Iranians. It was also decided that Iran would exert its influence to assist the Americans to free the hostages, as a counter gesture to the gesture of the Americans in supplying materiel and intelligence.

On February 28, Nir sent a small handwritten note to Peres. Referring to an upcoming meeting to be held on the Iranian island of Kish to discuss the next stage of the operation and apprehension over the CIA trying to exclude Israel: "At a meeting in Frankfurt, North tells me that it would be worth it for Shimon to write a letter to Reagan mentioning participation in the meeting because he is worried that the CIA wants to exclude us from the picture and to ignore the president's decision about our hostages."

Subsequently, Nir and Peres sat together and formulated a letter from the prime minister to Reagan, which read in part:

> I was very pleased to hear about the outcome of the meeting in Frankfurt. I believe that if what was finalized at the meeting indeed takes place, both our countries might be on the verge of a significant and strategic break-through. . . . You will appreciate, I am sure, that we have several problems regarding our two soldiers, as well as those Jews who are in a similar sit-uation. We believe that during the next meeting, this subject should be on the agenda, after your own expectations regarding your five men are ful-filled. I wish to express my greatest admiration for the courage and vision with which you lead this challenging project.

The ever cautious Nir delivered the letter to North, who wrote on the copy, in his surprisingly ornate handwriting: "Received: One letter from the Prime Minister of Israel to the President of the United States."

Another memo in the Hungarian Octagon file reveals that at a meet-ing in Paris on March 8, North and Nir decided that "out of awareness of the need for some kind of oversight of Ghorbanifar's activity as a medi-ator, the operations will be accompanied by a concentrated intelligence effort that will make possible at least a partial knowledge about Ghorba-nifar's activity and its reverberations in Iran and of the credibility of his reports to the American-Israeli side." At the same time, North and Nir decided that they would each examine other channels as possible alterna-tives to Ghorbanifar. From then until the end of July, Israel tried and tested four or five different options for establishing ties with Iran. But none proved to have anything like Ghorbanifar's access, however prob-lematic he may have been.

In the second half of March 1986, Ghorbanifar reported to Nir, who passed the word on to North, that he had visited Tehran and met with top officials, and that they were ready for a summit at which the whole deal would be finalized. The meeting would take place in Tehran, not on the island of Kish, as had been planned originally. Ghorbanifar also joyfully reported something that later turned out to be totally without basis: "one of the issues that was decided upon at Frankfurt—the Iranian undertaking to refrain from supporting international terrorism and aid in reducing it—had already been finalized with Khomeini himself, who would issue a *fatwa* against terrorism and the kidnapping of hostages."

In mid-May, Ghorbanifar and Khashoggi deposited a total of $15 million in the secret Swiss bank account, and Israel deposited $1.685 million there to cover the gap between what it was sending to Iran in the second shipment and what it was receiving from the United States. The delivery of weapons to Israel began, under General Secord's control. On May 22–24, spare parts for the Hawk missiles and 504 TOWs were flown into Israel, to replace those that had been sent to Iran. To the amazement of IDF officers who checked the consignment, it turned out that not only had Israel tried to supply Iran with faulty equipment, but the United States was trying to do the same thing to Israel. The TOWs had passed their use-by date and would have been a danger to anyone who fired them.

Until the bubble burst, neither the American nor the Israeli architects of the project realized the extent to which they were being used as tools in internal Iranian struggles. On May 24, at midnight, a Boeing 707 carrying the U.S.-Israeli team took off from Israel en route to Tehran. On board were McFarlane, North, Nir, and other intelligence personnel, as well as some 10 percent of the total package of materiel that had been promised at this stage, to be presented to the Iranians as a gesture of goodwill.

In Tehran, they were given pleasant rooms in a luxury hotel. Yet the delegation was not welcomed by high-ranking officials as promised. In fact, they were given a humiliating and contemptuous reception. Nir explained it euphemistically to Peres: "It soon became clear that the top echelon in Iran, although it was aware of the meeting that was to take place, had not prepared, or had not been prepared, for it properly and there were therefore delays, holdups, difficulties in reaching decisions or conflicts between the elements in the leadership that are involved regarding the desired outcome of the meeting."

In the coming months Nir, posing as an American, was present at four meetings with three senior figures in the Iranian government. The most interesting was with Dr. Hassan Rohani, then the deputy chairman of the Majlis and one of the most powerful men in the regime. Nir taped the meeting, which took place in Paris, as Rohani said some surprising things about his bosses: "They [the heads of the regime] sent three million dollars to Lebanon, and we in Iran don't have enough money to pay for our living and security requirements. [They want] to turn Lebanon into an Islamic state. What nonsense! I tried to put a stop to it but never succeeded."

Rohani went on: "I don't feel comfortable this morning, after the extremist speech that Imam Khomeini made yesterday. I think that it was his toughest speech since he took power. He demanded that all the people who do not take a tough line against the United States should be broken and chopped into little pieces. But it's you the Americans who are guilty. You sit on the sidelines and see what's happening between us and Iraq, and you don't lift a finger to help us. You won't get anything out of Iran as long as there is no movement on your part and you don't supply us with what we need.

"If we analyze Khomeini's character, we shall see that if someone strong faces up to him, he takes a hundred paces back. But if he's strong and someone weak is facing him, he takes a hundred paces forward. Unfortunately, you are taking an incorrect position. You have been too soft. If you were tougher, you would have been on top. You didn't show strength . . . first and foremost you must be tough against Khomeini. To stand up to him firmly."

Nir, pretending to be an American, engaged him in a dialogue. "Where should we show force against him?"

"If for example you would say to him, 'You must free all the hostages in Lebanon within five days. If not, we'll strike a military blow against you, and you will bear the responsibility for the consequences.' Do it. Show that you are strong, and you will see results."

"We are a great power," Nir responded. "Sometimes we are slow. But you saw how we acted against Libya [a reference to the American bombing of Tripoli on April 15, 1986, to retaliate for Libyan terror attacks against U.S. targets]. But we believe that if we use military force, it will push Iran into the arms of the Russians.

"You should use Muslim propaganda against Khomeini, with the help of Turkey and Pakistan."

During the month of July, contacts with the Iranians continued in an attempt to secure the release of at least one hostage. In the third week of the month, Nir told Ghorbanifar, and through him the Iranians, that the operation would be called off if there weren't a release in the next few days. Finally, Father Martin Jenko was released by Hizballah on July 26. Nir was informed a few days in advance by the Iranians.

What happened next, in late July 1986, has been vigorously denied by George H. W. Bush. The man who would become president in January 1989, and serve until he was succeeded by Bill Clinton, has always insisted that he was unaware of the "rogue" Iran-contra operation. Yet the Hungarian Octagon file suggests otherwise. Colonel North informed Nir that he had intended to meet with Vice President Bush, who was on his way to Israel, in Frankfurt, to brief him on the moves that had led to the release of Jenko, but Bush had left Frankfurt early for Tel Aviv. North asked Nir to brief Bush instead, in Jerusalem. Nir requested and received Peres's permission to do so, and he met with the vice president in the latter's suite in the King David Hotel on July 29. The meeting lasted from 7:35 to 8:05 a.m.

Most of Nir's report to Peres on the encounter is devoted to countering an erroneous summary of the meeting written by Bush's assistant, Craig Fuller, who was not familiar with the details of the operation and therefore did not quite understand what it was all about. The summary was meant for internal distribution, but Nir received a copy and found that it contradicted the notes he had made and what he remembered of the meeting. Nir explained it:

I said that the efforts to free the hostages was the test of the Iranians whom we were talking to, insofar as their will and their ability to establish a relationship with us was concerned. Important point: When I used the word "we" Fuller wrote "they" as if it was Israel I was talking about, although at the outset I had made it clear to Bush that I was speaking on behalf of the joint American-Israeli team, about both of our efforts and actions, according to North's request [to update Bush].

Later, Bush asked how the work was divided up and what Israel's role was, and I replied specifically. I told Bush that Israel was doing everything in order to provide "cover" and serve as a "disengagement squad" to protect the United States from exposure, dealing with logistical aspects, operating the channel [Ghorbanifar], providing a physical base for unloading and loading the materiel, and putting an aircraft at the disposal of the operation were precisely Israel's parts in the affair, and were all being done at the explicit request of the Americans. I do not see the logic that says that complying with the request of the United States and carrying out logistical steps that enable the United States to avoid exposure mean that Israel conducted the operation and ran it and dragged the United States behind it.

We sensed that the matter would die if we did not press to see what the Iranians we were in touch with were capable of delivering. The Iranians requested, claiming a lack of trust, to divide the deal up into four stages, and we—the United States and Israel—replied that there would not be any more talks or meetings before they began to fulfill their obligation to release hostages.

Fuller's report had insisted that "the vice president [Bush] did not undertake any commitment and did not give Mr. Nir any instructions. The vice president expressed his appreciation for the briefing and thanked Nir for continuing the efforts despite the doubts and reservations throughout the process." Nir, by contrast, wrote: "It is not clear to me now and it was not clear to me then what doubts and reservations Bush meant. He spoke in a rather optimistic tone, and I got the impression then that he was a supporter of the operation."

The disclosure of the Iran-contra affair and the subsequent break in the connection between the United States and Iran led to a new wave of kidnappings in Beirut. In the United States, the affair kept on snowballing. When it came out that the huge profits that Oliver North had garnered by overcharging the Iranians had been used to fund the contras, there was outrage in Congress, which had specifically barred the administration from so doing. Reagan's spokespersons hurried to blame Israel and specifically Nir. Furious, Nir phoned North. "How can you put out such a lie?" he asked in the taped conversation. "You know that it can be proved that it wasn't Israel that thought this up, but you."

"I had to do it," North replied. Nir protested but didn't respond publicly. One of the reasons for his silence was the phone conversation with Ghorbanifar on December 10, 1986, described at the beginning of this chapter. CIA chief Casey approved of keeping up the connection with Ghorbanifar, in the hope that it would lead to the release of the remaining hostages, thereby bolstering Reagan's position vis-à-vis the congressional inquiry, and serving to vindicate the entire operation.

But then someone leaked to *The Washington Post* that at the same time as it was dealing secretly with Iran, the CIA had supplied Iraq with intelligence information derived from satellite images about key targets in

Iran. The leaders of the Iranian regime angrily and immediately decided to break off the contacts.

Not only in the United States, but also in Israel, Nir was thrown to the dogs as the "fall guy" in the scandal. Most of the Israeli media related to him as an adventurer who had dragged the governments of the United States and Israel into an international political imbroglio. One cartoon showed Nir hovering in the sky, manipulating the strings of puppets representing world leaders. Although Nir remained the counterterrorism adviser to prime minister Yitzhak Shamir, who had taken over from Peres, he soon realized that he had been neutralized of his authority and could no longer continue to absorb the criticism and attacks and resigned. Until his death in the mysterious plane crash in 1988, he was in a private business.

In 1987, there was a severe escalation in the friction between Iran and the United States, over the so-called Tanker War in the Persian Gulf. The U.S. Navy intervened on behalf of freedom of navigation in the waterway and fired at Iranian vessels. The Iranians then instructed Hizballah to step up kidnappings of Americans in Lebanon. On July 3, the U.S. Navy cruiser USS *Vincennes* erroneously shot down an Iranian passenger jet, with the loss of all 290 passengers and crew. In response, Iran, acting through the Palestinian terrorist organization headed by Ahmad Jibril, launched a series of attacks against American targets in Europe, and even in the United States: the car belonging to Sharon Rogers, wife of the captain of the *Vincennes*, was blown up in San Diego on March 10, 1989, and her life was miraculously saved. The attacks in Europe were stopped thanks to "Operation Autumn Leaves," a joint effort by German intelligence, the CIA, and the Mossad in October 1988, which led to the arrest of a Palestinian terrorist by the name of Hafez Dalkamoni, who had previously been in an Israeli prison. He was caught with several barometric bombs which Ahmad Jibril's Popular Front for the Liberation of Palestine–General Command intended to use to blow up American and Israeli airliners.

Was Amiram Nir the "man who knew too much"? Was he murdered because of that meeting in the King David Hotel? Or was the plane crash in Morales in southern Mexico in December 1988 nothing but the accident that the Mexican police claimed it was? There is no definitive proof that Nir was eliminated. Three months earlier, however, he had told one of the people closest to him that he had met with two high-ranking members of the U.S. intelligence community, who said they represented the vice president and Republican candidate for president— George Bush. They asked Nir what he would say about that meeting at the King David, if and when he was questioned about it during the presidential campaign.

Nir told them he would keep the affair's secrets locked in his bosom forever.

# PART III

# THE GLOBAL WAR

# CHAPTER 9

# Assassins

In the long intelligence war between the West and Iran, there are many sharp distinctions between the two sides. Yet there are some ironic similarities as well. One of them is the peculiar attraction to code names drawn from ancient Rome and its wars.

"Hannibal," the name of the military commander from Carthage who taught the Romans a thing or two about tactics, was the code name that the Iranians gave to a senior Mossad operative in Paris in 1983. Conversely, the head of the Iranian station in the French capital was called "Gladiator" by the Israelis, and the surveillance operation against him was named "Herod," after the king of Judaea under the Roman Empire. Israeli Military Intelligence also used "Hannibal" for its own purposes, as the generic code name for the abduction of Israeli soldiers by hostile elements. The name of his home city, Carthage, later became the code name of the plan that was prepared by the Israeli army's Northern Command to crush Hizballah in the 2006 war, but failed. "Brutus" was the code name of a CIA mole in the Iranian nuclear program. And that's only a partial list.

On September 3, 1983, the headquarters of the Savama, the secret intelligence agency set up by Khomeini, sent a message to its clandestine station in Paris ordering it "to neutralize Hannibal." It was a direct instruction to kill a senior Mossad operative—the person responsible, among other duties, for Israel's link with the Iranian opposition in exile.

The content of the message reached Israeli intelligence, the first known case of a planned Iranian assassination in Europe. It was never actually carried out. Instead, the disclosure led to an intelligence gold mine for the West, and eventually pointed to a long string of follow-on assassinations in several European cities.

The mission was assigned to Gladiator himself, a man named Farhad Abdulghasem Mesbahi, the head of Iran's Paris intelligence station. He was a familiar figure to the Mossad and known to be an excellent operative. The order was given because Tehran feared the link between Israel and the Iranian exiled community. For their part, the leaders of the Iranian revolution saw it as their right, and even their holy duty, to wage an all-out war against dissenters, in order to deter them, both inside the borders and without. During this period, Israel was involved in a number of bids to overthrow the Khomeini regime, most of which were born out of the network of ties between Israel's intelligence and the Shah's loyal exiles, many of whose members had held senior posts in the Shah's administration and still enjoyed generous funding from the royal family. They were highly motivated to see Khomeini's regime overthrown. The Israelis' role in supporting the exiles' efforts had now motivated Tehran to target the Mossad's operative, Hannibal, in an effort to thwart further counterrevolutionary plots.

Shortly after the Shah died of cancer, his son and heir, Reza, led a number of attempts to overthrow the new Islamic regime, most of them with Israeli assistance. After his presence in Cairo became too heavy a burden on President Anwar al-Sadat, Reza moved his headquarters to Rabat, Morocco, and worked from there to plan the next attempt. He was surrounded by a large coterie of generals, among them Ghulam Ali Oveisi, the Shah's commander of land forces, and his son, who held the rank of colonel. Oveisi was murdered in Paris in 1985 by agents of the VEVAK, the Iranian Ministry of Intelligence and National Security.

In May 1982, Reza and the Israelis, along with the Saudi billionaire Khashoggi, initiated a scheme that was nothing if not ambitious. The plan they concocted called for the Saudi royal house, the Pahlavi family, and wealthy Iranian exiles to collect a billion dollars to buy arms in Israel and the United States. They would also pay the Sudanese ruler Jaffer Numeiri $100 million for his agreement to allow training bases and arms stockpiles to be set up in his country, to prepare Iranian recruits for the fight. Israel had the central role: to provide weapons and to train the Iranian recruits, to gather the intelligence, and finally to transport the Iranian fighters to Tehran, where they would seize key installations. Israel secretly informed the United States of the plan, through the military attaché at the Israeli Embassy in Washington.

The administration endorsed the operation, but without offering any material American involvement or support, apart from the approval of arms sales from both the United States and Israel for those items that included American components. The Pentagon was happy about the sales, which would bring in sizable amounts of money both to its own coffers, for items from the U.S. military stockpiles, and to several large American manufacturing corporations.

The plan reached a fairly advanced state of implementation. Two of Reza's generals went shopping for arms in Israel in September 1982, with $600 million to spend. But ultimately the scheme was dropped after Ariel Sharon was ousted from his post as minister of defense following Israel's entanglement in Lebanon.

Some of the details, though, as well as other Israeli moves in this field, became known to Iranian intelligence. Most of these initiatives were channeled through Paris and through Hannibal's network of contacts. Killing Hannibal would therefore send a strong message.

The Mossad decided to report the threat to Hannibal's life to the French external security agency, the DGSE, and a joint operation, code-named "Herod," was set in motion to thwart the assassination. The intended assassin, Farhad Mesbahi, was placed under constant surveillance. He was watched as he left his luxury apartment in the La Défense quarter and went to a nearby café for morning meetings, and then as he drove his green BMW to the Iranian Embassy. Mesbahi's wife was also followed.

In parallel to the close surveillance, information for Operation Herod was also gathered by other means, mostly through double agents run by French and Israeli intelligence from among the Iranian exiles in Paris who had enlisted for the new regime in Tehran. Gradually, Mossad and the DGSE learned that Mesbahi's activities were part of a major scheme to eliminate figures in the Iranian opposition whom Khomeini saw as a danger. Some of these figures were, in fact, busy planning moves to topple the ayatollahs. Others were dissidents guilty only of writing articles and making speeches harshly condemning the Islamic Republic. Eventually, Tehran assembled a list of over two hundred targets, among Iranians living in exile in France, Germany, Switzerland, and other European countries, as well as in the Middle East, Turkey, and the Philippines—in fact, almost everywhere that Iranians who opposed Khomeini were living.

Although in the years following the revolution there were signs of increasing dissatisfaction with the regime, the ayatollahs managed to maintain stability by establishing revolutionary institutions, by widespread indoctrination of their radical Islamic line, and by detention, torture, and execution of those who did not toe the line inside the country. Violent measures to suppress any opposition from Iranians abroad were also important. From the point of view of the government in Tehran, these elements not only endangered its existence by providing an alternative to the revolutionaries' ideas; some also advocated the use of force in order to destabilize the regime. These groups perpetrated a series of attacks inside Iran, and also harmed Iranian interests abroad. American intelligence estimated that the Iranian regime's motivation to hit opposition elements grew in direct proportion to the degree to which it perceived itself as vulnerable.

The attacks on opposition figures were generally carried out by Iranians, tenured agents of the Tehran intelligence services, or freelance mercenaries with Iranian citizenship. The perpetrators used a wide variety of weapons, and techniques of disguise, attack, and escape, sometimes engaging in sadistic abuse of their victims. They often used "Trojan Horse" associates to get close to their targets, in marked contrast to attacks on non-Iranian targets, which were almost always carried out by using large explosive charges—car bombs, for example. Bombing keeps the perpetrators at a distance (unless a suicide is involved) and makes detection more difficult for investigators. Close, personal involvement in a killing significantly increases the chances of leaving forensic evidence for investigators.

Most of the attacks against opposition figures were carried out in Europe. Iran chose not to operate on U.S. soil, as it no doubt estimated that terror attacks in America, even against Iranian exiles, would evoke reactions very different from the Europeans' nonchalant responses.

As far as was known to French intelligence, the first operation carried out by the Savama agents commanded by Mesbahi was the assassination in Paris in December 1979 of Shrihad Mustafa Shafik, a relative of the deposed Shah. Ayatollah Khalkhali, a Khomeini associate and head of the revolutionary court that was sentencing the regime's opponents to death, never even bothered to deny that the regime was involved in the slaying. In a public speech in Tehran, he said that "the fighters for Islam" had also wanted to kill the princess Ashraf, Reza's twin sister, who was living in Paris. No one was ever caught in connection with the crime. In July 1980, also in Paris, a Lebanese freelance hit man, funded by Iranian intelligence, made an attempt on the life of Shahpour Bakhtiar, the Shah's last prime minister, missing his target but killing a woman neighbor and a policeman. He was sentenced to life on March 10, 1982, but was pardoned and released in July 1990 by President François Mitterand, officially for health reasons and good conduct. Intelligence sources in Israel say that Mitterand had acted due to an Iranian threat to carry out terror attacks on French soil.

When French intelligence learned of another two Iranian oppositionists who were on the Tehran regime's hit list, the men were warned and immediately ceased their activities and left Paris. France's security agencies were determined to investigate these operations including a series of small bombings in June and July carried out under their noses, in their capital city. Admiral Pierre Lacoste, head of the DGSE, approached Mitterand several times asking for permission to take measures to put a stop to the assassinations, especially after both the French and the Mossad became certain that the Iranians were preparing to kill Hannibal. They had learned of an effort to locate where he lived. In December 1983, Mitterand was convinced. On Christmas Eve he ordered the Quai d'Orsay, the French Foreign Ministry, to declare Mesbahi, along with two other Iranian diplomats who were serving as his assistants, persona non grata, and to instruct them to leave the country immediately. One of the two assistants was Vahid Gorji, whose official title was "interpreter." He was responsible, French intelligence believed, for the bombings in June and July; they did not harm anyone but were aimed at terrorizing other dissident Iranians, who had also received threatening letters.

Mitterand's order did not put a stop to the killings; it simply prompted the relocation of Iran's center of European operations. Mesbahi was posted first to Vienna, then to Brussels. The Mossad kept its eye on him. He continued to try to get Hannibal eliminated, but eventually focused all his attention on exiled dissidents.

Throughout the 1980s and early 1990s, Tehran's targets were crossed off its list one by one. Europe's response was remarkably indifferent. The Mossad gave the intelligence services of Belgium, Austria, Germany, and France a lot of information about Mesbahi and his associates' actions against people living in those countries, his dealings in terror, and other criminal activities; but aside from the expulsion from France, none of these countries did anything about it. The ease with which Iranian agents shot, stabbed, and blew up the regime's enemies, while local police failed to stop them and intelligence agencies looked the other way, is reminiscent of the heyday of the Mafia in Prohibition-era Chicago. Certainly Europe's indifference sent a message to the Iranian government that the West was full of a lot of empty talk.

Some dissenters to the revolutionary regime were truly dangerous, carrying out guerrilla actions inside Iran and also harming Iran's interests abroad. The chief such element was the Mujahideen Khalq, the extremist socialist-Islamist organization that had fought alongside Khomeini against the Shah; the group broke away in fury after the revolution, when its leaders saw they were not getting their reward in terms of appointments and budget allocations. From 1980 on, the Mujahideen Khalq perpetrated a series of very ferocious terrorist attacks targeting the regime inside the country, as well as its representatives abroad.

Yet many of the dissidents who were assassinated by the regime's agents were not such violent elements, but just vocal critics, nothing more. Iran's attitude toward these inconvenient voices stood in marked contrast to its relationship with movements like Hamas and Hizballah. Officially, Tehran was and still is careful to speak of groups associated with terrorism in the world's eyes only in terms of granting them "moral support." The government is at pains to distance itself from violence. Yet when it came to the opposition in exile, Tehran's official policy was and is open and brutal. For example, the secretary of the Supreme Council for National Security and deputy speaker of Parliament, Hassan Rohani, declared in March 2004 that Iran "will not hesitate to crush the actions of groups abroad opposing the revolution."

Through the mid-1980s, in part thanks to Mesbahi, fifteen Iranian dissenters were killed and twenty-three wounded in France, Germany, Britain, Turkey, Austria, Pakistan, Switzerland, Belgium, Greece, and Italy, among other places, with no perpetrators ever caught. But the pace of killings did not satisfy Tehran, and it was soon to surge dramatically.

In 1988, in the course of a government reshuffle, President Rafsanjani ousted Mohammad Rayshahri from the post of minister for intelligence affairs, and appointed Hojjut al-Islam Ali Fallahian in his place. Born in 1950, Fallahian was a mullah and the scion of a prominent Islamic family. An ardent disciple of Khomeini, he had worked against the Shah, and after the revolution he was a magistrate in the city of Abadan. There he became known as "the hanging judge" due to his excessive fondness for death sentences. In 1982, he was made prosecutor general of Iran. Shortly after joining the cabinet in 1988, he intensified assassinations of opponents of the regime.

Becoming a sophisticated planner of operations, Fallahian was responsible for a new wave of terror that caused the deaths of many Iranian exiles. A German federal criminal attorney in 1993 ascribed no fewer than twenty-four murders of exiled dissidents to Fallahian's ministry since his appointment. Fallahian even boasted about the killings on Iranian TV in August 1992: "We also locate them abroad. Last year we succeeded in striking decisive blows against senior people."

Fallahian expanded Iran's foreign intelligence networks, planning assassinations through them. Many Iranian legations were substantially reinforced with "diplomats" who were in fact intelligence personnel. Within the Iranian Foreign Ministry, the Department for Islamic and Arab Movements kept track of the killing networks, providing funds and organizational assistance. In 1995 and 1996, some of these "diplomats" were declared persona non grata in Germany, Norway, and Turkey.

The networks operated through a number of cover organizations, including *Hilaal al-Ahmar* (the Red Crescent); *Jihad Sazandgi* (the Holy War for Building Purposes); the Office for Islamic Guidance, which deals with cultural activities and relations; Iran Air, the state airline; the Iranian News agency (IRNA); and the national Iran Shipping Lines.

In 1989, with Fallahian in place, Iranian intelligence decided to center all of its activities in Europe in the Iranian Embassy in Bonn, West Germany. Farhad Mesbahi was appointed deputy chief of the operation. He had become very close to one of the aides to President Hashemi Rafsanjani, who had supported, as early as the "Irangate" affair in 1986, the creation of secret links with European governments, the United States, and even with Israel. Rafsanjani now made Mesbahi his secret liaison with the German authorities, a "back channel," in intelligence parlance. With Rafsanjani's support, Mesbahi managed to negotiate the release of two German hostages captured by Hizballah in Beirut in 1990.

The Germans had a thick file on the man the Israelis called "Gladiator." They were aware that he was not just a back channel diplomat, but a key player in the Iranian terror that was running amok in Europe. The Mossad and the French DGSE had shared their files; armed with all this information, the Germans managed to recruit Mesbahi to work as their agent. Several explanations of Germany's achievement were given by people involved in turning Mesbahi. One is that the Germans blackmailed him, using information about some misuse of intelligence funds; another is that they threatened that they too would declare him persona non grata, a step which he realized would mean the end of his career in Europe, after he had already been barred from France. According to the third and simplest version, the Germans simply paid Mesbahi a lot of money.

Whatever means the Germans used, there is one point on which everyone agrees: he provided them with enormous amounts of information about Iran's intelligence and terror networks in Europe, and especially in Germany. The Germans listened attentively, documented everything thoroughly, interrogated him about every little detail, filed everything away—and made no moves.

The killings continued. The Iranian hit teams operated for years more in Europe, almost without interference. On April 24, 1990, the Iranian opposition's representative at the United Nations in Geneva, Professor Kazem Rajavi, was slain. According to a German intelligence report, Iran's Security Council had ordered VEVAK (the Ministry of Intelligence and Security) to have Rajavi eliminated. The reconstruction of the crime by the German investigators showed that two teams in two cars carried out the operation. One team followed Rajavi's car and fired two shots at it, causing him to swerve into another lane. The second team came from the opposite direction and forced him off the road. He hit a tree, and his head smashed into the steering wheel, activating the horn. The killers got out of their cars and pumped bullets into the unconscious Rajavi from several directions. The assassins then fled the scene.

A little over a year later, on August 6, 1991, a blazing hot afternoon in Paris, the Iranians struck again. Three dark-haired men approached an ivy-covered villa in the Suresnes neighborhood, the home of seventy-six-year-old Shahpour Bakhtiar, who had briefly served as prime minister after the flight of the Shah in 1979, and was now one of the leaders of the opposition to the Khomeini regime. The three men aroused no suspicions, as one of them, Faridoun Boirhamdi, aged thirty-eight, was a personal aide and confidant of Bakhtiar. The guards at the gate took their passports, frisked them, and allowed them to enter.

Bakhtiar and his personal secretary welcomed the guests in a ground-floor lounge. Immediately after the secretary left the room to make tea in the kitchen, one of the men leapt at Bakhtiar and, according to the autopsy findings, dealt him "a fatal blow" to the neck. The secretary was killed in the same way. Using two knives taken from the kitchen, the killers then cut their victims' throats and stabbed their chests and arms with such brutal force that one of the blades broke. One hour after their arrival, Boirhamdi coolly picked up the passports from the guards, who had not left their post at the gate to check if the people they were supposed to be guarding were unharmed, and the three men left in an orange BMW. The guards failed to notice that the shirts of Boirhamdi's two friends were bloodstained. There had been two previous attempts on Bakhtiar's life, but the guards were not particularly concerned about Boirhamdi, and they did not check on their client. They were not aware that he had been murdered until hours later.

The investigating judge appointed to handle the case was Jean-Louis Brugière, who specialized in probing terror organizations. What had at first looked like an unsolvable case to the French intelligence services eventually became, thanks to Brugière, a tortuous but successful inquiry that led via Switzerland and Turkey to the highest levels of the government in Tehran.

Nowadays, Brugière sits in a cordoned-off and heavily guarded wing of the Palais de Justice, the historic Paris law courts. The walls have been reinforced and the windows made of armored glass, ever since it was discovered that a Palestinian terror organization was planning to fire a shoulder-held missile into his office. The judge himself carries an enormous Magnum handgun, earning him the nickname "the Sheriff." He drives around Paris in an armor-plated limousine surrounded by police motorcyclists and protected by bodyguards. The bodyguards predate his office's armored glass; he has had them ever since agents of the Abu Nidal Organization booby-trapped the door to his home with a hand grenade in 1983.

Brugière is one of the most powerful judges in France. The French legal system bestows upon people of his status almost unlimited authority. This and the issues that he handles, combined with his flamboyant conduct, have made him a central figure in some of the stormiest affairs in France during the past twenty years. He gives the impression that he is quite pleased with all the fuss surrounding him, fully aware of his image as a troublemaker. "I love my work," he says, "and get huge satisfaction out of it, as well as much interest and a great sense of mission. It may be that there are politicians who would be happy if I did not solve the cases that I investigate. That is of no matter to me."

Of the Bakhtiar murder inquiry, Brugière says: "It was the classic case of the Trojan Horse. They recruited someone close to the victim, and linked him up with additional assassins. The security was faulty. They entered, killed, exited, took their passports, and 'bye-bye.' It was clear to me that time was against us, and that the killers were certainly trying to get out of the country. I immediately determined that they were Iranians, not necessarily French speakers, of foreign appearance, who would try to get to a more friendly country, perhaps one where Iranian intelligence is active, like Switzerland, for example. Since airports are relatively closed places, I presumed that they would choose a land route."

This was the pre–cell phone era, and Brugière also assumed that the fugitives would have to report to their controllers on the success of their mission and receive orders for further operations. He instructed his team to get printouts of all the calls made from all the payphones between Paris and the Swiss border, ascertaining that there were some 5,000 phones in that area, from which over 20 million calls had been made in the days following the murder. The call data was fed into a computer and sifted for patterns of calls made to foreign numbers. "We narrowed it down to something like two hundred calls that fit the bill, ruled out some of them, and it turned out that we had hit the bull's-eye," says Brugière. He managed to track down the identities of Bakhtiar's killers as well as their controllers. A Mossad operative explained, "With those phone numbers and a large number of documents that he managed to get hold of, Brugière actually uncovered much of the VEVAK network in France, Britain, Germany, and Turkey. He discovered their safe houses, their command hierarchy, and if the Turks had cooperated a little more, he also would have managed to arrest most of them."

"The Iranians had a special unit, over one hundred operatives strong, made up of VEVAK agents and members of the Revolutionary Guards, whose entire purpose was to eliminate dissenters," says Brugière. "The Turks didn't really help me at the outset. I sensed that they were afraid of Iranian terror. Later on they improved, but in the meantime some of the operatives managed to escape from Istanbul to Iran."

For two years, Brugière tracked down the Iranian network. His investigation earned accolades from law enforcement and counterterrorism agencies the world over. All of the Iranian agents that Brugière managed to trap, including those extradited from Turkey, Switzerland, and Germany, were tried, convicted, and jailed for long terms. This was the first time that so impressive an amount of solid evidence had been amassed to implicate senior Iranian officials in the murder of a political dissenter abroad.

"It's clear that Iran was involved in this crime," says Brugière. "The footprints led directly to the Iranian Ministry of Intelligence, to the close entourage of the head of the espionage and security services, and to Ali Fallahian, himself." As to the fact that the affair did not lead to a prolonged diplomatic crisis between France and Iran, Brugière adds: "I know that France has a negative image on the issue of the war on terror. I see great importance in my work and my declaratory judgments that link states like Libya and Iran to terror. Yet it seems that it's impossible to bridge the gap between the law and politics. The fact that France never broke off ties with Iran is a political statement about which I have nothing wise to say."

Brugière's 177-page classified report stated baldly that the Iranian espionage services took an active part in the execution of dissenters. The report also revealed the connection between Bakhtiar's murder and Iran's ministries of Foreign Affairs, Communications, Islamic Instruction, and its state television network, IRIB. A senior member of the logistical support team for the Bakhtiar assassins entered Switzerland with the orders for the operation typed on Iranian Foreign Ministry stationery and initialed by the foreign minister, Ali Akbar Velayati, himself. Brugière's report also mentions additional acts of murder committed at the behest of Tehran and even includes a "hit list" of future targets. "The government grants legitimacy to the murder of all opponents of the regime across the globe," it concludes.

When one government sends agents to murder a citizen of another government, it challenges that government's sovereignty. When it harbors those agents back in its own territory, and refuses to cooperate with a murder investigation, it insults that government's justice system. After Russian émigré Alexander Litvinenko was poisoned in London with polonium in late 2006, British investigators fingered Russian suspects. Moscow refused to extradite them, so the British expelled some Russian diplomats. Yet in Europe in the 1980s and 1990s, as Iran executed émigré after émigré, for the most part, Europe's elected officials did little to oppose the killings. In October 1992, for example, two of the Geneva-based killers of the Iranian opposition's UN representative, Ali Kamali and Mahmoud Sajedian, were spotted in Cologne while watching the home of another exile, a member of the Mujahideen Khalq opposition movement. The local police were informed, but were in no hurry to act. Kamali and Sajedian were arrested on November 15, together with two other Iranians, in France, after having been placed on the Swiss police's wanted list. They spent a year in jail in France, and were then deported to Iran, despite a Swiss extradition request.

European governments found it difficult to formulate clear policy in the face of a regime that employed terror against its citizens living in their countries. This kind of terror was perceived by some as part of an internal Iranian struggle and therefore better to avoid becoming entangled in. For both Germany and France, weighty economic interests were at peril. By the early 1990s, the volume of annual trade between Germany and Iran stood at $7.9 billion, and Iran's debt to Germany totaled $8 billion. Some 170 German companies, including giants like Siemens, Krupp, and Daimler-Benz, operated in Iran. In addition, some diplomats in Germany defended a velvet-glove policy, which had succeeded in securing the release of two of its citizens kidnapped in Lebanon by Hizballah and a third who had been accused of spying and was being held in Iran itself.

The official European Union policy toward Iran was one of "critical dialogue." Allowing relatively straightforward police investigations to peter out suited that policy. The Europeans preferred to leave channels of communication with Iran open, arguing that only thus would the way be clear to influence Tehran. The advocates of this approach contended that Iran was not incorrigible. They believed that sanctions, as some proposed, would only fan the flames of hostility.

Some European states, however, rejected the lenient line. One was Denmark, which in August 1996 broke off its dialogue with Iran. Foreign Minister Niels Helveg Petersen said he did not believe that "dialogue with Iran can lead anywhere. In fact, I cannot point at even one improvement that resulted from the critical dialogue that we held." Conversely, when a criminal investigation was launched in Belgium against former Iranian president Ali Akbar Hashemi Rafsanjani, on charges of wrongful imprisonment of dissenters who held Belgian citizenship, and of threatening dissidents living in Belgium by means of letters written by Iranian intelligence, Tehran responded angrily. President Mohammad Khatami declared that the probe against his predecessor was the work of "the enemies of the Iranian people," and warned that Iran would "spare no effort to protect its credibility, its strength and its honor."

But these cases of standing up to Iran were isolated exceptions. For most of the 1980s and 1990s, Iran enjoyed a forgiving, if not supportive, attitude on the part of European states. It seems that within the Iranian intelligence services the understanding was that as long as the targets were only dissenters in exile, Iran's assassins would not be given too hard a time by the Europeans. Meanwhile, within Iran, thousands of dissidents and persons deemed to be "offenders against the spirit of Islam" were being executed for deeds seen as immoral or transgressing religious law.

The killings that became known as the Mykonos affair finally broke the political impasse, culminating in the Iranian leadership being officially accused for the first time of involvement in international terror and murder. Just before midnight on September 18, 1992, two men armed with pistols broke into the back room of a Greek restaurant, Mykonos, in Wilmersdorf, a borough of Berlin, and opened fire at the eight clients dining there, killing three and mortally wounding a fourth. The victims were all exiled Kurdish Iraqis, leaders of the Kurdish opposition to the Iranian regime. As the killers sprayed the Kurds with automatic fire, they shouted in Farsi, "sons of whores." They made off in a BMW with a third man, similarly armed, who had stood watch at the entrance. The victims were Dr. Sadeq Sharafkandi, director of the Kurdish Democratic Party of Iran; Homayoun Ardalan, its representative in Germany; Fattah Abduli, its representative in Europe; and their translator, Nouri Dehkordi.

As the German police and secret services began their investigation, they discovered that German intelligence had been in possession of a great deal of material about the activities of Iranian government agents against members of the opposition in exile—much of it garnered from Farhad Mesbahi—dating back to 1989. The Mykonos affair caused much consternation and some contention in Germany's operational and diplomatic agencies. Two of the three perpetrators were caught on October 14: Abbas Rayal, one of the killers, and Yusuf Amin, who stood guard outside during the massacre. They were arrested along with two Lebanese residents of Berlin, as they attempted to cross the border to Holland with false documents. Rayal's fingerprints had been found at the scene of the crime.

A fifth perpetrator, Kazem Darabi, was also arrested on October 14 on suspicion of commanding and planning the attack, supplying the perpetrators with the money, cars, and weapons, and providing a hiding place in Berlin. In his indictment he was identified as a senior VEVAK agent, whose cover in Germany was that of a businessman and importer of agricultural produce.

Yusuf Amin turned state's evidence, so was not tried. He revealed that the killers had worked through a Trojan Horse: a member of the Kurdish Democratic Party who had served as a mole for VEVAK. Some in Germany demanded that the investigation be followed through to the end, while others wanted to make do with prosecuting only the remainder of those arrested, and not pursue those who had sent them. Two reports were prepared by German intelligence during the long investigation and trial of the four men. The first, dated June 29, 1993, stated that the murder of the Kurdish opposition members had been planned and carried out by the Iranian government in coordination with the Iranian Embassy in Bonn, under the code name "Bozurg Alawi." The second, dated December 19, 1995, asserted that "for a long time, official elements in the Iranian government have made it their goal to assassinate members of the Kurdish Democratic Party of Iran. At the beginning of September, the Iranian Ministry of Intelligence and Security, VEVAK, sent a team from Tehran to carry out the operation. The team acted in coordination with the VEVAK bureau in Berlin and began surveillance and drawing up a final plan for the attack."

The investigation of the case took three months, and the subsequent trial lasted three and a half years, comprising 246 hearings. Over 170 affidavits and testimonies were submitted, including classified intelligence material, tapes of broadcasts of Iranian TV, and the evidence of Iranian exiles.

The prosecutors said that there were three arms of Iran's secret services operating in Germany: the VEVAK, or Ministry of Intelligence and Security; the al-Quds force of the Revolutionary Guards; and the Iranian army's counterespionage branch. Each of these had its own separate objectives, but they cooperated with each other. All three maintained representatives in Germany. Their official offices were in the Iranian Embassy in Bonn, where they organized covert operations under the cover of straw companies. The VEVAK office was set up in 1986 and was housed on the third floor of the embassy. According to the prosecutors, this department was responsible for planning, management, and logistical supplies for espionage and terror operations carried out by the Iranian regime in Germany and other European countries. The Bonn office had a regular staff of twenty employees. During the same period VEVAK also maintained a branch in Düsseldorf, disguised as a small company dealing in bookbinding machinery. This branch brought the Mykonos assassins from Tehran. A list of Iranian diplomats in Germany who were actually intelligence operatives and assisted in planning the Mykonos attack appears in the German intelligence reports. These agents left Germany after the massacre.

This testimony was explosive; but the most dramatic development came from elsewhere: Farhad Mesbahi, the Gladiator, came in from the cold, seeking asylum in Germany. Mesbahi's close link to Rafsanjani was very useful to him, as it gave him not only prestige, but also an excellent salary and employment terms, but it also had its price. Certain sworn enemies of Rafsanjani, among them the speaker of the Parliament, Aya-tollah Ali Akbar Nateq-Nouri, heard about the "back channel" and tried to secure Mesbahi's arrest and prosecution for treason, during a visit he paid to Tehran in January 1993. But Mesbahi got wind of their plot and fled to Pakistan and then back to Germany, where he fell into the arms of his BND controllers and received political asylum.

As he was no longer able to serve as a mole within Iranian intelligence, there was no problem in making more open use of him. The Germans granted him asylum, and he was called as a secret witness in the trial of the four killers of the Kurds, though identified only as "witness C." His testimony served as the basis not only for the conviction of the assassins themselves, but also for the first clear accusation against the heads of Ira-nian intelligence and the revolutionary regime. Mesbahi made a power-ful impression on the court. On April 4, 1997, Darabi and Rayal were found guilty of murder, and the other two of aiding and abetting mur-der. The German court, in its ruling, asserted the "involvement of senior echelons of the Iranian government in political murders." The goal of the regime, the judges said, had been "to silence inconvenient voices."

Although Darabi and Rayal were sentenced to life in prison, they were released by the German government in December 2007, despite the fact that Germany had promised Israel not to do so. They were supposed to be part of a future deal between Israel and Hizballah, to be released in exchange for Israeli soldiers held by the organization. The Germans gave as their official rationale for the release the good behavior of the pris-oners, but officials in Israeli intelligence suspected that the real reason was a secret deal in which Iran promised to pressure Shi'ite militias in Iraq to release German hostages.

At the time of their conviction, though, the Mykonos affair was a rare stiffening of the West's backbone, and it provoked a strong response.

The Iranian deputy foreign minister, Javad Zarif, condemned the German court for a decision "based totally upon the evidence of terrorists and kidnappers, who are wanted by the Iranian law enforcement authorities." He added that "These elements are members of anti-revolutionary groups whose aim is to harm the good name of Iran." He referred to the entire legal proceedings in the Mykonos affair as a "show trial." President Khamenei also tried to belittle the importance of the trial, referring to it as a "puppet show about an attack in a café carried out by unknown persons."

Iran threatened to file a libel suit against the German government, and dispatched an official protest to the Foreign Ministry in Bonn, claiming that the judgment was not supported by the evidence heard in court and in any case it was the result of the ongoing Zionist campaign of incitement against Iran. In Tehran thousands of demonstrators, mostly students, took part in a protest procession to the embassies of Germany and the European Union. On several occasions, senior Iranian clerics even intimated that they would not hesitate to issue a *fatwa* against the prosecution team in the Mykonos trial, similar to the one issued against Salman Rushdie in 1988 by Khomeini.

Nonetheless, the regime backed off of further killings. The 1997 verdict in the Mykonos affair brought an end to seventeen years of assassinations carried out by Iran in Europe. From a list of five hundred-odd targets drawn up by Khomeini after the revolution, nearly two hundred dissidents had been killed. In the terror years of the Soviet Union, a few foreign assassinations made headlines (most famously, Trotsky's ice pick to the head in Mexico). But nothing on this scale had been perpetrated.

Although the Iranian assassinations of dissidents in foreign countries were not generally vigorously protested, other killings by Iran abroad *were* highly publicized—if they involved sensational acts of terrorism. Thanks to Iran's war with Mossad, there were more than a few of those.

# CHAPTER 10

# Operation Body Heat

On the night of October 16, 1986, Israeli air force pilot Yishai Aviram and navigator Ron Arad took off in their F-4 Phantom jet from the Hatzerim air force base in southern Israel. Their mission: to bomb PLO targets near Sidon, on Lebanon's Mediterranean coast.

The operation was a routine sortie for both men. For Arad, who was taking university classes as part of his service, this was the one day a week that he was required to perform flying duties, to keep up his operational fitness.

Twenty minutes after takeoff, they were over their target. Arad, who was also responsible for the fighter plane's weapons systems, released the bombs. Because of a malfunction, one of them exploded under the wing. The powerful explosion rocked the plane, breaking Arad's arm. A shrapnel fragment ripped into the cockpit, slicing off Aviram's ear. Arad was the first to recover his composure. He tugged at the handle that operated both men's ejector systems, yelling, "We're ejecting, we're ejecting!" into his radio mike. Aviram and Arad shot out of the plane and parachuted to the ground.

Aviram landed on a rocky hillside full of thorny bushes, rolling down the slope until he stopped. Using the radio in his survival kit, he managed to contact a Cobra attack helicopter sent in to locate the downed airmen, and describe his position. But as the chopper approached, it came under heavy fire, preventing it from landing. Aviram asked the pilot to fly as close as he could, and Aviram jumped up and grabbed one of the helicopter's runners, hanging on with one arm while keeping himself stable with his other hand. "Go!" he yelled, and the pilot took off. Aviram, today a pilot for El Al Airlines, clung on to the runner until they reached Israeli territory.

As for Ron Arad, due to a series of mistakes made by the air force and its 669 Rescue Unit, he was left behind and taken prisoner by the relatively moderate Shi'ite militia, Amal. Almost nothing is known about what happened to him after that, except that he probably fell into the hands of the Iranians. The failure to solve the disappearance is considered one of the most stinging intelligence defeats suffered by Israel in the struggle against Iran and Hizballah. It is impossible to comprehend the nature of the intelligence war between Iran and the West without knowing about "Operation Body Heat," as the search for Ron Arad was code-named. The search took on proportions and importance far beyond the fate of a single person, leading to high-level kidnappings and assassinations. It spilled over into terrorist bombings in Argentina, and led to economic warfare in Europe. Even so, it is still unsolved.

A Mossad commander who ran various stages of Operation Body Heat says, "Never in the history of the human race has so great an effort been invested in trying to locate a missing person; far more than in the case of Raoul Wallenberg, for comparison's sake. (Wallenberg was a Swedish diplomat in Budapest during World War II who saved thousands of Jews from the Nazis, but was arrested by the Soviets and was never heard of again.) There is no stone that has been left unturned, no source that we have not tapped, and no scrap of information that we have not examined. And it has all ended in nothing but disappointment. Zero information. Zero progress toward a solution of this tragic mystery."

This particular commander liked to play games of trivia with his colleagues, and he always won. General knowledge is his forte. He also used to tell his men about famous unsolved cases of disappearance: Wallenberg, Antoine de Saint-Exupéry, Josef Mengele, and others. "I hope that we succeed in solving ours," he would always end these talks, with a sigh.

The Jews as a nation have always ascribed great significance to what is known in the Bible as "redemption of prisoners." Their feelings for countrymen in enemy hands are intense, and members of Israel's intelligence and security communities are no exceptions. The inability of the government to reach solutions for the repatriation of prisoners and MIAs has caused damage to its approval ratings; interpreted as a reflection of general weakness and a dereliction of the moral duty toward those sent to battle who never returned from missions on the battlefield on behalf of the state.

In October 1986, Israel and Amal began negotiations that almost ripened into a deal. The negotiations were conducted by businessmen on either side. The Israelis were represented by Shabtai Kalmanovitch, a Jew formerly from Russia who traded in diamonds in Africa and offered his assistance to the Mossad in helping find Arad "as a gesture of good will." It soon turned out that this "gesture" was in fact the result of an order from Kalmanovitch's bosses in the KGB, for whom he worked as a senior agent in Israel. The Soviets were very interested in the Arad case and the complex ramifications of the various intelligence operations that it engendered, and they told Kalmanovitch to try to penetrate them. This, the KGB hoped, would provide valuable information about Israel's intelligence links with various European states, and with the United States. Because of the great sensitivity of the Arad affair, doors would be opened for him at the highest levels of Israel's defense and political establishments.

Kalmanovitch was put in touch with Uri Lubrani, who was the Defense Ministry official responsible for prisoners and MIAs at the time. Kalmanovitch told him that he knew a Lebanese businessman residing in Sierra Leone who was a distant cousin of Amal leader Nabih Berri. The businessman was code-named "the Tourist" by Mossad. Through him, three letters from Arad and two photographs of him were conveyed to Israel. They were examined by experts, including graphologists, photographic experts, forensic scientists, and Military Intelligence's code-deciphering specialists, and found to be authentic. But they were devoid of any clue whatsoever as to the airman's whereabouts.

"The Tourist" negotiated the terms for Arad's repatriation. They included the transfer of a sum of money, an agreement to allow arms for Amal to reach the Lebanese coast, and the release of a large number of prisoners by Israel. But the deal was shot down by Defense Minister Yitzhak Rabin, who felt that the price in released Palestinian prisoners was too high and feared that he would be assailed by the public, as he had been a year earlier, when 1,150 PLO security prisoners were freed in exchange for six Israeli soldiers.

From there, the affair became more complex. Soviet intelligence had a further interest in the Arad matter. One of Lubrani's aides handling Arad's case was a well-known Tel Aviv attorney, Amnon Zichroni, who for many years had dealt with security cases, both as a defense counsel and as a representative of the state in contacts over prisoner exchanges. When Shabtai Kalmanovitch was discovered to be a Soviet agent, and was put on trial for espionage in 1998, Zichroni defended him.

One day in 1989, three years after the repatriation negotiations were ended, a man appeared at Zichroni's office and introduced himself as Wolfgang Vogel, a lawyer representing the office of the East German leader Erich Honecker. He wanted to discuss the case of Dr. Marcus Klingberg, who had been deputy director of Israel's highly secret Biological Institute, located in Ness Ziona, south of Tel Aviv, and was serving a prison term for espionage on behalf of the Soviet Union. The work of the Biological Institute was among the most highly guarded secrets in Israel, on a par with the country's nuclear project. According to non-Israeli publications, for forty years the most deadly biological and chemical warfare agents had been developed there. Klingberg had been arrested in 1983 in a joint Mossad-CIA operation, tried, and sentenced to twenty years' imprisonment, all in total secrecy. He was the most important Soviet spy ever caught in Israel. At the time even mentioning his name was forbidden.

Zichroni told Vogel that he had never heard of Klingberg and hastily ended the conversation. But Vogel persisted, and Zichroni requested and received permission from the authorities to negotiate with Vogel about releasing Klingberg. Vogel also visited Kalmanovitch in prison, where he was by then serving an eight-year sentence after confessing to espionage.

In May 1989, Vogel and Zichroni signed a memorandum according to which East Germany and the Soviet Union would do all they could to get Ron Arad freed, as well as two other MIAs, and Israel would release Klingberg and Kalmanovitch. At a later stage the deal was broadened still further and its planners sardonically began referring to it as "the mother of all deals." It gradually grew to include American spies in Russian hands, and even the South African naval officer Dieter Gerhardt, who had spied for the Soviets for twenty years. The release of Gerhardt would have been particularly difficult for Israelis to swallow. He was deeply involved in the intimate military relationship between Israel and South Africa and had given the Russians the most highly classified Israeli information, including nuclear secrets. Nevertheless, Israel was prepared to see him go free in exchange for Ron Arad. In November 1989, however, "the mother of all deals" fell to pieces. The Communist bloc was crumbling, the two Germanies united, and Vogel, the Stasi, and Russian intelligence were no longer players in the international arena.

In hindsight, it is clear that all of these contacts were pointless. Amal's security officer, a man named Mustafa Dirani, had quarreled with Nabih

Berri over a year before the memorandum passed between Vogel and Zichroni. Relations between Berri and Dirani reached a breaking point in February 1988, when a group calling itself the Islamic Revolutionary Brigades, a front for Hizballah, kidnapped and murdered Colonel William Higgins. Dirani objected strongly to the hunt that Amal launched for the perpetrators, calling Higgins an American spy. His opposition to Berri and the Amal leadership led to his expulsion from the movement, and when he left the organization, he took Arad with him as a kind of severance pay.

Early in 1989, intelligence reached Israel to the effect that Dirani, not wanting to carry the hot potato around for long, had sold Arad to agents for the Iranian Revolutionary Guards. The reports said that in May 1988 Dirani had held Arad in a house in the village of Nabi Chit in the Bekaa Valley, and it was from there that he was handed over to the Iranians. The buyer, Ali Reza Askari, commander of the Revolutionary Guards in Lebanon, was said to have paid millions of dollars.

Then the trail went cold. Arad's whereabouts remained a mystery, despite the enormous resources and efforts invested by Israel, the CIA, and the intelligence services of Germany, Italy, Egypt, Jordan, and Britain to locate him. For several years, no clues turned up. Then in 1992, when Yitzhak Rabin was elected Prime Minister, he ordered the Mossad, which had for years not wanted to touch the case, to start getting involved, alongside Military Intelligence.

Yisrael Perlov was the head of the department that deals with prisoners and MIAs. He operated under the assumption that the missing navigator was still in Iran, or at least in Iranian hands, and Perlov and Mossad concentrated their major efforts on this front. The high point was an operation planned by Perlov and code-named "Autumn Days." The operation involved the recruitment of an Iranian about whom information had been received linking him—by virtue of his position— with the Israeli airman. Perlov's plan is still taught in the Mossad's course for information-gathering officers, and is said to be nothing short of a work of genius.

The Iranian came on board in exchange for a large amount of money. Perlov had posed as a Western businessman without the Iranian knowing that he had anything to do with Israel or that the object was to obtain information about the Arad case, which was only one of many subjects Perlov mentioned. In a method known in intelligence parlance as a "false flag operation," the Iranian never knew that Perlov was working for the country that the Iranian government saw as its number one enemy. After he was recruited, he said he had met Arad twice, once in Lebanon and once in Iran. A Shin Bet polygraph specialist was flown in to test the Iranian, and judged him to be speaking the truth.

The Mossad considered the man's tale to be a "golden nugget" of information. Rabin was so impressed that he awarded Perlov a special citation, an exceedingly rare event in the history of the Mossad. Perlov later left Mossad in a huff because he wasn't promoted, but to this day he keeps the citation in his living room and proudly shows it to guests.

Operation Autumn Days was afterward subjected to an exhaustive internal Mossad examination, an inquiry whose dramatic outcome is still fermenting within the organization. Some top officers claimed that the inquiry showed that the information supplied by the Iranian agent was *not* reliable, and came from a doubtful source whose polygraph tests were "adjusted" by Perlov. Perlov, one of the best agent controllers in the Mossad, but also one of the most controversial, reacts angrily to the idea. "These claims are founded mainly in envy and small-mindedness. I did many things in the Mossad, not connected with Ron Arad, that constituted breakthroughs. Because no one else managed to do them after me, some people claimed that perhaps it was all deception and fabrication. As for that 'golden nugget' about Arad—according to which he is in Iranian hands, and had been moved several times between Iran and Lebanon—firstly, it dovetailed and cross-checked perfectly with other intelligence that had come in, and not from me. Secondly, the source underwent polygraph tests twice."

Either way, in the wake of the Perlov operation, Israel's intelligence and diplomatic communities set their sights on Iran. The whole massive effort, overt and covert, of Operation Body Heat became focused upon Tehran. Prime Minister Rabin even went public, holding a special press conference in May 1993 to announce that Arad was in Iranian hands and that Israel saw Iran as responsible for the well-being of the missing air-man. In parallel, other endeavors were set in motion in the international sphere, especially the United States, where the goal was to get legislation passed that would make it possible for sanctions to be instituted against the Islamic Republic. The United States had already imposed a series of punitive measures against Iran, including the freezing of the Shah's assets and the inclusion of Iran on the list of terror-supporting countries. Israel's pressure led to a toughening of these measures.

And yet, to this day, Ron Arad has still not been released, begging the question: If Arad is being held by the Iranians, why haven't they admitted it and negotiated for his release? Israel would be prepared to pay a very high price, even for his body. In evaluation sessions of the Mossad's MIA team, some participants have expressed amazement at what one official called "the bizarre and irrational pleasure that certain circles in Iran derive from the prolonged torment of Israel and Ron's family." One former Mossad Iran specialist even admits he doesn't understand his subject of study: "The Iranian mind works in ways that do not necessarily connect to pure human reason as we know it."

One possible explanation is based on the deep understanding that the ayatollahs in Tehran have of Israeli society's weaknesses and sensibilities. They are aware of the State of Israel's unremitting commitment, fraught with symbolism, to bring every soldier home from the battlefield, alive or dead. The Iranians, according to various intelligence assessments, know that this is an important Israeli humanitarian and religious value. They have no desire to give the Israelis the pleasure of a moment of collective catharsis of the kind that has occurred when the remains of a long-dead soldier are discovered and brought to burial, or a prisoner is released from an enemy jail.

Another possible reason for the Iranians' behavior is that they are reluctant to give the world evidence of their links with a head of a Lebanese guerrilla organization such as Mustafa Dirani, the last man known to have held Arad. So far, the Iranians have always been careful to speak of their purely moral support for the Lebanese Shi'ites. They claim, however implausibly, to have only non-military relations with Hizballah and the Shi'ites in general. Admitting to having held Ron Arad would be tantamount to a confession of deep military and intelligence involvement in the internal affairs of Lebanon. At one level, it's an absurd game: *of course* Iran is deeply connected to Lebanese Shi'ites, especially Hizballah. But at another level, it's cagey public relations: the West often seems willing to ignore clear evidence of Iran's connections to terrorism.

There is also the intricate and delicate dance that Iran and Syria are engaged in around Lebanon. For years, the Syrians turned a blind eye to

Iran's support for Hizballah, and used it as a bargaining chip in their negotiations with Israel. They wanted to get the Golan Heights, conquered in 1967, back from Israel and they made it clear that the flow of aid from Iran to Hizballah through Syria would be stopped only as part of a general agreement, including the return of the Heights. However, the Syrians also have their red lines. Iranian confirmation of the claim that Arad was handed by Dirani to the Revolutionary Guards might well harm Tehran's relations with Syria.

Months after taking office and putting Mossad on the case, Rabin was still frustrated. In 1993, he took a fateful next step: he ordered that Mustafa Dirani be kidnapped and brought to Israel in order to extract the truth about the affair "by all possible means." Preparations for the operation took about half a year.

While Mossad geared up to snatch Dirani, Israel put pressure on Iran to give up Arad, though Iran refused to admit he was being held there. Then, suddenly, the Iranians came up with an impossible demand of their own. This was conveyed to Israel by Brend Schmidbauer, the German coordinator of the Intelligence Community at the Chancellor's Office, who served as a mediator between Israel and Iran and Hizballah on issues of prisoners and MIAs. The Iranians, he told Mossad officials in December 1992, say that you are holding four of their diplomats and that until you free them, there is no chance of progress in the matter of Ron Arad. What do I tell them? he asked.

The four men had disappeared in Beirut fully ten years earlier, in the summer of 1982, while Israeli forces were besieging West Beirut. They included the Iranian chargé d'affaires in Lebanon, Sayed Mohsen Mousawi, who was deeply involved in the establishment of Hizballah, and three aides: Taghii Rastegar Moghadam, Kazem Ahkavan, and Ahmad Motovaselian.

The Mossad flatly denied the allegation, but the Iranians never dropped it. They even made it public. In November 1994, for example, the Iranian ambassador in Beirut, Homayoun Alizade, claimed that the four men were alive in an Israeli prison. Relatives of the missing diplomats held press conferences and symposia and even travelled to Beirut on what were billed as private search missions but were actually Iranian government propaganda missions. As a counterbalance to the Israeli navigator, they now had four missing persons of their own. In each round of negotiations concerning prisoners and MIAs, Iran put the case of the four diplomats on the table as its number one item. Israel reiterated time and time again that it had nothing to do with their disappearance; but the Iranians persisted. The Iranian foreign minister, Kamal Kharazi, said over and over again that the four were "languishing in Israeli prisons."

In the Mossad's POW and MIA department, officers tried to look at things from the Iranian perspective. The claim seemed an obvious ploy, and a means to stall the Arad discussion, yet there were those who maintained that Iran's persistence was authentic. Deep delving into the files revealed that in fact Iran had received information back in 1982 that the diplomats had been secretly taken to Israel for questioning—but the report was false.

Israel told the German mediators that the four had been murdered in Beirut by the Phalange, otherwise known as the Christian Forces, and had never set foot in Israel—but Tehran refused to accept the story. Finally, in desperation, Israel approached an infamous witness from the bloody past in Lebanon: Robert Hatem, alias "Cobra," former chief hit man for the Lebanese Christian Phalange militia who now lives in Paris under the protection of French intelligence. "A friend in Beirut approached me," Hatem recalls, "and told me that in Israel they want to talk to me about the Ron Arad business. I told him that I don't know a thing about Ron Arad, but he persisted. I told [Elie] Hobeika [the Phalange commander] that I was taking a trip to Belgium. I bought a ticket and flew from Beirut to Brussels. At the airport there was someone waiting for me who took me to a suite in a luxury hotel, where there were three people waiting for me. They asked me a great deal of questions about the four Iranian diplomats. One of them had an up-to-date aerial photograph of what used to be the Karantina [the Beirut slaughterhouse that had been converted in the 1970s to serve as the Phalange HQ] and I pointed to the different places connected to this affair."

Hatem told the Israelis that during the siege of West Beirut in 1982, most likely at the end of July or early in August, the four Iranians were driving back to that city in their posh embassy Mercedes from Tripoli. "On the highway between Jounieh and Beirut, they were stopped at a checkpoint manned by Phalange militiamen, commanded by Rajia Abdo, whom we all used to call 'the Captain.' " The Captain didn't quite know what to do with the Iranians. He called headquarters, and Hobeika told him to bring them to the Karantina.

"They were placed in two separate cars. The Captain rode with them, with three other guards, and all the way they were yelling and protesting that it was forbidden to arrest them because they had diplomatic immunity. As if anyone cared that these four sons of bitches had immunity. Their Mercedes was also taken along with them. When they arrived at the Karantina, Asad Shaftari came into the office and told Hobeika they were there. Hobeika made a few calls to summon intelligence people and interrogators. They began to question them."

Needless to say, for a Lebanese militiaman in 1982, interrogations could get rough. "Our interrogations at the Karantina did not usually include coffee and light refreshments. They were very severe. There were many systems: electric shocks, beatings, hanging from the ceiling by a rope. Usually we killed them afterwards, but sometimes they died under interrogation."

When asked why they would let people die during questioning, since it was counterproductive as well as murderous, Hatem explained that "we never had enough experience in interrogation. We never knew how much pressure had to be exerted to get the information and leave them alive. So sometimes we slipped up. If he talked, well and good. If not, and a mistake happened, fuck him."

Taking my yellow pad, Hatem sketched, in great detail, the electrical torture device used on the four Iranians. Three of them were interrogated under torture for a week. As for the other one, says Hatem, "right at the beginning, we found that one of them spoke Arabic. I don't know why, but they killed him right away. They shot him in the head."

After the week of torture, the other three diplomats were executed and dumped into lime pits at the edge of the Phalange camp.

In his testimony to Israeli intelligence agents in 1993 and then again in 2000, Cobra said that to the best of his recollection, it was he himself who shot at least one of the Iranians, Ahmad Motovaselian. He now asserts that because of the large number of people that he killed during those years, he can't recall whether he himself or one of his associates shot the Iranians, although he does clearly remember their actual presence at the camp and their execution, because they stood out from the usual victims:

The four of them are dead. There's no doubt about that. Did I shoot them? That's not sure. If it was me, believe me, I would have no problem saying so. Four fucking Iranians, so what? But you have to understand how things were done. When they brought people to me, to the pit, they were in underpants, shaven, without any hair on their heads or beards or mustaches. The Israeli agents showed me photographs of the Iranians. I told them that if I erase the hair and the beard, then for sure it is possible that I know him and that I shot him.

About a month later, one of my men, a security man called Steve Naqour, got an order from the guy in charge of finance for the Lebanese Forces, Paul Aris, in Hobeika's name, to clean out all of the pits quickly, because the Iranians were looking for their people. Naqour got ahold of two Phalange truck drivers. They were supposed to make four trips to empty the pits, including the lime and the remains of the bodies. They took the trucks to a mountain in the area of Sakanta in the north where they dumped the loads into a deep wadi that since then we call "the wadi of the skulls."

In their negotiations with Iran over the Ron Arad affair in 1993, the Israelis put together a detailed file of information on the case of the four Iranian diplomats, based partly on Cobra's testimony. Perlov of the Mossad delivered it to German intelligence. He thought it would satisfy them, but the Iranians were not convinced, and to this day they demand the release of the four men.

As Cobra explains, "It doesn't really interest the Iranians what happened to the four. All that they want is to prove that Israel was involved in the affair. They just want to frame Israel, and to use the story as a counter to the Ron Arad case. Their representative in Paris offered me one hundred thousand dollars to change my story. I told him there was no chance. I will never accuse Israel."

Sources in French intelligence confirm that information in their hands shows that in February 2005 Hatem received a request from the Iranian Embassy in Paris. The approach was made by Sayed Ali Maojani, whose calling card says he is First Councilor at the embassy. He is suspected of serving in a senior capacity in VEVAK, Iran's intelligence ministry.

Meanwhile, in early 1993, while Israel tried to deflect Iran's gambit with the four diplomats, Mossad prepared to snatch Mustafa Dirani. A great deal of intelligence was required. In addition to the Mossad, most of the burden was taken up by the networks of agents run by Military Intelligence, both Unit 504 (HUMINT) in South Lebanon, and Unit

8200 (SIGINT), which listened in to telephone and radio signals in the vicinity of "Poison Sting," as Dirani had been code-named. Major General Uri Saguy, the head of Military Intelligence, said later: "In the planning stage we asked ourselves more than once if we had the capability of carrying out such a complex operation. We knew that we had activated most of the very impressive intelligence-gathering capabilities possessed by the State of Israel, but we were still faced by the fundamental question—Would bringing in Dirani provide us with information about the current whereabouts of Ron Arad? Ultimately, the school of thought which Ehud Barak [then chief of staff] and I supported won the upper hand. We believed that Dirani could close the large gap in intelligence that we needed to bring the navigator home."

The intelligence unit of Israel's elite commando force, Unit 269, gathered a great amount of information on "Poison Sting," as did the other branches of the intelligence community. Things reached the point where agents of Unit 504 were asked about the color of the bars on the windows of Dirani's home in the village of Kasser Naba in the Bekaa. Data on his medical condition was collected in Beirut. On October 20, 1992, the Mossad reported: "Information indicated that Poison Sting was supposed to undergo surgery due to shrapnel fragments in his back and buttocks that were affecting his personal life. Ultimately it was decided not to operate."

On the evening of May 21, 1994, a snatch group was ready for action, at a helipad near the border with Lebanon. Half an hour before takeoff, Uri Saguy was summoned urgently to the home of Prime Minister Rabin in Tel Aviv. Mossad director Shabtai Shavit, Ehud Barak, Rabin's chief of staff, and Rabin's military secretary, Major General Dani Yatom, were already there. Saguy recalled the scene: "No one touched the coffee on the table. I made a show of looking at my watch impatiently. Rabin began asking me the same old questions about the operation, as if we had never met during the half year we had been preparing for it. Once again he asked about the method of implementation. 'Are you, Uri, as head of Aman [Military Intelligence], sure that the operation will succeed?' I replied politely that I had already presented all of the excellent intelligence that we had to him, but I added, 'I cannot promise you about the future. I can only promise you that I am now sitting here with you.'

"I understood," Saguy continued, "that any hesitation, even the slightest, here in Rabin's home, would frustrate the whole operation. Rabin never gave up and went on asking the questions that were bothering him. 'So perhaps we shouldn't carry the operation out tonight?' I looked into his eyes and asked, "Why?' He quickly replied, 'You tell me that you can't be sure.'

" 'But tomorrow we won't have better intelligence,' I replied sharply, and I added, 'If you are not sure of our intelligence, then you must call the operation off, and if you do rely on it, there's no reason to do so.' "

Rabin, according to Saguy's account, lit another cigarette, one of the many that he smoked that evening, turned to Barak, and asked, "Perhaps we should postpone it?"

Barak replied, "If you aren't comfortable we can put it off to tomorrow, or the day after."

"I felt my blood pressure rising," Saguy recalled. "I thought to myself, what was that supposed to mean, to postpone it to tomorrow, or the day after? What exactly was supposed to happen tomorrow? If the operation was necessary, let's do it at the planned time."

Saguy recalls that both Yatom and Shavit also said, "If you don't feel comfortable about it, Yitzhak, then we'll postpone it." Saguy says he was boiling with anger. "In that room in the prime minister's apartment, a scene then took place that could have come straight from 'The Emperor's New Clothes.' People were suddenly saying things that I'd not expected, that I could never have expected them to say. Suddenly it became clear that they were looking at the matter in a completely different way than what I had heard them saying in recent months. It was more than embarrassing."

No one can know what was going through Rabin's mind during those moments, but the behavior was typical of the man—and not because he was indecisive. Yitzhak Rabin was a military man most of his life. He ended his army career as the commander of Israel's victorious forces in the 1967 Six Day War. He always insisted on knowing every detail of every operation and event, both in advance and in the aftermath. He always asked probing questions, never writing anything down, cataloguing everything in his phenomenal memory. His vacillation emanated from his knowledge of the very fine line between success and failure, and of the catastrophic consequences failure in an operation such as this could have. He had had similar hesitations over dispatching commandos to rescue the Israeli airline passengers hijacked to Entebbe in 1976. He ordered the commander of the unit, Yoni Netanyahu—who was killed during the operation—to rehearse it over and over until he was satisfied. In October 1994, he had to make a decision of the same sort to send the elite unit in to extricate a soldier, Nahshon Wachsman, who had been kidnapped by West Bank Palestinians from Hamas, inspired by the hostage-taking activities of Hizballah and Iran in Lebanon. That operation failed, and both Wachsman and the commander of the rescue unit were killed.

In his home that evening, Rabin turned to Saguy and asked, "What will happen if you arrive and Dirani isn't home?"

Saguy: "Then we'll be embarrassed; but rest assured that the level of risk to our force is not high. We're far from the nearest military forces in the area. I'll feel very bad if we don't bring him back."

Rabin, sharply: "You are responsible."

Saguy: "I am responsible."

Ultimately, Rabin was persuaded. The raid went ahead. The commando force got into Dirani's house, slipping noiselessly around the guards at the front gate. Dirani was woken up and he tried to resist, but a blow with a rifle butt silenced him. He was bound to a stretcher that the raiders had brought with them, blindfolded, and gagged. On the way to the choppers, Dirani, who by now must have realized who the abductors were, began trying to free himself. He fell from the stretcher and was wounded in the head. The guards at his house also became aware of what was going on and gave chase. They opened fire and one of the Israeli commanders, a lieutenant colonel, took a bullet in the buttocks.

Manacled, his head covered by a hood, Dirani was taken to the secret underground interrogation facility of Aman's Israeli Military Intelligence Unit 504 in central Israel. After being treated for the head wound, his scalp was shaved, and he was photographed and tagged "Prisoner 810554." Immediately after Dirani's capture, Rabin signed an administrative arrest order that was extended every few months by a judge as required by law, which enabled the government to take undemocratic measures in the name of security. All of the court hearings in the case were kept completely secret.

The interrogation of Dirani excited the heads of the intelligence community. Reports were sent directly to Prime Minister Rabin. The prisoner was held in harsh conditions, deprived of sleep, tied up, and beaten. It didn't do much good: "Poison Sting gave a confused and inadequate version" of the Arad case, according to a top-secret document summing up the interrogation. "At a certain stage he even named the place in Iran where the navigator is being held, but he retracted it later. He is believed to know more than what he has told."

Ultimately, Dirani's information merely confirmed what was already known by the Israelis. He said that on May 4, 1988, Ron Arad was incarcerated in a house belonging to his organization in Nabi Chit. Dirani himself had not been there. Zakharia Hamzeh, in charge of guarding Arad, was there at the time. When they heard that an Israeli raid was taking place in Lebanon on that day, the guards fled, leaving Arad locked up. Iranian Revolutionary Guards later entered the house, Dirani claimed, and they simply picked up their prize. Yet Military Intelligence didn't believe Dirani's version. They assumed that he had agreed with the Iranians that the guards would not be there and that the house in Nabi Chit was actually a Revolutionary Guards safe house, an agreed point of transfer. Dirani denied getting anything from the Iranians in exchange for the Israeli.

In the wake of Dirani's statements, Israeli intelligence carried out a series of operations aimed at getting information from or kidnapping members of the Shukhur family, the owners of the house in Nabi Chit. These bids all failed. One family member living in Germany was questioned by the security authorities there, and he denied the entire story. Israel asked the Germans to let them interrogate the man in the same facility as Dirani, so they could use less delicate methods to establish whether he was telling the truth. This time, the Germans, who usually complied with Mossad requests (a dividend of Holocaust guilt), firmly refused.

The art of interrogation is highly unscientific, and no amount of coercion can guarantee success against an obstinate subject. Despite the intense pressure used against him, Dirani managed to mislead his captors. They, in turn, tried various tricks with him. When they claimed he had conducted negotiations about Arad on a certain day with the commander of the Revolutionary Guards in Lebanon, Ali Reza Askari, Dirani at first flatly denied it. After being beaten, he confirmed it—but it later emerged that it had been technically impossible for this meeting to have taken place on that date. When the interrogators confronted Dirani with this, he agreed. "You said that I met him then," he responded. "What do you want from me?" Eventually, after other contradictions in his statements were discovered, it was decided not to ascribe any credibility to his statements whatsoever.

Dirani at least seemed to confirm that Ron Arad was in Iran. On an aerial photograph he even pointed out a camp near Tehran, commanded by the al-Quds force, where Arad was supposedly held. Israeli commanders began planning a daring rescue operation. Yet could Dirani's information be trusted? As a skilled captive, he managed to sow enough doubt in the mind of Mossad that none of his testimony was trusted. The plans to raid the al-Quds camp were dropped out of suspicion that Dirani was being deceitful.

In 1994, Unit 504 tried new ways to break Dirani. On August 7, he was taken to the best polygraph team in the country, that of the Shin Bet. It was headed by an operative code-named "Abu Sharif" who was later to become head of the investigation department of the Shin Bet. In his report, Abu Sharif wrote that his impression was that Dirani "is a cool-headed man, with a phenomenal memory, clever, pleasant, and doesn't hesitate to tell the truth even if it is unpleasant." Yet the polygraph did not move the investigation ahead significantly. Polygraphs can be beaten—they are no panacea against doubt.

Dirani, it seemed, was just as sophisticated as his interrogators. The summary of the Poison Sting file says that "As head of the security apparatus of the Amal movement, Dirani was familiar with the subject of interrogation and interrogations methods . . . and he let information out each time drop by drop in a controlled manner and that only after the interrogators had exposed to him what they already knew."

Another system tried by the interrogators was to intercept messages between Dirani and another inmate, Sheikh Abdul Karim Obeid, a senior Hizballah cleric who had been kidnapped from his home in Lebanon in 1989 by the Israelis in another fruitless bid to put pressure on Iran to free Ron Arad. When Dirani was allowed into the prison yard, his guards saw him hiding something under a stone. It emerged that he was sending notes to Obeid, whom he considered an important religious authority. It was decided not to stop the messages but to photograph them and put them back in the hiding place. But Dirani had evidently thought of this possibility and wrote the notes using hints and names that only he and Obeid could understand. They apparently did refer to Arad, but the Israelis could not derive any information from them.

Thanks to the Arad case and the Dirani interrogation, a profound legal debate took hold in Israel, in great secrecy, on issues relevant to the West's war on Islamic terror. Is it permissible to kidnap and secretly incarcerate citizens of other countries in order to extract information from them for use in the war? When it became clear that Dirani had given up all the information that it was possible to get out of him—such as it was—Israel was compelled to admit that it had no further need for him. Yet nobody wanted to put him on trial. Attorney Dvorah Chen, the state prosecutor who specialized in security cases, was compelled to explain to a District Court judge why the state insisted on holding him, at secret hearings held every six months to extend Dirani's administrative detention. She finally came out and admitted that Dirani and thirteen other Lebanese citizens were being held as bargaining chips that Israel was trying to trade for its missing aviator. A weighty legal and ethical argument ensued, with Dirani and his attorney on one side, and representatives of the intelligence community as expert witnesses on the other. At issue: Does a sovereign state have the right to hold hostages as a counter to the very same action committed by a terrorist organization? The court upheld the state's position at each hearing.

Another difficult matter—and another portent of future issues in the West's war on terror—arose out of a suit filed by Dirani in Tel Aviv District Court in 1997 against the state. He complained that he had been tortured brutally, and even sodomized during his interrogation. His statement to Military CID (Crime Investigation Division) investigators, which was kept under wraps in Israel to avoid embarrassment, makes chilling reading:

> They threatened me that if I don't tell them everything I know about Ron Arad they would bring a soldier who would fuck me in the ass. They brought a soldier who got completely undressed and said that I had better tell them everything or that soldier would fuck me . . . I told them again that I had nothing more to tell and I had told them all the truth and I wasn't hiding anything. Some soldiers took me and tied me up, lying on my stomach. They tied my hands and my legs and then the interrogators brought another soldier who raped me. During almost all the interrogations I was completely naked and the interrogators even photographed me naked because they saw how humiliating it was for me and they knew it was against my religion, which forbids nudity in the presence of other men.

A few days after I was raped, they threatened me that if I didn't tell them everything I know they would stick a police baton up my ass. The interrogator, who introduced himself as "George" [Unit 504 and Shin Bet interrogators always use false names, usually Arabic ones, with prisoners], threatened me again and again that I must tell him where Ron Arad is. He said that if I did not tell him, he would shove the club he was playing with into me. After I told George that I could not tell him anything more, that I had already said everything, he called some soldiers to tie me up. He inserted the club that he had shown me before into my behind. As a result of the insertion of the baton into my behind, I suffered a hemorrhage . . . they never took me to a doctor. There was a medical inspection every few days and when I was examined after they inserted the stick into my behind the doctor saw that I was hemorrhaging, but I was frightened to tell him, because they had told me that if I told anyone they would pay me back. The doctor never spoke Arabic, and when he examined me there was an interrogator with him who translated. The doctor never even asked how I got the hemorrhage and only gave me some ointment. After the thing with the baton, the interrogators forced me to drink large quantities of water with paraffin oil. They never allowed me to go to the lavatory but only to defecate into a diaper. They let me change the diaper only after a long time, when the interrogators themselves couldn't stand the stench.

A forensic pathologist, Lieutenant Colonel Chen Kugel, M.D., commander of the medical identification unit of the IDF, examined Dirani on March 26, 2000. After writing down Dirani's complaint, he added that there was "a linear scar on the anus, compatible with scarring due to a laceration following the penetration of the anus by a long foreign body (such as a baton or an erect penis)."

The Military Police encountered many difficulties in their investigation of the case. The MPs serving at the secret Unit 504 installation gave a number of contradictory statements about Dirani's diapers, the use of clubs during questioning, and the use made of MPs during interrogation for the purpose of deterrence. Some MPs attested that they had heard of threats of rape and the use of batons as an instrument of sodomy against prisoners. One of them even said that he had seen a baton smeared with blood. Later, Unit 504 personnel explained the matter of the diapers by saying that "the reason for the diaper was to prevent the complainant from defecating into his clothing in the course of his interrogations. It was not a system or method of interrogation and diapers were not used routinely."

The commanders of Unit 504 testified that "the actions which Poison Sting ascribes to his interrogators are by his lights the gravest of actions, which could serve as justification for cooperation and giving information on the Iranian involvement in the matter of the navigator Ron Arad and also about the involvement of Hizballah and the Revolutionary Guards. From the point of view of the Iranians and the Lebanese, he is considered a traitor. A complaint such as rape or the insertion of a baton, which is a grave complaint, could serve as a justification for his having given up much information." In other words, despite the physical evidence of his anal rape, the commanders claimed Dirani invented the story to justify talking to the Israelis. They left unexplained why he would humiliate himself to his Islamic colleagues, and why he had to worry about giving the Israelis information that was useless.

In his statement to the MP investigators, Dirani said that the soldier who raped him had a tattoo on his left arm and that he wore red underpants. "I know that his nickname was Kojak," he added. "I'm sure that if you search well, you will find him."

They did find him, and took a statement from him. Later, in a telephone interview from the Far East, where he is currently living, "Kojak" reconstructed the statement that he had given to MPs: "I served in the facility until March 1995. I was there when they brought in Mustafa Dirani. One day when George was questioning him, he asked me to come into the room. When I entered, I saw Dirani without a shirt and George was talking to him. Dirani looked scared. George asked me to open my belt and let my trousers down to my knees. It was clear to me that George was trying to frighten him. The whole thing seemed like a play to me and I couldn't hide my smile. George rebuked me quietly and said it was a serious matter and told me to wipe off my smile.

"I stood there facing Dirani with my pants down, and then George grabbed me and began to push me toward Dirani. He looked really, really scared and made gestures of no, no with his hands. George was shouting at him in Arabic and Dirani replied. After a few seconds George told me that it was enough and to leave the room. The whole situation was embarrassing to me, but I saw it as a kind of order from a commander and I thought that if I refused it could harm the investigation. In retrospect, I regret that I agreed. I should have told George no."

The case caused the Israeli military no small embarrassment. The interrogators, first and foremost George, had been led to understand that they had to do everything possible to extract information from Dirani. But they say that no one imagined that George would take a sexual tack in his interrogation. Eventually, George's contract was terminated and he was discharged from the military. Military Intelligence claimed, unbelievably, that there was no connection between his discharge and the Dirani case.

In the end, all the torture that Dirani underwent was for naught. He succeeded in casting doubt on his own credibility, and in any case, the information that he did provide did nothing to solve the Ron Arad mystery.

Fighting a terrorist regime forces every Western nation to confront its bedrock values. It also presents tactical dilemmas. In the pursuit of Ron Arad, Israel tried kidnapping and torture, without success. When Dirani's capture led nowhere, the Israelis tried again—and triggered an avalanche.

# CHAPTER 11

# Terror in Buenos Aires

The year of Yitzhak Rabin's ascension to prime minister, 1992, was a fateful one in the Arad case, for several reasons. After six fruitless years of searching for the captured airman, both sides were impatient. While Iran pressed about its four missing diplomats, and Mossad prepared to snatch Mustafa Dirani, Mossad operatives also decided to strike directly at Hizballah. They planned to kidnap the secretary general of Hizballah, Sheikh Abbas Mussawi, as a bargaining chip. The meticulously planned operation was to be carried out by its elite commando unit, and the order to snatch him was given on February 16, 1992, just days before Rabin became the head of the Labor Party. Mussawi was to be taken when his convoy was close to the village of Jibshit in southern Lebanon, away from the tight security environment of Beirut. In real time, an Israeli drone transmitted images of the convoy to the air force command post at military headquarters in Tel Aviv. But Mussawi was surrounded by too many bodyguards to be sure he could be seized alive. Reluctant to miss the chance, the chief of staff, Lieutenant General Ehud Barak, made a decision, with the approval of Prime Minister Yitzhak Shamir and Minister of Defense Moshe Arens: "If he's already in our sights, let's hit him." Suddenly the operation wasn't about getting Arad home, it was about an assassination. Few would argue that the head of Hizballah was anything other than a terrorist leader who was bent on killing as many Israelis as he could. Yet the possibility of his assassination raised the age-old question: Will it do more harm than good?

A videotape of an interview with an agent of Military Intelligence's Unit 504, the unit that tracked Mussawi's movements on the ground, is to this day locked in a safe in Israel. In it the agent firmly asserts that he had radioed to his controllers that in the car with Mussawi were his wife Siham and his son Hussein, who was then six years old. Nonetheless, two helicopters loosed rockets that blew the Mercedes and an escort vehicle to smithereens. Everyone in the car was killed. Hizballah's first response was to unleash a five-day barrage of Katyusha rockets at western Galilee, during which a six-year-old girl was killed.

The international media gave Mussawi's assassination extensive coverage, showing the smoking remains of his convoy. Watching TV in their home in Ankara in Turkey were Ehud Sadan, a Shin Bet operative and chief of security at the Israeli Embassy in the Turkish capital, and his wife, Rachel. "I hope this doesn't spark a war of assassinations," Rachel said. Her husband reassured her that nothing would happen. On March 7, 1992, he was blown up by a bomb planted under his car. Turkish authorities apprehended and prosecuted members of Turkish Hizballah for the crime, who were said to be acting under orders from Iranian intelligence.

It was just the beginning.

"You can have a cup of coffee or tea and some cookies if you wish, but I'm not going to give you a proper lunch. Every time I eat with an Israeli, there's a terror attack. Twice was enough for me, I don't want any more." Hugo Anzorreguy, the head of SIDE, Argentina's intelligence organization, from 1990 to 2000, is only half-joking. He is currently the senior partner in one of the biggest Buenos Aires law firms. Sitting in his wood-paneled fortieth-floor office, he recalled a March 1992 polo match and a magnificent luncheon with the head of the Shin Bet, Yaakov Peri, who was visiting the Argentinean capital. One week later, on March 17, the Israeli Embassy there was blown up. Four Israeli Embassy workers and five local Jews were among the twenty-nine people killed, many of them children in a nearby school, when a suicide bomber detonated a car packed with explosives next to the embassy. Over 242 people were injured.

"Yaakov and I spoke about the menace posed by terrorists," Anzorreguy recalls, "but neither of us imagined that a few days later Buenos Aires would become a target of theirs. We ate well, and then we went to the polo match. Then Yaakov flew back to Israel, leaving the catastrophe to me."

Israeli intelligence had no doubt the operation was revenge for the killing of Mussawi a month earlier. A team of Israelis, including operatives of the Shin Bet and the Mossad, as well as police explosives experts and ballistics experts from the Arms Development Authority, flew to

Argentina. The Mossad agents worked closely with the CIA's Counter Terrorist Center (CTC). One of the Israeli agents described what he witnessed: "It was one big mess. Buenos Aires was full of spies. It was clear to everyone that someone had changed the rules of the game. We, the Americans and the Israelis, soon understood that the attack had seriously embarrassed the local authorities, who were in a hurry to wrap it all up quickly and quietly. From then on, we acted on our own, and kept the findings of our investigation to ourselves."

The American intelligence community held an internal enquiry to establish whether in the days prior to the attack indications of the operation had been received but not interpreted correctly. The National Security Agency located a message from the Iranian Embassy in Moscow to Tehran that had been intercepted three days before the bombing but not translated in real time. It contained clear signs of awareness of an impending attack on an Israeli legation in South America. In addition, two messages, from the Iranian embassies in Buenos Aires and Brasilia to the Foreign Ministry in Iran, appeared in retrospect to contain coded signals about the approaching operation. These messages, which were passed to Israeli intelligence, indicated that Iran was deeply implicated in the embassy attack. Later, NSA supplied Israel with unequivocal proof—"not a smoking gun, but a blazing cannon," in the words of a Mossad official—that Imad Moughniyeh, together with another senior Hizballah member named Talal Hamiyah, were responsible for the execution of the operation. In a phone conversation between the two, Hamiyah was heard rejoicing over "our project in Argentina" and mocking the Shin Bet, which is responsible for protecting Israeli legations abroad, for not preventing it.

The Argentinean service agreed that Iran was involved, based on its own evidence. SIDE produced transcripts of an exchange that took place some time later in the home of an Iranian diplomat. In the course of a noisy family quarrel, the diplomat's wife was heard shouting at him that if he continued to treat her the way he did, she would tell everything she knew about his part in "what happened to the offices of the Zionists."

Ultimately, the CIA investigation report, written by Dr. Stanley Bedlington of CTC, presented the bombing as the model of an Iranian-led operation, with Iran working through Hizballah to avoid direct evidence of its involvement. The model had been used before: a Hizballah agent would leave Lebanon for the target zone equipped with forged papers supplied by the Iranian Embassy in Beirut. That agent would recruit Shi'ite residents of the zone, well versed in the customs and conduct of the local population, as a "local support cell." The cell would gather information on various targets, and then assist in the execution of a strike, after a target was selected by Beirut or Tehran. A unit of three or four agents would travel to the target zone to carry out the attack.

The Hizballah command in Beirut selected the Israeli Embassy in Buenos Aires as the best target for revenge for the Mussawi assassination. The Triple Frontier area—the border region shared by Argentina, Paraguay, and Brazil—at the Iguazu Falls was the staging ground, due to its large population of Shi'ite immigrants from Lebanon who maintain close links with their families back home and are ready to help when necessary. The Hizballah agent who ran the embassy attack was, according to intelligence assessments, Mohammad Abu Warda. The cell that carried out the bombing was part of Imad Moughniyeh's Special Operations Command, headed by a senior operative of the organization known by his nom de guerre, Abu al-Foul. The Hizballah squad came to Argentina via London and the Paraguayan city of Ciudad del Este, in the Triple Frontier area.

According to the CIA report, Iran and Hizballah had operated in this way in the United States, the Balkans, Cyprus, Spain, Mexico, Thailand, the United Kingdom, Austria, Germany, and Venezuela, as well as Argentina. Few people realize that Hizballah has attempted operations in these countries. The CIA maintains that Hizballah's activities have included the creation of sleeper cells and the gathering of information in preparation for carrying out operations in many countries in Europe and North America.

A Mossad team that visited the Triple Frontier area after the embassy attack came back with hair-raising reports from "a town named hell," as they called Ciudad del Este. "There is a clear and present danger that the next attack is on the way," they reported.

A visit to hot and humid Ciudad del Este nine years later, in late August 2001, revealed that little had changed since the Mossad checked it out. Hamid Nasrallah, a cleric in a Shi'ite mosque, told me he followed events in the Middle East via the satellite dish on the roof of his home, and was angered by the "atrocities" perpetrated by the "Zionist entity" in Lebanon. The Jews, he explained, ruled the world, including America.

Nasrallah's mosque is an unpretentious, gloomy place, with only a small sign reading *Mesquita*, or mosque, hanging over its doorway. It has been identified by Israeli intelligence as well as the Argentinean SIDE as one of the hubs of Hizballah activities in South America.

Like many other residents of this menacing city, Nasrallah carries a weapon—"for self-defense," he explains. His congregation numbers several hundred believers, almost all Lebanese, who visit the mosque with varying regularity. He firmly denies the claim that Ciudad del Este has become a base for the activities of Middle Eastern terrorist organizations: "That's all rumor, invented by the enemies of Paraguay together with the Zionists, in order to smear us." Nevertheless, like many other people in the city, Nasrallah has no problem in declaring his enthusiastic support for his relative, Hassan Nasrallah, head of Hizballah, and for the aims of the organization, which he calls "a respectable political movement," and for which he conducts fund-raising campaigns.

Ciudad del Este is a kind of murky mixture of Hong Kong, Gaza, and Beirut. It used to be called Puerto Presidente Stroessner, after the military dictator of Paraguay, General Alfredo Stroessner, who contrived a unique way to improve the economy of his country, squeezed in between the two giants, Brazil and Argentina. On top of its traditional crime, corruption, and smuggling, Stroessner allocated substantial funds to Puerto Presidente Stroessner, and with the agreement of the neighboring countries turned it into a free trade zone, exempt from export and import duties. At first it worked well. Droves of Argentineans came to visit the breathtaking Iguazu Falls and to buy discounted electrical appliances.

But the formation of a South American common market in 1991 and a tightening of Argentinean Customs regulations made the long trip to Ciudad del Este far less worthwhile. In the five years between 1995 and 2000, two thousand stores were closed in the city and the number of tour buses arriving there from Brazil dropped from three hundred a day to seven hundred a month. It gradually became a city without law. For the right sum, contraband and counterfeit goods of all kinds are still freely available: Rolex watches, CD players, cigarettes, TV sets, clothing, footwear, alcoholic beverages, cell phones, counterfeit hundred-dollar bills (sold for $40 apiece), the currencies (possibly fake) of various countries at very reasonable rates, stolen cars, and pirated copies of video games and movies. Most of the goods come from the Far East, by various routes, and from here they are distributed throughout South America.

You can also buy guns. Openly and over the counter, at a store called Personal Security Guns and Ammunition on Adrian Jarra Street, you can purchase a German Mauser semiautomatic rifle for $1,000. An Uzi submachine gun, or a mini-Uzi, costs $2,500. No questions asked. At another gun store, clerks offer to dismantle and pack each gun in several parcels, to make it easier to transport across the border into Brazil or Argentina. A lively traffic is conducted under the counter in more serious weaponry, such as assault rifles, bazookas, explosives, and for the well-heeled client, even TOW antitank missiles. Whatever can't be smuggled over the border on land is flown. There are some five hundred landing strips for private planes in Paraguay, many of them in the Ciudad del Este area.

The city is also the site of widespread extortion, bribery, money laundering, and trafficking in drugs of all kinds. At night, innumerable prostitutes of both sexes inhabit the streets and bars. No one asks questions. While the legitimate commerce in the city is estimated to reach a billion dollars a year, the volume of illegal trade is believed to be at least double that figure.

The population of the area is about half a million—a mix of Paraguayans, Brazilians, Argentineans, Indians, Chinese, Africans, Germans, Lebanese, Egyptians, and Palestinians. Some come to make money, others come to find rest and shelter after turning up on wanted lists in other countries. A few score are members of Hamas, Islamic Jihad, and Hizballah, according to SIDE, many of whom come here to escape the long arm of Mossad. Altogether there are some 20,000 permanent residents of Arab origin. The migration here from Lebanon began in 1944, and increased greatly with the outbreak of the civil war in Lebanon in the 1970s.

The Arabs have a very high profile in the city. The downtown area is full of hummus and shwarma stands. Lebanese flags, pictures of Lebanese scenery, and texts from the Quran are everywhere. One of the best known and well-liked city councilors is Sheikh Akhram Ahmad Barakat, the brother of Asad Barakat, who according to an investigation carried out by the Paraguyan newspaper *ABC* is the military commander of Hizballah in the Triple Frontier area. According to the same report, Sheikh Barakat represents the Iranian government in the region on various matters.

A senior SIDE official says that members of Hizballah and Hamas function with almost total freedom in the city: "It may be that in the Middle East there are serious differences of opinion between the various factions. But here, they cooperate with each other. We have observed periodical meetings between Hamas and Hizballah in the city's mosques."

The intelligence services of Argentina, the United States, and Israel agree that the financing and planning of the bombing of the Israeli Embassy in Buenos Aires in 1992 were carried out by elements of the Shi'ite community of Ciudad del Este, acting under the orders of Hizballah and Iran. The perpetrators set out from the city, and returned there. In the Mossad, there were some who demanded vigorous and aggressive action against the Shi'ite terrorists of South America. Unless we act, they warned, there will be further attacks. These demands were submitted to the Mossad director at the time, Shabtai Shavit, but he was firmly opposed. Shavit rejected the recommendation for a comprehensive operation in South America, arguing that "the Mossad has more important things to do."

A year and a half later, Shabtai Shavit would change his mind. On July 18, 1994, at 9:53 in the morning, a huge blast shook the bustling streets of Buenos Aires and sent smoke and dust billowing into the smoggy skies of the city named for its once clean air. A bomb had detonated under the seven-floor building that housed the offices of the Argentinean Jewish community organization—Asociación Mutual Israelita Argentina (AMIA)—killing 86 people and injuring 252.

The attack was planned and executed along the same lines as the one on the embassy, and Israeli intelligence officials assess that it was in answer to an Israeli operation known as "Knock on the Door."

In 1993, Israel and Iran did come to terms in a two-clause package deal that was formulated with U.S. agreement: Iranian assets that had been frozen in the United States since the Shah's regime was toppled would be thawed, and a favorable solution would be agreed to the arbitration underway in Switzerland over a $5 billion Israeli debt to Iran for oil and for pre-revolution advance payments for arms and sophisticated weaponry that was never delivered. But on the difficult issue of Arad's fate, and whether his life or his body are actually worth billions of dollars, no progress had been made. The Iranians had dug in behind their wall of silence, even though Israel offered billions of dollars in economic incentives.

If billions of dollars were the carrot, a stick was also brought into play at that time. By 1993, the Iranian economy was shattered. When the Iraq-Iran War ended in 1988, Iran entered a process of rebuilding and industrialization that required many external loans, obtained mainly from Europe. The Iranian banking system had underwritten immense debts, which began to fall due in 1993, while at the same time oil revenues that constituted 85 percent of the Iranian economy dropped drastically. The total debt was some $24 billion, and the Iranians simply could not pay.

Iran's income in foreign currency fell from $22 billion a year to $10 billion. A secret evaluation ordered by the heads of the Tehran regime indicated that it could not hold out for any prolonged period of time, and that famine would bring the masses out onto the streets. The situation had become so critical that according to some reports reaching Israeli intelligence, the military was sent in to attack the districts of Tehran where the black market in dollars was operating.

The head of Iran's central bank took a large team of advisers to Europe to ask government leaders and bankers there to reschedule the Iranian debts. Like a good Persian bazaar merchant, he cleverly manipulated the different European states, telling the one that the other had offered him better terms, and hoping in this way to maximize the profits from his journey. This ploy, however, had one weak point: The Israelis knew what he was up to. Military Intelligence's economics department, headed by Lieutenant Colonel Yitzhak Lev, carried out a detailed analysis of the Iranian moves and exposed the manipulation. The material was presented to Prime Minister Rabin and other top officials, and a plan was agreed upon, to use the information in an attempt to get Ron Arad home. "Operation Knock on the Door" was launched.

After experts who were recruited from the Bank of Israel confirmed that the suspicions about Iran's fraud were accurate, Tehran was told that if Arad was not released forthwith, its deception would be exposed and negotiations in Europe over the debt rescheduling would be sabotaged.

The Iranians did not respond, and MI concluded that they didn't believe Israel would carry out its threat. With Rabin's approval, it was decided to show them that Israel meant business. Deputy Foreign Minister Dr. Yossi Beilin organized and studied the evidence, and he and Foreign Minister Shimon Peres went on a trip, taking the file with them. They showed it to their hosts in several Western European countries, proving that the Iranians were intent on deceiving them; the Europeans, who were stunned, then stopped the negotiations and adopted a much tougher stance. The terms for the rescheduling of Iran's debt finally agreed upon were much more difficult than the Iranians had hoped for.

Beilin says: "Before every trip I would meet with the head of MI's POWs and MIAs department and get material from him. This included the economic material on Iran that you have mentioned. Together we would tailor the information we presented to the interests of each country."

A source who served in Military Intelligence at the time recalls: "It was amazing to see how everyone—without any exceptions, not even the most cynical and opportunistic people—harnessed themselves to Operation Body Heat. It was a tumultuous time, and everyone who touched this case . . . it was as if it did something to his heart, deep inside. Beilin, for example, was utterly dedicated. He took the material, studied it, physically carried it himself because of its sensitive nature, and briefed Peres about it before their meetings."

Knock on the Door did not end with the blow inflicted on Iran. Israel made it clear to Tehran that the Europeans' changed terms had been a direct result of Israeli action and warned: If you don't return Ron Arad, we will expose all of your lies. But Iran never said a word. Israeli intelligence concluded that Iran had interpreted Knock on the Door—together with Israeli anti-Iranian lobbying in the United States and Israel Radio's propaganda broadcasts in Farsi—as a kind of declaration of war. "Obviously the Americans would have taken steps against Iran without us," said a senior intelligence source, referring to various forms of economic sanctions and the blacklisting of Iranian companies and individuals by the State Department and the Pentagon. "But from the point of view of the Iranians—who were exposed to the lobbying activities in Washington, and who were fighting a Ping-Pong war, including speeches fraught with distress by their president and their spiritual leader countering items broadcast on Israel Radio about the tough economic situation in

Iran—to them, this was tantamount to the implementation of *The Protocols of the Elders of Zion*: the Jews were turning the world economy against them."

In July 1994, several months after Knock on the Door, the Iranians finally came up with their belated response.

The second terror attack in Argentina shocked the Israeli intelligence community. Mossad director Shavit shed his complacency and ordered a thorough inquiry into anti-Israel and anti-Jewish terrorism in South America. The Mossad probe, carried out with the cooperation of SIDE, took over a year, and the result sounded like a broken record: The network responsible for the attack was controlled by a veteran terrorist known only by the nom de guerre Abu al-Foul; the network belonged to the Hizballah offshoot run by Imad Moughniyeh; and it had operated along the same lines as two years previously.

In the United States, Secretary of State Warren Christopher laid direct blame on Iran for the AMIA attack. Argentina, too, hurriedly accused Iran. This was the easiest response, because Iran could not be prosecuted and put on trial. Only the insistence of the Jewish community and some journalists led to the launch of an investigation by the Argentinean authorities. The story of this investigation, its nebulous outcome, and its failure to solve the case could fill a book of its own. An endless series of arrests, announcements, leaks, alleged breakthroughs, and indictments all came to naught. No one has ever been convicted of perpetrating the attack.

The federal judge appointed to conduct the investigation, Juan Jose Galeano, issued arrest warrants against four senior Iranian officials in 1999, and also accused the Iranian ambassador, Hade Soleimanpour, and the cultural attaché, Muhsen Rabani, formerly imam of the al-Tawahid mosque in Buenos Aires, of complicity in the attack. None of them was actually detained, however, as they were conveniently out of the country at the time. Months and then years passed. Innumerable officers and civilians of fifteen different nationalities were arrested on suspicion of involvement, but none was convicted. Soleimanpour, meanwhile, went on to fill a series of senior posts in the Iranian Foreign Ministry. According to information reaching the CIA, he is actually a top official of the Intelligence Ministry.

The investigation became a highly sensitive political issue in

Argentina, due to allegations that neo-Nazi elements in the police and the military were implicated in the attack, which was why the police had neither prevented nor solved the bombing. The president of Argentina, Carlos Menem, was accused of trying to sweep the whole matter under the carpet, or of being involved in it, due to his friendly relations with the Syrian regime. When Menem's son died in a mysterious helicopter crash in 1995, these conspiracy theories were only strengthened. In a country which not long before had been ruled by a vicious totalitarian regime, that such theories would arise around the two attacks was natural. Some members of the Jewish community even attacked the Israeli government for papering over the investigation. None of these conspiracist claims has been proven.

Gabriel Pasquini, a journalist who covers the security services for *La Nación*, sums up the situation well: "Playing a central role here are the impotence of the Argentinean law enforcement and investigative authorities, which really do not know how to tackle this kind of terrorism, and also the terrible corruption that is deeply rooted in the governmental apparatus here. There is no doubt that the police made many errors in the investigation, but it is not clear whether these errors were made innocently or maliciously."

The story of how the police went about tracing the Renault van that was used by the attackers as a car bomb is a good example of the bumbling way in which the investigation was conducted. Soon after the attack, a man named Carlos Telleldin was arrested on suspicion of having sold the vehicle to the terrorists knowingly. He denied that he was aware that it was going to be used for anything illegal, and especially a terror attack.

The head of SIDE at that time, Hugo Anzorreguy, explains what happened next. "The Mossad requested, and to my mind completely justifiably, that a lie detector test be done on Telleldin to check whether the version he gave about the person who took the car from him was true. A Mossad crew even came here with a polygraph machine and they trained one of our men to take part in the test and ask the questions in Spanish. When we came to Judge Galeano with the request, however, he threw us out. It is very difficult to fight terror with your hands tied behind your back."

Brigadier General Yigal Carmon, counterterrorism adviser to Prime Ministers Rabin and Shamir, remains furious about the affair. "The interrogation of Telleldin was a disgraceful failure and I'm not convinced that it was the result of only negligence and lack of ability, and not a malicious intent to sabotage the investigation."

Telleldin was put on trial in September 2001, together with nineteen former and current police officers accused of varying degrees of involvement and complicity in the purchase of the vehicle and its preparation for the bombing. According to the indictment formulated by Judge Galeano, Telleldin had sold the van to four men, who were linked to Hizballah terrorists. But the entire web of the prosecution's evidence unraveled when a videotape of an interrogation session between Galeano and Telleldin came to light. In it, the judge was heard uttering statements that could have been construed as offering the suspect a large sum of money in exchange for evidence that would incriminate the police officers. Judge Galeano was sacked, and all of the indicted men were acquitted on September 7, 2004.

Galeano was replaced by the prosecutor general of Buenos Aires, a Jew by the name of Alberto Nisman. He decided to deemphasize local suspects and to concentrate on the complicity of foreigners. After two years of investigation, he submitted his findings in 2006, accusing eight senior officials of Iran and Hizballah, with Moughniyeh at their head, of responsibility for the atrocity. Nisman proposed trying the eight in absentia, and obtaining international warrants for their arrest. By early 2008, the matter was still under consideration.

Nisman's report was handed to the Mossad in July 2006, during a visit to Israel by the new head of SIDE, Miguel Angel Toma. Described as "courageous and professional" by Mossad officials, it is a highly detailed document that contains thousands of pages of surveillance reports, wiretap transcripts, and analysis of intelligence data. It suggests an additional motive for the terror attacks in Argentina: Iranian revenge for a broken Argentinean commitment to supply nuclear know-how and equipment for reactors. With Iran's resumption of its nuclear project after Khomeini's death in 1989, several contracts were signed with Argentina for the supply of nuclear equipment; but after the United States applied heavy pressure on Buenos Aires, they were not implemented.

The aftermath of the second bombing was not just devoted to investigations. Three months after the AMIA bombing, in October 1994, the CIA and SIDE launched a joint operation code-named "Centauro," to prevent further attacks and to crush Islamic terror in Argentina and elsewhere in South America. The funding was American, as were the technological equipment and the training. The operation began as a minor project, but expanded so that by the end of the 1990s it was one of the biggest intelligence operations on the continent.

Some idea of what they were up against, with their limited knowledge of the Middle East, was expressed by one of Centauro's Argentinean commanders. "We have good information on what's going on in South America, but who can understand the difference between Hamas and Hizballah? That's very important when it comes to telephones. We can listen in to the calls, but we have no idea what they are talking about in Arabic, or whom they are calling in Gaza, Paris, or Beirut.

"We gave a phone number to the DST, the French [domestic] intelligence agency," he added, "and it turned out to belong to a Hizballah agent that they had been tracking for two years. Elsewhere, we intercepted a call between [Hizballah secretary general Hassan] Nasrallah in Beirut and his cousin in Buenos Aires. There was one especially suspicious line in Ciudad del Este. Its owner, a Hizballah member, called all of the Iranian embassies in South America. The last call on the printout, ten days before the bombing, was to the personal number of Nasrallah himself in Beirut. After that the line was silent, and we never heard the man anymore."

Centauro's biggest success came in 1997, after SIDE managed to recruit a member of a Hizballah cell in Ciudad del Este as an informer. He reported that the cell was collecting explosives and other material in order to blow up the American embassy in Asunción, the capital of Paraguay. According to reports in the Argentine press, the Americans acted immediately, and in force. A special forces American commando unit was flown to Asunción at night, in several giant transport planes, and arrested the perpetrators. The operation was not reported in the American media, and no further reports have been made public about the outcome of the operation. That apparent success is only one of many hidden battles won by the West—no word of the operation reached the public at the time.

Nonetheless, Centauro was soon shut down. Upon Fernando de la Rua's election as president of Argentina in December 1999, he fired Anzorreguy and replaced him with Fernando de Santibanes, who soon ran into a head-on collision with the CIA. The agency's Buenos Aires bureau chief was recalled after being outed in the local press. Langley, in a snit, called a halt to Centauro. This move, SIDE sources say, also led to an end of the work of Mossad agents who were acting under the CIA's wing. Since then, they say, Israeli intelligence has drastically reduced its presence in Argentina. Members of the Jewish community maintain that senior officials of the American and Israeli embassies have warned that Argentina has practically stopped its intelligence efforts against terrorism, and that the community feels exposed.

One of the most complex, and to a certain degree most successful, operations against Iranian-sponsored international terror was aborted before term. The CIA pulled out because of ego struggles with Argentinean intelligence; the Mossad could not operate alone in the vast South American arena, and also felt that the danger had subsided. A vacuum resulted, and Iran entered it, reestablishing its agent networks, using Hizballah and its ties with Lebanese immigrants on the continent, and bolstering its relations with several states, most notably Hugo Chávez's Venezuela.

Despite the termination of Operation Centauro, there was one final break in the Buenos Aires bombing cases—a tantalizing yet ultimately frustrating defeat. In July 1998, the Jordanian General Intelligence Department, after a complex operation, trapped a Hizballah cell which was about to depart for Europe to carry out terrorist attacks. It was commanded by none other than Abu al-Foul, whom the Mossad considers one of the most dangerous terrorists to have sprung from the ranks of Hizballah, together with one of his subordinates, Yousuf Aljouni. In the course of his vigorous interrogation by the Jordanians (which, unlike its Israeli and American counterparts, is not limited in its physical ways of extracting information), al-Foul confessed that he and his cell had played the central part in the two bombings. He also provided a substantial amount of information on their planning and execution.

The Argentine government has not, however, given up its efforts to get convictions in the case of the attacks. With the acquittal of Carlos Telleldin and the police officers, Dr. Alberto Nisman was appointed head of a special task force that was to devote all of its time and energies to probing the events. In 2008, some fifty investigators were working on the team. President Kirschner even issued a special presidential order for the 1,700 pages of the SIDE probe to be handed over to the team. In fact, Nisman has been conducting two parallel investigations—one to discover the perpetrators of the attacks, and the other to determine who was responsible for the failures and cover-ups of the previous probes. He submitted a number of indictments against all of the heads of the prosecution and the investigators who were involved in the case, including Judge Galeano, SIDE chief Anzorreguy, police officers, prosecutors, and others. In December 2007, in the course of a lengthy interview for this book, he promised that he would also indict the man who had been interior minister at the time of the attacks, Alfredo Corach, and perhaps even former president Carlos Menem.

According to Nisman, the failures in the effort to prosecute Telleldin and the police officers (of whose criminality and corruption he harbors no doubt, but without connection to this case) originated in the wish of the authorities not to confront the Iranian regime. Nisman spoke at length of the evidence that he now has that the motivation for both of the attacks was indeed Iran's desire to wreak vengeance against Israel for its activities against Hizballah and Iran, and that they were carried out in Argentina because of the cancelation of the contracts related to the Iranian nuclear project. The Argentine government had been warned several times that Iran would retaliate, he says, and it was clear the Iranians did not mean only on the level of an international lawsuit.

Nisman was relying on the testimony of a number of witnesses who had held key posts in the Iranian government and intelligence community, including the former president Abolhassan Banisadr, and Farhad Mesbahi, the VEVAK operative who defected to German intelligence in the 1990s. He also has new evidence on the movements of Iranian agents in Buenos Aires and the testimony of their local contacts. In addition, he and his staff have analyzed all the phone calls coming in and going out of Argentina during the relevant period, and have exposed a network of connections between the Iranian intelligence agents and the units operating in the Tri-Border region, as well as Tehran and Lebanon. They have even discovered where the suicide bomber, Ibrahim Berro, resided in Foz do Iguazu, the Brazilian side of the triangle. From this house, calls were made to the Berro family in South Lebanon.

The material in Nisman's hands was sufficient to persuade the heads of Interpol to issue international arrest warrants in December 2007 against top Iranian officials and the field officers involved in the attacks, including Fallahian and Moughniyeh. This is a largely symbolic achievement, but nevertheless significant.

The Jordanians reported on al-Foul's arrest to Israel, and then shared these results. Yet despite Abu al-Foul's confession, at the end of the day the Jordanians decided that they didn't want to hold him. They had received menacing threats from people associated with Imad Moughniyeh, and they knew that putting al-Foul on trial would make them a target for Hizballah terrorism. Nor could they eliminate al-Foul secretly, now that Hizballah knew he was being held. They were even more fearful of handing him to Israel, with all the reverberations that would provoke in the Arab world. Despite all of the Mossad's protests, Abu al-Foul and his gang were freed in December 1998. As far as anyone knows, today they are back in Tehran.

# CHAPTER 12

# Exporting Terror

Denial of the significance of international terrorism was widespread in the 1990s, and indeed, many traditional sources of terrorism were less worrisome at the time. Most Palestinian organizations had by then adopted a moderate line that called for negotiations with Israel, and the PLO abandoned terrorism, at least on the international level. The CIA's Counter Terror Center brilliantly broke up the Abu Nidal Organization, sewing discord among its members by getting them to believe that they were being robbed by other operatives.

The IRA stopped detonating bombs in London, as the peace process ground forward in Northern Ireland. Once-feared ideological terrorist movements, including the Baader Meinhof Group in Germany, the Red Brigades in Italy, and the Red Army in Japan, had disintegrated. These developments led most states to lower their guard. Terrorism came to be seen as a low-grade threat, a problem for Israel but for hardly anyone else. Yet it was precisely during this period that Iran set up its worldwide networks of support for terrorism. These networks covered a variety of organizations, among them the one that would later become known as al-Qaeda.

Of course, 9/11 changed the West's attitude entirely. Yet that change has not made much of a dent in the dreams of terrorists. Osama bin Laden's organization and other extremist groups still harbor fantasies of a knockout punch. In all of the attacks since 9/11—in Tunis, Morocco, Saudi Arabia, Pakistan, Afghanistan, Indonesia, London, Madrid, Istanbul, and more—the degree of success and lethality has depended far more on the ability, daring, and breadth of imagination of the terrorists than on the strength of law enforcement. Some plots have been disrupted, but these spectacular strikes make a chilling progression. It is not a matter of one or two terrorists that somehow slip through the fingers of the CIA or MI6 or the Mossad to plant a bomb; it is a series of strikes, usually requiring meticulous planning and orchestration. Finding a suitable response has proven impossible, whether or not the perpetrators are linked to larger international networks.

We appear to be only at the outset of the conflict. When President George W. Bush declared a "war on terror" in the wake of 9/11, he inspired an increase in the level of attacks. On the face of it, those who blame Bush and the war in Iraq for the wave of terror are not wrong—the West launched an unnecessary war, and that war has resulted in more attacks. The United States, some European countries, and Israel all expend vast resources on the war against terror, but the West has not managed to come up with a viable alternative to extreme Islamic ideology; instead, it has only boosted the hostility and alienation felt in Muslim communities across the globe.

Yet despite the West's change in attitude, despite reams of paper devoted to studying international terror, one key fact is little understood. Iran—more than al-Qaeda even—stands at the center of the rise of modern terrorism. Since 1979, U.S. State Department reports have named Iran as a country that is involved in terrorism, and as of 1984, it has appeared on the list of states that sponsor terror. The addition of Iran to this list was concomitant with the declaration that it had been responsible for the terror attack on the Marines headquarters in Beirut in October 1983. In the wake of this decision, Washington froze $22.4 billion in Iranian government assets in bank accounts and other property in the United States. According to the State Department, Iran was involved in 133 terrorist operations in the nine years between 1987 and 1995.

Immediately after Khomeini's revolution, Iran's leaders adopted the Leninist doctrine which says that a revolution which does not export itself is doomed to implode. The market for this particular export business is vast—the twenty-one countries of the Muslim world. Although at the outset Khomeini naturally took an interest mainly in countries with Shi'ite populations, such as Lebanon, he very soon broadened the scope and began trying to export the Islamic Revolution to all the Islamic lands. He saw Iran as the center of this world and himself as the leader of all believers.

The revolution has irresistible appeal among the masses in those countries, and the resources required to pursue the cause are minimal. Khomeini had proved that it was possible to take over a powerful and wealthy country and impose an extremist Islamic rule upon it. For both Shi'ite and Sunni movements of all kinds, Khomeini was a dream come true and an ideal to be imitated.

The tool of the export drive is terror, and terror is the weapon of the poor—arming small groups of people with small arms and explosives is very inexpensive. It costs very little to employ people whose only concern is to secure a place in the hereafter and who are driven by blind fanaticism, in countries where $30 a month is a big salary. Amounts of money that are paltry to a country like Iran or to a multimillionaire like bin Laden can keep a terrorist cell going for many months. Even Iran's assistance to a major organization like Hizballah does not exceed $100 million a year (excluding 2006, after the July war with Israel), not a large sum for a country that earns about $50 billion a year in oil exports.

As early as the beginning of the 1990s, some Western intelligence services identified close links between Islamic terror elements in Egypt, mainly the local Islamic Jihad and al-Jamaa al-Islamiyya, and Department 15 of the Iranian Ministry of Intelligence and Security (VEVAK). Department 15 is the unit that is responsible for subversive intelligence activities abroad, and for exporting the revolution by undermining the governments of other Muslim countries in order to set up Islamic regimes there. Yet in Egypt as elsewhere, Iran was careful to avoid direct involvement. In most cases, Iranian intelligence demonstrated considerable concern over the possibility that operations may fail, perpetrators may be caught, and footprints may lead to Iran. That has not stopped Western intelligence agencies from spotting such footprints.

One target of Iranian activity has been its neighbor to the northwest, Turkey. There is a Turkish branch of Hizballah whose first function has been the systematic elimination of Iranian dissidents who had taken refuge in that country. The Turkish authorities did very little to stop them. The Iranians also began bringing Turkish Islamic extremists to training camps in the Tehran area.

One of these Turks was Irfan Cagarici, who was arrested in March 1996. He was convicted of murder and membership in a terrorist organization. In a confession, he explained how the Turkish branch of Hizballah was formed: "After the revolution in Iran, in the spring of 1982 I went there to try the Islamic way of life. On my return, I decided that Turkey was a suitable country for applying the laws of Islam. Under the influence of religious books and information that I obtained at religious schools we decided to establish the Hizballah-Turkey organization. We began our activity in Istanbul at the end of 1983 and the beginning of 1984. I was the leader. My friend Salim Goljan discussed our idea with Mohammad Tahiri, who was the Iranian consul in Istanbul at that time. The consul told Salim that he would not be able to help us himself, but he would give us the telephone number of someone in Iran who could help. We crossed into Iran through the mountainous area of Baskal on an illegal route. We were sent to a villa in northern Tehran. Then Ahmet Karimi, to whom the consul had sent us, arrived and we spoke a little. During our visit, which lasted five days, we met other Iranians. They were people from the Mahdi Hasimi group, which is the most active in the Iranian Revolutionary Guards and very involved in international operations."

After several more trips to Iran, Irfan Cagarici returned with an Iranian passport under the name Rahmani Pour. At meetings with agents of Iranian intelligence, he and his friends received orders to kill the journalist Chitin Amach, who had written severely critical articles against the revolutionary regime. "We put on ski masks to hide our faces. Thamer Aslan, another member of the group, blocked Amach's car. Muzafar Dalamaz was first to shoot, and then I fired. We saw Amach's driver, Sinan Arakan, running away toward the beach. Dalamaz ran after him and killed him. Then we went back to our car and fled. I and my friends carried out the action at the order of Ahmet Karimi, who had helped us with training and given us a place to live in Iran . . . twenty days after the assassination we met with Karimi. He congratulated us on our successful operation and gave us ten thousand dollars."

In a paper published in 2002, Turkish researchers Bulent Aras and Gohan Bacic observe that Hizballah's Turkey branch is a particularly lethal organization that has been involved in over a thousand operations, including hundreds of murders. One operation that failed was an attempt on the life of the Israeli diplomat David Golan in 1991. The terrorists fired an RPG missile at his car, but they only hit a tire, and he survived. Hizballah did succeed in killing the security officer of the Israeli Embassy in Ankara, Ehud Sadan, in March 1992. In 1995, they wounded chemistry professor Yuda Yurum, the head of the Jewish community in the Turkish capital, by booby-trapping his car. Department 15, according to Aras and Bacic, was behind the intensive activity of Hizballah-Turkey.

On May 23, 2000, under pressure from Israel and America, Turkish security forces carried out a rare operation against the organization, arresting a man with dual Turkish and Iranian citizenship by the name of Farhan Osman. He confessed to killing Sadan and to the attack on Yurum, saying that he had done so on orders from Iran, from which he had received weapons and where he had trained.

For years Iran pumped members of two Turkish groups into its training camps, something that bin Laden would also do later. The first group included Palestinian students at Turkish universities; the second, extremist Turkish Muslims who wanted to import the revolution to their homeland. Turkey's intelligence and police were aware of these activities, but did little about them until November 2003, when a coordinated strike in the capital made it impossible to ignore mass terrorism. In attacks on two synagogues, a branch of HSBC Bank, and the British Consulate in Istanbul, 62 people were killed and 750 were injured. Among those killed was the British consul general, Roger Short.

On November 15, in the evening, a few hours after the attack, the hands of Sarah Nigri ("almost nineteen," she answered when I asked how old she was) were still trembling as she recounted what had happened to her as she sat in the women's section of the synagogue during the bar-mitzvah ceremony for Aharon Cohen: the moving rites, the terrifying explosion, the screams of the wounded, the enormous glass chandelier that fell in pieces on the worshippers below, the dust, the shock, the flight from the building.

"I waited for a second blast, another huge explosion, that would kill me too," she said tearfully. But something else bothered her. "I couldn't find the man with a hole in his skull. I wanted to say I was sorry, but I couldn't find him." As she ran from the building, Sarah noticed a woman whose face and hands were full of blood. She was one of the members of the community. Sarah, who had suffered only a minor scratch, tried to find help for her but when she saw that there was none, she took the woman by the hand and walked with her to the nearby St. Patrick's Hospital.

"At the entrance to the hospital, they took her away, and then I saw another casualty, a not very old man who was holding a tallit [a Jewish prayer shawl] in his hand. He was alone. Only he and the tallit that he would not let go of. At first I didn't realize what was wrong with him, and then I saw he had a hole in his skull. Actually as if part of it had disappeared. I took his tallit and placed it on the terrible wound. It immediately got soaked with blood and I pressed it tightly on the wound, so that he would not lose more and more blood. The man only asked me if he was going to die. 'Only tell me this, does it look to you that I can go on living after something like this?' is what he said.

"We went into the E.R. and the doctors took him into a room. He held my hand, and I held the tallit to his head. But then the doctors told me to leave. The man said he didn't want me to go. He begged me to stay with him. He said that if I went, he would surely die. But the doctors shouted at me and I had to go.

"Afterwards I looked for him in the hospital to ask him to forgive me for agreeing to leave and leaving him alone, but I couldn't find him."

As soon as the perpetrators were identified, law enforcement authorities realized that they had undergone training in Iran and Afghanistan; in fact, all of the details of that training were already captured in law enforcement records. The authorities hadn't lifted a finger to stop them.

Some of the terrorists were known to Israeli intelligence for their links with the Palestinian Islamic Jihad and Hamas. If the Turks had bothered to share their information with Israel, cross-checking would have turned up some highly interesting facts. But the Turks had been largely indifferent to Israeli requests for information on Hamas.

Despite Turkey's close covert links with Israel on the matter of acquisition of weaponry, the government in Ankara saw Hamas as a local Israeli problem and not as a threat to itself. The Turks preferred not to get involved, for fear of what collaboration with Israel against Hamas would look like in the eyes of the Arab world, where the movement was greatly admired. Prior to November 2003, the Israelis sometimes had to act unilaterally in Turkey in order to protect themselves. In December 1992, a prominent businessman, Jak Kamhi, the head of the Turkish Jewish community, was urgently warned by Israel that Iranian intelligence was planning to assassinate him. An attempt on his life took place on January 29, 1993, but thanks to his bodyguards and other security measures, it was foiled and his life was saved.

Turkey was just one of the places where the Iranians used subcontractors to spread their network of terror. They also targeted the heart of Europe. In January 1987, Mohammad Hamadi, the brother of senior Hizballah official Abdul-Hadi Hamadi, was arrested in Germany while trying to smuggle liquid explosives into the country in three large bottles. The bottles were disguised as arak, the Middle Eastern anise-based liqueur. He was put on trial for that crime as well as his role in the murder of Robert Stethem, the Navy diver killed aboard TWA Flight 847, and was convicted and sentenced to life imprisonment. In 2005, he was pardoned and released. Chiefs of the Mossad station in Germany were not notified in advance of his release, and they were stunned. Hamadi had been considered one of the prime bargaining chips in Western hands for use in securing the release of Israeli hostages. The Germans never responded officially to Israeli requests for an explanation. The Mossad conducted its own investigation and reached the conclusion that Hamadi had been exchanged for a German hostage in Iraq, Susanne Osthoff, an archeologist. German intelligence had negotiated the deal with Iran. Under interrogation, Hamadi revealed the location of weapons caches near the German-French border. In retaliation for his arrest, Hizballah carried out terror attacks against German targets, including the kidnapping of two German citizens in Lebanon, Rudolf Cordes and Alfred Schmidt. Cordes, fifty-three, Beirut manager for the West German firm Hoechst AG, was kidnapped on January 17, 1987, as he was driving to West Beirut from the airport after arriving from Frankfurt. He was released on September 12, 1987. Schmidt, forty-seven, an engineer with Siemens AG, was kidnapped on January 20, 1987, and released on September 7, 1987.

In March 1989, another Hizballah activist, Bassem Raghib Maki, a student in Germany, was arrested. He was found in possession of pre-operational intelligence about Israeli, Jewish, American, and other sites in Germany that had been chosen as targets for attacks. Instructions in Arabic for the preparation of bombs were found in his apartment in Darmstadt. Similar operatives were discovered during the 1980s in Spain, France, Switzerland, and Cyprus. Iran helped raise money for Hizballah in Germany, Britain, Belgium, Switzerland, Italy, and Holland. In April 1994, the British government conveyed a stern warning to the Iranians to cut their links with the Irish Republican Army. According to reports in the British press, based partly on statements by the first secretary of the Iranian Embassy in London, who had defected, Iran had supplied the Irish underground organization with funds and weapons, and had possibly also trained its members.

Iranian audacity grew in inverse proportion to the weakness of European responses. In early May 1996, a shipping container unloaded at Antwerp was found to contain a special 300mm mortar that could fire shells containing 25 kilograms of TNT up to 700 meters. A quantity of ammunition was found with it. The shells were of a type fitted with fuses that would cause them to explode in the air over their targets. The container had been unloaded from an Iranian cargo vessel that had meanwhile sailed for Hamburg, where the German authorities detained the crew. At least two of them were identified as VEVAK personnel. The weapon was apparently meant to be used against Israeli or Jewish targets in Europe.

In August 1989, a Hizballah operative by the name of Mustafa Maza was killed in an explosion in a London hotel, when a bomb that he was making blew up in his hands. Two Iranian diplomats wanted by Argentinean authorities for the 1994 Buenos Aires attack have been traced in Europe even more recently. One, Saied Baghban, was arrested in Belgium in August 2003, but freed shortly afterward. The Argentinean report summing up the attack says that the same members of Hizballah and Iranian intelligence who carried out the Buenos Aires operation were also responsible for two "minor" terrorist attacks in Britain on July 26 and 27, 1994.

Widespread terrorist activity by Iran and Hizballah has spread to Asia as well. On March 12, 1994, an attempt to blow up the Israeli Embassy in Bangkok, Thailand, nearly succeeded. Disaster was averted only by the fact that the driver of a truck loaded with explosives, who was supposed to commit suicide in the act, apparently changed his mind at the last moment and ran away. The Israelis never determined exactly why Bangkok was targeted on that date. Highly reliable intelligence information links the operation to Imad Moughniyeh's network.

The Thai police arrested an Iranian citizen for the botched operation. He was sentenced to five years' imprisonment. But an investigation run by the Mossad came to different conclusions, and the Israelis told the Thai investigators that they had fingered the wrong Iranian. Mossad officials believe the Thais wanted to get rid of their suspect for reasons that had to do with other criminal activities of his, and to close the file on the terror attempt. In any event, Mossad's investigation led to no other arrests.

In 1995, according to Mossad sources, Hizballah agents from Lebanon recruited five Singaporean Muslims and formed a cell whose objective was to crash boat bombs into American and Israeli vessels. The cell also photographed the local embassies of those two countries. In 1999, Mossad sources say, the agency uncovered an attempt by Hizballah to recruit Malaysians and Indonesians to commit acts of terror in Australia and Indonesia.

Of course, Iran's targets weren't only distant. Moderate regimes among the Arab states were also considered ripe for revolution. The Revolutionary Guards established contact with extremist organizations in Egypt in the 1980s and arranged for some of their members to train in Iran. The most prominent Egyptian terrorist leader at the time was Ayman al-Zawahiri, and the story of his relationship with Iranian intelligence, on the one hand, and Osama bin Laden, on the other, is a chapter of its own in this history.

Elsewhere in the Middle East, Iran maintained links with exiled Islamic extremists from Bahrain who lived in Lebanon. In April 1996, the Bahrain Interior Ministry announced that Shi'ite terrorists from that country were in regular contact with VEVAK. As usual, President Rafsanjani emphatically denied any Iranian involvement in the internal affairs of other countries, in particular Egypt and Bahrain.

In Africa, Iran and Hizballah were active among the large Lebanese populations residing in certain countries. The Ivory Coast, from which large quantities of weapons were shipped to Lebanon, is just one example. Shi'ites in Johannesburg, South Africa, set up the Karbala Liberation Fund, which sent money to Hizballah in Lebanon. In Zaire, Hizballah activities were identified by Israeli intelligence sources at a mosque in Kinshasa, allegedly financed by the Iranian Embassy.

For its part, Israel attempted to take countermeasures against Iran and Hizballah in Africa. But it remained alone in this, as the Americans had lost interest in Africa as an arena for intelligence operations since the end of the Cold War.

During the 1970s and 1980s, Africa had been an important arena for the PLO's attempts to win international support, so Mossad was active there in its endless struggle with Palestinian extremists. Deep moles were recruited among the expatriate Lebanese and Palestinian communities in black Africa, moles who joined various PLO factions, such as those in Zaire.

In the 1990s, after the PLO became the partner in peace talks, the Mossad tried to use its former contacts and espionage networks against

Hizballah and Iran. The Ivory Coast was a key Mossad target, because it served as a back door to terrorist activity directed at Europe. Yet Mossad enjoyed only partial cooperation from the local authorities and intelligence services. When, for example, the Mossad tried to persuade the local authorities to start using stricter security measures at Abidjan Airport and to cooperate in foiling arms-smuggling operations, the refusal was polite but firm.

In short, anyone who thinks Hizballah is just an Israeli problem is fooling himself. And anyone who thinks Iran's VEVAK and Revolutionary Guards are not active outside the Middle East is terribly wrong. Iran, and its proxy Hizballah, are international menaces. They are mostly occupied with Israel and the United States, but they will do what they can, wherever they can, to spread the Islamic Revolution, including to the United States itself.

# CHAPTER 13

# Target: The Great Satan

For years, Iran has refrained from direct strikes at American targets, with one possible exception: the attack at the Khobar military complex in Dhahran, Saudi Arabia, on June 25, 1996, in which 19 Americans were killed and 500 injured. The building that was hit housed the U.S. Air Force's 4404th Wing, which was tasked with supervising the no-fly zone in Iraq. The Saudi authorities did very little to help, and in the opinion of some of the one hundred Americans who took part in the investigation at the scene of the attack, even sabotaged the American effort, led by the FBI, to understand what had happened.

A short while after it happened, Israeli Military Intelligence informed the CIA, via the Mossad, that five months before the attack, the Saudi Arabians had caught a Lebanese truck loaded with explosives on its way to Khobar. This information, which almost miraculously, one might say, reached the FBI, was shown to the Saudis who, mumbling guiltily, had to confirm it. The American investigators were beside themselves with rage. In addition to the story about the truck, more and more evidence connecting the attack to Iran began to accumulate.

For example, some senior officials of the American intelligence community claim that the interrogation of several Hizballah members arrested in Canada in March 1997 provided evidence that the attack was carried out by a Hizballah cell from Bahrain, acting on instructions from Iran. As the signs pointing to Tehran's involvement increased, the readiness of the Saudis to help, already minimal, receded still further. Unofficial information reached the FBI team from senior Saudi investigators who ignored the policy of silence, and the probe implicated Imad Moughniyeh's so-called Special Research Apparatus, acting on Iranian orders, in the attack. They had been aided by local residents, recruited within the kingdom.

In 1999, the Clinton administration asked for Iran's cooperation in investigating the event. To this day, the Americans are still waiting for a reply. Apparently, notwithstanding the intelligence officials' claims about Canadian Hizballah members, the U.S. government lacks absolute proof of Iranian involvement.

For the most part, at least until 2005, with the exception of financial warfare, Iran's links to terrorist threats to America are only indirect. In 2002, the report by the U.S. National Commission on Terrorism implicated Iran in the 9/11 attacks, but only indirectly.

Another indirect link can be found at the magnificent Islamic Education Center (IEC) in Potomac, Maryland. Its vast campus includes a huge mosque, a school from kindergarten to twelfth grade, a large library containing books in Arabic and Farsi, study halls for courses in religion, clubs, and more, all located on some of the most valuable real estate in the area.

This is a wealthy institution, perfectly maintained. Almost every student has his or her own computer terminal, among the many other state-of-the-art educational aids. They wear neat uniforms, the girls with their heads and limbs covered. Pictures of Khomeini are everywhere. Students greet each other in Arabic or Farsi. According to teachers, 50 percent of the students are from originally Muslim families, and the others from converted families. Graduates interested in higher religious studies usually go to Iran.

According to FBI officials, most of the Center's budget comes from sources connected to Iran. Sayed Naravi, one of the IEC directors, confirms that part of the funding for the construction came from Iran.

The IEC has never been linked to any terrorist acts. Yet Sheikh Mohammad al-Asi, a former imam of the IEC, is one of the most notorious preachers against Americans and Jews in the United States. In 2007 he still represented himself as the imam for the Center, though the institution itself denies this.

Al-Asi is a member of several extremist Islamic forums in Europe and the United States. He has also been hosted by the Islamic Republic of Iran: on January 30, 1990, he was a guest of Ayatollah Khamenei himself. On November 3, 1996, al-Asi appeared at a conference in London entitled "In Pursuit of the Power of Islam," which was sponsored by the Muslim Parliament of Great Britain and the Muslim Institute for Research and Planning. (Others present at this conference included Ayatollah Taskiri, head of the International Department of the Office of

Imam Khamenei, and representatives of FIS [the Islamic Salvation Front from Algeria], Hizballah, and Hamas.)

Al-Asi's message frequently focuses on the battle between Muslims and the *kufara* (infidels), and the necessity of an armed struggle for the victory of Islam. He is at pains to present himself as a liberal and moderate cleric, yet his rhetoric often belies that stance. Here are the liberal and moderate words he wrote in his biweekly column in the Canadian journal, *Crescent International*, in the issue of August 16–31, 1996:

> From the US to Poland, and Jordan to Argentina, the Jews are riding high. The higher they ride, the worse their crash will be when it inevitably shall occur. And Allah has spoken the truth: and you (the children of Israel) will reach unprecedented heights (on earth). . . . But when the last promise shall come to pass they [our subjects] will discredit your appearance, and they will enter the *masjid* [mosque] as they did the first time around and they will reduce to nil your celebrity status.

And here's what he had to say about the U.S. military presence in the Gulf, in a speech at a memorial service for Ayatollah Ruhollah Khomeini on June 4, 1994: "If the Americans are placing their forces in the Persian Gulf, we should be creating another war front for the Americans in the Muslim World, and specifically where American interests are concentrated—in Egypt, in Turkey, in the Indian subcontinent, just to mention a few. Strike at American interests there!"

Victor Marchetti, a former senior CIA official, has for years conducted a public campaign against AIPAC, the pro-Israeli lobby organization, and has even been accused of anti-Semitism as a result. At one point, Sheikh al-Asi approached Marchetti and suggested they work together to oppose AIPAC. Marchetti did not think much of the idea. "He apparently thought that I could serve him as a tool against AIPAC. He told me that he has an informant in the law office that represents AIPAC and showed me internal AIPAC documents that he had obtained, he claimed, from that source." Marchetti suspected al-Asi was working with Iranian intelligence. "He told me that he was interested in finding out what AIPAC's lines of action were, and in particular what they were planning to do on the subject of Iran and the sanctions against that country."

One man's opinion is only that, and there is no direct evidence what-

soever that al-Asi works with Iranian intelligence agencies. Yet his extremist rhetoric, aimed at Israel, Jews, and America, is toxic. It is like so much
of what comes from the Iranian government, when officials aren't pretending to be diplomatic.

If Iran has largely refrained from direct violence against America, a tactic it has engaged in instead is economic warfare, by illegal means.

Early in June 1992, two high-ranking agents of the U.S. Secret Service
arrived in Israel. In addition to protecting the president and vice president, and other designated individuals and sites, the Secret Service is
charged with defending U.S. currency against counterfeiters and other
financial crimes.

An American embassy official brought them straight from the plane to
the National Headquarters of the Israeli police in Jerusalem. There, in a
basement office, they met Israel's senior anticounterfeit team, headed by
Superintendent Avi Aboulafia, commander of the police document laboratory. One of the Americans explained their mission: "Everyone in the
anticounterfeit business knows how, toward the end of World War II,
Nazi Germany counterfeited sterling currency in order to damage the
British economy. They say the counterfeiting—thanks to the work of
Jewish money-printing experts recruited in the concentration camps—
was so good that it was impossible to distinguish between the real and the
fake. The Brits were lucky that before Hitler managed to print many of
these excellent notes, the war was over. That's all history now, but unfortunately we have reason to assume that it is being done again, in these
very days, against us, the United States of America. According to some
intelligence, it is the Islamic Republic of Iran which is forging hundred-
dollar bills of the best quality we've ever seen, and distributing them all
over the world, through the black money of the drug-trafficking trade
and terror organizations."

After a momentary silence, the second agent continued: "We discovered the first bill in 1990 and called it 'PN-14342.' Since then similar
bills have been found all over the world, from New York to Morocco,
from Macao to Uruguay. We have come here to explain to you how
to identify these bills and to ask for your help in combating this frightening thing."

There followed a brief explanation, illustrated by a greatly magnified
color photograph of both sides of a hundred-dollar banknote. Every

counterfeit has its own tell-tale signs. On low- or medium-quality counterfeits there are scores or even hundreds of such differences between the genuine bill and the fake one. Here, however, a Secret Service agent pointed only to four minute flaws, visible only with a magnifying glass, on the printing plate used by the Iranians. Such flaws, once discovered, are among the world's police forces' most closely guarded secrets—revealing them would enable the forgers to correct the error and make detection more difficult.

The Americans departed, leaving the Israeli experts one fake bill to work with. "Report to us immediately if you find more like this," they requested. The Israelis gave this superb forgery the code name "D-370." Within a few days, the lab's researchers began turning up similar notes from a variety of sources.

One of the signs of forgery detected by the Americans on PN-14342 was that the letter "o" in the word "dollar" was slightly truncated at the top. Several months after the meeting at the police headquarters, a message arrived from the Secret Service: "We don't know how, but the flaw we discovered on the 'o' leaked out and has been corrected by the counterfeiters. Now there are only three flaws. Attached is a sample." The Israelis called the new bill "D-470." In the years since then, it has become known in international police circles as the "super-bill" or the "super-note." By 2007, the Israeli police had seized several tens of thousands of dollars' worth of these counterfeits.

The dollar's centrality in the world markets makes it by far the most profitable currency to counterfeit. Until the discovery of the Iranian counterfeit, there were $360,831,314,979 in circulation in the world, according to U.S. Treasury spokeswoman Becky Lowenthal. Two thirds of that amount, she said, was presumed to be outside the United States. Some $215 billion of the total $360 was in the form of hundred-dollar notes. The international police organization, Interpol, knew of almost 19,000 different types of counterfeits of hundred-dollar bills. By comparison, Interpol knew of only 145 counterfeits of the German mark in 1995, not one of which even approached the quality of the super-bill.

The big question, of course, was: Who was manufacturing the phony dollars and trying to undermine the currency upon which the world's economy was based? A Republican congressional report in 1992, issued by Bill McCollum, a Florida congressman and chairman of the House Task Force on Terrorism and Unconventional Warfare, accused Iran. The

Secret Service and Interpol maintained an official silence on the subject. In a letter written in 1995 in response to a Government Accounting Office report on counterfeiting overseas, the Secret Service called the task force's allegations "unsubstantiated" and characterized its conclusions as being based on "rumor and innuendo."

In a July 2006 *New York Times* article, Stephen Mihm, an expert on currency counterfeiting, noted that in theory, only governments can buy the printing presses used for making money, and only a handful of companies sell them. Mihm maintains, however, that North Korea was behind the super-notes. Officials in the intelligence services of both the United States and Israel, by contrast, are focused on Iran, or at least elements in Iran. Hizballah has flooded Lebanon with the fake money. Many of the super-notes have surfaced in the Middle East, notably in the Bekaa Valley of Lebanon, and in Tehran.

"The dollar is not an easy bill to counterfeit. On the contrary, it is one of the most difficult on the market today," says Sadek Gardieh, who in the mid-1990s was in charge of anticounterfeit operations at Interpol headquarters in France.

Most of the countries in the world, the United States among them, print their currency using so-called intaglio presses, in which the design is cut into the printing plate, the ink fills the incisions, and the press comes down with enormous pressure, some 50 tons on every square centimeter of paper. That compresses the ink, hardening it enough to withstand all of the battering banknotes undergo in wallets, bundles, or even when run through the wash. The print on bills counterfeited using other printing methods would soon fade.

Intaglio presses cost from $10 million to $15 million and are manufactured in very few places. They are used exclusively for printing money and government documents like passports. Gardieh says that Interpol and national police forces see to it that the presses are sold only to governments, not to private bodies or individuals. This restriction strengthens the assumption that the super-bills are the work of a government and not an independent gang.

Yossef Bodansky, who was in charge of the research team for the House Task Force on Terrorism and Unconventional Warfare, says that in the mid-1970s a Swiss company, with the approval and financial support of the United States, supplied the government of the Shah of Iran with two intaglio presses. They were eventually seized by the revolutionaries. In a special report to the president of the United States, Bodansky wrote that it can be assumed that the high quality of the super-notes can be ascribed to the cadre of Iranian experts trained in the 1970s by the U.S. Treasury's Bureau of Engraving and Printing. They were put at the service of the Khomeini regime after the revolution.

Only about twenty people in the world know how to reproduce all of the tens of thousands of intricate details that there are on a dollar banknote plate. Interpol is in touch with each one of these craftsmen. No one knows if it was one of them or someone else who made the plates for the super-bill.

The congressional task force estimated that by 1995, Iran had distributed $15 billion in phony U.S. currency. A senior Israeli intelligence official said at the time that there wasn't a bundle of $1 million in used notes anywhere in the world that didn't have a few D-470 counterfeits in it.

The task force found that Iran had two main aims in counterfeiting the dollars: to help solve its own economic problems and to undermine the American economy. The decision to adopt this tactic was probably taken in 1989, because of a shortage of hard currency. Iran had become embroiled in a severe economic crisis. The cost of the war with Iraq was estimated at $600 billion. Because of the drop in oil prices and debts from Third World countries that it could not collect, the country was weighed down by heavy deficits. In early 1990, according to American intelligence sources, Iran began producing large quantities of counterfeit banknotes at two sites: the government printing works in Al Shuhada Street in Tehran, and in the city of Karaj, 20 kilometers west of the capital. The printed bills were stored at a building outside Tehran, on the way to Meharabad Airport.

A large part of the distribution of the fake currency was carried out by Syria, according to the House task force. Crates full of bills were flown to Damascus and then trucked to Zabadani, Iran's forward base in Syria, which was run jointly with Syrian intelligence. There they were packed into smaller bundles and prepared for shipment to distribution networks based in Lebanon. The man in charge of the currency-smuggling operation was Ghazi Kanaan, then commander of Syrian intelligence in Lebanon. He later became Syrian interior minister, and "committed suicide" in 2005 following the international inquiry into the assassination of former Lebanese prime minister Rafik Hariri.

In certain Lebanese banks, the going rate for one counterfeit dollar was 45–60 cents.

Hizballah, according to the CIA, had its own counterfeiting operation, employing expert forgers in a village near Baalbek, where there are ten to fifteen printing works that specialize in the various aspects of currency counterfeiting. The emphasis is on producing hundred-dollar bills of good quality, but not as good as the super-bills. In the past they also made twenty- and fifty-dollar bills, as well as banknotes of various Western and Arab states, of varying quality.

The House task force stated that since 1993, counterfeit Iranian money was distributed by organized crime gangs. Claire Sterling, a terrorism expert based in Italy, asserts that by the mid-1990s, the Sicilian Mafia was obtaining excellently counterfeited hundred-dollar bills. Another channel of distribution, according to the task force, was through organizations within the United States. Washington had cut off relations with Iran in 1981, but allowed a number of Iranian representatives to remain and function as an interest section in the Pakistan Embassy. In fact, the section is housed in a separate building, in which it occupies several stories. It serves as the local command post of Iranian intelligence, dealing with recruitment of personnel, support for extremist organizations in the United States, and the distribution of counterfeit money. In 1993, it had a staff of eighty. In the light of the reports on the true nature of these "Iranian Foreign Ministry" personnel, the State Department ordered that the number be cut by half.

The close connection between the counterfeit dollars and terrorism in the United States is clearly exemplified in the case of the Islamic network that tried to blow up the World Trade Center in New York in 1993. On May 18 of that year, Siddig Ibrahim Ali, commander of one of the cells in the network, told Imad Salem, an FBI agent, that he could get his hands on millions of counterfeit dollars. He offered to sell a million such dollars for $150,000. He identified the source of the money as "a good Muslim who wants to help." Quantities of counterfeit bills were found in the apartment of the cell's spiritual leader, Omar Abdul Rahman. Rahman, the blind sheikh, was one of those who called for *mujahideen* or *mutawineen* (volunteers) from all over the Arab world to come and help in the war against the Soviet presence in Afghanistan, a war organized by the intelligence services of Pakistan, Saudi Arabia, and the United States.

The sheikh received asylum in Sudan after the Egyptians put him on their wanted list because of another *fatwa* that he issued, in which he called for the assassination of President Anwar al-Sadat, who was in fact shot dead in October 1981. Rahman tried to emigrate to the United States, and was turned down six times by the American Consulate in Khartoum. The seventh time, amazingly, the CIA station there instructed the consulate to approve his request. To this day it is a mystery why this was done. Later on, the sheikh was convicted and sent to jail for life for his role in the bombing of the World Trade Center by his followers in 1993.

According to intelligence sources, the distribution operations are controlled from Iran by Mohsen Rafiqdoost, one of the leaders of the Revolutionary Guards and head of the Foundation of the Oppressed, Iran's largest holding company. He used some of the money to pay North Korea (which was aware that the notes were counterfeit) for helping Iran to build surface-to-surface missiles.

In 1997, following the discovery of increasingly large quantities of super-bills, President Clinton ordered the replacement of all of the hundred-dollar bills in circulation, a move that the Secret Service had recommended two years earlier.

The new bills were meant to contain so many new features and security measures that it would be impossible to counterfeit them within the foreseeable future. In 1995, Treasury spokeswoman Becky Lowenthal said that "the full replacement process will take years, and may never end at all."

Iran may also have engaged in some "counterfeiting proliferation." According to information gathered by the Secret Service and the CIA between 1999 and 2007, Tehran shared its secrets with Kim Jong Il's regime, and apparently even sent to North Korea one of the intaglio printing presses which the United States had given to the Shah. The North Koreans have been in dire need of cash due to international sanctions. Joint research by both Iran and North Korea has apparently enabled them to come up with a new super-bill, very like the new hundred-dollar bill that the Americans had begun to distribute. The similarity was not as close as that of PN-14342 but could nevertheless pass the scrutiny of most of the banks in the world. Counterfeiters and law enforcement engage in a constant arms race. The counterfeiting is improving constantly. Iran's benefit from the alliance with North Korea is threefold: Iran needs Pyongyang's missile technology very badly; Iran received some of the counterfeit bills of the new manufacturing line; and it was able to make use of an enormous distribution network for its own bills through the gambling industry and drug traffic at the disposal of North Korea.

For Hizballah, counterfeit bills are a lifeline. On August 17, 2006, three days after the end of Israel's Second Lebanon War, Hizballah started working at full steam to reconstruct its status in Lebanon. As part of the war for public opinion, the organization handed out packages of $12,000 to every family whose home had been destroyed by the Israeli military's bombardments of South Beirut and the villages of southern Lebanon. In Beirut alone, some 15,000 homes were destroyed. Hizballah made sure that its generosity received wide media coverage. But there was one question unanswered: Where did they get the $200 million to finance the operation? Israeli intelligence and the National Security Agency are convinced that the source was the intaglio printing presses where the super-bills are manufactured.

As 2007 was drawing to a close, the United States seemed to be taking a tougher line against Hizballah and Iran. There was talk of officially designating the Revolutionary Guards as a terrorist group. By contrast, the European Union still had not listed even Hizballah as such. Some European states with contingents serving with the UN forces in Lebanon were apprehensive about retaliatory attacks on their troops if Hizballah were added to the black list. (France seems to have undergone a certain change of heart since the 2007 election of Nicolas Sarkozy, who has called Hizballah "a terrorist organization," while his foreign minister, Bernard Kouchner, also expressed a more militant stance against the Lebanese militia's patrons when he said, "We have to prepare for the worst, and the worst is war," in remarks about dealing with Iran's nuclear program.)

Furthermore, Germany's intelligence services estimated in February 2007 that there were over a thousand Hizballah supporters living in Germany. Many of them were inactive, or active only in fund-raising—yet there may be many who could be called upon for more sinister purposes.

Alexander Ritzmann, senior fellow at the European Foundation for Democracy, is a former member of the Berlin State Parliament, where he was privy to a great deal of intelligence material gathered by German agencies. As he notes, "According to a German government report from February, the attitude of Hizballah supporters in Germany 'is characterized by a far-reaching, unlimited acceptance of the ideology and policy [of Hizballah].' Berlin is also aware that representatives of Hizballah's 'foreign affairs office' in Lebanon regularly travel to Germany to give orders to their followers."

On July 31, 2007, two of the organization's activists, both of whom were part of the Special Research Apparatus run by Imad Moughniyeh, placed bombs on trains in Dortmund and Koblenz. They failed to detonate due to technical hitches. Israeli intelligence provided crucial information about the two men to the German intelligence agency BND. Both were arrested after Israeli Military Intelligence intercepted a call from one of them to his mother in Lebanon and conveyed its content to the Germans. The men claimed that they had been motivated by the caricatures of the Prophet Mohammad published in Denmark and reprinted in other European periodicals. If the bombs had gone off, there would have been scores of fatalities and hundreds of wounded, said German officials.

Nonetheless, America is tougher than Europe on Hizballah. The Americans have known of Hizballah agents in the United States since at least the early 1990s.

In June 1992, three men—Mohammad Hammoud, Mohammad Attaf Darwish, and Darwish's cousin, Ali Fayez Darwish—arrived at JFK International Airport in New York after buying forged visas in Venezuela for $200. Hammoud, at nineteen, was the oldest of the group, and a protégé of Sheikh Abbas Haraki, the military commander of Hizballah in southern Beirut at the time. The three men destroyed their visas immediately upon landing, and asked for political asylum—claiming, ironically, that they were persecuted by Hizballah in Lebanon. Three previous applications for a regular visa by Hammoud had been turned down. They were allowed to stay pending a decision and promptly disappeared, never showing up for their hearings. They managed to create a number of fabricated identities for themselves, by acquiring or forging driver's licenses, credit cards, and other documents. It later emerged that they set up a cell in North Carolina.

They were not the only Hizballah members who arrived at JFK on that June day. A fourth was Haj Hassan Hilu Laqis, who came for a shorter visit and on a tourist visa. He was in charge of purchasing supplies for Hizballah in America and Europe. He would visit the United States three more times by 1996.

During the 1990s, most Hizballah activists in America settled either in Charlotte, North Carolina, or Dearborn, Michigan. Laqis ran the cells from Lebanon. The Michigan network, headed by Fawzi Mustafa Assi, was responsible for acquiring weapons and sophisticated items that the Iranians could not supply to Hizballah on their own. The North Carolina network was tasked with raising money, by any means that its members saw fit, legal or illegal, and transferring it, after deducting a commission, to Lebanon. A 1999 document drawn up by the terrorism section of Israeli Military Intelligence's Research Division explains that both cells were comprised of undesirables. "Hizballah in Lebanon saw the members of these networks as elements with criminal tendencies and was therefore happy to dispatch them to North America, so that they would not carry out these activities in the proximity of the members of the organization."

A number of Hizballah activists had also settled in Canada and set up their own cells there. As early as 1993, one was arrested. Under interrogation he admitted that he belonged to the organization and that he had sent photographs of strategic sites in Ottawa and Montreal to Lebanon, to serve as an intelligence reserve of potential targets, "in case there's a problem with Canada." The Canadian police gave regular closed briefings to the government to explain that Hizballah in 1997 began using Canada as a base country for raising funds through car theft and smuggling.

The relationship between the North American cells and Hizballah in Lebanon was more than just one of supplying material and funds.

One of the operatives in Canada was Fawzi Ayoub, a Lebanese Shi'ite who arrived in 1992 when he was twenty-eight years old. He became a courier for the networks there. A longtime Hizballah activist, he had participated in many of the organization's operations in Lebanon and abroad. He also served in Imad Moughniyeh's special highly secret apparatus. He lived in Canada for some years, keeping in touch with Hizballah's leaders and doing various tasks for them. On his return, he was recruited for a clandestine and dangerous mission in Israel. After an intensive training series, he was instructed to travel to Europe, where he would receive a false American passport and purchase an entirely new wardrobe and toilet kit, discarding any sign of his links with Lebanon. Then he would move to another European country from which he would fly to Israel. In Israel, he was told to observe certain strict rules of conduct, speak only English, and conceal his Arab identity. In short, his time in Canada had helped establish a disguise.

Ayoub arrived in Israel in October 2000, shortly before the intifada broke out. He checked into a hotel in downtown Jerusalem. After a few days he travelled to Hebron, where he met a man who was supposed to take him to a secret weapons cache. But in Hebron he was detained by the Palestinian security forces, who initially suspected him of working for Israel. When the Shin Bet (Israeli internal secret service) learned that he was planning terror attacks against Israel, it asked the Palestinian Authority to hand him over to Israel, but the PA refused. During Israel's massivie "Defensive Wall" campaign in the West Bank, launched after a particularly vicious suicide attack on a Passover seder festive meal in Netanya in March 2002, an IDF commando team "liberated" Ayoub from his jail cell in Hebron, and handed him over to the Shin Bet for questioning. Since then, he has been in an Israeli jail.

Until June 1997, the Hizballah networks in the United States and Canada functioned largely unhindered. Early that year, Israel managed to intercept some phone calls between Laqis and his Michigan cell. The monitors in Military Intelligence could pick up signals only from Lebanon to a satellite, so they heard only what Laqis was saying. He spoke in code, but it was clear from his words that he was instructing someone to purchase various advanced items, such as GPS and night-vision equipment and bulletproof vests. The Mossad asked the CIA station in Tel Aviv to have the phone calls looked into, and it turned out that Laqis was speaking to the cell phone of Fawzi Mustafa Assi in Michigan.

This was the start of "Operation Wicker Roof," run in cooperation with the FBI. The bureau secured court permission to tap into the phone calls of Assi and another fourteen persons with whom he was in contact. Heading the operation on the American side was Dale Watson, head of the FBI's international terrorism section, who visited Israel for a series of meetings with top Mossad officials and the director of the Shin Bet, General Ami Ayalon. In May 1998, after Assi had already purchased some of the items on Laqis's shopping list, he began shipping them by air from Michigan to Lebanon. The first shipment, which contained night-vision and GPS equipment, was seized by customs at Detroit International airport, acting on an FBI tipoff. Laqis, in a phone call, told Assi he believed that it had been a random search. Nonetheless, Assi panicked and tried to get rid of the items he had collected. He was arrested by FBI agents that July.

There was rejoicing in the Mossad, whose officials hoped that a brisk FBI investigation of Assi would lead to a roundup of other cell members and the disruption of Hizballah's acquisition and fund-raising activities in North America. Their hopes were dashed when Assi was freed on $150,000 bail, on condition that he wear an electronic monitoring anklet. This prevented the FBI from exerting any pressure on him or even trying to reach a plea bargain deal for information. As soon as he was released, Assi cut the anklet off, and crossed into Canada using a forged passport. He was soon back in Lebanon.

As for the North Carolina cell, most of its activity was criminal, centered upon credit card fraud and cigarette smuggling. It carried on without any problems until one day in July 1996. Robert Conrad, U.S. attorney for the Western District of North Carolina, testified before the Senate Judiciary Committee about what happened then. "An off-duty Iredell County deputy sheriff noticed young men coming into JR's Tobacco Warehouse in Statesville, North Carolina, and buying bulk quantities of cigarettes with bags full of cash. Then he observed them putting those cigarettes into a van and heading north on I-77. The only thing north of Statesville on I-77 is . . . a state line and once that van crosses a state line, a federal felony is committed. . . . The nature of this case was that in North Carolina, cigarettes are taxed at a 50 cent per carton rate, and no tax stamp is applied to those purchases. In Detroit, Michigan, the cigarette tax is $7.50 a carton, and so this provided the economic incentive to purchase bulk quantity cigarettes in North Carolina and smuggle them for resale in Michigan."

Conrad said that the deputy sheriff notified the Bureau of Alcohol, Tobacco and Firearms (ATF), which started a surveillance of the warehouse, leading to many details of the operation. The smugglers averaged about $13,000 per van load, and they made three to four van trips to Michigan a week. All told, they purchased approximately $8 million worth of cigarettes, making a profit of between $1.5 and $2 million.

At this point, without any connection to events in North Carolina, the

National Security Agency (NSA) intercepted calls from Laqis and his aides in Lebanon to cell members in Charlotte, and vice versa. Israeli intelligence officials had run into technical difficulties in monitoring the calls, and were reluctant to try to crack the codes of American communications satellites, so they asked for the NSA's assistance. Astonishingly, the NSA shared its information with the Mossad but not with the FBI, because of the rivalry between the two domestic agencies. The NSA had been able to ascertain the identities of some of the parties to the phone conversations. This was sufficient for the Israelis to piece together the puzzle. They discovered that all of the members of the Hizballah ring in North Carolina came from the same neighborhood in Beirut; some of them had been friends since childhood. Hammoud was immediately identified as a Hizballah activist who had undergone training by the Revolutionary Guards in Iran and Lebanon since the age of fourteen. In a photograph used later by FBI officials in lectures to closed forums, a fifteen-year-old Hammoud is seen brandishing an AK-47, with a picture of Khomeini in the background. The Mossad now shared its information with the FBI (it took a foreign agency to overcome NSA-FBI hostility), informing the bureau that a Hizballah fund-raising cell was operating under its nose. The FBI ran a check on the names and discovered that they were being investigated by the ATF.

Conrad described what happened next: "At about this time in the investigation, when charging decisions on the cigarette case were being made, the FBI walked in with news that they had, through their intelligence investigations, discovered a Hizballah terrorist cell. . . . And this case ceased to be about cigarettes and became about Hizballah. But these were intelligence sources, not sources we could use in a criminal case without burning those sources. And so a criminal investigation began on Hizballah."

As soon as it became a terrorism case, the investigation became much simpler. Phone-tapping warrants were issued under the provisions of the Foreign Intelligence Surveillance Act (FISA) against the suspects, producing a lot of evidence. Hammoud was taped speaking to his patron in Hizballah, Sheikh al-Kharaki, as they rejoiced over Israel's May 2000 withdrawal from Lebanon. A search of Hammoud's home turned up Hizballah propaganda, including videocassettes, in one of which Secretary General Hassan Nasrallah declares: "We will answer the call, and we will take an oath to detonate ourselves, to shake the ground under our enemies, America and Israel." The audience responds: "We will answer to your call, Hizballah. We will answer to your call, Hizballah." On another tape he incites the crowd to repeat "Death to America" and "Death to Israel."

The eighteen members of the ring were arrested and put on trial. According to the indictment, the members of the cell planned to acquire for Hizballah such items as night-vision devices, surveying equipment, global positioning systems, mine and metal detectors, video equipment, advanced aircraft analysis and design software, computer equipment, stun guns, handheld radios and receivers, cellular phones, nitrogen cutters (used for cutting metal underwater), mining, drilling, and blasting equipment, military-style compasses, binoculars, naval equipment radars, dog repellers, laser range finders, and camera equipment. In June 2002, a federal jury in Charlotte found the brothers Mohammad Hammoud and Chawki Youssef guilty, and they were sentenced to long prison terms.

Said Harb served as the liaison between this gang and the Hizballah cells in Canada, which were centered in Toronto, Montreal, and Ottawa, and commanded by Mohammad Hassan Dbouk and his brother-in-law, Ali Adham Amhaz. The entire operation was run by remote control from Lebanon by Laqis. In his phone conversations with cell members in both countries, Laqis would exhort them to do more for the organization, reminding them that their brethren in the Middle East were suffering from Israel's blows while they were enjoying the good life in America. Harb travelled to Canada and to Seattle to meet Dbouk and to hand him forged checks, with which he would later purchase goods for Hizballah in Canada. Laqis had begun to assign purchasing tasks to his men in Canada in 2000. They managed to buy some of the items that he requested and to ship them to Lebanon. In 2002, they purchased military equipment in Vancouver, and they also sought "rock blasting equipment."

After receiving information from the FBI, the Canadian Security Intelligence Service (CSIS) began to take an interest. Eventually, the heads of the Canadian network, Dbouk and his brother-in-law, managed to escape to Lebanon; but investigators had intercepted phone calls and faxes which were very helpful in understanding how the Hizballah network operated, and were also used in the North Carolina trial. Canadian officials gave U.S. investigators copies of eighty-one summaries of intercepted conversations, thirty tapes, and twenty photos.

Dbouk was an important Hizballah functionary. He asked Laqis and another superior officer five times to be allowed to become a martyr, but he was turned down each time. In one transcript, Dbouk tells Laqis that he's ready to do "my best to do anything you want. So please you must know that I am ready to do anything you or the father want me to do—and I mean anything." "The father," according to the FBI, was Imad Moughniyeh.

The Canadian Hizballah network also sought to take out life insurance policies for Hizballah operatives committing acts of terrorism in the Middle East. A memo from the CSIS to the FBI states that "Dbouk referred to a person down there [in southern Lebanon] . . . who might in a short period of time go for a 'walk' . . . and never come back, and was wondering if Said [the other cell member] could fix some papers and details . . . for him and put himself [Said] as the reference."

Laqis's network in the United States and Canada was wiped out in 2001–02. Yet Moughniyeh, and Hizballah, continued to try to use North America as an outpost. In March 2005, the CIA received information from Israeli intelligence about a new Hizballah network, based in Montreal. Some of its members had rented two apartments in New York City. The purpose of the network was to prepare for the execution of terrorist attacks, should the United States strike at Iranian interests. The cell had gathered information on a number of potential targets, including the FBI offices in the city and several large department stores.

Experts who analyzed the information about this group concluded that Iran was preparing for the possibility that the United States might attack its nuclear installations. Iran was once again making use of its two weapons—terror and the nuclear threat—to protect one another. Tehran knows that it has no chance in a frontal war against America. But that doesn't mean it cannot respond by other means, even in the heart of New York.

Officials in the United States, Canada, and Israel worked together to gather evidence against the new cell in 2005. The operation was dubbed "Double-Edged Sword," and it continued for several months, with hopes that the men could soon be arrested. But precisely when enough incriminating information accumulated to make that possible, in the late summer of 2005, all of the suspects vanished into thin air. They left their homes and jobs abruptly. Operation Double-Edged Sword was blown. The Israelis and the Americans are convinced that someone from inside the investigation must have tipped off the terrorists.

In November 2007, Rada Nadim Prouty, thirty-seven, a Hizballah agent inside American intelligence, was arrested by the FBI. Originally a Lebanese citizen, Prouty confessed to a number of offenses as part of a plea bargain. After managing to enter the United States, she married a U.S. citizen in 1990. Later, she was hired by the FBI and the CIA and used her security clearances to extract a great deal of information and pass it to Hizballah. Much of it dealt with the FBI operations against the Michigan Hizballah network, and it enabled some of the suspects to get away. In both Israel and the United States, intelligence circles were convinced that Prouty was not alone, and that within the system—on either the Israeli or the American side—a far more dangerous mole was at work, passing information to the sleeper cells. A probe into the source of the leak was launched immediately, and was still underway in mid-2008.

Imad Moughniyeh had lost a new cell in the West, but he still had his agents. And his intentions were very clear.

# CHAPTER 14

# The al-Qaeda Connection

"If we don't do it in Damascus, I've got no idea how and where we'll chop the son of a bitch's head off," said one operative glumly. "Maybe H. and the chief will go to the P.M., and get him to agree to have it done in Damascus after all." H. was the head of Caesarea, the Mossad's special operations division; the chief was Shabtai Shavit, director of the intelligence organization; the prime minister was Yitzhak Rabin; and the SOB was the leader of the Palestinian Islamic Jihad (PIJ), Dr. Fathi Shkaki.

"No chance," said someone else at the Mossad meeting in the fall of 1995. "Rabin won't let anything interfere with the talks with Syria."

"So then tell him that I don't know how to take him out."

Nine months earlier, on January 22, 1995, an Islamic Jihad suicide bomber had blown himself up in a crowd of soldiers at a hitchhiking post at Beit Lid, between Tel Aviv and Haifa. When passersby, soldiers, and civilians rushed to help, another terrorist detonated his device in their midst. The toll: twenty-one soldiers and one civilian killed; sixty-eight wounded, some of them gravely—the worst terror attack Israel had suffered in years. Prime Minister Rabin's blood boiled when he visited the site later, and he ordered the Mossad to eliminate Shkaki.

In the long history of terrorist violence sponsored by Iran, it is sometimes overlooked that Iran has used a wide range of proxies and partners. The government's Revolutionary Guard, and its Hizballah client, are the two terrorist organizations normally discussed. Yet beyond these, Iran has worked closely with the PIJ and Hamas in the Middle East and in Sudan, and even with al-Qaeda, al-Jamaa al-Islamiyya, the Abu Nidal Organization, and others operating in Afghanistan, Bosnia, Pakistan, and God knows where else. One of the myths of modern Islamist terrorism is that Sunni and Shi'a do not get along; but when it comes to common enemies or objectives or using force to replicate the Iranian revolution in

213

other localities, they work together quite frequently. The story begins with Palestinian Islamic Jihad.

PIJ arose out of a nucleus of Palestinian students at Zakazik University in Egypt, known as a hothouse of religious fanaticism. Fathi al-Aziz al-Shkaki went there in 1974, to study medicine. He joined up with a small group of other Palestinian students, including the man who was to inherit the PIJ leadership from him after his demise, Dr. Ramadan Shalah. They adopted the religious concepts of the Muslim Brotherhood, an international Sunni Islamist movement and the world's largest and most influential political Islamist group, founded in Egypt in 1928. After returning to the Palestinian territories, they drew enormous encouragement from Iran's Islamic Revolution. In 1981, Shkaki, who was working as a doctor—and a fairly successful one, it is said—in Gaza, began to set up a network of cells, known at first as the Islamic Vanguard, and later as the Islamic Jihad.

The members of these underground cells were enthusiastic supports of Khomeini, and a pro-Iranian orientation became the organization's trademark. The group aimed to escalate the conflict with Israel and turn it into an armed struggle; it was among the earliest participants in the First Intifada. Shkaki was in and out of Israeli prisons on convictions for his involvement in terrorist activities in 1986 and for incitement. When inside, he gave lessons in religion and other subjects to Palestinian inmates. In 1988, he was expelled from Israel—in hindsight, this was not only seen abroad as an immoral act and a breach of international law but also an egregious error on Israel's part. Shkaki settled in Lebanon, where he teamed up with his friend from his university days in Egypt, Abdul Aziz Oudeh, who has been involved in a series of terrorist acts, has never been caught, and still figures in the FBI's Most Wanted List, as Abdul Aziz Awda.

The two were soon noticed by the Iranian Revolutionary Guard's intelligence, and taken under its wing. Iran arranged a work permit and a job for Shkaki in Damascus and provided him with funds. Iran had in the past tried to link up with Hamas, which was already bigger and more popular than the Jihad, but its leader, Sheikh Ahmad Yassin, flatly refused to take the proffered assistance. He was worried that Iranian involvement would tarnish his fund-raising efforts broad, mainly in Europe and the United States, and in any case he wanted total independence for himself. Iran regretfully adopted Shkaki instead.

Thanks to Iranian support, PIJ established itself in Damascus, and under the guidance of the Revolutionary Guards it built up a network of activists in the Palestinian territories. During this time the PIJ, under Fathi Shkaki's guidance, launched a series of terror operations, including a well-organized assault on a busful of Israeli tourists 50 kilometers east of Cairo, in February 1990, killing nine and wounding nineteen. In another attack, a fourteen-year-old girl, Helena Rapp, was stabbed to death in Bat Yam south of Tel Aviv on May 24, 1992. These actions reached a climax with a suicide bomber killing three Israeli officers at a roadblock near Netzarim, a settlement in the Gaza Strip, on November 11, 1994, and then the double suicide attack at Beit Lid two months later.

When Rabin ordered the assassination of Shkaki, the Mossad had no trouble locating him at his Damascus headquarters. But Major General Uri Saguy, the head of Israeli Military Intelligence, who was coordinating the negotiations with Syria, warned that killing Shkaki there would infuriate the Syrians and undermine the talks. Rabin ordered the Mossad to come up with alternative plans.

Early in October 1995, Fathi Shkaki was invited to attend a conference of heads of Palestinian and other Arab guerrilla movements in Libya. Shkaki declined; but when the Mossad learned that Said Mussa Marara, better known by the nom de guerre Abu Mussa, would be at the conference, they were sure that Shkaki would change his mind. The leader of a faction that had broken away from the PLO in 1983, Abu Mussa was a rival of Shkaki's. "If Abu Mussa's going to be there, our client won't be able to resist it," said one of the Mossad men. "Tell our guys to get ready."

The Israelis didn't manage to find out in real time if Shkaki had set out for Libya. But they knew, based on his previous trips, that his route would take him to the island of Malta. They drew up two plans. The first was to intercept a ferry between Malta and Libya and grab him if he was on it; but Rabin turned that down, for fear of international complications. The second was to carry out the hit in Malta.

Mossad agents were waiting for Shkaki at Malta International Airport. On the first flight from Damascus there was no one of his description, nor on the second, nor the third. At headquarters in Tel Aviv, they were beginning to give up. "Hang on one second," the voice of one of the agents was heard over the radio; "there's someone sitting on the side, away from everyone. I'm going to check him out." Tension mounted. A minute later, the agent came in again: "I think it's him. He's got a wig on, but there's a high probability that it's the target." Shkaki waited a little while longer, and then boarded a plane to Libya, not knowing that his fate was sealed. When he returned to Malta on October 26, en route home after the conference, the Mossad already knew that he was using a Libyan passport under the name of Ibrahim Shawish. Agents had no problem identifying and tailing him.

At 10 a.m. he checked into the Diplomat Hotel in the resort town of Salima, where he had stayed on the nine previous occasions he had passed through Malta. He took a room for one night, and was given the key to No. 616. After leaving his luggage in the room, he left the hotel at eleven-thirty to do some shopping. He bought himself a shirt at Marks & Spencer, and then three sports shirts at another store.

Shkaki failed to notice anything unusual as he continued his stroll. A Yamaha motorcycle, license plate number QM6904, carrying two men, drew close to him until it was right alongside. The passenger took out a pistol fitted with a silencer and put three bullets into the commander of the Islamic Jihad, two in the forehead and one in the back of his head, splintering his skull. The pistol was fitted with a small pocket for collecting the spent cartridges, leaving very little physical evidence for Malta's investigators to gather. The motorbike, which had been stolen the previous day, was later found abandoned on a beach. The agents were extricated by sea, and they returned to Israel.

For years afterward, the assassination of Fathi Shkaki was seen as a model for hitting at terrorist organizations by eliminating their leaders. The PIJ replaced him immediately—two days later, when the reason for his failure to turn up in Damascus became clear, the Iranians summoned Dr. Ramadan Shalah—another star on the FBI's Most Wanted List—from his teaching position at the University of South Florida, in Tampa. But the PIJ under Shalah was no longer what it had been. Shkaki had acted independently under Iranian protection. Shalah was no match for him as a commander, and he became Tehran's puppet. Only after the outbreak of the Second Palestinian Intifada in 2000 would the PIJ return to full strength.

Yet even in its hurt condition, the PIJ made trouble.

•   •   •

On July 7, 1995, close to Addis Ababa, the capital of Ethiopia, a blue van veered across the highway, causing a motorcade of limousines from the airport to screech to a halt. Five men armed with AK-47 assault rifles and rocket-propelled grenade launchers, and carrying satchels full of ammunitions and explosives on their backs, jumped out of the van and a car that had been standing nearby. They began spraying one of the armored Mercedes limousines with bullets. Shots were also fired at the car from the roofs of two houses close to the road.

The target of the attack was the president of Egypt, Hosni Mubarak, who had just arrived in Ethiopia for a conference of the Organization of African Unity. "When we reached that road, I sensed that something unnatural was happening," he said later. "They approached our convoy as if they were on a picnic or an outing. . . . No one stopped them." Only several long seconds after the shooting began did Mubarak's bodyguards start firing back, hitting at least three of the attackers. As the gun battle went on, the convoy managed to turn around and extricate the president back to the airport, where he boarded his plane and flew straight back to Egypt. His life was saved apparently because the gunmen directed most of their fire at the wrong car, and because they failed to use their RPGs and explosive charges. Even so, twelve hits were found on Mubarak's car, and one of the rounds had penetrated the supposedly bulletproof vehicle.

The attack on the Egyptian president was one of the first terrorist operations of what has become known as the World Jihad. "From our point of view, it was the watershed," says Yoram Schweitzer, who filled a number of posts in Israeli Military Intelligence and the Mossad before going into academe. "We discovered something entirely new here. This was not an attack that was conceived one day and carried out the next, but was planned and executed on the basis of a new and ramified infrastructure."

It had actually been the Egyptians themselves who first raised fears of a new wave of international terror, emanating not from the interests of any particular state (such as Syria, Iran, Libya, or Iraq) but from the supranational phenomenon of extremist Islam. In semi-official publications in Egypt in 1992, mention was made of *al-Tanzim al-Dawli*, Arabic for "the international organization," a kind of board of directors of Islamic and Palestinian terror groups that opposed the Oslo accords and coordinated worldwide terror activities under various patrons, Iran among them. At that time, these reports were seen by Israeli Military Intelligence's Research Division as just another fake conspiracy dreamed up by the Egyptian media. In hindsight, it appears to have been a lot more than that.

Soon after landing back in Cairo, Mubarak blamed Iran for the attempt on his life. Egypt discreetly asked the CIA to help with an investigation. The Egyptians raised the possibility that elements operating from Sudan had been behind the attack. The CIA's resources in that country were meager, and the Americans therefore in turn asked Israel for assistance.

By the early 1980s Sudan had become the second country in the world, after Iran, to be ruled by extremist Islamists. Its spiritual leader was Dr. Hassan al-Turabi, a religious sage and a graduate of Oxford University. The government itself was controlled by General Omar al-Bashir, who led a military coup in 1989 and has been president since 1993. Al-Turabi was an enigma to the West. A pious Muslim, familiar with European culture, speaking fluent English and French, he explained in his books why there is no contradiction between religious rule and the modern state, and he advocated comprehensive legislation in the spirit of Islam throughout the Arab world. The Islamic state of Sudan would thrive under *Sharia* law, he promised, and other states would imitate it.

On the other hand, al-Turabi also had other aspects, which were interpreted in the West as indicative of a sort of liberalism. He was a great lover of music, appreciated the importance of art and culture, and even spoke of a degree of integration for women in society and activity, recalling that the Prophet Mohammad used to take advice from women. The *Sharia*, according to al-Turabi, would apply only to Muslims. What is more, in a quite revolutionary manner, al-Turabi advocated the creation of a common foundation for the Sunna and the Shi'a, and was ready to implement a series of theological and practical concessions to make such a move possible, though it appeared to many on both sides as unfeasible or even a grave heresy.

Iran hastened to offer oil and development aid to the new regime in Khartoum, ostensibly without demanding anything in return. In October 1990, diplomatic relations between Sudan and Iran were raised to the ambassadorial level, and Ali Akbar Mohtashemi-Pour was named Iran's ambassador to Sudan. In his previous post as ambassador to Syria,

Mohtashemi-Pour had been instrumental in the founding of Hizballah. On October 18, 1991, an international conference in support of the Palestinians opened in Tehran, with over four hundred delegates from sixty countries attending. One of them was Dr. al-Turabi, who was treated with a great deal of respect. Upon his return to Sudan he worked assiduously to boost the operational capabilities of the Islamic guerrilla and terror movements based there, with Iranian aid.

Sudan very quickly became a satellite of the ayatollahs' regime and, according to a U.S. congressional report, a distribution center for Iranian weapons for extremist Islamic organizations. Hundreds of members of the Revolutionary Guards took up residence in Khartoum. The government of al-Turabi and al-Bashir provided a refuge for members of a wide variety of groups: the Abu Nidal Organization, Hamas, the Palestinian Islamic Jihad, the Algerian FIS movement, the Tunisian al Nahda, and sundry Egyptian fanatics. At first they trained on Sudanese army bases, where they were known as "the guests," and not in separate camps. In the 1990s, over a dozen training camps were set up for them. The Revolutionary Guards provided their training, under the supervision of the Iranian Ministry of Intelligence and Security, VEVAK.

In 1990, Israeli intelligence began registering large shipments of arms from Iran being unloaded at Port Sudan—shipments that included weaponry that Sudan had difficulty in acquiring on the world market. According to a Military Intelligence officer who dealt with the matter, the Iranians made no attempt to camouflage the equipment. At that time, Somalia had become a no-man's-land controlled by armed gangs, and Sudan and Iran were preparing to pounce on the opportunity by supplying General Aidid, one of the two main contenders for power, with military and financial aid.

Islamist volunteers from Ethiopia, Eritrea, Kenya, Uganda, and Somalia were training in the camps in Sudan. Dr. Ali al-Hajj, one of al-Turabi's cronies, was responsible for managing the camps and the training of the foreigners. Some of the fighters embarked in fishing boats, landed on deserted beaches in Somalia, and were transferred from there to the war zone in Mogadishu; others were flown by light aircraft that landed at night at airstrips in Somalia; yet others infiltrated into Somalia across its borders with Kenya and Ethiopia.

Beyond securing a geographical basis for its activities, Shi'ite Iran had a further reason to work with the Sunni Muslim regime in Sudan. Every action taken by fanatical Muslims, wherever they are, requires a religious decree, a *fatwa*, issued by a mufti. No terrorist will lift a finger without such permission, and a *fatwa* issued by the Shi'ite leaders of Iran is not valid for a Sunni member of, say, al-Jamaa al-Islamiyya in Egypt, or the Algerian Islamic Salvation Front (Fis). The backing must come from a clergyman of the same persuasion. Therefore, the link with a senior Islamic authority like al-Turabi was vital for the Iranians.

Information about Hamas and Palestinian Islamic Jihad members training in Sudan had begun accumulating in Israel in 1989. Consequently, Military Intelligence, Mossad, and Shin Bet aimed both human and electronic resources at Sudan. After the attempt on Mubarak's life, the Israelis decided to utilize these resources to investigate the attack, and "Operation Sig Vasi'ah" (Hebrew for "Dealings"), a combined effort of the Mossad and Military Intelligence's HUMINT section, Unit 504, was born. The deeper the probe reached, the greater the Israelis' interest grew, and not just because of the help they would be able to give the Egyptians. When Military Intelligence's Research Division collated the findings, they were bound in a thick volume and sent to the CIA and Egyptian intelligence. In both Cairo and Washington, there were many who thought the Israelis were fantasizing—surely Iran wasn't working in Sudan, with a Sunni regime? But it was no fantasy. In fact, Iran was linked with Sunnis in many countries.

Long before the attack on Mubarak, Israeli intelligence had identified close ties between Islamic terrorist elements in Egypt and Department 15 of VEVAK, the Iranian Intelligence Ministry. At the time, the Mossad identified Ayman al-Zawahiri as the most prominent Egyptian "activist," and right up to the time of writing, he is number two on the American government's Most Wanted List, with a $25 million prize on his head, the same amount as for the number one. He had been imprisoned for his part in the assassination of Egyptian president Anwar al-Sadat in 1981, and, after his release, commanded the Egyptian Islamic Jihad (not the same movement as that of Fathi Shkaki, but one with similar ideological and theological characteristics) from abroad. The Egyptians had been trying to lay their hands on al-Zawahiri in order to settle accounts with him, but he managed to get away time after time.

Like many others of his ilk, al-Zawahiri too found asylum in Sudan. Its very long border with Egypt, which could never be sealed, made that country an excellent base to which Jihad members could escape from the Egyptian secret services, which hunted the radicals down ferociously; and from there terror raids could be launched into Egypt. In April 1991, al-Zawahiri paid a clandestine visit to Tehran and asked the Iranians to help overthrow the Egyptian government. In exchange, he offered the Iranians secret information on an Egyptian plan to seize certain islands in the Persian Gulf in a lightning raid, islands in which the Iranians themselves were very interested. The visit ended with the Iranians' promising a number of measures by Department 15 to support and assist his organization. The Egyptian government had scored a considerable number of successes against it, and al-Zawahiri needed money more than anything else. The Iranians agreed to finance him. They also undertook to train his men. Here, the Revolutionary Guard entered the picture, in Iran itself as well as Sudan and Lebanon. Al-Zawahiri sent many men to train in their camps, principally with the Hizballah in Lebanon, under Imad Moughniyeh, whom he met on that visit to Tehran, where he became convinced of the tremendous power of the suicide attack and that this was the method of operation that his organization should adopt. He also picked up from Hizballah the idea of videotaping a declaration by the *shahid* about to embark on his mission of martyrdom.

Following the push that al-Zawahiri's group got from the Iranians, al-Zawahiri unleashed a series of attacks in Egypt. The most ambitious was an attempt to take revenge on the man the movement considered to be responsible for persecuting it: the minister of the interior, Hassan al-Alafi. In August 1993, al-Zawahiri ordered a suicide attack against al-Alafi, to be carried out jointly with Iranians based in Khartoum. A motorcycle carrying two men exploded alongside the minister's car. They were both killed. Al-Alafi escaped with light injuries.

Nevertheless, this attack, together with another carried out by Hamas on April 16, 1993, in Israel, was of great importance, because both disregarded the religious ban backed by many top Sunni leaders against suicide. Although Ayatollah Khomeini had allowed such attacks long before, and although there had been some favorable statements about them by certain Sunni clerics, the taboo had not hitherto been broken. These two incidents broke the dam, and the Iranians achieved their goal of exporting the "poor man's smart bomb," first to the Middle East and then to the entire world.

• • •

It became clear to Israeli intelligence investigators that the gunmen who tried to kill Mubarak were Egyptians who had travelled from Sudan to Ethiopia, with support and funding from Iran. The operational commander of the action was Rifai Taha, operations chief of the Egyptian Jihad. Under him, as commander in the field, was Mustafa Hamza, known as Abu Hazem. But the Israelis realized that the plotters were part of a broader network. Further enquiries revealed that al-Zawahiri and his cohorts were part of a large group of Islamic extremists: veterans of the guerrilla war against the Soviets in Afghanistan who shared the goal of carrying out Islamic action all over the world. They had found refuge in Sudan. The Iranians were supporting them from afar.

These men are now famous, of course, in the wake of 9/11 and so many other battlefields in the global war on terror. Yet even now, the story of the emergence of al-Qaeda is usually told with only passing reference to Iran. Khomeini's 1979 revolution is often described as an inspiring event for Islamic extremists; but after that, the typical history connects the Soviet-Afghan War with Pakistan, Saudi Arabia, and the United States. From there, groups of Sunnis connect with one another from places like Yemen and Kuwait; they receive support from Sudan; they are inspired by (and involved in) places like Somalia and Chechnya, and so on. All are Sunni, working in Sunni countries. The Shi'a connections between Iran and Hizballah are treated as a sideshow that focuses only on Israel.

That history is wrong.

In Sudan, Ayman al-Zawahiri forged close links with various other elements who had found refuge there, and through him, ties were established between the Afghani vets and Iran. Superficially, it may seem that an alliance between these mostly Sunni fighters and the Shi'ites in Tehran is not logical. These are historical adversaries in Islam, and the Iranian regime never got along with the Taliban in Afghanistan, for example. Nevertheless, their common interests brought about an alliance of convenience under the aegis of al-Turabi's Sudanese regime.

Within this group of Afghani veterans, the Israelis identified one man in particular: a Saudi contractor who had been expelled from his country and became something of a well-connected mover and shaker in both Afghanistan and Sudan, while at the same time keeping up his building and trading business to double as a cover for his clandestine activities. His name was Osama bin Laden. The name of one of his construction companies was al-Qaeda. It became clear to Israeli intelligence that bin Laden was allied with al-Zawahiri and was deeply involved in the attack on Mubarak.

Mustafa Hamza, the commander of the operation, turned out to have been one of bin Laden's men, whom he dispatched to help his friend al-Zawahiri. A number of meetings took place in bin Laden's house, at which al-Zawahiri hosted the officers of his organization, the Jihad, along with their counterparts from the rival Egyptian movement, al-Jamaa al-Islamiyya, so they could join forces for certain assassinations and other attacks.

Further information strengthened apprehension that bin Laden saw Israel as a prime target for future attacks. Bin Laden himself, incidentally, had not been overjoyed about al-Turabi's having to take refuge in Sudan. As described in detail in the comprehensive history of bin Laden *The Looming Towers* by Lawrence Wright, he had reservations about some of al-Turabi's beliefs and customs, which seemed bizarre to him, but he certainly shared his main idea. In Sudan, he published a declaration to his followers informing them that the two rival factions in Islam must unite against their sole common enemy—the West.

Bin Laden responded favorably to al-Zawahiri's effort to get him to establish links with Iran, and the latter became not only his close friend but also his personal physician (the businessman-terrorist suffers from a number of ailments, including rheumatism). Bin Laden sent some of his senior aides to train in Iran and with the Hizballah in Lebanon. Imad Mougniyeh came to Khartoum to meet him, and told him about the enormous effect of the suicide attacks against the Americans and the French in the early 1980s in Lebanon.

From this point on, Moughniyeh became a major connection point between Iran and al-Qaeda. We know this thanks to the testimony of an Egyptian-born American and former Green Beret sergeant, Ali Mohammad, who was arrested on suspicion of involvement in the bombing of the U.S. embassies in Kenya and Tanzania. He confessed that for a long time he had tried to penetrate an American intelligence agency on behalf of bin Laden, but had failed. He had moved to the United States, obtained citizenship, and joined a special force of the U.S. Navy at Fort Bragg as an expert on the Middle East. In 1989, he travelled to Af-

ghanistan and joined the Islamic Jihad and bin Laden. He began training al-Qaeda terrorists in the use of explosives and in intelligence-
gathering techniques for use in attacks on American targets.

Mohammad testified to the FBI that he had personally taken care of
the security arrangements for meetings in Sudan between bin Laden and
Moughniyeh. As a result of this meeting, Hizballah supplied al-Qaeda
with explosives instruction, and Iran used Hizballah to provide bin
Laden with bombs. Much of the al-Qaeda training was carried out in
camps in Iran run by VEVAK, Ali Mohammad said.

The group in Sudan kept in close touch with Afghanistan veterans all
over the world and worked tirelessly to set up global links and networks
for terrorist training, fund-raising, infrastructure, and more. "The feeling was that something really big was cooking here, very different from
what we had known so far," says one of the Mossad officers who monitored Sudan at the time. "This wasn't a state dispatching terrorists, but a
terror organization that engendered itself." Mossad gave it the name
"World Jihad," and, in late 1995, created a special desk to deal with it.
Israeli Military Intelligence and the Mossad became the first Western
intelligence agencies to identify the menace of al-Qaeda. (The CIA
would not set up its own bin Laden station until 1996, just before bin
Laden's August 1996 decalaration of war against the United States.)

The conclusions of Operation Sig Vasi'ah were brought to the attention of political leaders, and in consultation with the prime minister, it
was decided that the Mossad should begin gathering additional intelligence and try to disrupt al-Qaeda in Sudan. It emerged that bin Laden's
secretary at the al-Qaeda Construction Company was a close confidante
of his. She had followed him to Sudan, leaving her family in a Middle
Eastern country with few overt ties to Israel, but many covert ones.
Despite the hostility between Israel and the Arab states, since its establishment Israel has maintained profoundly secret relations with some of
them—relations that are in stark contrast to the public policies and
declarations of those countries. Against a background of common interests and apprehensions, Israel formed regional alliances, with the Mossad
responsible for the covert links.

Senior intelligence officials of Israel and the secretary's home country
decided to launch a three-phase operation. First, the woman's family was
used to lure her home for a visit. During that visit, local intelligence operatives persuaded her to cooperate by giving her family a government per-

mit to open a business. In the second phase of the operation, she was supposed to gather as much information as possible on the activities of the al-Qaeda Construction Company and its boss. Finally, the secretary was supposed to kill Osama bin Laden, possibly by poison.

The woman agreed to carry out the plan. Tragically, however, the scheme fell victim to the Middle East "peace" process. Her home country froze all active cooperation with Israel, including the project to get rid of bin Laden, in the wake of a series of acts of terror and hooliganism by Jewish extremists against Arabs in the West Bank and Israel's failure to make progress toward a solution of the Palestinian conflict. Unit 504 tried to activate the secretary on its own, but failed. As far as Israel knows, this is the closest any intelligence service has ever come to the world's public enemy number one. Today, those in the know are still bemoaning the failure of Operation Sig Vasi'ah. "We could have saved ourselves many headaches, and the world great grief," says one Mossad officer.

Sudan's backing for terror had been uncovered two years before the attempt to kill Mubarak, when its intelligence service's involvement in a plot to blow up the UN Building in New York City was exposed. The plan was part of Sheikh Omar Abdul Rahman's grand scheme.

Following this, the United States declared a boycott of Sudan, and placed it on the American blacklist of terror-supporting states. The uncovering of its role in the Mubarak attack and other operations only made matters worse. The aid from Iran never had any impact on the country's dire economic situation, especially as Iran itself was approaching financial catastrophe and had asked the Sudanese to pay back some of the large amounts Tehran had invested in the Sudanese road system and industry and in the Sudan-based terror organizations. The treasury in Khartoum was so empty that the government found it difficult to pay its debts to bin Laden himself for the road paving and earthworks that his company carried out there.

For its part, Egypt threatened that if Sudan didn't throw al-Zawahiri out and close down his training camps, it would take military measures. In southern Sudan, a civil was war raging, with the government army fighting the rebels of the SPLA (Sudan People's Liberation Army). This assumed the proportions of a humanitarian catastrophe in early 1996, and the non-Muslim population demanded political and religious autonomy, and a share of the country's oil revenues.

Omar al-Bashir and Hassan al-Turabi realized that if they did not take immediate action, they were at risk of losing control of the government, or Sudan would cease to exist as a unified political entity. As a first step, despite the pleadings of the Iranians, al-Zawahiri was expelled. Al-Turabi used a death sentence that the mass murderer had issued against two children who were caught spying for the Egyptians as a justification, claiming that it had been an act of heresy. Then, in May 1996, after heavy American and Saudi pressure, Osama bin Laden was also told to leave, and he returned to Afghanistan. At the same time, the training camps were closed down, and the members of the organizations had to find other asylums.

Yet the link between Iran and the incipient al-Qaeda was strong, and independent of Sudanese hospitality. Iranian intelligence and bin Laden began moving the "refugees" from Sudan to five other countries: Yemen, Pakistan, Afghanistan, Iran, and Lebanon. In the camps where they were housed, al-Qaeda as we know it today was born. Bin Laden himself set up his new headquarters in Afghanistan.

Iran's attempts to export the Islamic Revolution were not limited to the Middle East and North Africa. Seizing an opportunity to aid a Muslim minority in distress, Iran became involved in the various conflicts in the Balkans as well. Here too, Tehran's interests converged with those of bin Laden.

On December 5, 2001, a senior Mossad official came to the office of Munir Alibabic, chief of the intelligence services of Bosnia and Herzegovina. He was there to be briefed on the preliminary findings of an investigation conducted in Bosnia into the World Jihad movement in the wake of the 9/11 attacks. Alibabic spoke of his urgent need for the West's assistance. The Mossad man was surprised at the depth of Iran's penetration into Alibabic's vulnerable nation. "Our country has become a playing field, an arena in the struggle for influence between Shi'ite Iran and Sunni Saudi Arabia," the Mossad official was told. The two men agreed that Israel and Bosnia would cooperate in the war against terror.

The roots of an Islamic terror base in the Balkans can be traced to the civil war of the 1990s, when the Western world was standing on the sidelines. Daniel Korski, a graduate of Cambridge University's International Relations Center, has researched Balkan terror in the wake of the civil war. "The world in general and the United States in particular," Korski says, "is not comfortable when it recalls the circumstances that made the Republic of Bosnia-Herzegovina dependent upon Arab generosity and Iranian weaponry during the war, not to mention what made it welcome up to three thousand Muslim volunteers into its armed forces, in the absence of any other saviour. Outside of that country, there is very little public awareness of the circumstances in which Bosnia found itself with a heritage of mujahideen."

Beginning with the rule of Khomeini, Iran has continued to preach and practice the export of the revolution through assistance to "liberation movements" in the Muslim world, but only after the end of the Cold War did this begin to seem possible in Europe. Iran was not interested in "crawling like a worm [into other countries] but wish[ed] to enter through the front door, like an invited guest," said Khomeini. The invitations picked up after the collapse of the Soviet Union.

The Communist and atheistic one-party state in Yugoslavia fell in its wake, in 1991. Delegations from the Muslim world promptly came to Muslim areas in the Balkans. Predominantly from Iran and Saudi Arabia, they brought large amounts of money with which to restore and rebuild neglected and ruined mosques, and to construct classrooms for religious instruction. In many cases, the Muslim aid was much more abundant and effective than that given by the West. James Woolsey, director of the CIA at the time, said, "We looked with great concern at the very great amount of money coming in, especially from Iran, for the promotion of a very particular type of Islam in the Balkans."

There are many more observant Muslims in Bosnia today than there were in 1992. Historical mosques are no longer museums for tourists, but houses of worship. New mosques, along with centers for Islamic study, have sprung up all over, built now in the ornate style of the Persian Gulf rather than the local tradition. Anyone walking the streets of Sarajevo or Zenica today will see, alongside the girls in shorts, quite a few in traditional garb. Pork is a rarity in restaurants.

The well-known turmoil of the Balkans in the 1990s—ethnic cleansing against Muslims, civil war, the intervention of Serbian dictator Slobodan Milosevic, and the perceived indifference of the West—led the leader of the Bosnian Muslims (and the first president of Bosnia and Herzegovina) Alija Izetbegović to appeal to Muslim states for assistance. Iran and Saudi Arabia responded happily, and helped circumvent an embargo that was preventing Bosnia from legally arming itself. Funds from Iran were channeled through the Iranian embassies in Sarajevo and Vienna, and according to Mossad sources, arms deals were arranged there. The airfield at Visoko, northwest of Sarajevo, served as a secret landing place for arms shipments from Iran, bringing light arms, anti-aircraft ammunition, and antitank missiles to Muslim fighters in the growing three-way civil war between Muslims, Serbs, and Croatians.

According to British intelligence reports, some two hundred advisers from the Iranian Republican Guard were in Bosnia during that period, and from 1,000 to 3,000 volunteers—including some from Hizballah—came to help the Muslims. At first, they fought as disorganized militias; but soon a special unit was established for the volunteers: the al-Mujahid Brigade, part of the 7th Division of the Bosnian army's Third Corps. The Iranian Revolutionary Guards took it upon themselves to train these recruits. Izetbegović named himself an honorary commander of the brigade. "No one asked them to come to Bosnia," he said of these volunteers, "but it was impossible to ask them to leave, because most of them had good intentions: to help a people that had been attacked and were facing danger."

The Islamic volunteers made a valuable military and moral contribution to the Bosnian army. They were trained; most of them were disciplined; and they inspired the local soldiers with their enthusiasm. Some of the volunteers had been eyewitnesses to what had happened only a few years before—how highly trained and motivated guerrillas had managed to drive the mighty and aggressive Red Army out of Afghanistan.

Bosnian intelligence is in possession of a videotape showing the mujahideen in training and in action. The images are very similar to those of al-Qaeda's training camps. There are also records of combat with Serb forces, with a special section devoted to martyrs, including photos of them alive and then pictures of their corpses.

During that time in Bosnia, Iran's relationship with al-Qaeda expanded, though it was tinged with suspicion. It entered a new phase after the Dayton Peace Agreement of August 1995 brought an end to the fighting in Bosnia and transformed the state into a federation between Bosnia-Herzegovina, with a two-thirds Muslim majority, and the Srpska Republic, with a Serbian majority. The accord provided for the breakup of the foreign volunteer units, which was carried out; but Bosnia did almost nothing, until 9/11, to oust the mujahideen themselves from the country. Some one thousand of the foreign volunteers remained there after the war. Some were in the cities and villages; others established their own new communities, taking in hundreds of local supporters and building an infrastructure based solely in *Sharia*. In the village of Bocina, for example, the mujahideen settled in the homes of Christians who had been driven out, and instituted a strict religious regime, closer to that of Taliban-controlled villages in Afghanistan than to anything in twenty-first-century Europe.

To this day, Bosnia is an ideal location for the activities of Iranian intelligence and Osama bin Laden. The country is a magnet for international crime, including the drug trade, trafficking in humans, smuggling of all varieties, and money laundering. There are four hundred land crossings connecting Bosnia to its neighbors, only about ten of which are under real police control. Even the airfields came under proper border control only in 2002, thanks to the gift of an advanced computer system from the United States. "I have to admit regretfully that Bosnia is indeed a dangerous place," says its director of intelligence services, Munir Alibabic. "There's a group of terrorists here that is connected to extremist Islamic organizations across the world, and to Iran, and who present a serious problem not only to us but to all of Europe."

The networks set up by the Revolutionary Guards in the Balkans, especially in Bosnia and Albania, continuously initiate attempts at terrorist operations and supply shelter to wanted terrorists. Among those who have found refuge there are the wife and son of Sabri al-Banna, better known as Abu Nidal (whose death in Baghdad in 2003 was presented as a suicide). Abu Nidal had been the former leader of the Fatah Revolutionary Command, considered the most dangerous terror organization in the world during the 1980s and early 1990s.

Hiyam al-Bitar, Abu Nidal's wife, moved to Bosnia in 1998. In that year, the Swiss attorney general and public prosecutor Carla del Ponte ordered a secret investigation into an account in a Zurich bank, where some $15 million had been deposited under the name of Hiyam al-Bitar. Del Ponte suspected that the money came from Iran, and was to be used to fund terror operations. The Swiss were about to issue an international warrant for the woman's arrest, but at the last moment, astoundingly, she received Bosnian citizenship. Bosnian law forbids the extradition of its citizens to other countries. Abu Nidal's son-in-law, Adnan Buzar al-Banna, also wanted by Switzerland, is the deputy head of the Careva mosque, one of Sarajevo's most important houses of worship. The chief imam at that mosque was, according to Bosnian testimonies, responsible for particularly cruel atrocities against the Serbs.

An indictment submitted in 2003 against three former senior officials of Bosnian intelligence (AID), including its former chief Bakir Alispahic, and two of his top aides, describes how they are alleged to have arranged the citizenship for Nidal's wife. The three are also charged with maintaining illegal links with the Iranian Intelligence Ministry, selling secrets to Tehran, and planning terror operations. When Munir Alibabic took over as chief of Bosnia's intelligence services, he ordered that all of his predecessors' links with Iran be investigated. The findings of the probe, in a 100-page report, revolve around raids carried out by SFOR, the UN's stabilization force, at a number of mountainous locations in Bosnia, among them the small village of Pogorelica. There, in an enormous wooden hut, which from the outside looks like a ski lodge, the Bosnian intelligence chiefs are alleged to have run their own private school for terror, under Iranian sponsorship.

Inside this hut there were classrooms and a large armory containing explosives, pistols, sniper rifles, rocket launchers, grenades, and ammunition. Some of the bombs found there were concealed in plastic playthings, such as toy cars and helicopters and ice-cream cones. A glass jar of beans had a detonator activated by pressure under the lid. It was a simple device—water was added to the beans so that they would swell up and activate the charge. The weapons and ammunition were many and varied, ranging from Russian AK-47s with regular rounds to rifles with telescopic sights and silencers, explosive dumdum bullets, and unmarked magazines, so that their owners could not be traced.

In a file on one of the tables were plans for kidnapping a Serbian liaison officer in the UN Building in Sarajevo. There were photographs of the building, which was guarded by French UN troops, as well as detailed sketches of escape routes and defenses inside the building. Also found in the hut were cardboard models of houses and buildings, used as instructional aids in the planning of attacks on civilian targets.

At first, the Bosnian authorities denied that all this meant that the hut in Pogorelica served as a school for terror. They maintained that it was a legitimate espionage training facility for government agents. But piles of documents in Farsi, photographs of the Ayatollah Khomeini, and the fact that three Iranians were caught there, indicated otherwise. One of the Iranians carried a diplomatic passport.

Sudan and Bosnia were not the only places where Iran and al-Qaeda worked together. In February 1998, when the veterans of the Egyptian Islamic Jihad, headed by Ayman al-Zawahiri, united with the al-Qaeda movement, the link between al-Qaeda and Iran was strengthened. Al-Zawahiri was responsible for planning the attacks on 9/11, and is marked as the successor to Osama bin Laden in the event of his death. He is the chief go-between for that organization and Iran. According to information gathered by NSA and Mossad, he travelled to Iran several times after the war in Bosnia, as the guest of Security and Intelligence Minister Ali Fallahian and the chief of Iranian operations abroad, Ahmad Wahidi. Materiel and men were transferred from Iran to al-Qaeda in Afghanistan, using Hizballah as the mediator. The Revolutionary Guards also gave financial and logistical assistance to an al-Qaeda terror cell that was active in Hamburg, Germany.

American intelligence agents believe that Iranian aid is vital to al-Qaeda. Despite the organization's good relations with Pakistan until 9/11, every now and again, Pakistani intelligence (ISI) would decide to toss a bone to the Americans in the form of terror suspects in that area. Ramzi Ahmad Yousef, who was involved in the 1993 bombing of the World Trade Center, was arrested in Pakistan in February 1995 and extradited, as was Mir Amal Kanzi, who opened fire at CIA headquarters in Langley and killed two security guards. Bin Laden and his movement found Iran to be more reliable. After al-Zawahiri's arrival in Afghanistan, he was helped on many occasions by the Iranian authorities to pass weaponry and reinforcements to the al-Qaeda forces across the border between the two countries.

In Tehran itself, al-Qaeda's interests were represented by a man named Gulbuddin Hekmatyar, no stranger to American and British intelligence. In the 1980s, he had headed one of the mujahideen factions in Afghanistan, and he had been one of the first to be recruited by British and American secret agents to wage guerrilla warfare against the Soviets. Like most of the mujahideen, however, he felt no need to show gratitude to them for their help. He saw them as heretical interlopers who were to be driven out someday. After the Russian retreat, Hekmatyar clashed with the Taliban and was not included in the government that they set up. But neither did he get on well with the rival Northern Alliance. Instead, he found a place for himself in Tehran.

Another case in which the Americans believe that al-Qaeda received assistance from Iran was the operation for the assassination of Ahmad Shah Masoud, the supreme military commander of the Northern Alliance in Afghanistan, who was at the time being backed by the United States.

Bin Laden gave the order to eliminate Masoud as a kind of gesture to his Taliban allies, and also because Masoud had warned the Americans of a terrorist attack of vast proportions that bin Laden was planning, and that indeed occurred two days after the assassination, when the Twin Towers were brought down and the Pentagon hit. Iran's help was extended to him, according to information that reached the FBI in the course of the investigation, despite its bitter rivalry with the Taliban.

The Iranian Embassy in Brussels helped two Tunisian al-Qaeda assassins obtain counterfeit Belgian passports and other documents, which they used to enter northern Afghanistan in the guise of journalists come to interview Masoud. This was a highly professional assassination operation, in which daring, planning, originality, sacrifice, and a great deal of patience all came into play. The Iranians also sent the two men to procure the camera used for the assassination, which had been stolen from a French journalist, and in which the explosives used in the hit were concealed. Soon after their interview with Masoud began, the two blew themselves up, taking Masoud (who died at the hospital later) and one of his top aides with them.

Since 9/11, Iran has been perceived as behaving cautiously vis-à-vis al-Qaeda, for obvious reasons. Investigation of the 9/11 attacks has not found any Iranian involvement and Iran has no desire to be linked to al-Qaeda activities. On the other hand, neither does it refrain from granting shelter to members of the organization. The Saudi-owned Arabic newspaper published in London, *Asharq Alawsat*, has reported that senior al-Qaeda members have spent long periods of time in Iran, including Osama bin Laden's son Saad; Saif al-Adel, the head of al-Qaeda's military wing; and Abu Khaled, the brother of Khalid al-Islambuli, the killer of Anwar al-Sadat. According to the paper, al-Islambuli spent five years in southeastern Iran under the protection of the Revolutionary Guards, with Mustafa Hamza, who headed the assassination attempt against Mubarak in Ethiopia. Another Egyptian who found shelter in Iran was Ahmad Hussein Agiza, leader of the extremist Egyptian movement Talaa Fateh al-Islami. After five years he was deported to Sweden, which extradited him to Egypt, where he was sentenced to life imprisonment.

Several Arabic sources reported that Iranian president Khatami was surprised during 2003 to discover that al-Qaeda networks were operating in Tehran and two other Iranian cities. He ordered his intelligence minister Ali Yunesi to round them up—an important fact that shows disagreement within the Iranian government on this issue. In another instance of such tensions, *Asharq Alawsat* reported that following the discovery of the role of Saif al-Adel, number three in al-Qaeda, in the attacks in Saudi Arabia early in 2003, Yunesi ordered his arrest together with the other al-Qaeda members—yet they managed to get away, with the help of the Revolutionary Guards, on May 14, 2003. The same report said that in June 2003, President Khatami learned that Ayman al-Zawahiri was living in a government-owned house controlled by the intelligence arm of the Revolutionary Guards on the Iranian-Afghani-Pakistan border. Khatami immediately ordered the arrest of al-Zawahiri and his transfer to a military prison in Tehran; but he, too, managed to flee the country with the help of his friends in the Revolutionary Guards. Iranian foreign minister Kamal Kharazi had declared in February 2003 that Iran had expelled over five hundred infiltrators suspected of being linked to al-Qaeda. It appears to be true.

Iran has been careful to keep its distance, but there is no question that many of its officials sympathize with al-Qaeda. So, how should the West interpret Iran's distancing itself from the world's most famous terrorists? Is it purely tactical? In early October 2006, Sunni Muslim Web sites associated with the Jihadist movement in Iraq published an Iranian document classified as "top secret." Dated May 2001, it reveals high-level links between the Iranian intelligence apparatus belonging to the office of the Supreme Leader, Ali Khamenei, and al-Qaeda. Both Israeli and American intelligence agents who examined the document said that it appeared to be authentic, and that its publication was probably meant to embarrass the Iranians, who had dared to cut off their relations with al-Qaeda around that time. Signed by Ali Akbar Nateq Nouri, Khamenei's intelligence chief adviser, it reads:

The Islamic Republic of Iran, the Intelligence Apparatus of the Supreme Leader—Top Secret.

Date: May 14, 2001

Reference: 4-325-80/s/m

By: Head of the Intelligence Apparatus of the Supreme Leader

To: Head of Operations Unit No. 43 [in the Iranian Intelligence Ministry]

Re: Orders regarding the decisions of the Honorable Leader [Khamenei]

[Dear] Hujjat Al-Islam Wal-Muslimin [Mustafa] Pourkanad [director general of Operations Unit No. 43]

We wish your dedicated and courageous team every success. The results [described] in your recent reports have been examined, along with other opinions. After consideration, and in order to remove the existing lack of clarity regarding support for al-Qaeda's future plans, the Honorable Leader has emphasized that the battle against the global arrogance headed by the U.S. and Israel is an integral part of our Islamic government, and constitutes its primary goal. Damaging their economic systems, discrediting all other institutions of these two allied enemies of the Islamic government [in Iran] as part of political confrontation [with them], and undermining the stability and security [of the U.S. and Israel] are obligatory duties that must be carried out.

The Honorable [Leader Khamenei] stressed the need for each of you to be vigilant in his field of activity, and asks you to be particularly attentive. He also stressed [the need] to be alert to the [possible] negative future consequences of this cooperation [between Iran and al-Qaeda].

The Honorable [Khamenei] said that this struggle must be stepped up by tightening the collaboration with other security and intelligence apparatuses in Iran and with supporters outside Iran, thereby hindering the enemy's steadily expanding activities.

[Khamenei further instructed] that in carrying out your duties, you must operate under the direct supervision of the security division of the headquarters of the organization [i.e., the intelligence apparatus of the

Supreme Leader]. Naturally, identifying [potential] damage is the responsibility of the vigilant and diligent Unit [No. 43].

It has also been decided that, in the upcoming meetings, discussions must be held in order to formulate clear goals and remove the main obstacles and difficulties in achieving these goals and in promoting the issue of expanding the collaboration with the fighters of al-Qaeda and Hizballah [Lebanon].

Finally, I wish to convey [Khamenei's] full satisfaction with Unit [No. 43] and his full support in the implementation of its future plans. The Honorable [Khamenei] is aware of the important and dangerous [nature of] the tasks you perform. [He] emphasizes that, with regard to cooperation with al-Qaeda, no traces must be left that might have negative and irreversible consequences, and that [the activity] must be limited to the existing contacts with [Hizballah Operations Officer Imad] Mughniyeh and [bin Laden's deputy Ayman] al-Zawahiri.

May Allah grant you success . . .

[Seal and Signature] Ali Akbar Nateq Nouri

PART IV

# THE SECOND COMING
# OF HIZBALLAH

# CHAPTER 15

# A Divine Victory:
# Hizballah Takes Lebanon

The figures tell the whole story.

In 1986, Imad Moughniyeh began bolstering his power as the man in charge of Hizballah's special operations. Backed by the guidance, money, trust, and cooperation of Iran, he orchestrated more and more attacks that inflicted more and more casualties, many of them fatal, on the Israeli forces in Lebanon. It was a gradually escalating process until the end of 1988, a year in which twenty Israeli soldiers were killed. Then, under pressure from Syrian intelligence, which feared that he was slipping out of its control, he was forced to flee to Iran. In 1989, with Moughniyeh out of commission, the Israel Defense Forces' fatalities dropped to two. Contributing to this decline, no doubt, was the civil war between Hizballah and Amal; but Israeli intelligence sources are convinced that Moughniyeh's absence had just as much to do with the relative quiet.

In May 1991, a truce of a kind was reached between the two Shi'ite factions, Amal and Hizballah, enabling Hizballah to go back to channeling its energies against Israel. Shortly afterward, Hizballah's spiritual leader, Ayatollah Mohammad Hussein Fadlallah, proclaimed that the Islamic resistance was back on track. "It would not be wrong to presume that the Islamic resistance will be able to cause the enemy so many casualties that they will be forced to withdraw from the Security Zone, just as they withdrew from the other parts of the south in 1983 to 1985," he stated. He assured the fighters of the Islamic resistance that it was they and not the diplomats who would write the next chapter of history.

In mid-1990, Moughniyeh returned to Lebanon, with an entourage of fellow terrorists. From then on, the number of Israeli casualties began rising, peaking in 1997, when thirty-three soldiers were killed and hundreds wounded. Altogether between June 11, 1985, when Israel completed its first withdrawal from Lebanon, and November 26, 2000, when it vacated the Security Zone, 250 Israelis were killed. Moughniyeh has a lot of blood on his hands.

In August 1990, about a month after Moughniyeh came back to Lebanon from Tehran, Saddam Hussein invaded Kuwait, sparking the first Gulf War between the United States and Iraq. Moughniyeh's beloved brother-in-law, Mustafa Badr al-Din, was still in jail in Kuwait at the outset of the invasion, but he took advantage of the chaos, managing to escape and find refuge in the Iranian Embassy in Kuwait City. Members of the Revolutionary Guards conveyed him to Tehran and then back to Beirut, where he was reunited with Moughniyeh at long last.

Badr al-Din immediately resumed working with Hizballah, and also took part in the negotiations with Giandomenico Picco, the UN Secretary-General's special envoy, for the release of hostages held in Lebanon in 1991. In Hizballah's internal code, Badr al-Din was known as "Elias." Moughniyeh's second deputy, Ibrahim Akil, was "Tahsin." Also operating with Moughniyeh was Haj Khalil Kharb, who was Hizballah's commander in the south of Lebanon. Later, he would set up Unit 1800, which was responsible for Hizballah's war against Israel.

It was this group that established the secret body known as Hizballah's Special Research Apparatus, which was behind most of Hizballah's "quality" operations both inside and outside Lebanon in the early 1990s. The men of "Special Research" were the pride of Iranian intelligence, Hizballah's crack special forces, the ones who had attacked French and American targets in the 1980s. Altogether, they were some two to four hundred of the best and toughest fighters, all trained in Iran.

Moughniyeh was determined that the Special Research Apparatus would be impenetrable to Israeli intelligence, so he isolated it from the rest of Hizballah. Only the top echelon was aware of its activities. Moughniyeh believed that Israel monitored the militia's cell phones, so he ordered his men not to carry them, or to change them frequently. Iranian intelligence built Moughniyeh two independent telephone exchanges, in a bid to avoid surveillance. And conversely, the Special Research Apparatus set up its own small team of Hebrew-speaking Palestinians to tap into Israeli networks.

In Israeli Military Intelligence, Moughniyeh was spoken of as a "field security psychopath," meaning he was absolutely crazy about maintaining security. They meant it as a sign of respect. Whenever he suspected that the Israelis knew something about an upcoming Hizballah operation, he would switch the entire communications setup, lest the enemy listen in.

Israeli attempts to listen in on Hizballah communications were foiled time and again by Moughniyeh's preventative steps. Without useful signals intelligence—when intercepted messages are in unreadable code, or when an enemy stops using electronic communication—human intelligence is the only alternative. Unfortunately, there was none to be had, because Israel had neither agents nor informants inside Moughniyeh's unit.

Throughout the 1990s, Moughniyeh's fingerprints were spotted on many operations. An internal "top-secret" Israeli Military Intelligence document from 1995 reads: "Iran is aided by Hizballah's operational infrastructure abroad, which is based mainly on Shi'ite expatriates through the Islamic Jihad apparatus of Imad Moughniyeh, for the purpose of attacks. It is to be noted that recently links have been tightened between Iranian intelligence and Moughniyeh's apparatus, which helps Iran locate candidates from Islamic and Palestinian organizations for training in Iran or Lebanon. It appears that Imad Moughniyeh has a role in the organization of this training."

Sources in British intelligence claim that Moughniyeh was used by the Iranians to supply funds to the Palestinian Islamic Jihad. He also supplied the Islamic Jihad with operational intelligence that enabled them to plan an attack on a convoy in which the commander of Israel's Lebanese Liaison Unit, Brigadier General Micha Tamir, and other senior officers, were travelling on April 6, 1992. It was a very carefully planned military operation, which, luckily for the Israelis, was thwarted only thanks to the quick intervention of the crews of two Merkava tanks that shelled the house where the guerrillas had set up their ambush. Tamir himself directed the Israeli forces under fire. Two Israeli soldiers were killed, and several others wounded, including a colonel. The guerrillas apparently had been told by an informant that the head of Israel's Northern Command, Major General Yitzhak Mordechai, would be travelling in the convoy. Mordechai had indeed planned to be there, but changed his mind.

By late 1994, Mossad had had enough. On December 21, 1994,

Fouad Moughniyeh, Imad's brother, a shopkeeper and a low-level Hizballah operative, was the target of a car bomb in South Beirut. It was nine years after another brother, a bodyguard for Sheikh Fadlallah, was killed in a botched attempt on his boss by the CIA. This time, the damage wasn't accidental. Fouad was the intended victim. He and three other people were killed, and fifteen seriously injured, at about 5 p.m. in a crowded Shi'ite neighborhood. Police investigators said that a 50-kilogram explosive device had gone off under a car parked outside Fouad's store. Lebanese intelligence later gathered evidence which stated that the car's owners, a local couple, "parked the car near Fouad's store. Then the man entered the store to make sure Fouad was there, shook hands with him and went hastily back to the car, and then detonated the charge."

Fouad's funeral was held the next day. Imad, sensing a trap, did not go. Hizballah issued a statement: "There is no doubt as to the identity of the criminal hand that committed this crime against civilians in a shopping area in the al-Safir neighborhood in Beirut. Today, after repeated threats, the Zionist enemy and his destructive agencies carried out a despicable crime against a number of people while they were doing their shopping."

Accompanying the long struggle between Israel and its terrorist enemies has been a running debate about the morality of both sides. Israel's defenders cannot stand it when critics charge that each side is equally culpable in the cycle of violence. They insist that there is a crucial distinction between targeting civilians, as terrorists often do, and targeting militants, notwithstanding any "collateral damage" caused by strikes against Hizballah or Hamas leaders. In practice, however, each side often borrows methods from the other. Hizballah often targets the Israeli military. And in the case of the 1994 operation, Mossad killed a low-level brother in hopes of luring Moughniyeh to a crowded funeral. It was the brainchild of Major General Meir Dagan, who was then head of the operations branch of the IDF. He would be appointed Mossad director in 2002. There are still those who criticize the "idiotic operation" of 1994.

A joint investigation by Hizballah and the Lebanese military focused on a number of suspects in the killing of Fouad Moughniyeh. Two had already left the country. Another, by the name of Ahmad Khalak, left Beirut for the Far East because he sensed that he was in danger. He was a Palestinian of enormous bodily dimensions who had, according to the indictment against him, been recruited by the Mossad after Israel's invasion of Lebanon in 1982 and had served the Israelis in a number of special operations.

Imad Moughniyeh had a long memory. One day in March 1996, an agent of Moughniyeh's, a Lebanese policeman, invited Khalak (who had meanwhile returned to Lebanon) to lunch at the home of a drug dealer, Ramzi Nahara, in the village of Ein Ibel. Nahara had been a longtime Israeli agent, and Khalak trusted him. He was not aware that by that time, Nahara had crossed over to work with Hizballah. (Israel would settle accounts with him a few years later, when he turned the ignition in his car and was blown apart.) During the luncheon, Khalak was drugged and put into the baggage compartment of the policeman's van. Moughniyeh wanted to ask him a few questions, and then have him prosecuted in a show trial. The policeman had free passage at the roadblocks between the south and the rest of the country, and he smuggled the sleeping Khalak to Beirut.

At the same time, Lebanese police rounded up several of Khalak's fellow suspects and his wife, Hanan. She was on her way to the airport to flee to Cyprus when they grabbed her. A Beirut newspaper reporting on her arrest cited "knowledgeable official sources" as saying that she was part of the ring that had planned Fouad Moughniyeh's assassination at a meeting in Cyprus with a senior Mossad officer, who had paid Khalak $100,000 for the job. Khalak was grilled by Hizballah and Lebanese Military Intelligence, prior to a trial at which he was found guilty of murder and treason.

On September 21, 1996, Khalak was executed by firing squad in Beirut. His wife was tried separately as an accomplice in the plot and an Israeli agent and sentenced to fifteen years' hard labor.

Imad Moughniyeh now had had two brothers killed by American and Israeli assassination operations. He himself remained at large, and in control of Hizballah's elite special forces. The attention of the CIA had been diverted by the 1993 attack on the World Trade Center, when a crude but massive truck bomb detonated in the garage beneath the towers. As the agency would uncover, the attack was the work of the elements who would later form al-Qaeda, not Hizballah. In the years ahead, Osama bin Laden would replace Imad Moughniyeh as America's most wanted terrorist.

Yet the CIA did not forget about Moughniyeh. On April 7, 1995, the Americans learned that he was flying in a Middle East Airlines plane

called for strikes at Hizballah bases within civilian centers, in order to drive the population northward out of the area.

The operation lasted a week. During the first few days, the international community reacted with restraint, but as the number of civilian casualties mounted, so did the criticism of Israel. When Israel and Syria reached the brink of a clash, U.S. secretary of state Warren Christopher managed to engineer a cease-fire. Syria claimed that Hizballah agreed not to fire any more rockets into Israel, and Israel promised to refrain from shelling Lebanese villages north of the Security Zone, "unless IDF forces had been fired at from that location." These understandings were vague and unwritten, and no supervisory or enforcement apparatus was provided for. Syria refused to take responsibility for Hizballah's compliance, however, claiming that its influence over the organization was limited. Hizballah never obligated itself to cease attacks, including rocket fire, at the Security Zone.

After Hizballah once again stepped up attacks in the zone, Israel launched "Operation Grapes of Wrath" on April 11, 1996. The Syrians had made no attempt to curb the Shi'ite militia and to block the escalation. The Israelis' aim was to destroy the Hizballah infrastructure and to pressure the Lebanese and Syrian governments to restrain the guerrillas. Yet Grapes of Wrath ran out of steam after one week, on April 18, when Israeli artillery erroneously targeted a group of civilians who had taken shelter in a UN facility at the village of Qana, killing more than one hundred people. The tragedy led to an eruption of anger and condemnation from the international community, especially in the Arab world. On April 27, the American secretary of state again managed to arrange a cease-fire and new terms. This time they were in writing, and a monitoring group was set up whereby Israeli officers met with Syrian and Lebanese counterparts under American and French auspices. Yet Hizballah still had room to maneuver, and time was on its side. Nasrallah continued to send agents into Israel; to sponsor suicide attacks; and to target Israeli forces in the Security Zone.

During the 1990s, Hizballah's great fear was that a peace deal would be struck between Syria and Israel. Israeli Military Intelligence's 8200 SIGINT unit and the American National Security Agency discovered that Iran was not pleased by such talks. But it saw great importance in keeping its ties with Syria stable, because without them it would be very difficult to provide assistance to Hizballah, and the Iranians were always very careful to make their rebukes gentle. In any case, the longer the negotiations between Israel and Syria dragged on, the stronger Nasrallah's self-confidence became, and he was convinced that Hizballah could defeat Israel in a prolonged war of attrition and force it out of Lebanon.

On his way to achieving his goal, Nasrallah displayed originality and daring, never hesitating to carry the war deep into enemy territory. From the mid-1990s, Hizballah began dispatching intelligence agents and spies as well as terrorists into Israel, on Iran's behalf, a phenomenon that became a veritable flood after the Israeli withdrawal. Hence, for example, Steven Smyrek: thirty-two, a British-educated, German-born man who had converted to Islam in 1994 and taken the name Abdul Karim. He contacted Hizballah two years later after deciding to become a martyr by carrying out a suicide bombing in Israel. On November 28, 1997, the Shin Bet arrested him when he arrived at Ben Gurion Airport on a flight from Amsterdam. He was sentenced to ten years in prison and released in 2004.

There were also agents imprisoned by Israel who had been controlled directly by the Iranians. One of these was Hussein Mikdad, thirty-three, a Lebanese Shi'ite accountant recruited to carry out a suicide attack in Israel, who accidentally detonated a bomb he was assembling in a Jerusalem hotel in April 1966. His legs and one arm were blown off, and he was blinded and half deafened. He had entered Israel on a forged British passport in the name of Andrew Newman carrying a large amount of plastic explosive in his luggage.

Shortly after he was found in a critical condition in the wreckage of his room in the Lawrence Hotel in East Jerusalem, it became clear to the police and Shin Bet investigators what had happened. Mikdad was rushed to Haddassah Hospital, and the best of its doctors were called in to try to save his life. This hospital has had much experience with cases of people with similar wounds from suicide bombings. When he came round, two weeks later, into a world of darkness, the Shin Bet placed two Lebanese Jews next to him, and they spoke Beirut Arabic. Mikdad was hoodwinked into believing that he had been returned to Beirut, as part of some exchange, to his Hizballah controllers, and he began talking. When he realized his mistake, it was too late, from his point of view.

Mikdad told interrogators that he had been trained by the Iranian Revolutionary Guard instructors how to shake off surveillance and how to conduct surveillance, both solo and in a team. He learned how to shoot a 9mm pistol and an Ingram submachine gun and how to make bombs out of dynamite and plastic explosives. After shaving off his beard, he was photographed in the Iranian Embassy in Beirut, and the picture was placed by experts into the Andrew Newman passport. He was also given other documents to bear out his cover story.

The course of Hussein Mikdad's life up until the blast in the Lawrence Hotel in East Jerusalem intrigued not only the Shin Bet investigators but also the team of psychologists that the agency had set up to try to solve the conundrum of the suicide bomber's profile. This project was conducted in cooperation with the CIA's behavioral sciences department, and its conclusions were supposed to help in the war against suicide terrorism.

The dissemination of the "poor man's smart bomb" to other countries in the Middle East, chiefly Israel, was perhaps Hizballah's greatest success. A suicide bomber can select his target, zero in on it with great precision, and choose the exact place and time when his or her bomb will cause the greatest damage. In the 1980s, intelligence analysts in Israel and the United States believed that only a group of melancholic fanatics ("The Oppressed of the Earth" was Hizballah's first name) could produce such an insane phenomenon, and that it couldn't spread to other environments.

Throughout the years of their stay in Lebanon, the Israelis never managed to find a remedy against suicide bombings, neither did they try to do so. No attempt was made to get down to the root of the matter: How was it that sane people, aware of their actions, would blow themselves up in order to kill as many other people as possible?

Then came the two blasts in Argentina; but they were still construed as extensions of what went on in Lebanon. On April 16, 1993, a car bomb went off at the Israeli settlement of Mehola in the northern West Bank, killing only the driver. The Israelis never bothered too much about it. They were convinced that it was an unsuccessful onetime event that would not be repeated, the whim of a crazed individual, certainly not a new trend.

For some time, this assumption seemed correct. But then something changed the course of history. It was the return from Lebanon, in December 1993, of 415 prominent Hamas and Islamic Jihad activists from Gaza and the West Bank. Israel had deported them a year earlier, after Hamas terrorists abducted and murdered an Israeli Border Police-man. They set up a camp at Marj al-Zuhur, and with Iranian intelligence assistance—Ali Reza Askari of the Revolutionary Guards playing a key role—a connection with Hizballah was established. The deportees were taught how to make car bombs and other explosive devices.

When Israel, under heavy U.S. pressure, agreed to allow the activists to return, they were very carefully searched to make sure they had no weapons or explosives on them. Nothing was found, because all the tick-ing time bombs were in their minds. They had learned of the effective-ness of suicide bombing from their Hizballah mentors. No less important, under the tutelage of Iranian intelligence agents they had also learned the techniques of assembling powerful explosive devices. The number one expert to emerge from this training course was one Yihya Ayash, born in 1966, and a 1988 graduate in electrical engineering of the University of Bir Zeit on the West Bank.

Shortly after the deportees returned, Hamas launched a series of attacks. Yihya Ayash made the bombs and planned the attacks, earning himself the nickname "the Engineer." In little over a year, the graduates of the camp at Marj al-Zuhur, headed by "the Engineer," caused the deaths of almost a hundred Israelis. When the suicide bombings started, teams of Israeli psychologists and other experts, set up in various depart-ments of the defense establishment, began trying to sketch the profile of the perpetrators. Analysis of the résumés of the early cases led the Shin Bet to believe that the phenomenon was the result of cynical exploitation of weak, ignorant, frustrated, poor, and sometimes even mentally unbal-anced people. But quite soon it transpired that there were also well-educated people, with bachelor's and master's degrees, who chose this way to win blanket forgiveness for all of their sins, as well as access to no fewer than seventy-two virgins in Paradise.

The profilers found again and again that the issue of life after death was of the greatest importance. Thus, for example, Shin Bet investigators documented the case of an Islamic Jihad would-be suicide bomber in Jerusalem in January 1997 whose explosive belt failed to go off, except for the detonator. He was lightly wounded by the small blast and lost con-sciousness, waking up in hospital later under heavy police and Shin Bet guard, with doctors and nurses coming and going. He opened his eyes, sat up in bed, lifted the arm that wasn't connected to an infusion, and said in Arabic: "You can tell them to come in now."

"Tell who?" asked the Shin Bet man, who hadn't expected the interrogation to begin like this.

"It's okay," said the failed suicide. "You can bring them all in. I can see them all at the same time now." Seeing that the interrogator still hadn't gotten his drift, he made it clearer: "Where are the virgins?" he asked, and could not be persuaded that he was in Haddassah Hospital and not Paradise until the investigator showed him his Shin Bet ID card. "Do you think that in Paradise you'll be interrogated by the Shin Bet?" he asked the disappointed man.

The Israelis soon learned, the hard way, that the suicide bombings did not grow in a vacuum but had a direct connection with Israel's own actions. On January 5, 1996, one of the few people who knew where Yihya Ayash was hiding in the Beit Lahiya in the Gaza Strip came to visit him. The Engineer knew that Israel rightly saw him as the person most responsible for the suicide terror that had begun after the return of the deportees from Lebanon. He was worried about Israeli eavesdropping on his mobile phone, and he had asked the contact to bring him a new one. The man complied with the request, forgetting only to tell him that he had not bought the new phone, but had obtained it free of charge, from his controller in the Shin Bet. Ayash made his first call to his father, and after he had said enough for the people listening in to be sure it was him and not someone else on the line, the concealed 340-gram plastic explosive charge (in those days the phones were still fairly bulky) was detonated, and his file at the Shin Bet was closed for good.

Hamas speakers promised the huge crowds at the funeral a wave of suicide attacks on Israel, the like of which it had never experienced. "The gates of Hell have been opened," they declared.

They kept their promise. The Engineer's students, including some of the deportees who had returned with him, staged a series of lethal terror attacks in February and March 1996 that demonstrated how suicide bombing can change the course of history. In the Israeli general elections in May, the hawkish leader of the opposition, Benjamin Netanyahu, who had been lagging behind incumbent Prime Minister Shimon Peres, caught up and won by a very narrow margin. Netanyahu owed his victory to Hamas.

For the last decade of the twentieth century, the initiative, the daring, the originality—and the luck—were almost always on Hizballah's side. As the years went by, the Ron Arad case became more and more important for the Israeli intelligence community and their Iranian counterparts, and Hizballah took the maximum advantage of their sensitivity and sense of urgency over the issue. On January 14, 1998, an agent of the security apparatus of the South Lebanese Army brought a videocassette wrapped in paper to his controller, Samir Raslan, and told him: "There are pictures of Ron Arad on this." An excited Raslan hurried with the cassette to his Shin Bet contacts, meeting them at Fatma Gate, a crossing on the Israel-Lebanon border. Orders forbid the opening of packages from unknown sources without an X-ray examination. But the machine was broken, and the sapper in charge said it would take hours to repair. The Israeli operatives were in a hurry because of the importance of the matter and insisted on having the package opened. The sapper agreed that he and the Lebanese would do it, with the Shin Bet men waiting in an adjoining room. The package was booby-trapped, and Raslan and the sapper were badly wounded. The two agents, who were peeping through the open door, each lost one eye.

One of Hizballah's goals was to eliminate senior officers of both the Israeli military and the South Lebanese Army. Over the years it succeeded in killing a brigadier general, two colonels, and two lieutenant colonels of the Israel Defense Forces. Many of the SLA top brass were also hit, including the commander, General Antoine Lahad, who was badly wounded in a joint operation by Hizballah and Syrian intelligence in November 1988. The deputy commander, Akel al-Hashem, was taken out by a bomb in the yard of his home in January 2000, an action that was videotaped by Moughniyeh's men. A short time before his demise, al-Hashem boasted in an interview with me of all the times that Nasrallah had tried to have him killed, calling himself "bulletproof."

Israeli commanders in South Lebanon drove around in Mercedes sedans, which were fairly common in the area, to avoid identification by the enemy. It didn't always work. On February 28, 1999, around noon, the senior Israeli officer in the Security Zone, Brigadier General Erez Gerstein, was killed when a roadside bomb blasted his Mercedes. His driver and radio operator, and an Israeli journalist accompanying him, were also killed.

Major (Res.) Ehud Eiran, a Harvard research fellow, was Gerstein's intelligence officer and later his biographer. Eiran says that Hizballah's greatest intelligence success was the organization's ability to learn the psychology of their Israeli rivals. "Hizballah understood how very sensitive the Israeli public is to casualties, and made effective use of the basic tools of psychological warfare, like taping and screening its attacks on Israeli targets."

The assassination of Erez Gerstein, one of the most charismatic and courageous of Israel's officers, was both a military and a political blow. Israel had occupied southern Lebanon for eighteen years, and had lost hundreds of men; now it had lost a man of great strength of character and confidence, a famous and beloved officer. The price of the occupation seemed too high. Directly after the incident, prime ministerial candidate Ehud Barak promised that if elected, he would "take the IDF out of Lebanon."

In fact, for the last three years of the IDF's presence in South Lebanon, there was a decline in the number of fatal casualties: twenty in 1998, twelve in 1999, and eight in 2000. This drop, and a number of successful operations before the eventual withdrawal in May 2000, contributed to a feeling in the IDF that the retreat had occurred "on the verge of victory." Similar claims have echoed throughout modern history—by the U.S. military after the pullout from Vietnam; the French in Algeria; the Russians in Afghanistan; and even by Prime Minister Ehud Olmert in the 2006 Lebanon war. Just another few months, officers believed, and the guerrilla movement would succumb.

It's a popular but usually a false belief. In any case, the battle for public opinion in Israel had been lost.

Two weeks before the pullout from Lebanon, Israeli intelligence's gun sights locked on to Imad Moughniyeh. He was using a cell phone, and they positively identified him and knew his location. Sources in Military Intelligence's counterterrorism department say that Prime Minister Barak vetoed taking him out. On the verge of Israel's withdrawal, he didn't dare heat up the region. Barak, they said, had been traumatized by the attacks on the Israeli Embassy and the AMIA Jewish community headquarters in Buenos Aires that followed the assassination of Sheikh Mussawi. As chief of staff in 1992, he had ordered the hit on Mussawi, and he did not want to repeat history. Barak claims that the decision not to liquidate Moughniyeh was taken at the military level and not by him, though he approved it.

On May 24, 2000, the IDF pulled out of Lebanon. Nasrallah

described it as "a divine victory," and declared that the anniversary would be celebrated every year as the most important date on Hizballah's calendar.

It was a hurried, shameful, woebegone retreat. Its greatest victims were the men of the South Lebanese Army and their families, who had to flee into Israel, leaving their homes and all their belongings behind them. They were mostly Christians who had linked their fate to Israel, and they would have been killed had they stayed behind.

People who held key positions during the eighteen years of Israel's presence in Lebanon look back at the period with great sadness over the blood spilled in "the war after the war." Many wonder what was gained. Patrick Seale, an expert on the Middle East and an admirer and biographer of Hafez al-Assad, predicted in 1999 that if Israel got out of Lebanon, its Hizballah problem would be solved. Yet in March 1999, when Nasrallah himself was asked what would happen if Israel retreated, he gave no reason to be hopeful: "Our reply is that we do not speak about the future. This is a matter to be kept secret, because secrecy on this issue is to the benefit of the Resistance and of Hizballah. The future of our activities will remain concealed. We think that the less we speak about it, the more powerful it will make the Resistance and Lebanon . . . I believe that Palestine is conquered land, and the Israeli presence is an occupying and an illegal entity. There is no end to the struggle against this regime."

# CHAPTER 16

# Hizballah Prepares

On May 24, 2000, Israel complied fully with Security Council Resolution 425 of 1978 and withdrew its forces from Lebanese territory to the complete satisfaction of the United Nations and the international community. The Lebanese government, acting on Syrian orders, refrained from deploying its army in southern Lebanon, apart from a symbolic presence, and from enforcing its authority in the vacated areas. Yet it also later refrained from implementing Security Council Resolution 1559 of September 2, 2004, which called for the imposition of control by the Lebanese government over the entire area of the country, and the disbanding and disarmament of all militias.

The vacuum created by Israel's withdrawal was filled by Hizballah, under the command of the Iranian Revolutionary Guards. The militia took control of what had been Israel's Security Zone, established itself in a line of fortresses along the border, and created new pretexts to justify continued terror operations. One such pretext was the liberation of an area known as the Shaba Farms near Mount Hermon. Israel had not withdrawn from that area because the United Nations considered it part of the Syrian Golan Heights, and not Lebanese territory. Another pretext was the release of Lebanese prisoners in Israel.

Hizballah worked steadily to build up its military power. Throughout the years, Iran supported Hizballah in every way, and controlled it. From Iran's point of view, Hizballah was the perfect way to export the Islamic Revolution. "This is Iran's Southern Command," said a source in Israeli intelligence. According to a report on May 11, 2006, in *Asharq Alawsat*, the Arabic newspaper published in London, a senior Iranian official told a group of Western diplomats at a closed meeting in London that Hizballah is "one of the foundations of our strategic security. It serves as the first Iranian defensive line against Israel. We do not accept that it must be disarmed."

Back in 1996, according to intelligence data collected by Israel, arms shipments from Iran to Hizballah were stepped up sharply, with the aim of making the militia a significant military machine, not just a terrorist and guerrilla force. American intelligence managed to recruit some individuals who were working in Iran's military industries, and they confirmed to the CIA (which in turn informed Israel, in July 2001) that since Israel's withdrawal from Lebanon, arms shipments from Iran to Hizballah became a flood.

According to a CIA report in 1999, the shipments included Zilzal rockets, with a range of 125–210 kilometers; Fajr 3 and Fajr 5 rockets, with ranges of up to 75 kilometers; Nazaat rockets with ranges of 80–140 kilometers; antitank missiles produced in Iran, with tandem warheads for use against reactive armor; land-sea missiles of the 802 C class, made in China; Ababil drones developed by the Iranian aircraft industry, both a recon version and another that carries substantial explosive warheads; SA-7 and SA-14 antiaircraft missiles made in Russia; 250 advanced night-vision kits sent to Iran by Britain in 2003 as part of their joint effort against drug smuggling; as well as equipment and weapons for use in small-scale naval warfare.

The weapons and other equipment from Iran were usually flown to an airport near Damascus and then trucked overland to Lebanon. The Iranians asked President Assad to let them fly directly to Beirut, but he turned them down. Later he even took steps to reduce the flow of weapons through Syria, in parallel to the secret talks that he held with Israel, and because of quarrels between the Syrian government and Iran. Yet the relationship changed when Hafez Assad was succeeded by his son, Bashar Assad, on July 10, 2000.

Hafez Assad had treated Hassan Nasrallah, the secretary general of Hizballah, as a subordinate. Bashar Assad saw him as a mentor. Bashar agreed with Nasrallah's theory that "Israel is as weak as a spiderweb." Syria suddenly became a major arms supplier of Hizballah. The turning point came in the summer of 2001, after the Israeli air force twice attacked Syrian targets in Lebanon in response to Hizballah operations. From then on, Syria began supplying weapons and assistance to Hizballah, with or without coordination with Iran. In October 2003, the Israeli air force attacked targets in Syrian territory and even buzzed Assad's residence, complete with supersonic booms. This prompted Assad to order a significant increase in the transfer of weapons to Hizballah, and in some categories Syria became the militia's chief supplier. It was Bashar's injured pride that led to a substantial change in Syria's approach to Hizballah.

In 2002, the National Security Agency intercepted a cell phone call from a senior representative of Iranian intelligence in Lebanon, to Tehran, informing his superiors that the Syrians had given Hizballah a gift of Chinese-made 220mm rockets, along with the latest antitank missiles, notably 9K115-2 Metis-M and Kornet models, which Russia had supplied to Syria. Says Uri Chen, a former chief of research for the Mossad, "There can be no doubt that President Assad himself approved the shipment of those missiles. A short time later, he allowed Nasrallah's people to hold a demonstration of support for Syria in the city of Qardaha in the north. Is it conceivable that his father would have allowed Hizballah to set foot in Syrian territory?"

Syria's enlistment as another patron of Hizballah was a significant boost to the organization's power, partly because of the geographical proximity between Syria and Lebanon, and Syrian intelligence's ability to provide the militia with real-time assistance, something that would prove useful during the 2006 Israel-Hizballah war.

In the six years following the IDF's withdrawal from Lebanon, the Iranians invested great effort in preparing the fighters of its "Southern Command." Hizballah men underwent training at Revolutionary Guard camps in Iran and in Lebanon. Iranian aid to Hizballah was coordinated by the al-Quds force, the elite unit of the Revolutionary Guards. Iran gave Hizballah $100 million a year, via that unit. From 2003, in addition, Hizballah got involved indirectly in the Iraq War, as members of various Shi"ite groups fighting the Americans and the central government in Iraq trained with Hizballah personnel, sometimes under veteran Hizballah instructors with experience fighting Israel, at those same bases.

The two main camps used by the al-Quds force to train foreign terrorists and guerrilla cadres are the Imam Ali base in Tehran and the Bahonar base in Karaj, north of the capital. During the 2006 war, a Hizballah fighter by the name of Hussein Ali Sliman, who was involved in the July 12 abduction of the Israeli soldiers that led to that war, was taken prisoner. Under interrogation, he said that he had undergone training in Iran with forty to fifty other Hizballah men. Their passports had not been stamped in either Syria or Iran, to hide the fact they had gone there for training. He also related that about a year and a half before the war, while he was on guard duty at a position in South Lebanon, two Iranians came to visit, together with two Hizballah officers. He later recognized one of the Iranians as a Revolutionary Guard member who gave him antiaircraft instruction in Iran.

From 2000 to 2006, a military formation akin to a division was set up in South Lebanon, following the model of the Revolutionary Guards; it included a number of territorial brigades and antitank, artillery, logistics, engineering, and communications units. It was subordinate to a kind of general staff—the general command of Hizballah, located in the Shi'ite southern Beirut neighborhood called the Dahya. This general staff included a "strategic weapons" department in charge of ground-to-ground missiles, an air unit in charge of drones, a naval unit, and more.

*Asharq Alawsat* in London published further details of the assistance supplied to Hizballah by the Iranian Revolutionary Guards on July 29, 2006, quoting a senior officer in the Guards who trained Hizballah naval units. He said that the militia had units of frogmen and naval commandos. He also reported that the Revolutionary Guards had helped Hizballah construct underground installations, including command-and-control bunkers, operated by both Hizballah and Guards. "Hundreds of Hizballah personnel who are today fighting the Israeli military [in the Second Lebanon War] took part in special training courses in Revolutionary Guards bases in Tehran, Isfahan, Mashad and Ahvaz," the officer said.

"Thanks to the presence of hundreds of Iranian engineers and technicians, and experts from North Korea who were brought in by Iranian diplomats," he continued, "Hizballah succeeded in building a 25-kilometer subterranean strip in South Lebanon. Each entrance is 12–18 square meters. The four openings are connected to each other by means of a passage through which the fighters can easily enter and reach the next opening.

"The Revolutionary Guards also built underground storerooms for Hizballah in the Bekaa, eight meters deep, that contain huge amounts of missiles and ammunition," the officer said. "There's also a central operations room in the Bekaa, that is run by four Revolutionary Guards officers and four Hizballah fighters. The Hizballah missiles units include some 200 technicians and experts who were trained in Iran. Hizballah has three missiles units, under a control team comprising 20 people."

In addition to the assistance of the Revolutionary Guards, Hizballah also enjoys assistance from the Iranian Foreign and Intelligence ministries, operating out of the Iranian embassies in Beirut and Damascus. The embassy in Beirut is a vast complex, most of which is devoted to intelligence activity, including operational and intelligence coordination between Iran and Hizballah. The embassy also carries out innumerable planning and operational tasks on behalf of the organization.

Between the Israeli pullout and the 2006 war, Iran greatly expanded the activities of the so-called Center for Culture and Islamic Studies which operates out of the Beirut Embassy, including Hebrew lessons for Hizballah fighters. It was here that a large group of Hizballah personnel were trained to monitor Israeli communications networks, pagers, and telephones, in order to gather as much information as possible on the enemy.

Alongside its military effort, Hizballah has continued a propaganda war. Dozens of books and pamphlets published by the organization have spewed hatred for Israel and the United States, and glorified the values of the jihad and martyrdom, as well as fostering personality cults around Ayatollahs Khomeini and Khamenei. These publications mostly offered Iranian propaganda material translated into Arabic, with almost no references to Lebanon.

Israeli troops found massive amounts of such propaganda alongside the Iranian weaponry in the quarters of many Hizballah fighters and in the organization's command posts when they occupied them in the 2006 war. Many of the men had the book entitled *Qaidi* or *My Commander*, published by the Hizballah youth organization known as "the Scouts of the Imam al-Mahdi." It is a brief biography of Iran's supreme leader, Ali Khamenei. A second popular book was *al Jihad*, published in 2004 by the Khomeini Cultural Center in Beirut. It analyzes the significance of holy war according to Khamenei, who sees the fight as a struggle against the "imperialist greed" of the West. Another booklet, entitled *The United States is the Source of Terror*, contains the text of a speech by Khamenei on March 17, 2002, according to which the United States is the root of oppression, corruption, imperialism, and terrorism in the world, and Israel is its ally and partner.

In addition to weapons and propaganda, Hizballah continued to expand its social services. A broad infrastructure of institutions and organizations conducts a variety of social welfare activities among the Shi'ite communities of Lebanon. The Lebanese government, with its sparse resources, cannot compete. These operations are integrated with Hizballah's propaganda machine. Funds come not only from Iran but from Shi'ites around the world, including those in Detroit, where there is a large Shi'ite population originating in South Lebanon. The collection of contributions is done through moneyboxes in mosques, clubs, and restaurants.

Hizballah's youth movement was set up in 1985, after the Israeli army withdrew into the South Lebanon Security Zone. It received a license from the Lebanese Education Ministry in 1992. In 1997, it had some 42,000 members between the ages of eight and sixteen. The aim of the movement, as stated on a calendar issued in 2006, is to raise an Islamic generation on the concepts of Khomeini. At their camps, the young men receive basic weapons training as well as physical education and marching drills. Some of the members of the militia are recruited from the ranks of this movement. According to the calendar, more than 120 of the Scouts of Mahdi had sacrificed their lives in Hizballah operations, including suicide bombings. Units of the Scouts appear at various Hizballah events and on Islamic and Iranian holidays. They parade in uniform, carrying plastic rifles and trampling on American and Israeli flags.

Hizballah's major media organ has been its television station, Al Manar, which Nasrallah uses to deliver speeches to the Shi'ite masses. The channel covers the organization's activities, presenting it as "the shield of Lebanon." The channel also fosters hatred toward America, the Jews and Israel, and encourages the Palestinian resistance. Its broadcasts treat Nasrallah and Khamenei as objects of worship.

In addition, Hizballah has a radio station, newspapers, Internet sites (in a variety of languages, including Arabic, English, French, Spanish, and Hebrew), and publishing houses that bring out journals and books. All of these enterprises are under the direct control of Nasrallah.

During the six years after Israel's 2000 pullout, while Hizballah built up all this infrastructure, it never completely abandoned its military actions against Israel. Altogether Hizballah carried out sixty-four attacks during this period, killing eleven Israeli soldiers and civilians. There was a kind of balance of terror between the two sides. Hizballah knew that its antiaircraft guns were not effective against Israeli warplanes, so each time there was an overflight, the militia turned its antiaircraft cannons against Israeli settlements near the border. Meanwhile, Hizballah threw its weight around politically. A Hizballah member of Lebanon's Parliament warned that if the government wanted to reach a political agreement with Israel, "it would have a problem with the organization and with other elements in Lebanon."

Hizballah kept up the tension with Israel, using small-scale attacks, attempts to kidnap soldiers, and even provocations such as tossing eggs and bags of urine and feces over the border fence at Israeli personnel. As usual, Imad Moughniyeh maintained strict field security and intelligence, changing the frequencies of communications networks whenever he suspected that Israel was listening in.

On October 7, 2000, Hizballah attacked an Israeli border patrol in the Shaba Farms sector on the northwestern slopes of Mount Hermon and snatched three soldiers—Adi Avitan, Benny Avraham, and Omar Souad—to be used as hostages to secure the release of Lebanese prisoners in Israel. It was the most sophisticated and complex operation ever mounted by the Shi'ite militia, and it took Israeli intelligence by surprise. Agents were shocked by the guerrillas' deep understanding of the Israel Defense Forces' weak points. Imad Moughniyeh planned and commanded the kidnapping. He code-named it "Operation Montazeri," after his good friend Ayatollah Montazeri, with whom he had trained in camps run by the PLO for Khomeini's supporters before the Iranian revolution. Once again Moughniyeh proved that he has no match when it comes to high-end guerrilla and terror operations.

With consummate ease, the attackers abducted the three men from inside Israeli territory, blocked rescue forces, and whisked their captives deep into Lebanon. Their fate remained unknown for a long time. Even as Hassan Nasrallah used the three soldiers as bargaining chips, Hizballah refused to reveal their true condition or allow anyone access to them. Israel assumed they were alive, although they could easily have been killed in the attack. Only long afterward did it become clear that they had died at the start of the operation—which meant, for Hizballah, that the operation was ultimately a failure. But there would be many others.

On the morning of the abduction, Israeli intelligence received information indicating that there was *another* operation in the works, involv-

ing Iran and Hizballah, not connected to the three soldiers. What it v
exactly could not be ascertained until Nasrallah appeared live on Hizba.
lah's al Manar television three days later and announced: "We have an
Israeli colonel in our hands."

Nasrallah's statements are always taken seriously. Special field security
teams were set up to check if any IDF unit was missing a colonel. Each
unit was instructed to establish contact, by telephone or in the flesh, with
all of its colonels (of whom there are several hundred) to make sure they
were not spending the night in a Hizballah interrogation cell. After all of
the colonels in the regular army were accounted for, the army's comput-
ers printed out lists of all officers of that rank in the reserves, or who had
ever served in the past, and investigators began checking each one.
Some had passed away; others were amazed to be woken up in the middle of the night.

The search produced nothing, apart from yet another snafu: to the
army's surprise and anger, it turned out that the Mossad had been aware
for some time that Hizballah was aiming to kidnap an Israeli colonel but
had not shared this information with the other intelligence agencies.
Hizballah had even picked a target: a reserve intelligence officer by the
name of Yom-Tov Eini, who had served in a number of senior posts.
After leaving the regular army, he had gone into business, dealing in various commodities with Arab countries. Agents working on behalf of
Hizballah tried to lure him to Cyprus, with a gigantic deal as bait. He
agreed, but on arrival at the rendezvous, his old intelligence instincts
kicked in and he suspected a trap, so he returned to Israel. Hizballah
moved on to another target.

Uri Tannenbaum heard about Nasrallah's speech on the radio at home
in Tel Aviv. "I was in bed, and I switched on the radio. I was half asleep,
listening to the news. The first item was that the leader of Hizballah had
announced that his organization had taken an Israeli colonel prisoner.
The name wasn't mentioned, but I jumped out of bed, shaking. I ran to
Mom and I said, 'Dad's been kidnapped.' " Two days later, Uri's sister
Keren called the Military Police investigations chief and told him that her
father, Elchanan, was missing and could be the colonel Nasrallah had
spoken about. Shortly after that, on October 16, the Shi'ite media wiz-
ard himself took to the airwaves again, when the suspense was at its
height, and announced that the name of the Israeli prisoner was indeed
Elchanan Tannenbaum. The riddle was solved.

Tannenbaum had been kidnapped after being lured to Dubai by the prospect of making a massive drug deal. He remained in Hizballah's hands for more than three years, until he was returned, together with the bodies of the three abducted soldiers, in exchange for 436 Arabs who had been held in Israeli prisons. Moughniyeh's human trafficking proved just as useful as ever.

Although Hizballah mounted a number of other operations between 2000 and 2006, the abduction of Tannenbaum proved to be one of its most important. In the Israeli defense establishment, when the news broke that it was Tannenbaum who had been taken hostage, the first reaction was one of relief. An artillery officer in the reserves, they thought, what secrets can he know? But closer scrutiny disclosed that this rather obscure officer had been privy to the very latest and the most carefully guarded of Israel's military secrets.

Only five days before his abduction, Colonel Tannenbaum was on reserve duty, serving as one of the commanders of an exercise codenamed "Northern Resident," the largest and most important such war game conducted by the IDF in recent years. It was a simulated total war with Syria and Hizballah. The secrets shared among participants in this simulation were vital to Israel's security and strategy—including how it would deploy its forces in the next war. Tannenbaum was involved in the simulated use of Israel's most advanced weapons systems, those that were supposed to surprise the enemy in future combat. During the exercise, he had spent much of his time in the command bunker near the Galilee city of Safed. From there, using secret state-of-the-art systems, he controlled the firepower of the combat forces. Tannenbaum had been responsible for the planning and management of large components of the exercise.

Colonel (Res.) Moshe Cohen, who was chief staff officer of the IDF's directorate for exercises, explained that "we worked on this exercise for about three months. Elchanan took part in the whole process, and was acquainted with the plans, the capabilities, the lot." He added that it was all "very sensitive information."

Assessing the magnitude of the security breach caused by Tannenbaum's abduction, Cohen commented, "The enemy knowing this information—I'd define it as irreparable damage to the security of the

State of Israel. When I heard that it was him, I was in shock. Like a punch to the stomach. It was clear to me that the information would not remain with him in captivity."

Cohen said there could be no doubt that Tannenbaum gave Israel's enemies information that caused grave damage the security of the state. He was very emphatic in his reply when asked what he would have done if it were he who had been abducted: "Understanding that I would not be able to keep the information inside me, I would probably have killed myself, if I could have done so."

Among the secrets that Tannenbaum knew was one called simply "the project." It has to do with Israel's most advanced weapons system, one that was supposed to have decided the next battlefield confrontation. The system has many top-secret American components and parts of it are manufactured in the United States. When the IDF attaché in Washington reported to the Pentagon on the Tannenbaum affair, therefore, there was considerable consternation.

That consternation only increased after the U.S. invasion of Iraq in March 2003. There were those who feared that some of the information on the technologies used in "the project" would be transferred by Hizballah to the forces fighting against the Americans there.

Investigators assume that whatever information Tannenbaum might have divulged, it was given under interrogation, and he did not set out to sell it to Israel's enemies. If, however, he had been a professional spy, he was well qualified. His interrogators in Israeli intelligence have all remarked upon Tannenbaum's ability to live separate and parallel lives, with those involved in each circle unaware of the existence of the others, and with Tannenbaum himself functioning perfectly in each, as if he were devoted only to its members. Says one senior military source: "He lives at home with his wife, he has two mistresses, and he has a child with one of them that none of the others knows about. In his reserve duty he appears to be a man of values, a giver; he always looks fine, well dressed, drives a luxury car. But at the same time, he gets heavily into debt, as a result of bad business deals and gambling."

To help him improve his economic situation, Tannenbaum's friends in the army top brass had him called up for reserve duty, on regular army terms. He served 150 days a year, earning a colonel's salary. Absurdly, the deeper he got involved in dubious business deals, the more he was exposed to classified information. The last time a security check was run on him was in 1988.

Ultimately, it was Tannenbaum's friendship with the Obeid family that got him, and the State of Israel, into trouble. The Obeids live in the Arab town of Taibeh. They are one of the most prominent Arab clans in Israel. Its members are doctors, scientists, Knesset members, businessmen, community functionaries—and drug dealers. Among the entire clan, Keis Obeid stood out. A young man, he was a brilliant businessman who dabbled in drug dealing as well as serving as an agent for Israeli Military Intelligence. Tannenbaum saw in Keis Obeid the ideal partner for the deal that would save him from ruin.

Tannenbaum, Obeid, and a Lebanese drug dealer by the name of Kaid Biro, whose father was in an Israeli prison for drug trafficking, planned a massive operation to smuggle tons of heroin and cocaine from Lebanon into Israel in shipping containers. Tannenbaum claimed later to have played only an advisory role, but the police and the public prosecution are convinced that he was the driving force behind the deal. All the while, Obeid and Biro were plotting with Hizballah's special operations unit to turn this ostensibly straightforward drug deal into a kidnapping.

Shortly after Tannenbaum was abducted, information reached Israel that it was Keis Obeid who had organized it on behalf of Hizballah. Further investigation revealed that the Shin Bet was aware that Obeid was about to go abroad, and had even approved of his trip, but it knew nothing about his links with Tannenbaum. Major David Barkai, of MI's Unit 504, says that Obeid had never been considered anything special as a spy, "but we must have been wrong. Listen, he was so good, he was a superstar who could recruit a colonel in the IDF, no? Hizballah turned Keis Obeid, and Keis Obeid recruited Elchanan Tannenbaum via a drug deal trap, and in the end Hizballah's guys went home. No doubt about it, a stunning success."

The Israelis believe that the Tannenbaum sting was Obeid's ticket into Hizballah. Today, he is the militia's number one contractor for staging terror attacks from the territories against Israelis. As for his friend, Kaid Biro, investigators believe that he wanted to get his father out of prison, as part of a general prisoner exchange that would follow Tannenbaum's release.

• • •

The story of the three years and three months of Tannenbaum's captivity is one of intelligence failure, frustration, and tremendously costly negotiation. To this day, it is not clear how Iranian intelligence's Department 5, which handles Israel, managed to get the drugged Tannenbaum from his capture in Dubai to his first makeshift prison in Beirut. Some months after the kidnapping, Israeli intelligence learned that he was being held in an apartment in one of Beirut's northern, Christian neighborhoods. It was decided not to try to rescue him by force. Israel did not want to risk its soldiers' lives in a bid to rescue someone who had fallen into captivity because of his own avarice.

In the meantime, the Israeli government and Tannenbaum's family launched a massive international effort to get him released. The precious store of information in Tannenbaum's head motivated the Israeli defense establishment to back the effort. They understood that if he told his captors about "the project," great damage would be done—damage that could prove irreparable. The military exerted pressure on the prime minister to get him back so they could find out exactly what he had told his interrogators. Ariel Sharon understood the implications and was determined to reach a deal.

Sharon brought the proposed deal to the cabinet for approval, and threw his weight behind it. At a crucial meeting, Major General Ilan Biran, who had represented Israel in the contacts, told the ministers: "There is no chance of reaching an agreement that will include Ron Arad. Dirani and Obeid [Sheikh Abdul-Karim Obeid, the Shi'ite cleric and Hizballah activist who had been abducted before Dirani to serve as a bargaining chip for Arad] aren't worth anything. If you want to save Tannenbaum and get the bodies of the three soldiers back for burial in Israel, this is the only way."

The deal was approved and carried out on January 29, 2004. It was an enormous achievement for Nasrallah. Nasrallah had proved that he kept his promises and that he was the only Arab leader who did more than just speak about the Palestinian issue. Hundreds of families in the territories owe him a huge debt as a result.

Tannenbaum was returned to Israel through Berlin, along with the bodies of the three soldiers. The same plane that brought him out had flown the released Lebanese prisoners to Berlin. The IDF was vigilant up to the last moment. Dirani and Obeid and the others were chained, with masked guards from the Military Police special intervention unit, armed with electroshock weapons, patrolling the aisle. Not one of them even dared to ask to go to the bathroom. Later, in the German plane that flew them to Beirut, they celebrated—to the extent that they caused damage to the cabin.

A special interrogation team was set up to question Elchanan Tannenbaum. Everyone wanted to be part of it. The United States had pressured Israel hard to find out definitively whether American technological secrets had fallen into the hands of hostile elements, adding urgency to the investigation, as well as prestige to those conducting it. The Shin Bet, the police, and the military never stopped squabbling over the case. Dvorah Chen, director of the Department of Security Matters and Special Affairs in the District Attorney's office at the State Attorney's office, who had overseen the affair from the start, wanted to bring back the legendary interrogator, known as "the Sheriff"—who had broken Nahum Manbar* and had interrogated Dirani—to question Tannenbaum. Yet the new head of investigations refused, and kept Chen away from most of the details of the interrogation.

One of the first questions that arose was what to do with Tannenbaum when he arrived back. He was suspected of a large number of offenses, including espionage and treason, the most serious crimes in Israel's criminal code. The police wanted to get a court order to have him detained in custody in a police cell until the end of the proceedings. But the IDF and the Shin Bet—who were responsible for the fact that a drug dealer with links to Hizballah had kidnapped a senior Israeli officer implicated in criminal activities who was nevertheless given access to highly sensitive material, and therefore had a great deal to lose from the affair—decided to hold him at a police rest-and-recreation facility, in hotel conditions. In such surroundings, it was not difficult for Tannenbaum to keep his secrets to himself—after all, he had just come back from prolonged captivity by the Hizballah.

Tannenbaum amazed the interrogators by sticking to a totally deceitful story for fourteen days, according to which he had been on a legitimate business trip and gone to Lebanon to collect information on Ron

---

* Manbar is the Israeli businessman who sold chemical warfare to Iran, as described in Chapter 18.

Arad. He claimed that he had not given away any information on anything to the Hizballah interrogators. He underwent no fewer than sixteen
polygraph tests, and "his lies almost burned the fuses in the national electricity grid," according to one source.

On the fourteenth day, he changed course and admitted that he had
cooperated with his Hizballah interrogators on a number of topics. He
said that he had been questioned throughout by two men, one of whom
spoke Arabic and Hebrew while the other spoke Arabic and English.
Most of the questions were in Hebrew. There were two rounds of questioning, the first very brief and general, the other much more intensive.
He said he was grilled on a wide variety of topics, both military and civilian: his army service, his participation in Israel-Arab wars, Israeli politics,
Jewish-Arab relations, and more. Hizballah was very interested in the
atmosphere and the mood in Israel, it seemed. He said he was held in a
narrow cell with a light burning twenty-four hours a day. Some of the
time he was tied up, and every time he was moved from the cell to
another room where he was given food, he was blindfolded. He said that
he passed the time by humming Israeli songs to himself.

Eventually, he insisted, instead of being broken by his Israeli interrogators, he broke them by sticking unwaveringly to his lies. The IDF
and Shin Bet investigators, without the knowledge of the State Attorney's
office, offered him a tempting deal. In an unprecedented "investigation
arrangement," Tannenbaum was promised that if he came clean about all
the crimes and scams he was involved in, and if it indeed emerged that he
had not give Hizballah any vital secrets, especially the one supremely
important secret, he would be granted a full pardon and immunity
from prosecution for all prior offenses and embezzlements, as well as the
drug deal he had plotted. Tannenbaum signed on the dotted line, and
came up with a new story: He said he went to Dubai as an adviser in a
drug deal, and gave Hizballah some information on the IDF's deployment against the Syrians on the northern border—but told them nothing about the secret project.

The Shin Bet believed that Tannenbaum was telling the truth and that
he had not given away information on "the project," but some people in
the army and the police never bought Tannenbaum's final story. They
claim that evidence exists that he *had* given Israel's worst enemies some
of its most highly classified secrets. Major General Dani Yatom, who
served as Mossad director from 1996 to 1998, even believes the Shin Bet

was covering up the truth. "The embarrassment in the intelligence community is so great, and the disgrace is so great, that there was someone who tried to cover it up. . . . That was apparently the main motive for the deal with Elchanan. Anything to quiet everything down, especially the consciences of the people who failed so very badly and calamitously."

When the immunity arrangement was signed, Tannenbaum was released from prison, and has since been a free man. Some of his associates in alleged criminal conspiracies to defraud Israeli Customs—offenses in which he was involved before being abducted—have been prosecuted, on the strength of evidence that he has provided. In mid-2008, he was studying law and making a living as a cab driver. The only action taken against him was a special law enacted by the Knesset, which made it possible to have him demoted to the rank of private.

On January 6, 2006, the New York correspondent of the *Al-Hayat* international Arabic newspaper published "Scenarios for 'Inviting' an Israeli Offensive Against Lebanon." She raised the possibility that Syria and Iran would try to drag Israel into war by using Hizballah, in order to lessen the international pressure that was being exerted on both of those countries.

As she wrote:

It may well be that the leaders of these two countries will find that they have an interest in provoking Israel through Hizballah and the Palestinian factions, either to divert the pressure that's being exerted on them, or to stir up hostility against Israel that will serve their interests locally and regionally. . . . The greatest responsibility in the Lebanese arena is Hizballah's as it has to decide whether it is really a Lebanese party or a soldier who obeys the orders of Syria or Iran and to drag the region into war and to turn Lebanon into a hell in order to serve the Iranian nuclear program or in order to get Syria off the hook of the investigations of the assassination [of Lebanese prime minister Rafik Hariri].

Nassrallah, in 2006, made that strategic decision: He went to war.

# CHAPTER 17

# Oil on the Flames

On December 29, 2001, the freighter *Karin A* set sail from Iran, en route to the Suez Canal. In the Red Sea between Egypt and Saudi Arabia, 500 kilometers south of Eilat, Israeli naval commandos boarded the ship from helicopters, without opposition from the four crewmen, who were members of the Palestinian naval force. When the commandos examined the ship's cargo, they discovered launchers and rockets with a range of up to 20.4 kilometers; mortars, antitank weapons, mines, 2 tons of explosives, assault rifles, machine guns, sniper rifles with telescopic lenses, hand grenades, and hundreds of thousands of rounds of ammunition. If the massive haul of weaponry had reached its destination, the violence emanating from Gaza would have reached new heights, bringing population centers and strategic installations within range of the rockets of Palestinian terrorist organizations. The range, quantities, and nature of the weapons could have tilted the balance of terror with Israel, which would undoubtedly have found it necessary to take very strong measures to redress it, with all of the repercussions that such an escalation would entail.

For years, Iran had regarded the Palestinian Authority as a treasonable body because it wished to reach a settlement with Israel. The more progress the peace process registered, the greater the suspicion grew. After the signing of the Wye River memorandum between the Palestinians and the Israeli government of Benjamin Netanyahu in 1998, which included a pledge to prevent acts of terror, Iran's Supreme Leader Ali Khamenei attacked Yasser Arafat and accused him of having replaced Israel as the oppressor of the Palestinians. Hizballah secretary general Hassan Nasrallah went further: "From the moment that he cast down his gun and decided to take the path of negotiations on the Palestinian issue, Arafat proved that he is a Jew."

The outbreak of the new intifada in September 2000, however, caused a change in Iran's attitude to the Palestinian Authority, and especially to Arafat. Khamenei even issued a religious ruling permitting cooperation with the PA and with Arafat's Fatah movement. Iranian foreign minister Kamal Kharazi declared at a press conference that the June 1, 2001, suicide bombing at the Tel Aviv Dolphinarium nightclub, where twenty-one people, most of them young people out for a night on the town, were killed, was not an act of terror "because Israel is an occupying power." Israeli intelligence estimated that "At the bottom line, Iran derives much satisfaction from the Authority's turn to terror and sees the situation as a historical window of opportunity to weaken Israel."

But the shipment of arms on the *Karin A* represented a significant escalation in Iranian support for Arafat and the Palestinians, making that conflict a newly central theater in Iran's war with Israel. The contacts prior to the voyage of the *Karin A* were between the Palestinian naval force and Hizballah. The weapons were loaded onto the boat on the Iranian island of Kish. Captain Omar Akawi said he had been told that in order to deliver the weapons, special sealed containers were necessary, and they could not be manufactured in Lebanon but only in Iran.

Israeli intelligence officers insist they have incontrovertible evidence that it was the Revolutionary Guards, acting with the approval of the Supreme Leader, who were behind the smuggling attempt. The identification markings on the weapons were filed off, but experts who examined them determined beyond doubt that many of the items were manufactured in Iran. It is inconceivable, according to Israeli sources, that so large a shipment could be assembled and consigned from Iran without the knowledge and support of the higher echelons of government. According to information gathered by Israeli Military Intelligence, Iran and the Palestinian Authority reached a secret agreement, providing that in exchange for the weapons, the Revolutionary Guards would be allowed to establish and operate bases in the Gaza Strip and the West Bank.

Each of the four crew members said the same thing under interrogation: The voyage of the *Karin A* was organized and financed by Fouad Shoubaki, head of the financial directorate of the PA's General Security and a close Arafat confidant. The captain and crew of the vessel belonged to the Palestinian Naval Police. Yet shortly after the ship was seized, Arafat told Egyptian TV: "We'll see if anyone can prove that this boat belongs to the Authority. Everyone knows that there's no link between us and the Iranians on this matter. . . . If we wanted to bring in weapons, we could have done so from all of our Arab brothers. No Arab country would say no. So why should I have to bring weapons from Iran?"

George W. Bush was furious at Arafat's denial of any knowledge about the *Karin A*. Later, Arafat would gradually retreat from most of his denials in the matter. But it wasn't so easy to repair the damage. According to State Department officials interviewed for this book, President Bush was not prepared to forgive Arafat, even after his death, for his blatant lying.

The *Karin A* incident strengthened the president's belief that Iran was one of the main threats to world peace, a belief that had led him to include that country—together with Iraq and North Korea—in the "axis of evil" that he first denounced in his 2002 State of the Union speech.

How much has Iran helped Palestinian terror groups? The full answer is: A great deal. Often, it came in the form of direct assistance to terrorist cells. But it has also come indirectly, in the form of intelligence sharing. For the most part, Iran has worked through Hizballah and, to a lesser extent, the Islamic Jihad. Yet even Hamas, which rebuffed Iranian overtures in the 1980s and the early 1990s, began a significant flirtation in the latter part of that decade, and has cooperated much more since then. The story of one such flirtation, in 1997, grew into one of the most embarrassing debacles in the Mossad's entire history.

September 1997: Some of the more observant shopkeepers in Tel Aviv's Ibn Gvirol Street couldn't help noticing two typical Israeli youngsters who came back day after day. If it were not for one peculiar aspect to their behavior, they would not have stood out from the thousands of similar youngsters in cafés and restaurants, and on sidewalks of the busy thoroughfare. Walking close behind random passersby, they would shake up a can of Coca-Cola and snap it open. Their victims would be hit by the spray. There was often some angry shouting, in which case the two would apologize politely and offer to clean the soiled clothing. But when the target did not realize that he'd been sprayed, the two would slip away quietly.

Unbeknownst to any observers, these youngsters were practicing for the deadly serious business of assassination. They were members of the Mossad's "Bayonet" Unit, responsible for violent operations. They were training to eliminate the head of Hamas's political bureau, Khaled Mashal. Mashal was coordinating Hamas's ties with the intelligence branch of Iran's Revolutionary Guards, and Mossad wanted to sever the relationship and also sought revenge.

Much has been written in Israel about the consequences of the abortive attempt to kill Mashal. But very little has been published about the operation itself, and the little that has come out is riddled with inaccuracies. An internal Mossad inquiry that examined the operational failure tells the true story. Its conclusions, published here for the first time, make it possible to reconstruct the catastrophe.

July 30, 1997, was the usual quiet Wednesday in the Mahaneh Yehuda produce market in central Jerusalem. At about twelve noon, two young men dressed in suits and ties and carrying heavy bags joined the thousands of shoppers walking among the stalls. Their bags concealed massive explosives. Within seconds, two enormous blasts shook the market's alleyways. Sixteen people were killed and some two hundred injured.

Immediately, while angry voices called for revenge, the Shin Bet began to investigate. Great efforts had been made to conceal the identity of the two terrorists. Among other things, they had cut the labels off their clothes so that the stores where they had been purchased could not be located. Before detonating their bombs, they held them close to their bodies, so that as little as possible would remain for postmortem examiners. Nonetheless, there were body parts. On the day after the bombing, the two were identified as members of the military wing of Hamas. It emerged only later that they had acted according to instructions from Jordan and Syria, based on advice from Iranian intelligence.

In the wake of the identifications, Prime Minister "Bibi" Netanyahu convened an emergency meeting of the security cabinet, which approved the assassination of Hamas leaders as a response. The cabinet authorized the prime minister and the defense minister to set the specific targets. The next day, Netanyahu called in Mossad director General Dani Yatom. The prime minister demanded a hit list. Yatom went back to his advisers, and soon the Mossad proposed a number of Hamas representatives in European countries and elsewhere as targets. These were men responsible for acquiring weapons or raising funds, whose elimination would be relatively easy. Netanyahu angrily rejected the list. Bring me some serious figures, not these minnows, he demanded, adding, "I want leaders, not merchants." In a conversation ten years later, Netanyahu recalled that he also insisted that the burgeoning connections between Hamas and Iran be severed, and demanded to know who was in charge of them.

The Mossad officials explained to the prime minister that in the upper layer of those Hamas officials not resident in the occupied territories there were four salient figures: Khaled Mashal, Mohammad Nazal, Ibrahim Usha, and Mussa Abu-Marzook. Netanyahu, the Mossad officials later recalled, did not understand why they gave him the names in this order. He hadn't heard of Mashal, but he was very familiar with the name of Abu-Marzook, one of Hamas's top officials and an American citizen who had been deported to Jordan. He was wanted in Israel for terrorism charges already.

Manipulating Netanyahu, the Mossad had put Abu-Marzook's name last because they did not want to hit him. As a famous leader, living in Jordan by an agreement between Jordan and the United States, his assassination would infuriate the Jordanian government, which was one of Israel's most important quasi-allies. A team was sent to investigate the potential targets, and they went down the list in order. The Mossad wanted them to pay as little attention as possible to Abu-Marzook. When the team came back, they had enough material on Mashal to make killing him possible, but little on Abu-Marzook. They knew where Mashal lived, where he worked, what car he drove. Netanyahu accepted their recommendation and gave the go-ahead for the elimination of Mashal.

Mishka Ben David was head of the intelligence department of the special operations wing of the Mossad. The Bayonet Unit was part of his department, and so Ben David was put in charge of intelligence for the operation.

"It was an unfamiliar arena, because since the peace treaty with Jordan, Rabin had forbidden the Mossad to work there," said Ben David. "Netanyahu did not want a bomb or shots fired in the street, and demanded a silent operation, something that we were not accustomed to."

A number of alternative methods of assassination were considered. Netanyahu had not just ruled out anything noisy; he had demanded an operation that could not be identified as Israeli and perhaps not even as an assassination. The Mossad unit responsible for technological and scientific solutions for operational problems was called in. One agent, a doctor in biochemistry who was an authority in quiet ways of killing, proposed the use of a certain nerve toxin so lethal that a drop or two on the skin is enough to cause death. It is also very hard to identify in post-mortem examinations.

The next problem was how to administer the poison. After a series of meetings, it was decided to spray it onto Mashal in the street. Two operatives would approach him from behind. One would open a well-shaken can of soda while the other sprayed the toxin onto him. When Mashal turned around to see what had made him wet, he would find two embarrassed tourists with a can of fizzy soda. The technology unit told the operatives to make sure they took along some of the antidote to the poison with them, in case any drops fell on them by mistake.

After the plan was approved, a team began practicing it on the side-walks of Tel Aviv. Just as they were spraying passersby with Coca-Cola, however, on September 4, three suicide bombers blew themselves up on Jerusalem's Ben Yehuda pedestrian mall, killing five—among them three young girls, one of them a fourteen-year-old visiting from Los Angeles—and wounding two hundred. Netanyahu, speaking at an impromptu press conference, declared: "We are not prepared to go on like this. From this moment, our path will be different."

The prime minister instructed Yatom to proceed immediately with "Operation Cyrus." Not only was the operation to be silent, untraceable, and situated in the unfamiliar terrain of Jordan, but now it had to be hasty. The Mossad feared that the haste that Netanyahu demanded would harm execution of the plan. But despite the criticism and the reservations, none of the Mossad's leaders told Netanyahu that the organization was not ready to carry out the operation.

Dani Yatom refuses to evade responsibility. "True, I could have refused to operate in Jordan, but after we examined it, we found that it could be done. I do not accept the claim that we set out on the operation unprepared because of Bibi's pressure, although that would be easiest for me. If I had not agreed, there would not have been an operation. I was convinced that it could be carried out cleanly and quietly."

In mid-September, the Bayonet team travelled to Jordan for final preparations and execution of the mission. The two operatives selected for the actual engagement had already used their usual cover identities as Europeans on a visit two weeks earlier, so they were given Canadian papers as Shawn Kendall, twenty-eight, and Barry Beads, thirty-six.

These identities were not nearly as well tested as the usual covers used by the agents.

Also in Jordan under non-Israeli cover were the commander of the Bayonet Unit, the commander of the team, one female operative, and two male ones. Separately, travelling on Israeli passports, intelligence officer Ben David and a female doctor came to Amman with the antidote, in case one of the Israelis was affected. According to the testimony of senior agency officials, it was one of the Mossad's best teams, which had racked up a number of successes in other operations. This was the team that had eliminated Fathi Shkaki in Malta in October 1995; settled accounts with PLO terrorist Atef Bseiso for his part in the 1972 Munich Olympics massacre in Paris twenty years later; and removed the threat against Israel posed by Dr. Gerald Bull, the Canadian engineer who was developing a "super cannon" for Saddam Hussein, in Brussels in 1990.

Most of the team checked into the Amman Intercontinental Hotel. They hired a green Hyundai and cell phones, and hurriedly began filling in the gaps in their intelligence. They established that Mashal went to the Hamas office—called the Palestinian Assistance Center—in the Shamiyeh Center every morning.

The plan was for two team members to wait outside Mashal's home in the Hyundai in the morning, and follow him on his way to work, alerting the others when he was due to arrive. When he parked near the office, the Hyundai was to pass by, drop off one of the team to serve as a lookout, and then drive up the road and wait there as the getaway vehicle.

Meanwhile, another lookout was to be stationed near the building, waiting for a sign that the target was approaching. Upon receiving it, he would give a signal to "Kendall" and "Beads," who were waiting at one end of a long arcade on the ground floor. They would then begin walking at a pace timed so that they would meet Mashal at a specific spot, and spray the poison. As a safety net, two more operatives were to follow Mashal along the arcade and hold him up if the timing was disrupted.

On September 21, as the team in Amman was making its preparations, the Shin Bet received fresh information tying Iranian intelligence and Hamas to the terror attacks in Jerusalem. Netanyahu stepped up his pressure for the assassination to be carried out. Another day passed. By complete coincidence, King Hussein of Jordan then notified the Israeli government (via the Mossad) that Hamas had proposed a cease-fire, in exchange for negotiations with Israel. It remains unclear whether the king's message was held up by the Mossad or whether Netanyahu himself decided to ignore it until after the assassination.

On the morning of September 25, the team set out to execute the hit. The decision to go ahead was problematic, because of a fear that one of the surveillance men had aroused the suspicion of a worker in the Shamiyeh Center. But the botches that followed were far more serious.

The team had managed to carry out only one full surveillance of Mashal on his way to the office. They therefore were unaware that sometimes Mashal's driver also took his children to school. That is what happened on the day set for the assassination. The children were sitting low in the backseat. The Israelis never saw them there.

At 10:35 a.m., Mashal's car arrived at the Shamiyeh Center, and the Bayonet commander in the tailing car gave the final go-ahead signal. It was passed on to the two operatives in the arcade, who began walking toward the target. They were not carrying any means of communication. Once they had set off, there was no way of aborting the mission.

Mashal got out of the car and started walking toward his office. Suddenly, his little girl, whom the driver was supposed to be taking to school, opened the car door, jumped out, and began running after her father, calling out: *"Ya baba, ya baba"* (Daddy, Daddy). The driver began running after her. The hit men, who did not see the girl, neared their target. One of them lifted the canister of poison, which was taped to the palm of his hand, aiming at the nape of Mashal's neck. The other began to snap open the Coke can.

The driver caught sight of Mashal, and assumed that the man raising his arm behind him was about to stab him with a knife. He yelled out, "Khaled, Khaled!" Mashal heard him, and turned around. The jet of toxin hit him in the ear instead of the back of the neck.

This made no difference as far as the effectiveness of the poison was concerned, but the element of secrecy was lost. Mashal stared at the Bayonet agent, knowing that he had been sprayed from a strange cylinder. He grasped immediately that he was in danger of his life and began running away. The driver picked up the girl and ran back to the car. The hit men also ran, in the direction of the getaway car.

Dani Yatom, speaking about the case for the first time, blames the screwup entirely on the two agents, saying that they "blatantly disobeyed my orders. I had delineated a playing field, and they played on their own field. I had made it unequivocally clear, both in writing and verbally, on the two occasions that I observed their practice runs, that if there was anyone at all next to Mashal, they must not go ahead. But they did nevertheless. They claim that they never saw the child because some pillar obscured their vision. That's all blabber. They were simply overmotivated to execute, after all the days that they had not been able to."

The screwups continued. While the two operatives were making good their escape, in another coincidence, a Hamas arms and currency courier and a trained guerrilla fighter by the name of Mohammad Abu Sayaf turned up in the arcade. Sayaf did not immediately understand what was happening, but he saw Mashal and the two men running in different directions. He followed the two. As the Israelis got into the Hyundai and drove off, he took down the number and ran after the car.

The driver saw him writing the number down, and told the two operatives. The car got caught up in heavy traffic. The Israelis didn't realize that Abu Sayaf was still following them, and a few hundred meters further on, they made a critical decision that ultimately led to the total collapse of the mission: They told the driver to stop and got out of the car.

They later claimed that they thought that once the registration number had been taken, it was better for them to separate from the car. Yet had they remained inside, they might very well have escaped in time to ditch the Hyundai. Instead, as they emerged from the car, Abu Sayaf arrived. He had been trained in Afghani terrorist camps, and was an expert in hand-to-hand combat. He was apparently very worked up.

Without much ado, screaming in Arabic, he jumped one of the Israelis and ripped his shirt. The operative fought to free himself while the other Israeli landed two karate chops on Abu Sayaf's head, which began bleeding profusely. The sight of two foreigners beating up on a local created a major uproar in the street. Instead of taking advantage of the tumult to escape as fast as they could, the operatives spent some time throttling Abu Sayaf until he lost consciousness.

A policeman who arrived at the scene extricated the two agents from the angry mob. He listened to their claim that someone had attacked them for no reason, and also to the stunned Abu Sayaf's explanations, and decided to take the two Israelis to a police station. They did not resist, explaining later that they were confident that their cover stories would hold up. At the station, they were arrested. They used their right to make a phone call to contact "relatives abroad."

Two hours after their arrest, the Canadian consul in Amman came to the station. He entered their cell, asked the men where they had grown up and other questions about Canada, and came out to tell the Jordanians: "I don't know who they are. Canadians, they aren't."

The other members of the team heard of the arrests through the phone calls to "relatives." The female member of the team went to the Intercontinental to notify Ben David. "I was at the hotel pool," he later explained. "Suddenly she came up to me, though she wasn't supposed to be in touch with me at all. From her face I could tell that something was very wrong. We exchanged a few words and I realized that a grave hitch had occurred. I contacted Israel and was instructed to collect all the members of the team from their hiding places and to bring them to the Israeli Embassy."

When Netanyahu was notified, he immediately called King Hussein and asked him to receive General Yatom for an emergency meeting, without mentioning the subject to be discussed. Hussein assumed it had something to do with Hamas's cease-fire proposal. Yatom flew straight to Amman and told Hussein the whole truth.

After hearing him out, a fuming Hussein stormed out of the room. Yatom recalls: "It was [Jordanian intelligence chief General Samih] al-Batihi who got the king angry, because he was personally offended by me. Without him, we would have been able to finish the matter much more quietly with the king, and at a much lower price. During the discussions, Batihi started complaining to me for not telling him, saying that we could have planned the operation together, etc., etc. That's pure nonsense."

Meanwhile, in Mossad headquarters near Tel Aviv, Uri Chen, in charge of relations with the American intelligence community, called in Stan Moskowitz, the head of the local CIA station. Moskowitz was very surprised to hear the news, and very unhappy about a request that the Americans should intervene with the Jordanians to help get the Israeli agents released. But even before he could report to Langley, CIA director George Tenet had been informed of the incident by the agency's Jordan station and had issued an order not to intervene.

Netanyahu and Yatom realized that if Mashal died, King Hussein would have to order the two agents tried for murder. They would very likely get the death penalty. Ben David recalls what happened next: "All this time I was walking around with the antidote which was not needed, because none of our guys was affected. . . . I decided to destroy the stuff because I didn't want to get caught with it. I called in and left a message saying that I wanted to destroy it. Then I got a call from the commander of Caesarea. At first, because what he said was so fantastic, I thought that I had heard wrong and I asked him to say it again.

"He asked if I still had the antidote, and when I said yes, he told me to go down to the lobby, where a captain from Jordanian intelligence would be waiting, and to go with him to the hospital, where the doctors would administer the antidote to Mashal and save his life.

"I understood from him that this was being done as part of a deal between Netanyahu and Yatom and the king. The Mossad would save Mashal, who was already unconscious and on a breathing machine, well on his way to the world hereafter. In exchange, the arrested operatives would be freed."

Ben David did as he was told and found the Jordanian captain, whose eyes were blazing with anger. "I still remember the hostility in his glance. But he had his orders and he carried them out." Ben David and the Israeli woman doctor went with the Jordanian officer to the hospital. She wanted to administer the antidote, but the Jordanian did not trust her and would not let her approach the dying Hamas leader. A Jordanian doctor took the container and injected the substance. Mashal recovered rapidly.

The attempt to assassinate Khaled Mashal had grave diplomatic repercussions. Israel's relations with Jordan and Canada were severely strained. Prime Minister Netanyahu, Ariel Sharon, former Mossad deputy chief Ephraim Halevi, and Attorney General Elyakim Rubinstein all made trips to Amman to try to placate the king. But Hussein was convinced that the Israelis were trying to get him overthrown. He refused to meet them, and they were received by his brother, Crown Prince Hassan. The two imprisoned operatives were released, but the price was very high. Israel was forced to release none other than Sheikh Ahmad Yassin, the founder of Hamas, along with many other Palestinian prisoners. A short while later, the four other operatives were allowed to return to Israel.

The Mashal affair caused serious damage to Israel's intelligence relationship with its neighbor to the east, driving the Jordanian services into the arms of the CIA, a connection that would become far more intimate after 9/11. For the Mossad, this was a great loss. Instead of the Israeli organization being the Jordanians' first and most important partner, the CIA is now Jordan's closest ally. Israel gets its information from Jordan only indirectly, if at all.

"Our friend from Taibeh is bombing again."

This sentence was heard over and over again in the corridors of Israel's intelligence-gathering agencies in the years 2001–08. The "friend" was Keis Obeid, the Israeli Arab who had crossed over from helping the Israelis to attacking them. The story of Obeid reveals the nature of Hizballah's efforts to work with Palestinian terrorists. As in so many arenas, Iran has done most of its pro-Palestinian dirty work through the proxy of Hizballah.

Obeid was given an important role in Hizballah's Unit 1800, set up in cooperation with Iran to support Palestinian terror. He became the most prominent and influential contractor for terror attacks against Israel, earning himself a very high spot on the hit list of Israeli intelligence. But because he was located in Lebanon, Prime Minister Sharon decided not to have him liquidated for fear of reprisals.

Under interrogation, many perpetrators of terror acts, or people caught before being able to carry out such attacks, have implicated Obeid and Hizballah in the organization and financing of their operations. One example was Ahmad Sari Hassan, of the West Bank town of Tulkarm, who abetted a suicide bombing on the promenade in the seaside town of Netanya, in which thirty-two people were injured on March 30, 2003.

He said that he was given 10,000 shekels (about $2,000) by the head of the Islamic Jihad in Tulkarm, who received it from Hizballah in Lebanon. Iran contributes money to Palestinian organizations through the "Martyrs' Fund" which also supports Hizballah.

Hizballah has launched some of the most lethal attacks, like the double suicide bombing in a Tel Aviv pedestrian mall on January 5, 2003, in which 23 people were killed and 105 injured. According to Shin Bet statistics, Hizballah was involved in 21 percent of all terror attacks in 2004. In 2005, 90 percent of the terror operations of the militant Fatah faction known as Tanzim were at least partially funded by Hizballah. In many cases, the perpetrators' motives were financial rather than ideological. Numerous field operatives make a reasonable living out of their part in the attacks. Suicide bombers themselves often agree to undertake their missions because the organizations that send them to their deaths promise to take care of their families afterwards.

In contrast to the strict enforcement of field security in most Iranian operations abroad, the Revolutionary Guards and Imad Moughniyeh never even tried to maintain secrecy when it came to their dealings with the Palestinians. They were aware that the Palestinian networks were riddled with Israeli agents, so they opted for quantity over quality. They assumed, correctly, that at least some of their operations would succeed despite the vigilance of the Shin Bet. This is why Keis Obeid made no attempt to hide his name or the nature of his activities in the phone, fax, and Internet contacts that he conducted with Arabs in the occupied territories and in Israel. He distributed money by means of bank transfers to the families of terror operatives, adding a bonus for every attack. The same rather cavalier attitude was evident in the wholesale recruitment of Palestinians who had come into contact with Iranian and Hizballah agents, in full knowledge that most of them would be caught by the Israelis.

Alongside the activities of Keis Obeid and Hizballah, Iran also recruited Palestinians directly. During the Second Intifada, hundreds of wounded Palestinians were taken to Iran for medical treatment. There, many were contacted by various agencies, with a view to enlisting them for intelligence or operational purposes: gathering information in Israel and the territories, setting up infrastructures of operatives to carry out terror attacks, and smuggling arms and ammunition into the territories. Some of the wounded men were given military training during their stay in Iran, after they recovered.

In the late 1990s, before the intifada began, Iran's preferred Palestinian client, Islamic Jihad, was at an operational low point following the elimination of its exiled leader, Fathi Shkaki, in Malta in 1995. But when Israeli prime minister Ehud Barak attempted to reach a final settlement with Yasser Arafat at Camp David in 2000, Iran decided to resuscitate the group. A secret internal document of the Palestinian General Security Apparatus, dated June 1, 2000, reveals that on the eve of Israel's withdrawal from Lebanon, Shkaki's successor, Ramadan Shalah, met with the

Iranian ambassador in Damascus, Sheikh al-Islam, who demanded that the group carry out terror operations "inside Palestine," without admitting responsibility.

Early on in the intifada, the Islamic Jihad launched many attacks against Israeli civilians and soldiers. Unlike Hamas, Islamic Jihad has almost no social or communal goals or functions; it is devoted solely to military operations. A small organization, it is very difficult to penetrate or obtain intelligence about it, and it is heavily influenced by Iran. Hizballah gives Jihad members advanced training in making explosives, assembling bombs, and smuggling weapons and money. In April 2001, Ramadan Shalah visited Tehran and met with Ali Khamenei, who praised the courage of Jihad's members and promised him that its budget would be increased by 70 percent, to enable the recruitment of Palestinian youngsters for suicide operations.

In March 2002, during "Operation Defensive Shield," two senior Jihad activists were captured in the West Bank town of Jenin. Ali al-Saadi and Thabet Mardawi both admitted responsibility for or involvement in innumerable terrorist operations, many of them suicide bombings. According to Shin Bet sources, the two said during their interrogations that they had been in constant contact with Ramadan Shalah at the organization's headquarters in Damascus, and had received large sums of money from him. Iran provided the Islamic Jihad with generous funding, and it soon became one of the most persistent and lethal terrorist groups.

For years, with the chief exception of intelligence sharing, Hamas kept its distance from Iran. Its leader, Sheikh Ahmad Yassin, wanted its fundraising to be as legitimate and as unhampered as possible, and he therefore made sure that Hamas's actions would always appear to be part of a broad struggle against the Israeli occupation of the Palestinian territories. Both Hizballah and Iran wooed him ardently, but they were politely rebuffed. "We're coping, thank you," Yassin and his cohorts would say, while they raised millions of dollars from sympathizers all over the world.

Early in 2004, however, after Yassin was assassinated by the Israelis, Hamas began accepting aid from Iran and Hizballah. The Shin Bet and the IDF were applying more and more pressure, and Hamas leaders abroad—particularly in Damascus and Tehran—were gaining influence at the expense of the local leadership in the territories. It was through them that financial and logistical support began flowing in from Iran and Hizballah. This newfound cooperation reached a peak with the visit of the Palestinian Authority prime minister, Ismail Haniyeh (a Hamas member), to Tehran in December 2006. On his return to Gaza on December 11, Haniyeh announced that Iran had undertaken to give his government $240 million in aid in 2007. The Hamas Web site said that $100 million of this would be a direct grant to the government; another $45 million would go toward salaries of civil servants and the families of Palestinian prisoners in Israeli jails; $60 million to the unemployed; $20 million to the rebuilding of homes destroyed by Israel; and $15 million to libraries and cultural programs.

During the same visit, Haniyeh declared that "Iran is the strategic depth of the Palestinians." Addressing an audience of thousands at Tehran University, he proclaimed: "The braggart of the world [the United States] and the Zionists want us to acquiesce in the plunder of the Palestinian lands, to stop the jihad and the resistance and to accept the agreements that were signed with the Zionist enemy in the past. We will never recognize a Zionist government. We will carry on with the jihad until Jerusalem is liberated."

Though at first support for the Palestinians was provided in secret, as time went by, Hizballah began boasting about it publicly. On April 27, 2007, when an interviewer for the Beirut daily *Al-Safir* asked Nasrallah if the organization was supplying arms to Palestinians, he said that at the beginning of the intifada it had done so, but after an attempt to smuggle weapons through Jordan was discovered and political problems ensued, the Palestinians, "asked us to transfer them money, and they would conduct their own affairs." Nasrallah added that the Palestinians had the capability of purchasing or making their own weapons, including missiles, "but they need financial, political and informational support. We do not deny that we help them with this."

An example of "informational support" came to light after the Shin Bet arrested a man named Yunis Shadi Abu al-Hassin in the Gaza Strip on December 15, 2003. He was planning, and had almost completed, a model aircraft that was designed to deliver an explosive device onto one of the Israeli settlements in the Strip, at the instigation of Iranian intelligence. He told his interrogators that he had learned of the possibility of joining Hizballah while watching the movement's al Manar TV station,

which screened e-mail addresses and phone numbers for those wanting
to enlist.

The Israelis made several attempts to combat the funding of Palestinian
terror by Iran and Hizballah. A few months after Ariel Sharon became
prime minister in March 2001, he met with Major General Meir Dagan,
who had been his close associate in the early 1970s when Sharon ran a
brutal operation to wipe out terror in the Gaza Strip. Sharon asked
Dagan, who had been decorated for bravery during the Gaza operations,
to set up a new counterterror body within the Prime Minister's office,
reporting directly to him, to concentrate on gathering information on the
finances of terror. The new department was code-named "Harpoon." Its
offices were located in a closed, secure compound. What Sharon really
asked Dagan to do was to disrupt Arafat's financial setup, and Dagan
soon broadened his activities to take in the funding of other organizations, mainly Hamas and other Islamist groups. In the wake of Harpoon's
researches, all of the organizations holding funds from Hamas or Iran
were outlawed. A series of proposals for the disruption of these financial
activities were considered, some of them particularly wild, in keeping
with Dagan's reputation as a loose cannon. One was to torch the computer center of a Swiss financial institution that held and laundered
Iranian money. (Military Intelligence representatives at Harpoon
scotched that one.) In August 2002, Sharon appointed Meir Dagan as
the new director of Mossad.

The activities of Harpoon and a parallel unit in the CIA did not
escape the attention of the Iranians. In February 2006, attempts to
smuggle their currency reserves out of Europe were detected by the
Israelis and the Americans. The Iranians feared that their accounts might
be frozen because of their support for terror and in the wake of anticipated sanctions over the continued development of their nuclear project.

In late 2005, a group of terror victims had filed suit against Iran in
Italy, leading to the freezing of an Iranian government bank account containing some half a billion dollars. Because of a bureaucratic slip-up,
however, the Iranians managed to withdraw the money and transfer it
elsewhere. But they feared that the same thing might happen in other
European countries. After a series of consultations with the head of
Iran's central bank and senior economic officials in Tehran, the govern-

ment ordered that as much as possible of the reserves be moved out of Europe and into banks in countries that were considered less accessible to international institutions. Some of the money was placed in accounts under the names of private individuals, or of straw companies, in order to make it more difficult to locate and confiscate.

Hizballah's deep involvement in the financing of Palestinian terror was the reason for "Operation Green Torch," carried out by Israeli security forces in February 2004. The army, the Shin Bet, and the police came up with a simple solution that caused a lot of very negative responses abroad and in the media: Special forces raided the premises of the Arab Bank and the Cairo-Amman Bank in the West Bank city of Ramallah, and ordered the astonished staff to help them locate certain accounts and to determine the balance in each account. A very senior army source said that certain clerks who at first balked at helping the Israelis were "persuaded" to do so. He swears that physical force was not used.

Armed with the figures, the Israelis then ordered the clerks to open the vaults, and took out cash equaling the total amount of the accounts, telling the banks to settle matters with their clients themselves. This entirely novel method of confiscating monies was an original Israeli invention. It yielded no less than 37 million shekels, or some $9 million in various currencies. Most of the four hundred-odd accounts belonged to various societies connected to Hamas and the Islamic Jihad.

"Green Torch" was severely criticized by some Israeli intelligence officials. Very soon after the operation started, large numbers of armed Palestinians began firing at the forces securing the banks. "The second problem," said a former operative involved in the planning of the operation, "was that it was very difficult to seize the contents of the accounts. You can put a gun to the temple of the bank manager and demand that he show you how much is in the account, but what then? The Israeli force decided to take the sum in cash from the banks' safes, but that is a very problematic measure. First of all, it was seen in the world as a bank robbery in broad daylight carried out by the State of Israel. Secondly, the money was clearly the property of the bank, and not of the account owners. And on top of that, how do you confiscate an overdraft? After all, some of the accounts were in the red." In the wake of devastating criticism, Israel decided against any repeat operations, at least for the time being.

Very quickly, Iran and Hizballah tried to repeat their success in boosting the Palestinian uprising, this time in an uprising against the Great Satan himself.

As the dawn light began to rise, a cat appeared suddenly on the windowsill. After creeping out of a pile of junk, it was looking for a ray of sun to rid it of the night's chill. An alley cat, shabby and filthy, it had once been white but now was wearing the same gray shade as the alley itself. It was 4:30 a.m. on April 15, 2004, at the corner of Salah al-Din Street and Cinderblock Alley, in the heart of the casbah of Nablus, the largest city in the West Bank. Early peddlers were dragging their carts piled with vegetables and fruit, and the smell of baking pita bread was in the air.

The cat, with all of its feline instincts, did not notice that less than an arm's length away, on the other side of the closed iron shutter, someone was watching it through the sights of a sniper's rifle.

The awakening street shared the cat's ignorance.

Inside the apartment overlooking the street was a team of elite Israeli soldiers, men of Viper Company of Paratroop Battalion 202, heavily armed and daubed with warpaint, waiting for the start of "Operation Swamp King." The objective: to kill wanted, armed terrorists of Hamas and the Iranian-backed Islamic Jihad based in the casbah. The method: creation of an artificial provocation that will irresistibly tempt them out of their hiding places to attack Israeli troops operating in the streets, thus exposing themselves to the waiting ambush, of a kind code-named "Grass Widow."

In April 2004, as part of the research for this book, I managed to persuade the IDF's land forces command to allow me to join a special commando operation, one of a series that the army had been staging since early in 2003.

The American military in Iraq has been conducting similar actions since the end of 2005. At the beginning of that year, twenty-three senior and middle-level U.S. officers had been in Israel studying the "Grass Widow" technique. They watched videotape footage filmed during operations, heard lectures, and participated in training sessions for the special forces of the IDF's counterterror unit, as well as "dress rehearsals" for the real thing.

They could not join actual raids, because of the political repercussions if one of them were to be killed in an attack on Palestinians in the occupied territories. But they learned the method, and passed it on to their troops, first at training bases in the United States and later to the forces in Iraq, who began to make frequent use of it.

The operation that I observed was planned over a number of days and based on aerial photographs of the densely populated casbah. Two "widows" were to be placed in the dead of night in the very heart of the locality in the West Bank most hostile to the Israelis. "The objective," explained Captain Omer, commander of the company and of the operation on the ground, "is to put the widows at places that give the snipers as great a 'killing ground' as possible." The positions were decided upon in light of past experience, overlooking long stretches of narrow alleys from which the gunmen generally appear to open fire at the Israeli soldiers.

After the two days of planning and discussion groups, the combat orders are drawn up, providing for a large force, including tanks at the ready outside the casbah in case a widow is discovered and there's an urgent need for the troops to be extricated. "After all, it's only a group of eight men, and the last thing we want is a case of 'Blackhawk Down,' " says one of the officers, immediately reassuring his guest, who cannot hide his apprehension, that the chances of our being stranded in the hostile zone are very small, "really zero."

The regional Shin Bet intelligence coordinator reports to the final orders group on the up-to-date situation in the target zone and the most recent information obtained on a Hamas weapons laboratory/workshop whose destruction is one of the objectives. It is concealed in a secret room in one of the casbah buildings, and it is guarded by an aide to the Hamas commander and number one on Israel's wanted list in Nablus.

After the rehearsal comes the real thing. The troops who are to take up positions near the windows and do the killing smear black and green paint on their faces. At 2 a.m. there is a last inspection parade at the Samaria Brigade headquarters. Company commander Omer reminds his men that "there may be many opportunities to kill gunmen in operations like this one, but we can't afford to miss even one, so focus on your sights, and don't blink too much. Fire at the center of the body and a little higher. That's the best. We can assume that the gunmen have fewer ceramic bulletproof vests than we do. If one falls, take another shot to confirm the kill. Don't forget, we want him to come out of this dead."

A long convoy heads for the casbah. It's now 2:30 a.m. The Israelis make as much noise as possible. Very soon, the other side is awake. The vehicles begin to take scattered hits from small arms and Molotov cocktails, and a large explosive device that is tossed from somewhere goes off with a huge bang. The force that I am attached to identifies itself in code on the radio. The vehicles stop for a few seconds at one particularly dark corner. The force jumps out and the convoy moves on, as if it had not left anyone behind. We enter the apartment that had been marked off on the aerial photograph.

Two women are woken up: an elderly widow and her daughter, who had arrived from Jordan on a visit. The two are panicked, especially the visitor, who is not used to the harsh reality and suffers a slight asthma attack brought on by anxiety. The women are shut up in the kitchen. Their cell phones are removed. "Please let us go to the neighbors, we're frightened," they plead. The soldiers are compelled to refuse.

The snipers begin setting up the ambush. We are at No. 2280 in the casbah, and another four hours must pass before the action begins. During this time, the snipers have to settle in and prepare themselves firing slits. This is no easy task with large iron shutters covering the windows. Removing them would reveal our presence because of the noise. Opening them would expose us from a certain angle. For lack of other options, the snipers use small tools to make holes in the shutters and bend the iron back slowly with infinite patience so as not to wake the neighbors. They create two openings—one for the telescopic sights and the other for the muzzle of their rifles. The hours go by with nerve-wracking slowness. An orange streetlight outside leaves stripes on the ceiling. The men take turns to sleep and to smoke in the toilet, the only place where the commander has permitted them to do so. Gradually, the casbah begins to wake up. When the snipers finish their work and have hung their rifle barrels from cords slung over the tops of the blinds, the company commander whispers into his radio: "The widow is ready. The moon [vehicle] can be sent."

The overall principle of Grass Widow is very similar in most operations. It was born mainly out of the tremendous difficulty of securing freedom of movement in heavily populated zones, freedom that is critically important in preventing terror attacks on civilians inside Israel or in the settlements as well as against military forces. Before Grass Widow was devised, every Israeli incursion into a Palestinian refugee camp or city became a real war. Lieutenant Colonel Amir, who is given credit for developing and streamlining the Grass Widow tactic, calls it "Giving guerrilla to the guerrillas." The commander of Paratroop Battalion 890 during most of the confrontation with the Palestinians, Amir used a sabbatical period at the IDF's Command and Staff College to compose a paper on the principles of such warfare. Today, a translation of this document into English serves as a basis for the U.S. military's operational plans as they endeavor to apply Grass Widow techniques in Iraq.

According to the IDF's "open fire procedures" in terrorist-infested areas like Nablus, soldiers must shoot to kill at anyone holding any kind of firearm, Molotov cocktail, or explosive device, without any warning, and then confirm the kill. Almost every day, new variations of the Grass Widow technique are tried, tempting gunmen out of their hiding places and exposing them to fire from a concealed sniping position: an object "falls" from a truck; someone is arrested and the gunmen attack the force carrying out the arrest; an armored car drives up and down the street, sometimes with a loudspeaker broadcasting a tape prepared by the Shin Bet in Arabic with someone chanting challenges like: "So where are all the big heroes of Izz al-Din al-Qassam [the military wing of Hamas]? Why don't you come out and fight? Let's see if you are men." Or more provocatively: "All the Jihad are homos," or: "Hamas are sons of whores, your mothers work in the streets and give it out free to anyone who wants it" (others are even less printable). Surprisingly, it has worked, with the gunmen coming out to spray the offending vehicle and getting picked off by a sniper concealed in a nearby apartment the night before.

Lieutenant Colonel Amir says: "The idea is to make the gunmen think twice before coming out to fire at IDF forces in the alleys. The terrorists have learned that all of sudden a price tag has been fixed to this whole story of firing sporadically or throwing a bomb at our forces, that it's suddenly become risky, that suddenly you can take a bullet in the back.

"What we set out to do was cancel out the built-in asymmetry of a big, heavy, clumsy, predictable army with routine procedures, and guerrilla forces, which are generally seen as shapeless, amorphous. By studying the characteristics of the guerrillas, I can force them into a certain pattern of behavior. I give them a shape. I make them respond where I want them to, and then I hit them."

In a number of simple provocation actions, an armored jeep was positioned on the outskirts of the Balata refugee camp near Nablus. Lieutenant Colonel Guy says: "An armed man came out into one of the alleys and opened inaccurate fire, while running, at the jeep. The jeep did not fire back. The gunman felt safe and came a little closer, shortening the range and getting braver. Every now and again he'd let loose a burst of fire, standing in the middle of the alley for a longer spell each time. The jeep didn't respond. The guy apparently thought he'd found some idiots, and in the end he just stood there, in the middle of the alley, like he was in some American action movie, firing bursts into the window of the jeep, just to impress his buddies. Seconds later, he took a round in the forehead.

"After that, the gunmen learned the trick with the jeep, and they were careful of it. We moved the jeep away, about 500 meters from the camp. They felt more secure again to walk around and show themselves in the alleys of the camp, knowing that the M-16 isn't accurate at a range of more than about 150 meters. But this time we had a sniper in the jeep with a more powerful rifle and we hit them again."

The use of Grass Widow proved itself again and again in the war against Hamas and Islamic Jihad. Dozens of wanted terrorists were killed, and the others began showing a lot more caution combined with fear of the IDF's snipers. This significantly reduced their freedom of movement and the time that they had to prepare terror attacks.

The "widow" that I joined is not so successful. It seems that one of the neighbors has reported to the armed organizations that some suspicious movement had taken place during the night. They send people to go around knocking on doors to check if there are soldiers in the nearby buildings. They knock on the door of the apartment we are hiding in. We do not respond and they go away, but we have left the shutters closed and this arouses suspicion. More and more people in the street are staring at the windows. A large stone hits one of the shutters. The soldiers fear that a grenade or explosive charge may be tossed at the window, and they close the shutters as tightly as possible. Captain Omer reports over the radio: "Fear that widow is exposed. Repeat. Fear that widow is exposed," and some code words which indicate that the large forces should be prepared in case a catastrophe occurs and we have to be extricated urgently.

Then we see that the locals below are now looking at the side of the building where we are hiding on the second floor. It is clear that something is going on, but in the absence of a lookout outside, we can only guess what it is. The onlookers appear to be really interested, but they also are moving away from the building. The battalion intelligence officer reports over the radio that the Shin Bet has just warned that a Hamas detachment is laying demolition charges.

Minutes later, it turns out they were right. A mighty blast shakes the building, deafening us. Windowpanes shatter and we are covered with glass fragments. Dust fills our mouths and nostrils.

There is no longer any doubt. "We have been discovered," Omer reports. Soon, a large Israeli rescue force reaches the house. But the entrances have been booby-trapped and its fire detonates the charges that could have led to a completely different end to Operation Swamp King than the one planned. The force discharges large quantities of tear gas, through which eight soldiers and a nervous journalist stumble to a jeep, weeping and coughing, and are driven off.

The next day, a Palestinian woman sets out to execute a suicide mission in the Jewish city of Ariel. She is carrying 25 kilos of explosives from the laboratory that was supposed to have been destroyed in the operation. By sheer luck, she is stopped on the way. But what better illustration could there be of the price of failure?

The most astonishing thing about Operation Swamp King was that in the street below, life continued more or less as normal. The incidents did draw the attention of the casbah residents, but they are so accustomed to this sort of thing that some of the peddlers, although they knew that explosives had been readied and a full-scale battle was about to take place, never even bothered to move their wagons of oranges and tomatoes. Even the cat, which survived the explosion and appeared from somewhere a few minutes later, didn't seem to be too upset.

Today, Grass Widow and various refinements added by special forces of the U.S. military (such as scattering explosive items that terrorists are likely to be interested in) are a leading element in the warfare against the "subversives" in Iraq. According to data conveyed to Israel by the Americans, with expressions of gratitude, 146 terrorists were killed in 2006 using this technique. Impressive; but no more than a drop in the ocean compared to the tidal waves of terrorism that are sweeping that country with the support of Iran and al-Qaeda.

Iran's attitude to the American invasion of Iraq was ambiguous even before it happened. Iran wanted to see Saddam Hussein disarmed of his weapons of mass destruction, but believed that it should be done by peaceful means alone, in accordance with UN resolutions, and without unilateral U.S. military intervention. The Iranians saw Saddam as an embodiment of evil, but the Americans were no less an evil in their eyes, and the presence of their army on its doorstep was the last thing the regime in Tehran wanted to see. The ayatollahs were beginning to feel an American ring closing around them: the new U.S.-backed Hamid Karzai regime in Afghanistan; increasing American cooperation with Turkey in the northwest and Pakistan in the southeast; the bolstering of the American presence in Saudi Arabia and the Gulf Emirates; and a massive American military buildup in the Gulf.

The moment the Iranians reached the conclusion that the U.S. invasion of Iraq was inevitable, they began making preparations of their own, in a number of spheres. First, the Iranian regime stopped being wary of giving public support to the Iraqi opposition and extended its patronage to opposition groups of both Shi'ites and Kurds. About a month and a half before the invasion, some 3,500 Iraqi Shi'ites belonging to the opposition forces crossed the border from Iran into northern Iraq. This formation was trained by the Revolutionary Guards and was called the Badr Brigade. The Iranians issued scattered warnings against the Americans. Supreme Leader Khamenei declared that Iran would not allow "the American highway robbers and savages in civilized clothing to rule our country again." Ayatollah Ahmad Janati, a close associate of Khamenei, whose many roles include that of Tehran's Friday prayer leader, attacked the American administration in a sermon in February 2003, saying, "A number of naive people in Congress support the moves of their administration, which is acting like Stalin and Hitler and Genghis . . . the people will soon take care of them."

Iran's Lebanese proxy Hizballah also adopted a much harsher tone toward the United States after the American campaign against terror began in the wake of 9/11 and the invasion of Iraq. In a "Martyrs' Day" address broadcast on the militant Shi'ite organization's Al Manar TV station on November 11, 2001, Hassan Nasrallah said: "This is the war of a tyrannical, despotic, arrogant country against everyone who refuses to submit to it." At the mass rally in Beirut that same day, Nasrallah railed against the United States and called out: "Death to America." The crowd replied: "Death to America," and the leader's response was, "That won't make America die. Louder!" An example of the virulent anti-American campaign launched by Hizballah was a clip broadcast daily by Al Manar during the second half of October 2002, showing the figure of the Statue of Liberty with the face of a skull, holding a dagger, and with two cannons at her feet.

Iraq after the invasion became the new meeting point between Iran and and the World Jihad. Both saw the torn country as a fertile field for activity—the Jihadists as part of their war against everything American, and Iran as part of its efforts to show the Americans that their wish to impose democracy by force was not worthwhile, and that President Bush had better not contemplate doing to the ayatollahs' regime what he had done to Saddam Hussein.

Day after day, the number of American and Iraqi casualties mounted. The U.S. military's enormous efforts to overcome the terrorists produced some isolated results, but made no significant overall impact.

As in other cases, the Iranian involvement in Iraq was led by the al-Quds force of the Revolutionary Guards. It trained the personnel of the Badr Brigade that had entered the "no-fly zone" in northern Iraq before the invasion, and then dispatched them on suicide missions inside the country. It also provided training, funding, and weapons to another Shi'ite force, the al Mahdi Army, that was established in June 2003 to fight the American presence under the Shi'ite leader Muqtada al-Sadr. The subject of assistance to terror activities against the Americans also came up in the Iranian media. For example, the Sharq press agency Web site reported that a senior source in the Bassij (militia) had disclosed that a group calling itself the al Karbala Battalion had been dispatched on May 27, 2004, to Karbala to fight the Coalition Forces.

In January 2004, Israeli intelligence informed the CIA that a new unit had been formed by Hizballah with the purpose of stirring up the rising in Iraq. Called Unit 2800, with headquarters in Beirut, most of its personnel came from the militia's own Badr Brigade (not to be confused with the Shi'ite force mentioned above), deployed north of the Litani River in South Lebanon.

Because it was not within immediate engagement range of Israel,

Unit 2800 was considered more available for the new task. Hizballah's Unit 1800, which deals with the Palestinian uprising, is only able to work by remote control, using phones and the Internet, or through couriers, because of Israel's tight border controls. In contrast, Unit 2800 could easily send personnel into Iraq, usually via Iran, to put their experience and expertise at the disposal of the forces fighting the Americans. Even earlier, in November 2003, the National Security Agency had monitored a message from the Iranian Embassy in Beirut to the al-Quds headquarters in Tehran reporting that Imad Moughniyeh (or "Tahsin," as he was code-named in the message) was pressing to be "as involved as possible in the subject of Iraq." The instruction and the weaponry that came from Hizballah and Iran caused dozens of American and British fatalities and left hundreds wounded.

In June 2004, there was an escalation. An American soldier was killed when a powerful projectile fired from a roadside ambush penetrated the armored vehicle he was travelling in. U.S. Army demolitions experts identified a new type of weapon, dubbed an explosively formed penetrator (EFP), which soon began appearing in more and more attacks. By the end of 2006, it had killed 170 Coalition troops and wounded 620. Early in February 2007, the Americans intercepted a shipment of EFP devices thanks to accurate intelligence obtained from the former commander of al-Quds, General Ali Reza Askari, who had defected to the American side. These sophisticated devices were manufactured by the Revolutionary Guards, on the basis of Hizballah's experience in its long years of war against the Israeli military. They had been smuggled into Iraq by Guards personnel and members of the Northern Badr Corps. The report of the intercepted shipment came out soon after Askari's disappearance from his hotel in Istanbul.

There is disagreement between the intelligence services of the United States and Britain over whether these sophisticated bombs were manufactured in Iran or Lebanon or whether Hizballah had given the know-how to the Mahdi Army, which was already capable of making them in Iraq. Either way, it was clear that Iran or its emissaries were doing everything to strengthen the ability of the Shi'ites in Iraq to harm Coalition Forces there.

Askari had been in touch with the CIA long before his actual defection, giving them the information that made possible the American commando raid in the northern Iraq city of Irbil on December 22,

2006, when dozens of Revolutionary Guard members were detained, including the commander of al-Quds in Iraq, Hassan Abbassi, one of Askari's former aides. Also taken prisoner were a brigadier and a colonel from the force. The raiders seized infrared sensors, electronic detonation devices, and information on specifically Iranian explosive materials, as well as ten Strela antiaircraft shoulder missiles originating in China and repainted in Iran.

Hizballah's contribution was vital. In July 2005, the newborn Iraqi intelligence service, set up under CIA aegis, produced information to the effect that ten Mahdi Army specialists had been given a half-year training course in the building of roadside bombs and other powerful devices by the Lebanese militia. A year later, Israeli Military Intelligence reported that the sum of information in its hands indicated that by then a total of some 1,200 Mahdi Army men had taken part in various Hizballah training programs. The organization had also supplied the Iraqi guerrillas with RPG-29 shoulder-launched missiles, as well as Metis and Kornet missiles, which it received from Syria.

In February 2007, British media reports said that one hundred snipers' rifles sold to Iran by the Austrian Steyr Mannlicher concern in the years 2004–05, ostensibly for use against drug smugglers on the border with Afghanistan, had reached Shi'ite subversive elements and were being used against Coalition Forces in Iraq. These rifles are highly accurate, and their rounds, some of which are manufactured in Iran, can penetrate armor at a 1,500-meter range. Two senior commanders of the Mahdi Army told an Associated Press correspondent in March 2007 that hundreds of members of the Shi'ite militia had gone to Iran to be trained by the al-Quds force, and that Iran provides most of the funds for the army.

In March 2007, the U.S. Army reported that it had apprehended a senior officer of the organization by the name of Abu Mussa Dakduk, who had been one of the personal security officers of the secretary general, Hassan Nasrallah. He was captured in a raid in the city of Basra in southern Iraq, with two Iraqi subordinates. The Americans stated that he had been sent two years earlier to Iran, to help train Iraqi Shi'ites in guerrilla warfare. Upon completion of their training, these men joined the forces fighting the Americans in Iraq itself. After some time Dakduk himself was sent to Iraq to command operations there.

It seems that Iran took courage and self-confidence from the successes against the United States in Iraq. In parallel to the rise in the number of body bags being sent home to America, the tone of the declarations ema-nating from Tehran about the American presence in the Gulf became blunter. In May 2004, a senior officer of the Revolutionary Guards threatened that "Our missiles are ready to strike at the Anglo-Saxon civilization, and when we get the order from the leader we will launch them. . . . There are twenty-nine sensitive targets in the United States and the West. We already . . . know how we will attack them. We have a strat-egy for destroying the Anglo-Saxon civilization and to eradicate the Americans and the English. Iran has the means to attack Israel's nuclear facilities so that no trace of them will remain."

The previous day, the secretary general of the International Commit-tee of Support for the Palestinian Intifada, Ali Akbar Mohtashemi-Pour (who initiated the attacks on the U.S. Embassy and the U.S. Marine headquarters in Beirut, and whose fingers were blown off in a CIA revenge operation), said: "We, the Muslim states, must form a storm front against the United States and Israel. The association of half a mil-lion formed in Beirut [Hizballah] is not enough. After all, there are many Muslim youths who are ready to carry out suicide attacks against the American crusaders."

In June 2005, a rally was held in Tehran to register volunteers for sui-cide missions in Iraq and Israel. It was organized by a body known as the Headquarters for the Perpetuation of the Memory of the Shahids (Mar-tyrs) of the World Islamic Movement. Taking part were various public figures, commanders of the Revolutionary Guards, and representatives of jihadi movements from a number of Islamic countries. Volunteers were given registration forms offering them three alternative tracks: to kill Salman Rushdie; to undertake suicide missions against the Americans in Iraqi cities holy to the Shi'ites such as Najaf and Karbala; and to attack Israelis in "Palestine." A spokesman said that two thousand people had registered. The missions, he said, would begin when the Supreme Leader, Ali Khamenei, gave the signal.

It seems that the best summation of the Iranian involvement in Iraq is to be found in the Annual Threat Assessment that the director of National Intelligence issues to the the Senate Armed Services Commit-tee. There, on February 27, 2007, Michael McConnell stated that

> As a result of last summer's hostilities, Hizballah's self-confidence and hos-
> tility toward the U.S. as a supporter of Israel could cause the group to

increase its contingency planning against U.S. interests. . . . Iran's lethal support for select groups of Iraqi Shia militants clearly exacerbates the conflict in Iraq, as does Syria's continued provision of safehaven for expatriate Iraqi Ba'athists and less-than-adequate measures to stop the flow of foreign jihadists into Iraq.

Iran uses radio, television, and print media to influence Iraqi public opinion and help promote pro-Iranian individuals in the Iraqi government at all levels. . . . It seeks a capacity to disrupt the operations and reinforcement of U.S. forces based in the region—potentially intimidating regional allies into withholding support for U.S. policy—and raising the political, financial, and human costs to the U.S. and our allies of our presence in Iraq. Tehran views its growing inventory of ballistic missiles (it already has the largest inventory of these missiles in the Middle East) as an integral part of its strategy to deter—and if necessary retaliate against— forces in the region, including U.S. forces.

# PART V

# THE FIRST SHI'ITE BOMB

CHAPTER 18

# The Termite File:
# How an Israeli Arms Dealer
# Gave Iran a Chemical Arsenal

In the headquarters of the Mossad's Caesarea Division, the organization's elite operational unit, there is a small memorial room to commemorate agents ("warriors," in Mossad terminology) who have fallen in the line of duty. Despite the innumerable perilous actions carried out by Caesarea since it was established, there are only three photographs on the wall. One is of Eli Cohen, the heroic Israeli spy who penetrated the upper echelons of the Syrian government and was caught and executed in 1965. The other two are much newer and less romantic—their demise was the result of a motorcycle crash in Vienna on May 27, 1993, during one of the least dangerous Caesarea operations ever, the surveillance of Nahum Manbar, the man the Mossad had code-named "Termite." A businessman and native Israeli, Manbar had betrayed his country and sold chemical weapons to Iran.

At the time, he was playing a double game, offering to help Israeli intelligence on two different fronts—illicit arms trades *and* the case of missing Israeli airman Ron Arad.

The two Mossad operatives were tailing an associate of Manbar's, Dr. Majid Abbaspour, a leading figure in the Iranian Ministry of Defense, after a meeting between the two of them. Manbar later described the scene:

"Abbaspour contacted me and said that he could help [on the Arad case]. The subject is extraordinarily sensitive, or so he said, and we will have to find a way of presenting Arad's release, when and if it happens, as something that has no connection whatsoever with Iran. It is impermissible that Iran's name be involved."

Manbar set up a meeting with Abbaspour at the Marriott Hotel in Vienna. "When he came to my suite he was very angry, and he said, 'Nahum, do you know that I've been followed from the airport? I'm certain that these are your guys, because only you and I know that I am here,' " Manbar recounted. "I tell the doctor that it could not be so, but I know he is right. I went down and saw two guys with earphones . . . I went up to the first one, who was sitting to one side with a cup, and I stirred his coffee for him. I asked him in Hebrew and English what he was doing there. His face went red and then white. He didn't say a word. I went up to the other one and did the same thing. I asked if that was all the allowance the Mossad gave. Not even enough for a little cream cake. The two got up and left. I went back up. Abbaspour was also pale. He said, 'I can't go on like this. I have to get to the Iranian Embassy. I need an escort and bodyguards. My journeys are always secret, and now I've been discovered, which means that I am in danger.' I said good-bye and flew back to France."

The two Mossad agents raced off on a motorcycle after Abbaspour, who left the hotel in a great hurry and made for an Iranian Embassy safe house. It was pouring with rain, making it particularly difficult for the agents to keep up with his speeding car. As they emerged from an underpass, they overturned, and a woman driving a Mazda ran over and killed them both.

It may not have been a heroic moment, but their mission was part of a crucial one—and apparently, crucially bungled. Manbar's arming of Iran stands as one of Israel's greatest embarrassments, and it could have been prevented.

Nahum Manbar was born on April 18, 1948, at Kibbutz Givat Haim. His family were among the founders of the settlement. Ostensibly the model *sabra* (literally, a "prickly pear," the term for natural-born Israelis), at age sixteen he was in the reserve squad of Israel's national basketball team, his determination making up for his lack of height. He then became an outstanding soldier, a combat officer and instructor at the army's officers' college. Manbar fought in both the Six Day War in 1967 and the Yom Kippur War in 1973; during the latter he saved the life of Hanoch Saar, who was a defense counsel at his trial and among the last of his friends to remain loyal to him to the end.

After his military service, Manbar moved to Tel Aviv and opened a series of businesses. These ventures generally ended with police investigations and indictments. Passing bad checks, fraud, and theft of checks from the government employment service were just some of the crimes of which he was suspected or convicted. The last straw came in 1984, when he was indicted for fraud, imposture, and theft. He fled to Britain and was declared a fugitive from justice in Israel. He began buying and selling agricultural produce in London's Covent Garden market, but soon switched to a much bigger market, trading in arms and military materiel.

Manbar befriended Joy Kiddie, perhaps the most mysterious figure in the whole affair. Kiddie ran a series of charities based in Cambridge, helping wounded people and children all over the world, sending toys and food to Rwanda, Angola, and Uganda, and aiding needy children in the United Kingdom.

Kiddie has delicate features and a face that shows her abundant kindness. She declares that she is a devout churchgoing Christian. But she also has another side, that of a shrewd businesswoman, trading not just in charitable donations but in almost any commodity worth her while. She has maintained a close link with MI6. Kiddie met Manbar through her dealings as a broker on European commodities markets. "I traded in everything then, from sugar to diamonds," she recounts. "Nahum called me one day when I was in Paris. At the time I was trying to find some red mercury, which my connections in the international arms trade had told me was used in improving missile boosters. I knew that a lot of intelligence agencies were looking for the stuff, and I realized how valuable it would be. Nahum said that he knew I was in the market for it, and suggested that we cooperate." Red mercury, incidentally, is also used in nuclear weapons and missiles.

Business blossomed between Manbar and Kiddie, and his circle of associates grew. Manbar linked up with Bari Hashemi (alias Farschi), an Iranian Defense Ministry purchasing agent who had homes in Britain and Austria and headed a Vienna-based company. At the time, he was implicated in some of the deals involved in the Iran-contra scandal. Manbar later defined his relationship with the Iranians as a "mutual meeting of wills. They found me just when I was looking for them."

Initially, after coming to power, Ayatollah Khomeini maintained a strict policy against developing or acquiring weapons of mass destruction; but Saddam Hussein's horrendous use of poison gas against Iran in the 1980–88 war forced Tehran to take a different line. In 1983, the Revolutionary Guards were instructed to develop offensive chemical weapons.

Four years later, in order to boost the spirit of the Iranian people and to deter Iraq as the war dragged on, Tehran announced officially that it possessed chemical warfare capability, although it had not yet made use of it. In a speech in the Majlis or Parliament, Prime Minister Hussein Mussawi stated that "If one day Islam permits us, we will have no problem in using this weaponry and going into serial production of it." In point of fact, this declaration was pure propaganda. Despite its efforts, Iran had hardly any actual chemical capability.

Yet its determination did not waver, even as the war drew to a close. Manbar's arms trade with the Iranians expanded steadily. He bought weaponry, some of it from the Polish army, and sold it to Iran, shipping it via Poland, where he set up his headquarters in Warsaw and spent most of his time between 1987 and 1992. At first, the weapons were conventional, a small consignment of shoulder-launched antiaircraft missiles. Through this deal he became acquainted with the Polish defense minister, General Florian Siwicki. "I would buy, say, T-55 tanks from the Polish army for $35,000 apiece, install some fire-control system that I had brought from Israel for $20,000 apiece, and sell them to the Iranians for $200,000," he explained in an interview with the author. "The profits were fantastic."

In addition to such offensive weaponry, Manbar sold the Iranians protective gear against atomic, biological, and chemical arms, setting up a plant in Poland to manufacture it. He insists he informed Israeli authorities of his activities. "All of the competent [Israeli] authorities who should have known, did know all about everything, and they said nothing. All of the items that I imported from Israel and sold to Iran had the full approval of SIBAT [the Israeli Defense Ministry's division for military aid and exports]. At a certain stage, the Iranians . . . began asking for some completely different items. I refused to handle the requests, and I reported them to the appropriate authorities. The Iranians wanted medium-range missiles that could be fitted with chemical warheads. They wanted certain materials. They wanted me to set up a chemical weapons plant in Iran. I transmitted all of their requests that looked suspicious to the appropriate factors in Israel, and I'm speaking about suitcases full of papers. Acting on the instructions of those factors, I asked the Iranians to give me more details about what they wanted, to submit more blueprints and sketches. Everything was conveyed to Israel."

At least, so he claims. As the record would eventually show, Manbar sold chemicals and even chemical weapons designs and manufacturing equipment to Iran. The question is, when did Israel discover it, and why did they take so long to stop it? The full story has as many twists as a Le Carré novel.

Thanks to his arms trade, Manbar became a wealthy man, and many companies and businesspeople wanted some of the action. Or at least they wanted some information. Through Brigadier General Amos Kotzer, his representative in Israel, Manbar offered to supply Israeli intelligence with information on military subjects, as well as on the missing airman Ron Arad. Manbar claimed that with the excellent links he had created with the heads of the Iranian arms industries he would be able to garner information on Arad, and even reach a resolution of the tragedy and bring the airman home. The Mossad, like the rest of the Israeli intelligence community, was by then in an advanced state of despair. They had failed to come up with any information about Arad and were being subjected to extreme pressure to solve the problem by the political leadership, who appeared more and more helpless in the eyes of the public. They were ready to grasp at anyone who seemed able to help. Manbar knew this, and exploited it to the hilt.

He gave the Mossad a videotape which he claimed showed Arad, still alive. In fact, the tape—and his other leads on the Arad case—proved worthless.

In another matter, however, not less important, Manbar proved able to help, this time thanks to romantic connections. His girlfriend and wife-to-be, Francine, had previously been married to an aviation engineer by the name of Herman Schmidt. Schmidt had held a senior position in a combined Argentinean-Iraqi-Brazilian-Egyptian effort to build a long-range ballistic missile, a source of grave concern to both the United States and Israel. Francine was not at all happy about her husband's occupation, "because the missile was liable to kill children." But, as she put it later, he told her that "he only wanted to make a few million and to retire." As Schmidt's trips to Iraq became more frequent, he started to get many threats on his life, and the offices of his firm in Salzburg were torched. Eventually, under pressure from American intelligence, the couple was expelled from the principality of Monaco by order of Prince Rainier. In February 1990, Schmidt contracted lung cancer, although he had never suffered from medical problems before. He died in November. Francine believes he was killed by a Western governmental agency, "perhaps the Mossad," she reported in an interview for this book.

Francine may have had good reason to believe her husband was murdered. Nonetheless, she opposed the arms industry and was sympathetic to Israel. Manbar brought Francine to Israel, where she had a long talk with experts from the Mossad and the technical side of Military Intelligence's Research Division. She supplied many important details that contributed to Israel's understanding of the project.

Yet even as Manbar helped Mossad, he helped himself with its enemies. In mid-1990, on a visit to Austria, Manbar was introduced by Hashemi to Dr. Majid Abbaspour, who was acting as a special assistant to the Iranian president, Ali Akbar Rafsanjani. Abbaspour has had several titles, and he eventually became a cabinet minister. He was and still is one of the strongmen of the Iranian arms procurement system. At that time, he was the head of Iran's chemical weapons program. He headed a Ministry of Defense department known as Unit 105, comprising hundreds of officials, experts, logistical staff, and intelligence personnel, whose job it was to procure the components and the know-how to enable the country to produce chemical weapons. Toward the end of 1990, Abbaspour and Manbar formulated a contract under which the Israeli was to supply the Iranians with the know-how for the production of substances used in chemical weapons, to set up a production plant, to install the necessary equipment, and to train teams of employees. Manbar was to be paid a total of $16.23 million for fulfilling his obligations under the contract.

The process leading to Manbar's prosecution began two years later, after information reached the Mossad that the Iranians were trying to recruit Manbar for their chemical weapons program. A report arrived that did not mention his name, but did specify the name of one of his companies. It could easily have gone unnoticed were it not for the alertness of "Ruth," a Mossad staffer. She read the information, realized that it was about Manbar, and requested his files from various branches of the intelligence services. She did some cross-checking and realized that something was very wrong. Pursuing Manbar became an obsession, in some cases leading her into battle with her own direct superiors. All the while she wondered, "How can an Israeli do a thing like this?"

On July 16, 1992, in the wake of the misgivings raised by Ruth, Shin Bet internal security agents met with Manbar and ordered him to cease all activities with Iran and to hand over all the documents connected to them.

He delivered some documents, which were handed to Ruth and another Mossad official, "Ilan," then in charge of the scientific aspects of the chemical weapons department. But Ruth and Ilan were not satisfied. In the words of Ilan's later testimony at Manbar's trial: "All of the data referred to things that had been done in the past. Our sense was that these things were ongoing, and that it was possible that they were even at the early stages."

For six more years, Manbar operated with varying amounts of freedom. He still had the stain of his bad checks and fraud in the 1970s and early 1980s, so he launched a vigorous campaign to rehabilitate himself. A multimillionaire, he built two magnificent villas, one at Lugano on the Swiss-Italian border, and the other on the French Riviera, where he entertained many of the Israeli power elite, showering them with the best of everything. He lived like a very wealthy man and made sure that everyone took note. He surrounded himself with advisers and publicists whose job was to create for him the image of a philanthropist and investor in Israel's economy. Another aim of course was to erase the memories of his checkered past.

He began visiting Israel again and buying Israeli basketball teams, eventually claiming investments of $7 million in them. He also began contributing to charitable organizations, hospitals, and various politicians. He became a sought-after guest at parties thrown by members of Israel's high society. A smiling Manbar can be seen in photographs with the likes of Foreign Minister Shimon Peres and other cabinet ministers, Labor Party leaders Dalia Itzik and Uzi Baram, future Prime Minister Ehud Olmert, as well as Yitzhak Rabin's wife, Leah, and others, during the years 1989 to 1996. At the same time, he began trying to streamroll the Israeli Ministry of Justice and President Ezer Weizman, who had pardoning powers, into wiping his record clean of past convictions. "He used the heaviest possible guns, so that he would not only be forgiven, but also have his record cleared," the Mossad director Shabtai Shavit would recount later.

His efforts were initially somewhat successful. In 1991, a plea bargain was reached in which Manbar paid a small fine and received a suspended sentence. There was no erasing of convictions, but he got off lightly nonetheless. It would take six more years before he was brought to justice for his gravest crimes—treason, and arming the enemy. All along the way, the intelligence services debated what do to about him, and made astonishingly meek decisions. Ruth and Ilan led the charge, taking their suspicions to Shavit at the time of Manbar's plea bargain, in 1991. Six years later, in classified testimony at Manbar's trial for treason—disclosed here for the first time—Shavit recalled: "The people who are considered experts on the subject by the Mossad came and told me about the sale [to Iran] of constituent materials and technology for the production of mustard gas from thionyl-chloride and also told me of the accused's connection with the supply of know-how for the production of tabun, or nerve gas. Of all of the substances in the chemical weaponry arsenal, these are the two that are lethal on a mass scale, to entire populations. If we were talking only about a constituent substance, it would be open to discussion, perhaps, what the purpose of the sale was and what the purpose of the substance was. But when it is a matter of the sale of technology, of production lines for factories, the debate about the end use of the substances becomes altogether redundant. . . .

"This case seems exceedingly grave to me, perhaps the gravest in my entire experience of crimes committed by Israelis against the security of the state . . . I decided that we must expose the truth about this man's involvement in the supply of the know-how, the materials, and the technology to Iran. . . . From the first moment, and because of the fact that he was an Israeli, I deemed it necessary to bring the matter to the attention of the prime minister and defense minister, the late Yitzhak Rabin."

Shavit passed what had become known as the Termite file to the Kidon (Bayonet) Unit of the Mossad's Caesarea special operations division. Kidon handled the most complex and covert tasks, including assassinations. The two operatives who lost their lives in the pursuit of Abbaspour were members of this unit, and their deaths were one of the tragic twists of the Termite file.

After 1992, and especially after these two were killed, Mossad pursued Manbar much more actively. The secret services of France, Italy, Holland, the United States, Germany, and Britain were also after him. MI6 tried to exploit the network set up by Manbar in order to penetrate the Iranian arms industry. A young agent named Richard Tomlinson was given the mission. In time, Tomlinson was fired and decided to take revenge on his former employers by publishing a sensationalist book purporting to reveal the failures and illegal actions perpetrated by MI6.

Tomlinson was jailed for six months for trying to get his book, *The Big Breach*, published. After his release he broke his parole terms, fled from Britain, and began distributing parts of his work by mail and via the

Internet from a hiding place in Switzerland. One chapter was devoted to his involvement in the Manbar affair. In an interview granted as part of the research for this book, he maintained that "We never intended to interfere with Manbar's work. On the contrary, the whole thing was a classical British intelligence operation: to allow authentic private businessmen, not straw companies, to enter into relationships with hostile countries like Iraq, Iran, and Libya, and later to penetrate their networks in order to gather information on the target country."

Tomlinson dismisses concerns about the damage Manbar caused, arguing that not all WMD are equally dangerous: "Equipment and material for the production of chemical weapons don't count to MI6. It's easy to defend against chemical warfare agents and they don't have a decisive effect on the battlefield. The conception is that it is permissible to supply something in this area in order to collect important information on many other subjects."

He is absolutely certain that Manbar acted on behalf of Israeli intelligence in his arms deals with Iran: "We had no doubt about it. I wasn't a liaison officer, but I know that Manbar's name kept cropping up in talks our people had with their Mossad counterparts. Officially, the Mossad never admitted that Manbar was acting on its behalf, but it was clear that the Israelis knew about everything that he did. We received the reports of the DST [the French interior intelligence service] on their surveillance of Manbar's house on the Riviera. There were dozens of calls to the Israeli Embassy and the Mossad headquarters in Tel Aviv. These calls could be interpreted in only one way." He also claims that Mossad stonewalled them on any hard information about the weaponry, saying that Mossad "kept on trying to disrupt our work and didn't hand over all the documents that it had."

Tomlinson's assertions are astounding. If in fact the Mossad not only knew about Manbar's work but gave him permission to continue, then why was he eventually tried for treason? Tomlinson has no explanation, commenting: "Just as it happens often in intelligence services, this time too the Israeli services decided, for reasons unknown to me, to get rid of Manbar, break off the connection and make him a scapegoat. The Mossad kept all the documents that could have proved his innocence to itself, and anyone who tries to get them out will be punished."

MI6's profound conviction that Manbar was working for the Mossad was shared by the CIA. By the early 1990s, that agency too had marked

Abbaspour as a subject and had placed him under surveillance. In the course of their inquiries, Manbar's name cropped up, so the Americans began an intensive investigation into him as well. On July 16, 1994, the State Department issued a statement that Manbar had been placed on its blacklist, noting that Manbar and two of his companies, Mana International Investments and Europol Holdings Ltd., had sold chemical weapons components to a state which appears on the list of countries that support terrorism, in contravention of an American embargo. Manbar and the two companies were to be boycotted by the American government, and none of their or their subsidiaries' products were to be allowed into the United States. "Manbar's dealings . . . helped the Iranians to leap several stages forward in their efforts to develop chemical weapons. If it were not for Manbar's involvement we believe that it would have taken them several years more," commented a State Department official in charge of the prevention of proliferation of non-conventional weapons.

On the covert level, the Manbar affair cast a shadow over the relationship between the CIA and the Mossad, and even over the entire American-Israeli partnership. Senior officials in the U.S. administration were convinced that Israel was conducting a massive operation behind Uncle Sam's back, yet it made no sense. The Israelis were investing huge efforts in trying to persuade the Americans to take strong measures against Iran and its endeavors to obtain non-conventional arms. So why was Jerusalem supplying Tehran with precisely what it needed to produce such weaponry? As Brigadier General Amos Gilad, deputy military secretary to Prime Minister Rabin, explained later at Manbar's trial: "The Americans were altogether bewildered by us. They believed that we were activating him in order to wipe ourselves out. It all appeared irrational to them. . . . When you come to an American and demand vigorous action against the Iranian strategic threat, your own hands seem to be dirty when you yourself are turning a blind eye on or covering up for someone who is an Israeli citizen and is helping to build the gravest threat against you. We were perceived in a bewildering light."

In late 1993, Mossad director Shavit met with Rabin to discuss prosecuting Manbar. As he later testified, "We were certain beyond any doubt that we had all of the intelligence evidence that the accused was indeed doing what we suspected that he was doing. . . . This discussion was not a typical discussion with the prime minister and defense minister. The purpose of this discussion was to take a decision as to how to proceed. We presented intelligence information which was in the nature of intelligence proof about the charges. We brought a legal opinion that said that there was not yet enough evidence for an indictment. Eventually, the prime minister decided that the next time the accused came to Israel he would be summoned to the police and warned by a senior official of the Israel Police, to cease his activities with the Iranians. . . . Another decision taken by the prime minister and defense minister at that meeting was that we would bring the Americans up to date and disclose all of the details to them so that they would not, God forbid, suspect us of running an operation the ultimate result of which would be Iran's possession of chemical weapons capability." If they couldn't convict him, they decided to settle for a stern lecture—hardly the typical Israeli response.

In October 1993, Manbar was summoned to Israel and told to report to Brigadier General Avi Cohen, commander of the national unit for investigation of serious crimes. Cohen informed Manbar that he was known to be selling chemical warfare materials to Iran despite previous warnings to desist, and that if he did not cease, he would face prosecution. There was no arrest. Manbar's shipments were not sabotaged. A year and a half after the first warning in July 1992, there was only another talking to.

Manbar claims he did cease all connections with Iran at the end of 1993. Yet in 1995, by his own testimony, he came to Shimon Peres, who was then foreign minister, and gave him Abbaspour's calling card. "I told Peres that this was the man who could do anything for us in Iran. He is a pragmatist with a very moderate attitude. . . . Peres took the card and told me that the matter was being dealt with." Two weeks later, Manbar contributed $200,000 to Peres's campaign fund.

On November 3, 1995, I met Nahum Manbar for a long conversation, in which he completely denied the charges leveled against him by American intelligence. In the same meeting, which—without our knowledge—was photographed and monitored by the Shin Bet, Manbar said that Israel had missed a historical opportunity by not allowing him to continue the dialogue with Abbaspour. The next day, Prime Minister Rabin was assassinated, and the Manbar case was put on hold.

Finally, in April 1996, a meeting was held in Prime Minister Peres's office to debate the case against Manbar. The Shin Bet representative said Israel should not submit to the American pressure to indict him, in order to prove that Israel has no part in the business that he was doing with Iran. Others disagreed and argued that it was time to arrest him. Nothing happened.

At the beginning of the following year, Dvorah Chen, deputy attorney general for security related affairs, reached the conclusion that she could get Manbar convicted for harming the security of the state and aiding the enemy in its war against Israel, offenses carrying the death penalty. Meanwhile, Mossad officials finally persuaded Manbar's right-hand man, Kristof, who had been a party to the deals with the Iranians, to come to Israel from Poland and testify. On March 27, 1997, Manbar arrived in Israel to watch one of his basketball teams, Hapoel Jerusalem, compete for the State Cup. On the runway when his plane landed were officers of the police's serious crimes unit and the Shin Bet. He was arrested, and a court ordered him held without bail. A blanket gag order prevented the media from reporting the details of the case.

When Manbar went on trial on May 15, the story launched several political scandals that shook the nation, including Manbar's large donations to Labor Party leaders and unconfirmed reports that Prime Minister Netanyahu had tried to influence the court against Manbar. Also unconfirmed were rumors that the president of the court, Judge Amnon Straschnov, had had an inappropriate relationship with a female member of the defense team. It was a secure trial held behind closed doors, and much of the testimony was classified.

The defense case was largely based on the claim that Manbar did not act alone. The Israeli arms industry, Manbar's lawyers asserted—including Israeli businessmen who functioned with the ostensible permission of the security authorities—had sold and were still selling vast quantities of material to Iran. The judges partially accepted the defense arguments on this point and leveled sharp criticism at the state's conduct: "Even if there have been only a few instances and they were of an altogether dissimilar nature, and even if these facts did not clear the accused of the responsibility for the disgraceful crimes that he has committed, they nevertheless constitute a weighty consideration for not punishing him to the fullest extent of the law, as would have been appropriate had these circumstances not existed."

Witnesses testified that Manbar was fully aware at the time of the gravity of his actions, and tried to blur his tracks. Kristof, his assistant and right-hand man in Poland, recounted how Manbar had secretly given the Iranians diskettes containing information for the construction of the thionyl-chloride plant. "He used to yell at the Iranians at meetings for sending us things directly to the office," Kristof told the court. "All of the correspondence was addressed to the company's 'cover' name."

In his decision, Judge Straschnov poured eighty-six pages' worth of fire and brimstone onto Manbar: "I regret to say that my impression of his testimony and his personality was utterly and absolutely negative. His testimony was replete with contradictions, peculiarities and self-rebuttals, not to say outright lies. It was evasive, tortuous and devoid of . . . even the most basic credibility. The accused has impressed me as a liar, a manipulator, a profiteer, who only rarely can be caught telling the truth."

The panel of judges determined that from 1990 to 1994, Manbar provided the Iranians with 150 tons of thionyl-chloride in very high concentrations, most of which was acquired by Joy Kiddie, the patron saint of needy children, from China. The court also found that he sold Iran the equipment needed to produce more thionyl-chloride, shipped from Europe to Iran on a fleet of twenty-four trucks. Manbar was convicted of supplying know-how and equipment for the building of factories for the manufacture of four different types of nerve gas, including VX, the most lethal chemical warfare agent that there is.

Manbar was positive he would be acquitted, just as he had once seemed to think he could get into the good graces of Mossad by offering a forged videotape in which a man not at all resembling Ron Arad says, in a heavy Persian accent, "I am Ron Arad, I am Ron Arad." Manbar had ordered a private jet to fly him to France on the day the trial ended. But the only trip that he took was to Ramle Prison, to serve out his sixteen-year sentence.

The materials and the factories that Manbar supplied have undoubtedly served as a key component of Iran's chemical weapons capability. A senior Mossad official said in his testimony in the trial: "Because of the accused's actions, an extremely hostile state, which openly advocates the destruction of Israel, is today equipped with chemical weapons of mass destruction and with the practical ability to use them against the population of Israel."

According to a series of reports submitted by the CIA to the House Permanent Select Committee on Intelligence during the latter half of the 1990s, Iran had by then stockpiled thousands of tons of chemical agents, including mustard gas, phosgene, and cyanide. Its production capacity was estimated at 1,000 tons a year, with the main plants situated at Damghan, 300 kilometers from Tehran. It was to Damghan that Manbar's lethal and lucrative materials were shipped. Moreover, despite the protestations of the Israeli defense establishment that it never traded with post-revolutionary Iran, in fact Manbar was never prosecuted for selling Iran conventional weaponry, though he repeatedly admitted doing so.

Even in prison, Manbar has continued winning people's confidence, although he has quarreled with almost all of his former friends and acquaintances, including his wife Francine. During furloughs, he carried on a hot romance with his lawyer for a time. Manbar gives lessons to inmates in several subjects, including chemistry, in the prison library. He has also tried to keep his business going, trading by telephone with African states in various products. Somehow, he was given permission to acquire unlimited phone cards, and has held long conversations with the defense minister of Uganda. On occasion, he has needed to explain the background noises made by the prison's public address loudspeakers, and he was once heard to say to the minister: "It's all right for you sitting comfortably in your air-conditioned office in Kampala, with all your aides and secretaries. But I have to work hard for you, waking up in a different country every morning and suffering the nerve-wracking noise of the loudspeakers in airports."

In June 2007, after serving ten years in prison, Manbar asked to have the remaining third of his sentence commuted for good conduct. There was no disagreement that his behavior in jail had in fact been good, but the Mossad and the Shin Bet submitted secret reports to the parole board, expressing sharp opposition to his release.

The Mossad was so anxious for Manbar to remain behind bars that it hired as an adviser former prosecutor Dvorah Chen, who had left government service and gone into private practice as a defense attorney, representing particularly well heeled clients. Mossad director General Meir Dagan sent the head of the organization's agent control division to represent him and the agency at the hearings. In his affidavit and in testimony, he was referred to as "Daniel." In the Mossad, behind his back, he is known as "the model" because of his good looks ("Good enough to appear in Marlboro ads," says one coworker) and his fashionable taste in clothes, from Europe's top designer brands. In the classified affidavit that Daniel submitted to the court, he wrote that he was a trained and highly experienced senior intelligence and operations agent of the Mossad. "At the time, as part of my duties, I took part personally in the investigation, both intelligence and criminal, of the prisoner, and I served as a prosecution witness in his trial." The Mossad and the Shin Bet were worried that Manbar's information—"along with the great knowledge that he has in the area of setting up a secret proliferation system," as Daniel testified, and the connections, monies, and operational networks that he had left in Europe—would enable him to recover and begin again. He would have only one goal in mind: to make as much money as possible. Since Manbar had never confessed his crimes or expressed regret, there was a grave suspicion that he would soon be back at his old tricks. Manbar's application was denied.

Many column inches of newspaper headlines have been devoted to Iran's nuclear weapons program. Yet hidden in plain sight is the fact that Iran possesses huge quantities of chemical WMDs.

Only time will tell if Iran will dare to make use of these weapons either in the battlefield, or—and herein lies the great fear of the United States and Israel—through its "long arm": Hizballah, Hamas, and Islamic Jihad, as it has done previously with many weapons developed in the past. Hamas had already tried to produce chemical and biological weapons, without help from the outside, but failed. The Iranians could solve the problem for them.

# CHAPTER 19

# Importing a Russian Bomb?

Iran's desire for weapons of mass destruction was not born of the 1979 Khomeini revolution. On the contrary, the revolution actually delayed the process. The Shah was very fearful of the Soviet Union, which shares a border with Iran, and wanted to position his country as an international superpower. He tried to acquire nuclear energy technology, and he signed a huge military agreement with Israel for the joint acquisition and manufacture of "missiles capable of carrying nuclear warheads."

An internal top-secret CIA document from 1993 asserts that Iran owes the start of its nuclear program to the United States, which had in the mid-1960s sold it a small research reactor that was installed at Tehran University. The facility was called the Tehran Nuclear Research Center (TNRC), and it included a 5-megawatt reactor and auxiliary laboratories. The Americans also provided 6.5 kilograms of uranium of a very high quality, almost weapons grade, for the reactor. Later, after he gave in to American pressure and signed the Nuclear Non-Proliferation Treaty, the Shah decided to purchase ten nuclear reactors from the United States, for the production of electricity.

The Shah may have been interested in alternative energy sources to replace oil when it ran out; but he was also keenly interested in the military applications of nuclear technology. He set up the Atomic Energy Organization of Iran to pursue the Bomb.

In 1974, Siemens, the West German company, had begun building two reactors near Bushehr. About 60 percent of one and a smaller part of the other had been completed before the 1979 revolution. They were both scheduled to be operational by 1981. In addition to Siemens, contracts for equipment, services, and raw materials were signed with companies in France, Germany, Argentina, and mine owners in various African countries. In Israel, senior officials familiar with the nuclear issue studied the reports of Iran's purchases and came to two main con-

316

clusions: The Shah was not counting pennies when it came to his nuclear product, and he wanted a bomb, as soon as possible.

Immediately after the revolution, payments from Iran ceased, and Siemens stopped building. At first, it was simply a matter of the general post-revolutionary chaos, and the fact that the state budget had very soon to cope with a series of new tasks, like the war with Iraq and the establishment of new defense and intelligence organizations.

But then, the interim prime minister appointed by Khomeini, Mehdi Bazargan, suddenly announced that all the contracts were annulled. He did so at the orders of the Ayatollah who, according to several sources, saw nuclear weapons as "anti-Islamic." Khomeini spoke of America's use of atom bombs at Hiroshima and Nagasaki and the killing of innocent civilians as evil deeds that were sharply opposed to the spirit of Islam. He did not want to replicate that sin, and so he issued a *fatwa* cancelling the entire project and forbidding the production of nuclear or other weapons of mass destruction. Until the end of the war against Iraq in August 1988, Iran did nothing to develop its nuclear potential further.

The death of Khomeini in 1989 brought about a dramatic, although at first secret, change in Iranian nuclear policy. Khomeini's successor, Ayatollah Ali Khamenei, was a middle-of-the-road and far more pragmatic politician. Once he took over, Iran again began trying to get its hands on unconventional weaponry. In closed forums, the new spiritual leader announced that it was possible to resume the nuclear project. As early as 1987 Khamenei said at a secret meeting of the Atomic Energy Organization of Iran: "Our nation has always been subject to external threats. The little that we can do to stand up to this danger is to make our enemies aware that we can defend ourselves. Accordingly, any step that we take here will serve the defense of our nation and your revolution. With this aim in mind, you must work hard and fast."

It was only in February 2006 that Iran dared to openly announce the *fatwa* that explicitly contradicted the commandment of the Imam Khomeini. Extremist clerics from the city of Qom reportedly ruled that "there is no religious law against using nuclear weapons." In real time, when Khamenei took power, and for several years after that, the West did not discern this change in policy. One of the reasons for the CIA's blindness was the downright stupid conduct of its Bonn station, which operated agent networks inside Iran. On one occasion, in July 1989, letters were sent to all the agents in a certain network containing coded messages in invisible ink, all on the same day, from the same address, in the same handwriting. Iranian counterespionage was already watching one of the members of the network, surveillance that included close scrutiny of the agent's mail. As soon as the letter arrived, all the Iranian investigators had to do was to check who else had been sent similar letters, and then pick up the agents like apples under a tree. They were interrogated under torture and most of them were executed. The CIA had suffered a major blow.

Beginning in 1989, Iran approached innumerable scientists who had left the country since the revolution, offering them hefty amounts of money to come back home and help "rebuild the motherland." Some of them were physicists and chemists who had undertaken advanced nuclear studies in America and Europe. Many of them returned and set up nuclear studies departments in Iranian universities.

Iran tried to get Siemens to come back to complete the Bushehr installations, in compliance with the terms of the contract with the Shah, but the United States managed to thwart this plan. Another German firm, Kraft-Werke Union, proposed replacing the nuclear reactors with natural gas turbines, but Iran was not interested in anything other than nuclear technology. It turned, next, to a rich potential source: Russia.

The disintegration of the Soviet Union had turned Russia and the other former Soviet republics into lawless territories. Yitzhak Yaakov, a former Israeli brigadier general who became a high-tech entrepreneur, recounts that "in 1993 I visited a company called Lutch in the city of Podolsk in central Russia. It developed products based on exotic materials like crystals and precious metals that are widely used in the development of nuclear weapons, and the technology is usually classified. Before *perestroika* there were over 10,000 scientists and engineers working for the company. When I was there, the number had dropped to about 1,000. The other 9,000 were wandering around looking for work. Some of them were working in the company dining room and served us lunch. I suggested that they set up technological hothouses, using the Israeli Trade and Industry Ministry model. I also met officials of the Russian security services. They admitted that they had no idea of the whereabouts of the scientists who had worked in the non-conventional weapons field. At that time it became known too that an Iranian agent had been going around in Russia, hiring scientists to work in his country. They could be bought, for $1,000 a month."

The recruitment didn't stop in Russia. Israeli intelligence learned of a flow of Iraqi nuclear experts to Iran, especially after the American invasion in 1991. Hussein Shaharastani, for example, a past head of the Iraqi nuclear program, has crossed over and is today employed in a senior position in Tehran. Ironically, many of these scientists were trained in the United States. Before the first Gulf War, relations between America and Iraq were good, and many Iraqi scientists even attended closed conferences of the U.S. scientific community that dealt with the development and production of various parts of atomic weapons. In August 1989, for example, there was a conference on detonators for nuclear bombs in Portland, Oregon, whose participants included M. Ahmad of the Iraqi government installations at al Qa'aqa, and his colleagues S. Ibrahim and H. Mahad. Israel was well aware of this, because among the others present were senior members of Department 24 of Rafael, Israel's arms development agency, which (according to non-Israeli publications) builds Israel's nuclear warheads.

Apart from the recruitment of unemployed experts, another serious cause for concern was the leakage of dangerous materials from the former Soviet Union. The Arms Control and Disarmament Agency (ACDA), a branch of the State Department, claimed that it had evidence that the Iranians tried to obtain fissile materials for military purposes in the former Soviet Union, through a number of private purchasing agencies. A senior ACDA official said that during a visit to Russia he was amazed by the ease of access to fissile materials. The Russians, he said, do not know how much such material there was before the collapse of the Soviet Union or what kind of material it was, so they cannot know how much has been stolen. Laboratories are not adequately guarded and there are places, including important Moscow institutes, where there is only one lock protecting fissile materials.

In order to assuage international anxiety, Iran agreed to allow the International Atomic Energy Agency (IAEA) to inspect all of its nuclear facilities. But IAEA inspection has proved to be only a very partial means of preventing the development of nuclear weapons.

With the approval of the IAEA, Iran made aggressive efforts to acquire nuclear technologies from Russia and China. As early as 1993, China agreed to install two 300-megawatt reactors at Esteghlal, near Bushehr, on the shore of the Persian Gulf. The project was cancelled due to American pressure, so Iran sought another supplier. The Russian Ministry for Atomic Affairs, MINATOM, which suffers from acute budgetary problems, leaped at the opportunity. Overtly, the Iranians asked the Russians for reactors for civilian purposes. Yet plutonium is a byproduct of the process of making electricity with nuclear fuel rods, and once plutonium has been extracted from uranium, it can be used for more sinister purposes.

In January 1995, Russia contracted to supply Iran with a reactor for electricity production, to be erected at Bushehr, for $800 million. From the start Russia asserted that it was a light water reactor, of the sort that the United States undertook to supply to North Korea, that could not be used to produce enough plutonium to manufacture nuclear weapons. In December 1998, however, American intelligence sources claimed that Russia was about to sell Iran a 40-megawatt heavy water reactor, for "research purposes." Such a facility would significantly increase Iran's ability to produce plutonium for use in a nuclear weapons program. It later turned out that at the same site, Arak, the Russians were helping to build a heavy water production plant.

Although the sale of the heavy water reactor was delayed, there was great anxiety in both Israel and the United States over the proposed deal. The two countries launched a massive campaign to block the nuclear relationship between Russia and Iran and the Bushehr project, in which they perceived a threefold danger:

First and foremost, the construction of the reactor and activating it would give the Iranians a great deal of nuclear experience and know-how, including in areas that could be used for military purposes.

Second, the large number of Russian ships sailing to the Bushehr site could have been carrying prohibited materials and equipment.

Third, in a complex on the scale of that rising at Bushehr, with its vast volume of activities and personnel, even if it were subject to international inspection, it would be possible to conceal a plutonium production plant. According to non-Israeli sources, Israel managed to hide a vast underground structure from American inspectors who visited its plant at Dimona in the 1960s. Why should the Iranians not be capable of doing the same? Bushehr is therefore perceived with suspicion as a place where Iran's real intentions are disguised.

Iran claims that these reactors, and nine more that it intends to acquire, are meant to supply electricity to its citizens, a contention that aroused great puzzlement in the West. A look at the figures on Iran's abundant oil and natural gas reserves does not make it clear why it feels a need for nuclear energy. The country is sitting on 92.86 billion tons of crude oil, or 9.3 percent of the world's reserves. It also has 73 billion cubic feet of natural gas, second only to Russia. It is far easier, safer, and cheaper to produce electricity from gas than from nuclear reactors.

Iran is aware that its activities are a difficult pill for the Americans and Israelis to swallow, and it fears an Israeli or an American attack. Iran has purchased an enormous number of antiaircraft missiles from Russia, some of which, according to Mossad reports, are S-300 missiles, considered among the most advanced in the world. These missiles have been deployed around Bushehr and other strategic targets.

The Iranians also began developing close relationships with certain elements in Russia in the field of missiles, and with a number of companies from a large number of countries for the supply of dual-use technologies, for use in its nuclear program. The data bases of ACDA, the U.S. Arms Control and Disarmament Agency, are full of the names of such companies from China, Germany, Pakistan, and Britain, who signed fat contracts with the Iranian government and Iranian agencies.

Just as in the affair known as "Iraqgate"—in which Western companies sold Saddam Hussein equipment and technology that almost enabled him to build nuclear weapons—so too in the Iranian case. Sales personnel from profit-hungry German firms led the amoral parade of businessmen ready to do anything for money. Since the Russian reactors were to be housed in German-built structures and based in part on German technology, the Iranians had to get assistance in addition to that given by Moscow. One of the concerns that hastened to provide such assistance was based in Potsdam and called VERO; it served as a pipeline through which some fifty German companies shipped equipment for Iran's nuclear program worth a total of about $200 million. In 2004, the Potsdam prosecutor general ordered a raid on the company's offices and the confiscation of its documents and computers. The managing director was in Moscow at the time, and by the end of January 2008 he had not returned to Germany. The investigation was still underway when this book went to press. VERO and the companies that worked through it claimed they had transferred the equipment to a reactor in Rostov, Russia, thereby attempting to circumvent the ban on sales of such equipment to Iran.

Late in 2001, former president Rafsanjani made an unusual statement. "If one day the Islamic world too acquires weapons such as those in Israel's hands," he threatened, "the strategy of the imperialists will be at a dead end, because dropping just one nuclear bomb on Israel will destroy everything, while such a bomb will only cause damage to the Muslim world."

Statements such as this have not been voiced in the years since then, apparently because Iran has grasped that they only increase international pressures. The official line on the nuclear issue taken by Iran's leaders until late in 2007 was generally very conciliatory, notwithstanding statements by President Ahmadinejad about "wiping Israel off the map."

"Iran is not seeking any kind of military-grade nuclear material, neither plutonium nor enriched uranium," said Iran's permanent delegate to the IAEA, Mohammad Sadeq Ayatollahi, in 1995. "Neither do we intend to build an atomic bomb, since that is ideologically contrary to our policy. We do not believe in weapons of mass destruction. We also do not believe that nuclear weapons bring power. . . . If you give a country nuclear weapons, you will not be making it stronger because the deterrent value of nuclear weaponry has been undermined in recent decades."

Very few in the West are convinced by these statements. After 1993, no one in Israeli intelligence doubted that Iran was seeking to obtain nuclear weapons, by any means. The combination of these intensive efforts and Iran's expansionist revolutionary ideology, even before Ahmadinejad's bizarre arrival on the scene, has caused Israeli intelligence to take the Iranian nuclear threat very, very seriously. This does not mean that the Israelis fear that someone in Tehran will be in a hurry to drop an atomic bomb on Tel Aviv. States and their leaders, even if they are dictatorships ruled by mad despots, are not suicidal. Hitler may have wanted to destroy what was left of Germany together with himself, but he was the exception. The Iranian regime over the past three decades has demonstrated a remarkable will and ability to survive, although it has brought economic ruin to its land. The Iranians believe that Israel has nuclear warheads and bombs and the means to deliver them. They know that using WMD against Israel would mean mutual destruction.

Yet the Iranians fear an American attack, and they need a "Samson option." Iran needs the shelter of a nuclear umbrella—one that would make any American president think twice before doing to Iran what Bush did to Saddam's Iraq.

In the early 1990s, uranium deposits were discovered in Iran. A team of IAEA inspectors who visited the mines in Saghand, in the central region of the country, in February 1992 estimated that there are 500,000 tons of natural uranium in these deposits. Two years later, intelligence reaching Israel indicated that Russia was supplying the Iranians with mining and uranium ore crushing technologies. It was also training substantial numbers of Iranian physicists and engineers at a nuclear research center in Moscow and at nuclear power stations. At first the Russians denied the IAEA allegations against them, but eventually the Russian Ministry for Atomic Affairs admitted that it had in fact planned to mine uranium on a limited scale on Iran's behalf.

It also transpired that Russia was giving some aid to the Iranian long-range ballistic missiles program, this time jointly with North Korea. Thanks to the technology it acquired, Iran managed to carry out several successful launches of its Shihab 3 (an upgraded version of the North Korean Nodong), a missile with a range of 1,300 kilometers, enabling it to cover all of Israel and parts of Europe.

Further, Iran is engaged in a serious effort to convert its missile engines from liquid to solid fuel. According to information reaching the Mossad, at least two private Russian firms supplied Iran with the technology used to build its missile engines. Russia denied this in spite of the fact that a number of shipments were stopped on the way, some in Austria, in interdictory operations by Western intelligence agencies. No one knows how many shipments were actually delivered to their destination.

In early 2006, Iran dedicated a heavy water production facility at Arak. Satellite photographs taken by American intelligence in July 2006 showed that the plant was working at full capacity and, more gravely, that the construction of the heavy water reactor was proceeding at a tremendous pace. Late 2006 satellite photographs clearly showed the reactor building and the structures to house the hot cells or fuel rods. Missile batteries were in place to defend it against air attacks. If building continues according to plan, Iran will be able to make its first plutonium nuclear bomb by the middle of the coming decade.

Meanwhile, at the Bushehr site, the Russians were building an entire nuclear city around the two reactors, one of which was at an advanced stage. The second remained in the same condition it had been in since 1979, and was slated for rebuilding by the Russians after they complete the first one. Satellite imagery showed that in their spare time, the Russian engineers enjoy swimming pools and tennis courts. One source, code-named "Brutus," who supplied a great deal of information to the West about Bushehr, also told of the enormous gap between working and living conditions for the Russians and their Iranian colleagues.

At the center of the Iranian residential quarter, a large bunker had been built, apparently to serve as a central command-and-control post. Perhaps as a deterrent to Israeli raids, the Iranians were careful to leave the two fishing villages on either side of Bushehr—Haleila and Bandara—in place. They also greatly reinforced the naval units protecting the site from the sea. Iran purchased ten fast Houdong-class missile boats from China, capable of firing C802 antiship missiles. The failure to persuade the Russian government to take steps against those of its citizens selling problematic technology and raw materials to Iran wasn't the only Russian problem faced by Israel and America. In September 1994, a file from Moscow marked "Top Secret" reached the Mossad and Military Intelligence, and through them, the Americans. According to the documents in the file, obtained by an Israeli representative in Moscow, Dr. Alexander Libin, very senior officials in the Russian ministries of Defense and Nuclear Industries had signed a secret contract with Iran for the supply of centrifuges for uranium enrichment, behind the back of the rest of the government. Russia has much experience in the manufacture and installation of centrifuges, and Iran could not have hoped for finer assistance than this. The documents revealed that top Russian officials, including ministers, had received bribes totalling $50 million, a gigantic sum in Russia in those days. The Russians made the deal on the side, without approval from the top echelons of Russian intelligence or the Kremlin.

The secret was so well kept that Sergei Primakov, the head of the SVR, Russian's external intelligence organization, heard about it only from his agents in Tehran. The furious intelligence chief decided to leak the story to the outside world, via Israel, which he knew would raise hell. The

United States turned to President Boris Yeltsin, who did not go as far as to fire those involved but did nip the centrifuge deal in the bud. That affair ended well; but from then on, the Russians were marked as "bad guys" by most of the influential figures in both American and Israeli intelligence. The Israelis kept on banging on the Russian door, openly and secretly, demanding an end to Russian aid to Iran's missile and nuclear programs. From the point of view of Israeli intelligence, Russia had become the primary locus of evil, as the supplier of both missile technology and nuclear know-how to Iran.

Together with China, the Russians have blocked and frustrated the attempts of the international community to build a coalition against Iran. They have worked constantly to soften the sanctions imposed on that country. Russia has signed more and more deals, including substantial arms deals, with Tehran. In addition, it has insisted that the construction of the Bushehr reactor be specifically excluded from the provisions of UN Security Council Resolution 1737, which dealt with sanctions.

On the other hand, the Russians never intended to supply the Iranians with nuclear weapons or the means to make them. They have secretly promised Israel that they would find excuses not to complete the work at Bushehr. As time went by, the Iranians also began to catch on to this, and from the end of 2005, a crisis evolved in the relationship between the two countries. There were reports in Iran, based on sources in Russia, that some of the Russian engineers working on the reactor had flown out of the country in a special plane, following an instruction from Moscow, without even informing the Iranians.

Iran responded sharply to the new Russian position, emphasizing its negative implications regarding the relationship between the two countries. Ali Larijani, the secretary of Iran's Supreme National Security Council, said in a threatening tone that "any delay at all in the activation of the reactor at Bushehr will damage Russia's commercial future. . . ." In his wake, the Iranian media came out with attacks on "the immorality of Moscow" and "the unreliability of Russia as a trading partner in the Persian Gulf region and all over the world." Iran also emphasized its determination to carry on with its nuclear program, even without Russia's support.

As far back as 2003, the Israelis began to sense that there was more than a grain of truth in the Russian contentions that they would take care not to help Iran acquire the Bomb. A discussion held during that period in the Israeli Military Intelligence Research Division concluded that "It is a fundamental Russian interest, both economic and strategic, to know exactly what is happening at Bushehr, to control events there, and to be certain that Iran is not developing nuclear weapons there. The last thing that Russia wants is Iran with an atomic bomb."

Yet Iran was clearly on the way to getting the Doomsday weapon. "If it isn't the Germans, or the Americans, or the Chinese, and not the Russians, and not even we who are helping them," asked the head of the WMD division of the Mossad's intelligence wing, "then who the —— is it?"

# CHAPTER 20

# The Countdown

I, Dr. Iftikhar Khan Chaudhry, was born on April 12, 1971, in Chakwal, Pakistan. I make this affidavit in support of application for political asylum in the United States. I have reasonable fear of persecution if I return to my home country, Pakistan, and if returned would be killed immediately. My wife Munza Iftikhar Khan, and our child Mehdi Murtaza would have joined in this application for political asylum—however they are outside of the United States and are in jeopardy. . . .

I know, from firsthand knowledge, of significant nuclear efforts that the Pakistani government is utilizing in order to enscourage strife between several nations in that region. Files and records which came under my purview and to my attention as a nuclear research officer, indicated that Pakistan was supplying nuclear technological assistance to Afghanistan, Uzbekistan and Iran.

On June 1, 1998, a top-secret meeting was held in the FBI offices at 26 Federal Plaza in Manhattan. Joining special agents Robert Washington and Christos Sinos were Michael Wildes, an attorney specializing in political asylum, and his client, Dr. Iftikhar Khan Chaudhry, a former research officer in Pakistan's nuclear project. The agents were amazed by what they heard. For hours, Chaudhry told them a shocking tale of Pakistan's plan to launch a preemptive nuclear attack against India, and its role in helping other countries, including Iran, to acquire nuclear weapons.

A U.S. source familiar with the affair says that at first the Americans were highly suspicious of Chaudhry's story. They assumed that the Pakistani asylum seeker had made it up to bolster his case. "Many of us did not want to believe that this was the truth, because after all we have a warm long-term relationship with Pakistan," says the source. But what Chaudhry revealed in 1998 proved to be true. It would become known to the whole world only five years later. The villain of the story was the head of Pakistan's atomic project, Dr. Abdul Qadeer Khan, who under the noses of the world's intelligence agencies had set up an enormous clandestine international network that sold nuclear expertise, equipment, and raw materials to Libya, Iran, Iraq, and North Korea. The huge progress made by these countries toward acquiring atomic bombs was to a large degree his responsibility. Khan and his agents also offered their services to Syria and Saudi Arabia. Dr. Khan's actions have had a critical, almost existential, effect on Israel.

As Chaudhry's affidavit makes clear, the United States had profound and intimate knowledge of what Pakistan was up to. Yet for several years it turned a blind eye, in part out of deference to President Pervez Musharraf, the Americans' ally in the war on terror.

In his affidavit, Chaudhry described Khan's marketing and distribution of his Doomsday playthings all over the world. Most in demand was the P-1 centrifuge, designed by a company called Urenco, which was jointly owned by Britain, Holland, and Germany. In the early 1970s, this company had employed Khan as a metallurgist. He stole the plans for the centrifuge and went on to become the father of the nuclear program in his country. He was treated with reverence in Pakistan for achieving a balance of terror with Pakistan's mortal enemy, India. The country's national nuclear center, the Khan Laboratories, was named after him. Later, Urenco centrifuges turned up in Libya and North Korea. Khan also helped sell designs for a later-model centrifuge, the P-2, and he even helped sell sophisticated bomb designs.

Dr. Khan in fact became a salient example of that rare phenomenon when a person without any position of political leadership has a critical impact on human history.

Chaudhry recounted exactly how the secret channel between Pakistan and Iran was set up. The two countries had signed a cooperation agreement for the exchange of nuclear technology:

I was present in May 1997, to witness a minimum of 5 Iranian scientists who were conducting an instructional study-tour of the Nuclear Research Center in Kushab. After reviewing documents it was apparent that a conference took place between Dr. Hussain [a senior official of the Center], and an official Iranian scientific delegation [at which] the Iranian scientists entered negotiation on the subject of: what was the level of development of Pakistan's nuclear research; what was the material used in producing nuclear weapons; what sources for the procurement of nuclear technology were being exploited; and what was the possibility for further cooperation between the governments of Pakistan and Iran. These and other Iranian scientists were introduced to the method in which uranium is processed for the purpose of creating a nuclear bomb.

For good measure, Chaudhry added: "it is also apparent that Iran intends to utilize a nuclear weapon—in the future, when a nuclear weapon would be operational—against the State of Israel."

Chaudhry recounted how he had quarreled with the Pakistani secret services over the country's intention to strike a preemptive nuclear blow against India. After he was informed that he and his family were in danger of losing their lives, Chaudhry managed with the help of connections and bribes to get on a plane to Canada from Islamabad on May 18, 1998. He crossed into the United States and contacted the FBI.

An American intelligence official says that the details supplied by Chaudhry were checked and found to be accurate. He was granted political asylum, but his affidavit, as well as the comprehensive interrogation that he underwent by intelligence experts from several agencies, was buried. The White House and the Pentagon just didn't want to hear about all this.

It was not only American intelligence that knew but never acted. A number of German intelligence documents (obtained with the kind help of the journalist Oliver Mayer-Rueth) show that German middlemen acting for Khan's distribution network—who had earlier helped Pakistan acquire the equipment and the expertise for producing its own bomb and are today on trial in Germany—offered top Iranian officials centrifuges for uranium enrichment as early as 1987.

A man by the name of Gotthard Lerch represented Khan in contacts with Masoud Naraghi, a senior Iranian official who had been sent by Hashemi Rafsanjani to examine the possibility of buying nuclear equipment. These contacts were kept under wraps in Iran also because at that time Ayatollah Khomeini was still alive and had banned the development of atomic weapons. When Khomeini died, the deal was struck at a meeting between the two sides in Dubai, where the Iranians received the blueprints for the P-1, as well as a list of companies that could produce the various parts.

German intelligence shared this material with the United States, which responded in a detailed document and with its own observations, but never took any meaningful action against the Khan network. Naraghi was dismissed from his post as head of the enrichment project in 1992, and the next year he defected to the United States. But even his detailed testimony didn't change anything in the Americans' conduct.

For fifteen years, Abdul Qadeer Khan worked at setting up a tremendously profitable, wide-ranging operation, selling the technology and means of production for the manufacture of nuclear weapons to Iran and several other states. According to assessments made after the fact, Iran paid between $4 and $8 billion for his playthings, including the blueprints for centrifuge manufacture.

The United States has never admitted that it was aware of what was going on between Iran and Pakistan. Says Dr. Robert Einhorn, who served as under secretary of state for arms control: "Israeli and American intelligence failed to crack and to comprehend the Iranian effort to get nuclear arms. The great irony is that throughout the 1990s, and until very recently, both countries invested huge efforts, overt and covert, in order to find out what exactly Russia was supplying to Iran, and in attempts to prevent that supply. We were convinced that this was the main path taken by Iran to secure the Doomsday weapon. But only very belatedly did it emerge that if Iran one day achieves its goal, it will not be by the Russian path at all. It made its great advance towards nuclear weaponry on another path altogether, a secret one, that was concealed from our sight."

Only in September 2003 did the United States confront Pakistan directly about Khan's activities. It happened at a meeting in New York between Pakistani president Musharraf and CIA director George Tenet, who threw onto the table the blueprints for centrifuges and other nuclear installations that Khan had sold Iran and Libya. And it was only with a lot of luck—and the alertness of a Mossad intelligence collection officer—that the Iranian site at Natanz, where the Iranians had set up a uranium enrichment centrifuge operation, was discovered. When this information was verified, a great hue and cry went up in Israel. Some demanded that the site be bombed at once. Other voices in the Mossad thought that different methods should be used, and that even if the Natanz site was destroyed, in the intelligence fog in which Israel finds itself vis-à-vis Iran, it was very possible that there were other sites about which nothing was known. This assumption later proved to be correct.

Somehow, amazingly, the information also reached an Iranian dissidents' group, the National Resistance Council, which in October 2003 announced publicly that Iran was building a centrifuge installation at Natanz. The statement appeared to be well founded and serious, unlike most things the Iranian opposition had previously published. This led to a visit to the site by a team of inspectors from the IAEA, headed by Mohammad al-Baradei. They were very surprised: Iran had advanced far farther than it had admitted and was well on the way to completing the "nuclear fuel cycle," the series of processes for the enrichment of uranium that is a critical stage in producing a bomb.

This disclosure came at the same time as a secret order was issued by the head of MI6, Sir Richard Dearlove, to keep track of Khan's international distribution network. Her Majesty's intelligence services came across this matter by chance, while investigating another subject. The operatives of SIS (Secret Intelligence Service, the official name of MI6) were surprised by the size of the network and the potential for evil which it encompassed. As Dearlove put it in a conversation with an Israeli counterpart: "We pulled one thread, and the whole [lot] fell on our heads."

Dearlove was a central player in an additional effort that was launched as a result of the Armageddon bazaar opened by Khan: the highly successful British-American attempt to persuade the Libyan ruler, Muammar Gaddafi, to drop his advanced nuclear program. (Incidentally, this was one of the Mossad's most difficult moments, not having known anything about Libya's nuclear efforts, although it was considered a prime intelligence target, and not having heard a word about the unprecedented deal between Gaddafi and the Americans and British. The first time the director of the Mossad heard of it was from a newspaper.)

In the wake of these disclosures and, later, Libya's abandonment of its nuclear program and transfer of all its components to the IAEA, the network built by Abdul Qadeer Khan across the globe was exposed. The Pakistani government could no longer give him its backing. In February 2004, he made a carefully choreographed public confession on Pakistani television. He admitted that he had indeed marketed forbidden nuclear technology from the labs named after him in Pakistan to other countries, via middlemen. He asserted that he had done it all at his own initiative, without the knowledge or approval of the state leadership. He concluded his confession with a heart-rending plea for forgiveness from President Musharraf, who immediately appeared on the screen and granted the errant scientist a pardon. Khan was confined to house arrest. He is reported to have given his daughter, who lives in London, documents that clearly prove that the highest echelons of the Pakistani military were aware of his activities and had even facilitated them.

Meanwhile, after the discovery of the centrifuges at Natanz, a cat-and-mouse game developed between Iran and the IAEA. The agency asked Iran to supply it with all the information on its nuclear program to date. Iran responded by providing only sparing and contradictory details. But even the partial picture stunned the West. It emerged that as early as 1989, when the IAEA was repeatedly reassuring the world that all was well, Iran had already committed innumerable breaches of the Nuclear Non-Proliferation Treaty at different locations. It had concealed the importation of large amounts of uranium, as well as the existence of various nuclear facilities and large numbers of tests. In 2004, Iran admitted that it had been developing its program for the centrifugal enrichment of uranium for seventeen years. It had already produced a small amount of enriched uranium. It had failed to report many other activities, including the extraction of a small amount of plutonium. The Iranian government told the IAEA that all of these activities had been conducted within the framework of "experiments to study the nuclear fuel cycle and to acquire experience in chemistry."

With each round of questioning, the Iranians owned up only to what they were forced to own up to. When the IAEA inspectors found traces of uranium fluorides, the Iranians said that the material "had evaporated because of leaky valves on the cylinders that held the gas," only to "remember" later (when faced with contradictory evidence) that it was in fact stored somewhere.

Some of the minutes of the IAEA's meetings in Iran reached Western intelligence agencies. Reading this material, it is difficult not to be impressed by the sophistication and audacity of the Iranians. When asked in January 2005 about their connections with Abdul Qadeer Khan, the Iranians presented a single handwritten page from 1987, when Khan had proposed via an intermediary that they acquire two thousand P-1 centrifuges and the accompanying equipment. The agency asked for all of the documentation of the negotiations with Khan, including blueprints to which the handwritten proposal had referred. In January 2006, Iran informed the IAEA that the page was the "only remnant" of those negotiations. Ali Larijani, secretary of the Supreme National Security Council of Iran at the time, and the chief negotiator with IAEA, claimed that the reason for this arose from the secrecy of the project and "the management style of the Atomic Energy Organization of Iran."

The IAEA inspectors told the Iranians that they knew that five hundred more centrifuges of the same type had been delivered to Iran in the mid-1990s. May we see the paperwork on that? they asked. No, said the Iranians at a meeting in February 2006. We have no papers.

In April 2004, the Iranians cleaned out the installations of the al-Kalaya company, ostensibly a private concern, but actually the place where various items for the Natanz site were made. When finally the IAEA inspectors were allowed in, they found empty halls, freshly painted and shining white. Just days before, according to clear-cut evidence conveyed to the inspectors by U.S. and Israeli intelligence, they had been humming with activity. Even so, the inspectors found microscopic traces of weapons-grade uranium—which the Iranians explained by saying it had stuck to the machines when they were being used by their previous owners. The IAEA discovered a large number of other violations and actions that Iran had not reported, such as a radioisotope laboratory in Tehran, and sites that had been set up especially to store nuclear waste on a large scale.

The IAEA also received a great deal of information about nuclear and missile activity at a site called Lavizan, a military camp north of Tehran. It eventually turned out that it was here that most of the development and testing of the Shihab missiles had taken place, under Iran's Aerospace Industries Organization, AIO. Shortly after IAEA inspectors asked to visit the site, and were turned down under various pretexts, the satellites of the U.S. National Reconnaissance Office (NRO) began to record large-scale demolition and excavation work there. The Iranians razed buildings, removed the debris, and excavated a huge pit, removing to distant sites every trace of vegetation and earth, which were apparently contaminated by radiation or forbidden substances. When they finally allowed the inspectors in, there was nothing left to inspect.

During the first half of 2007, the Iranians several times prevented inspection of bunkers at Natanz, claiming that the inspections were "too frequent." Iran also refused to discuss its testing of explosives, and its plans for missiles suitable for carrying nuclear warheads. In the inspections that were carried out, traces of several suspicious substances were found, including weapons-grade uranium. Iran's reply: The uranium was not ours, but had stuck to machines at the place where they had previously been in use, possibly Pakistan.

Another subject that required clarification was an apparently inadvertent remark by President Ahmadinejad about centrifuges that are more advanced than those known to be in Iran's possession. Experts understood him to be referring to the P-2 model. This slip of the tongue embarrassed Iranian representatives, who offered several different and contradictory explanations.

An excellent example of the dance of lies, deception, fabrications, and stalling that Iran has been carrying on to mislead the West can be found in the tale that could be called "The Affair of the Smoking Laptop." Toward the end of 2003, a former colonel in the Shah's army, who now lives in Germany and has played a leading role in the Iranian opposition's efforts to topple the ayatollahs, handed over to German intelligence a laptop computer which he said belonged to a nuclear scientist employed by the Atomic Energy Organization of Iran and contained blueprints for an atomic bomb. The Germans passed it on to the CIA, which had it examined by Israeli and American scientists as well as by the IAEA.

The investigation never discovered the source of the material, but determined that the computer did indeed contain blueprints and much information, in Farsi, about the methods for building an atomic bomb.

The Iranians at first denied the entire story and claimed that it had been concocted by the CIA or the Mossad, only to change their position and admit that the computer did belong to them but did not contain what Western intelligence was claiming. After the IAEA insisted on explanations, the Iranians, as they always did on all such matters, owned up to what they had to own up to. In November 2007, they informed the IAEA that the material and blueprints in the computer were outdated, devoid of any scientific value, and could be downloaded from the Internet; the information had reached them by chance, they said, and in any case was of no use to them because they were not occupied with developing nuclear arms.

•   •   •

The tale of the Iranian bomb is a study in the art of deception. By the time the world caught Iran in one lie, the regime was already ten steps ahead in its bomb development. Iran denies carrying out certain nuclear activities and refrains from reporting them to the IAEA. When those activities are exposed, it confirms them—but claims that they do not violate the Non-Proliferation Treaty. On the other hand, in order to neutralize international pressure and avoid having the IAEA transfer its case to the UN Security Council—where sanctions could be imposed—Iran launches diplomatic efforts to persuade Britain, France, and Germany that the issue can be resolved between them, without the involvement of other parties, that is, the United States.

The U.S. government decided in late 2003, with silent but fervent Israeli support, that the only way to ensure that Iran won't get a bomb is to prevent it from completing the fuel cycle, although that may be permitted under the Non-Proliferation Treaty. Washington claimed that because Iran had cheated the international community and behaved like a neighborhood bully, it should not be given any credit, and much more must be demanded of it than of the other signatories to the treaty. The Americans wanted to turn the suspension of uranium enrichment into an indefinite stoppage.

In the meanwhile, they left it to the moderate Europeans to conduct the negotiations and even agreed to certain concessions in the boycott of Iran, including allowing the Europeans to sell Iran airplane parts with American technological components. The Iranians announced their flat refusal to an indefinite halt to enrichment. After innumerable contortions, they in fact rejected every compromise proposal, including a package of benefits from Europe that was very tempting in terms of the Iranian economy and could have ensured a slightly better life for the millions of poor in that country.

Since 2003, every time that the Iranian leadership feels they are approaching a point where the international community is about to impose meaningful sanctions on their country, they hasten to announce that the enrichment of uranium is being suspended, or they promise to allow close IAEA inspection, or some other security arrangements. They promise, but each time find pretexts to get out of the commitments they have undertaken.

Thus, for example, in June 2004, after being condemned by the

European states for not supplying the IAEA with full information, Iran announced that it was cancelling its commitments and renewing the assembly of the centrifuges and the enrichment of uranium, and withdrawing its ratification of the additional Protocol (new part of the NPT which was added after the failure to discover Iraq's nuclear project in the 1980s and permits IAEA's inspectors to run surprise visits to suspicious sites). It also made an economic threat: The deputy chairman of the Majlis and member of its foreign policy and national security committee said that if Europe supported the transfer of Iran's case from the IAEA to the UN Security Council, it "would lose more than Iran . . . the European economy is more fragile than that of the United States and it depends on oil . . . we believe that the Europeans will adopt a wise policy and ensure their own national interests."

In August 2006, one week after the Security Council called on Iran to stop enriching uranium by the end of the month, chief nuclear negotiator Ali Larijani declared that Iran would *increase* its production of nuclear fuel as it saw fit and according to its needs. He also threatened that if sanctions were imposed, Iran would not hesitate to use its oil reserves as a weapon against the West. "We do not wish to make threats on the matter of oil, but the West is forcing us to do so," he said.

Iran's threats were not only economic. Defense Minister Ali Shamakhani hinted in an interview on Al Jazeera that the option of a preemptive attack was on the table. Hassan Abbassi, a senior Revolutionary Guard intelligence officer, said in a secret meeting, according to a report that reached French intelligence, "We have identified twenty-nine sensitive sites in the West and conducted observation of them with the aim of bombing them in mind. Our intention is that the 6,000 nuclear warheads in America explode in America. We have located the weak points and passed the information on them to the guerrilla organizations, and we work through them." Abbassi added that "We have also set up a department for Britain, and the debate over toppling it is on the agenda. We are also active amongst the Mexicans, the Argentineans and everyone who has a problem with the United States." Fortunately, Hassan Abbassi found himself in American custody after a targeted attack by the Delta Force in Irbil, Iraq, in February 2007.

In October 2007, three days after President Bush had warned of the danger of the outbreak of World War III if the international community did not manage to prevent Iran from acquiring nuclear armaments, the commander of the Revolutionary Guards missile section, General Mahmoud Karabagi, threatened on Iranian TV that "Iran is capable of launching eleven thousand [missiles] in one minute if it is attacked." Iran had mapped all the bases of its enemies and was capable of responding immediately to any attack, he said.

On December 23, 2006, the UN Security Council decided to impose sanctions on Iran. It was a weak resolution, which underwent many changes, and which ultimately included only a ban on any trade relations that could assist Iran with its nuclear and ballistic missile programs. Iran responded the next day, aggressively, when President Ahmadinejad said: "They will soon regret their superficial action. . . . The technology of the nuclear fuel cycle is a matter for Iran, and no one can take it from the Iranian people. If they like it or not, Iran is a nuclear country, for the good of those who stand by its side . . ."

It's hard to find a politician or diplomat anywhere in Europe who does not believe that Iran is building an atomic bomb. Even sources in Russian intelligence, speaking off the record in September 2006, said they had no doubts about what was going on in Iran. Nevertheless, the Iranians were allowed to push on, practically unhindered.

In August 2006, during the war in Lebanon, Israeli satellite photograph decipherers detected changes at several locations in Iran, suggesting strongly that Iran was stepping up its nuclear project. Moreover, many additional antiaircraft missile batteries were deployed at nuclear sites, and existing ones were replaced with S-300 missiles, one of the most advanced generations that Russia has produced, virtually the equivalent of the American Patriot. By September 2006, no fewer than twenty-six antiaircraft missile batteries had been placed around the centrifuge installation at Natanz, which is not particularly large. Israeli experts said that there are few sites in the world that are so densely protected.

The *Sunday Times* of London has reported that in October 2005, a consignment of uranium 238 from Africa to Iran was intercepted in Tanzania—evidence that even as it was engaged in serious discussion with the Europeans on the future of its nuclear program, and was trying to convince the international community that it wanted nuclear technology only for electricity production, Iran was continuing to act covertly and smuggling in nuclear raw materials. The report said that the uranium came from a mine in Congo and was shipped to Tanzania via Zambia. It

was seized in the port of Dar al Salaam on October 22, 2005, while waiting to be loaded onto a ship bound for the Iranian port of Bandar
Abbas. A Tanzanian customs official said that the uranium was concealed
in a large shipment of coltan, a mineral used to make computer chips.

The most worrisome reports, however, related to a familiar name, that
of Dr. Majid Abbaspour, Nahum Manbar's associate. According to intelligence information reaching the West and conveyed to the IAEA, a
group of Iranian scientists at the Parchin military complex, operating
under the aegis of Abbaspour's Department 105, was conducting tests
with conventional high explosives needed to detonate an atom bomb.
The activities underway at Parchin are called the Weapon Group by the
Israeli intelligence. In late 2007, the activities of the Weapon Group
became a point of contention between the intelligence services of the
United States on the one hand, and those of Israel, Germany, France, and
Britain on the other.

What is the "Weapon Group"?

Iran's main path to nuclear weaponry goes via the centrifuges. It has
four stages:

Stage 1. The mining and milling of the uranium ore and turning it
into yellowcake, a not very complicated chemical process. The Iranians
have plenty of their own ore and have passed this stage successfully.

Stage 2. Uranium conversion—the transformation of the yellowcake
into pure uranium hexafluoride (UF6) gas, a long and complex process.
The Iranians have managed to do this at a plant in Isfahan, despite
IAEA inspection. Before IAEA started looking at the plant and before the
Americans pressured China to stop providing assistance, the Iranians had
already managed to produce some 10 tons of the gas, enough for one and
three-quarter bombs. In other words, at least as far as this stage is concerned, the train has already left the station on the way to the first
bomb.

Stage 3. Enrichment, the hardest stage of all, entails feeding the UF6
gas into clusters of connected high-speed centrifuges known as cascades.
The circulation of the gas through the cascade increases the concentration of the uranium.

By July 2008, there were 2,952 centrifuges in 18 cascades installed at
Natanz, operating under great technical difficulties, according to Mossad

reports. In another part of Natanz the Iranians had begun building the plant itself, which would house 30,000 to 50,000 centrifuges.

Satellite photos of Natanz show that this huge facility is being built underground protected by a meters-thick layer of reinforced concrete and antiaircraft batteries, out of fear that the scenario played out by the Israeli air force, when it bombed the Osirak reactor in Iraq in 1981, will be reenacted.

After the discussions about sanctions against Iran began in the UN Security Council in February 2006, following the decision by the IAEA board of governors that Iran had violated the Nuclear Non-Proliferation Treaty, Iran began boasting of the achievements of its nuclear scientists at the same time as it continued denying that it intended to make a bomb. Iran also started making the work of the IAEA inspectors inside its country much more difficult.

On April 9, 2007, after several delays, President Ahmadinejad gave a much-heralded announcement that would "make all Muslims happy," at celebrations marking Iran's "Nuclear Energy Day." Speaking at the Natanz facility, Ahmadinejad said that Iran was now capable of producing nuclear fuel on an industrial scale; in other words, the centrifuge plant was operational.

The announcement was intended to achieve two goals. First, to show that Iran was capable of making progress despite the sanctions and international pressures. And second, to blunt internal criticism aroused by the increase in the pressures and sanctions against the country.

On exactly the same day, the editor of the conservative daily *Kayhan*, Hossein Shariatmadari, a close associate of Khamenei's, said in a lecture that "A country that has obtained the expertise and the technology for the enrichment of uranium is only one step away from the production of nuclear weapons. This step is neither scientific nor technical [but a matter] of a political decision."

Stage 4. The last stage in the process is the emplacement of the enriched uranium, shaped like a ball, into the device that will start the chain reaction. This is the duty of the Weapon Group. The Iranians are believed to have made considerable progress in this sphere, as well as in acquiring the expertise required to manufacture nuclear warheads that can be fitted to their missiles. These missiles can reach Israel, but still have to be adapted for carrying nuclear warheads. This stage is underway at Parchin and there have been reports that much progress has been made.

In order to set off a chain reaction, a number of charges around the core of the bomb must be exploded at exactly the same split second to implode the core inward, a highly complex process. IAEA inspectors tried to gain access to the Parchin facility several times to check the intelligence information, but were repeatedly rebuffed by the Iranians. When a visit was finally allowed, their movement was restricted. They did manage, however, to locate a high-speed camera of the sort used in tests of the high explosives used in implosion-type bombs. Despite this discovery, the issue of the Parchin complex received only an ambiguous mention in al-Baradei's report.

Satellite images showed that a great deal of expansion had taken place at Parchin, including vast underground bunkers and tunnels, judging by the amount of earth excavated. Also visible in an area to which the inspectors were denied access were structures that could be used for the assembly of the explosives needed in nuclear warheads. Identical structures had over the years been spotted close to the installations where the Soviet Union developed and manufactured its nuclear warheads.

Another worrying development has occurred in relations between Iran and North Korea.

The North Korean precedent has rendered the Iranian threat even more dangerous. It is a twofold menace. First, on the international level, Iran has been careful not to cross the red line and blatantly breach the Nuclear Non-Proliferation Treaty inspection regime. From the technological point of view, it would have been much easier to kick the inspectors out, and to move full steam ahead toward the bomb, but Iran feared a very sharp international response to such a step: it feared becoming another North Korea. But the impotence of the West following the North Korean test in October 2006 and its failure to penalize Pyongyang beyond the sanctions that were already in place, may give Khamenei a sense of security and the feeling that he can emulate Kim Jong Il.

An indication of the Iranian attitude to the precedent can be found in an article entitled "Lessons from North Korea" that appeared in *Kayhan* on October 12, 2006. "How does a state become nuclear?" it asks, and continues: "What brought North Korea this far was its perseverance against the United States, which refused to talk to them face-to-face or to undertake not to act to topple the North Korean government. . . . Korea built a bomb under the Americans' eyes, and although it was subject to great pressure and years of harsh international sanctions, no one could do anything."

The second danger is the potential for closer nuclear cooperation between Iran and cash-strapped North Korea, a state which has achieved a fairly advanced military-technological level and has not hesitated to share it, especially in the sphere of ballistic missiles. Iranian scientists were present at the North Korean nuclear test, according to information reaching a Western intelligence agency. They were invited—or invited themselves—to witness the realization of Kim Jong Il's dream.

While all this was happening, international cooperation on the matter of Iran gradually strengthened. On this subject, unlike the Iraqi case, for example, there were no or very few disagreements between the United States and its allies in Europe. The effort had a number of goals, which added up to an attempt to prevent the nuclearization of Iran.

To the credit of the Israeli intelligence services, it must be said that after the discovery of what was happening on "the Pakistani track," they did begin to act more energetically (while drastically neglecting other spheres, such as the global activities of al-Qaeda). These efforts led first of all to the discovery of many details about what was happening at Natanz. Israel knew that the Iranians were setting up a nuclear facility there, and in 1996 they even sent two Mossad agents, in the guise of tourists, to the region. The men took soil samples, which they brought back in their shoes for analysis in Israel. But although the tests revealed that there was some nuclear activity underway, Israel never managed to discover exactly what until 2003.

Since Meir Dagan became Mossad director in 2002, Israel has significantly improved its knowledge about goings-on inside Iran, and has even taken certain preemptive actions, entailing a vast investment of effort and great risk.

The result of one of these efforts, implemented jointly with the United States, was evident in a serious of mysterious explosions due to faulty equipment at both the Natanz and the Isfahan sites. In one blast, in April 2006, which was reported in the Iranian media, two transformers blew up during the first attempt to enrich uranium at Natanz. Fifty centrifuges that were near the transformers were wrecked, and the highly important enrichment attempt was put on hold for a lengthy period.

Since much of the equipment that Iran purchases is illegal and cannot be bought off the shelf in the international market but only from dubious elements, the Iranian buyers cannot conduct the necessary quality tests or thoroughly check the backgrounds of the sellers. The Iranian investigation revealed that the transformers were actually in good working order, but that someone had "handled" the pipes that connect them to the centrifuges.

Another case occurred in January 2007, when many units of the insulation used in the connections between the centrifuges purchased from a middleman on the black market in Eastern Europe were found to be flawed and unusable. The Iranians concluded that some of their suppliers were actually straw companies set up by Western intelligence agencies (the Iranians suspected MI6 specifically) in order to sabotage the Iranian effort by hoodwinking them into using faulty equipment, so that they will never actually be able to get a production process running.

Between February 2006 and March 2007, at least three (and if exiled oppositionists are to be believed, four) planes belonging to the Revolutionary Guards crashed in Iran, while carrying personnel connected with the security of the nuclear project. It is possible that the aircraft were badly maintained, or, as the Revolutionary Guards suspect, that the crashes were not accidents.

Another modus operandi associated with Israeli intelligence was the assassination of nuclear scientists themselves. In the late 1970s, three top Iraqi nuclear scientists who had played a central role in Saddam Hussein's effort to make a bomb were eliminated. A former Mossad cadet who published a book on his (very brief) experiences in the organization, Victor Ostrovsky, claims that they were killed by the organization.

On January 18, 2007, Professor Ardeshir Hosseinpour, a world expert on electromagnetics who was employed at the Isfahan enrichment facility, was found dead in his apartment, apparently from having inhaled cooking gas. Some Western publications, including some put out by exiled Iranians, said the Mossad had killed him. Other publications also reported that there had been an explosion in his laboratory, and some of his staff were killed or wounded.

The efforts of the United States and Israel to slow down the Iranian nuclear project created a substantial gap between the Iranians' success in developing and producing the means of delivery for the warheads, the Shihab missiles, and the relatively slow pace of their progress toward the production of the weapons themselves. In the field of missiles, the Iranians showed remarkable technological ability and determination.

The deputy director general of the Israeli Atomic Energy Commission, Dr. Eli Levite, who is an accepted top authority in the eyes of the American intelligence community, had this to say at a closed forum in April 2007: "[The action taken against Iran] gained time for us and has doubtless caused significant delays in the project. The process has led to revealing of large parts of the program in the areas of sources of supply, of the infrastructure, and of the goals, which were not known or were known at a different resolution."

But at the end of the day, despite specific intelligence and diplomatic successes, much was still shrouded in confusion, and in any case there were not many operational options.

As for the sanctions against Iran, those that were imposed by the Security Council were very weak and mainly concerned the export of equipment and expertise that could help the Iranian nuclear project. Much more effective were the sanctions enforced by the United States and American companies.

This subject was of prime importance to Benjamin Netanyahu, the man who made Iran into the number one issue, and who has never neglected it, or Islamic terror, for one moment even after he lost the premiership to Ehud Barak in the 1999 elections. He has also made it the main plank in the platform from which he hopes to regain power, something which according to early 2008 polls appears likely.

The most articulate of Israel's political leaders in the eyes of outsiders, with his polished American English, the charismatic Netanyahu never stopped threatening the public with visions of apocalyptic prophecies about what would happen if Iran and radical Islam were not halted. Netanyahu's wide network of connections, headed by the American Jewish billionaires Sheldon Adelson and Ron Lauder, has racked up some real successes. More and more pension funds of the employees of American state governments, funds that control $10 trillion, have announced that they would boycott not only Iran but also any company, bank, or economic institution that maintains links with Iran. The pension fund of the public service workers in the state of Ohio, for example, is invested in 102 companies trading with Iran.

Netanyahu did not start the process, but his involvement gave it a big boost.

It can be assumed that if Netanyahu is elected prime minister, the Israeli defense establishment will receive higher budget allocations and much support from him to prepare to confront the Iranian threat, both defensively and also in preparing for a tactical raid on Iran's nuclear facilities, in Netanyahu's words, "in the event that we fail and Iran has managed to get the bomb." He went on to say: "Against lunatics, deterrence must be absolute, perfect, including a second strike capability. The crazies have to understand that if they raise their hand against us, we'll put them back in the Stone Age. At second thought, back to where they won't even have stones that they can throw at us."

The economic and political pressure that the United States and other Western countries are exerting on Iran has had the effect of reducing investments there and stepping up the crisis in its fuel economy. Iran is one of the world's greatest oil producers and has vast reserves of natural gas. Nevertheless, it has been finding it difficult in recent years to prevent its fuel supply system from deteriorating. Since Ahmadinejad's election to the presidency and his spate of declarations about achieving nuclear weapons capability, Iran has had trouble obtaining contracts in the sphere of energy. Its production and refining capabilities are receding. In the light of all this, Iran is not able to meet its economy's demands for energy and has been forced to import most of its gasoline from abroad. In order to prevent political unrest in the nation, the regime subsidizes fuel costs; in fact, the price of gasoline in Iran is one of the lowest in the world. An announcement in June 2006 by Ahmadinejad that subsidies were to be cut caused violent protests across the country.

The international sanctions deter companies from trading with Iran. Oil companies say that investment in Iran bears little if any profit. Even Chinese firms that Iran tries to tempt by using oil and natural gas as bait are hesitant about operating in Iran.

On the other hand, black market arms dealers are always there to fill Iran's every need, and some countries, headed by Russia and China, which trade with Iran in huge quantities and in almost every possible commodity, make the sanctions a lot less effective. They are not alone; India, Turkey, and Austria have also signed massive contracts with the ayatollahs' regime to supply gas and build infrastructure despite harsh criticism from the West. The biggest concern in Austria, OMV, which is partly owned by the government, has signed on to the largest gas and oil deal ever in European history, worth a total of 22 billion euros.

What is more, a number of states, including Greece, Turkey, India, Belgium, Italy, and to a lesser degree China, South Korea, and France, depend on Iranian oil supplies. It is clear that they will not be interested in stepping up the sanctions in a manner that will affect their own energy supplies.

While all this was going on, American and Israeli teams, together and separately, were working assiduously on plans for a massive aerial attack on Iran's nuclear sites. This was not a simple task, and was dependent first of all on a political decision by the president and/or the prime minister whether even to give the order for so risky a venture. From a purely military point of view, such an attack would require the deployment of large numbers of bombers and support aircraft, which would simultaneously drop the massive amount of ordnance—smart bombs with high-penetration capability—needed to smash the deep bunkers in which the Iranians conceal most of their nuclear installations. At the same time, it must contend with the thick antiaircraft missile defenses that the Iranians have placed around these sites.

The great problem facing Israel and America is that there is no way of knowing whether the Iranians, who have displayed such tremendous sophistication and guile, are not hiding another site like Natanz. At a careful estimate, in mid-2008 there were seven central nuclear project sites, and another fifteen places, mostly laboratories, where additional research on various aspects is being conducted. Any attempt to destroy them all, even in a highly complex, combined, simultaneous attack, would not be assured of success, because some of them are fortified, and/or underground, and/or well protected by batteries of missiles. But even if such an attack succeeded, it is possible that other, secret parts of the project would remain unharmed.

And those initiating such an attack would have to take into account the response of the Iranian regime. Alongside the expressions of determination to carry on with their nuclear program, in the light of the possibility of military action by the United States and Israel, Iranian security factors have loosed the harshest possible threats of retaliation in four spheres: The Gulf States assisting the United States would be hit; al-Qaeda and other terror organizations would be permitted to operate using Iranian territory freely, enabling them to strike at any state in the region, in addition to operating in Iraq, Lebanon, and the occupied Palestinian territories; U.S. military bases in the area would be attacked; and Iran would cause the price of oil to reach $250 per barrel, leading to the "economic ruin" of the West.

Speaking of the prospects for a military attack on Iran, Eli Levite, who is familiar with all the details of Israel's planning vis-à-vis Iran, took a very shrewd look at the harsh reality: "The Iraqi trauma is resonating in everyone's head, and the world will therefore not accept a military move that is based only on intelligence information. . . . The relationship between Israel and the United States is more complicated today than ever before. The situation could arise, and this would be the worst possibility in my eyes, that the American president tells us: 'I do not want to draw the necessary conclusions. You want to attack? Attack. I won't stop you. But if you attack, you pay the price. It's up to you.' I characterize such a situation as the worst possible because of life after [the attack], with all the implications on so many different levels."

Levite was speaking in March 2007, and it seems that his prediction of a sharp clash between Israel and the United States on the possibility of a military strike against Iran came true long before he anticipated.

In December 2007, the U.S. intelligence community released a dramatic report stating that Iran had ceased its military efforts to produce a nuclear bomb back in 2003. The National Intelligence Estimate (NIE) report created an uproar both in the United States and internationally, and led to a rift between the intelligence services of America and those of Britain, France, and Israel. Actually, the report changed nothing in the estimates already made by the CIA of the time by which Iran could acquire the bomb—between the beginning and the middle of the coming decade, as opposed to the Mossad's estimate of 2009–10. But it stirred up a mighty storm in the world, got a tremendous welcome in Iran, and was termed "a putsch by the intelligence community" by John Bolton, the former American ambassador to the United Nations, because of a certain statement that it made, and because that statement appeared prominently at the beginning.

Israel had claimed that the Weapons Group operating at Parchin was active, and that Iran was doing everything it could to get nuclear weaponry. In a stunning reversal, the NIE report said that the group had ceased functioning in 2003. The report came as a huge blow to many of the people in Israel's intelligence community involved in the relationship with their American counterparts. They had never heard from their American colleagues any such clear-cut estimate.

Earlier that year, on February 27, the director of National Intelligence, Mike McConnell, in a classified briefing to the Senate Armed Services Committee, had stated precisely the opposite of the NIE report that he signed just ten months later. Among other points, he observed that "Iran and North Korea are of particular concern, and these regimes have pursued nuclear programs in defiance of United Nations Security Council restrictions. We assess that Tehran seeks to develop nuclear weapons and has shown a greater interest in drawing out the negotiations rather than in reaching an acceptable diplomatic solution. This is a very dangerous situation, as Iran—a nuclear Iran—could prompt destabilizing countermoves by other states in this volatile region."

So, what changed between February and November that caused McConnell to realize that he had conveyed information to the Senate that was so totally wrong? According to one version, it was because American intelligence understood that the "smoking laptop" really contained outdated and useless information and that it could not constitute evidence of the activities of the Weapon Group.

The report does not explain—unless it is made clear somewhere in the 130 pages that remained classified—how the analysis of the contents of the computer in 2004, which led to a strongly worded report in 2005, suddenly became irrelevant. According to other observers, the reasons are also to be found in the computer, but not only there. They say that U.S. intelligence claims to be in possession of recordings of conversations between senior officials of the Iranian nuclear project that speak of the cessation of the Weapons Group project in 2003.

According to leaks published in the British media, it was the GCHQ, the SIGINT branch of Her Majesty's intelligence services, that provided these recordings to the Americans. A very senior British official responded in a closed conversation in January 2008 to these reports by saying that "they were intentionally leaked by the Americans who wanted to harness us to the wagon of lies that is known as the NIE. We never provided any such information. On the contrary, we believe that the conclusions are totally incorrect. The American intelligence estimate has caused unprecedented international damage to the effort to boycott Iran, and we have no idea, to this day, what ostensible proof upon which the report relies and why it was phrased the way it was phrased. Its content was so illusionary that there are those amongst us who believe that whoever wrote it simply doesn't know English and does not understand the significance of what was written and the implications were. Our senior intelligence officials say that the Iranians were fully aware that the Americans were listening to them, and this is why they said what they did about dismantling the Weapon Group in 2003."

The NIE report aroused an unprecedented wave of criticism against the American intelligence community—criticism in which the same stand was shared by elements on both the right and left, who usually accuse the intelligence services of being too alarmist. One of the heads of the Israeli intelligence community said: "This is a report whose sole aim is to prove to the American public that the intelligence community has a will and opinions of its own and that it has cleansed itself of the charges of false reporting about the WMD efforts of Saddam Hussein. The report is illusionary and lacking in any internal logic, even without access to the classified information. Iran's nuclear project stands on four legs: the development of long-range missiles capable of carrying nuclear warheads; the enrichment of uranium by centrifuges at Natanz; the construction of a heavy water reactor that can produce plutonium at Arak; and the Weapon Group, which is meant to manufacture the actual bomb. The first three legs are expensive and very difficult, and have very conspicuous intelligence signatures. The fourth, the Weapon Group, is less expensive and requires far fewer personnel and efforts. In fact, the American intelligence report says that Iran has given up on the fourth leg, but is carrying on at full steam with the other three, the existence of which, incidentally, Iran itself does not deny and even boasts of. It is as if Ford would set up an expensive plant to produce cars and after a few years would announce that it will not produce cars, but will complete the construction of the plant."

Following the publication of the NIE report, senior officials in the United States and Israel estimated that in the situation that had been created, President Bush would not be able to order an American attack on Iranian targets. As far as the Israelis knew, Bush had not decided upon such an attack before the report was released, but neither had he decided against it. He was still weighing the issue, having ordered his people to make every effort to step up the sanctions against Iran in order to achieve a halt to their project through peaceful means, but at the same time instructing the Pentagon to prepare comprehensive plans for attacking the nuclear sites, with the help of other states.

However, two weeks after the NIE report was issued, Vice President Dick Cheney sent a message to Prime Minister Olmert through an associate to the effect that despite the report's contents, the possibility of an American military operation against Iranian nuclear targets and military infrastructure had not been discarded. The Mossad's estimate of May 2008 was that President Bush, out of religious and ideological motives, will order a strike.

Only time will tell what President Bush's plans were, and, no less interesting, what made the heads of the American intelligence community totally ignore a number of cross-checked items of information—some of which were presented to the president during his January 28 visit to Israel, from sources that the Americans themselves described as most reliable—to make a U-turn and alter the global agenda.

# CHAPTER 21

# Ghost Raid

The nuclear threat from Iran is not just a question of what may or may not be happening inside Iran's own secret nuclear facilities. There is also the question of Iran's unholy triple alliance with North Korea and Syria. In 2007, Israeli concerns about Iranian-sponsored proliferation came to a head.

It began in February 2007, when a man disappeared from his hotel room in Istanbul. General Ali Reza Askari was a top intelligence adviser to Iranian president Mohammad Khatami, in addition to his duties as deputy minister of defense. Long a predominant figure in the Iranian defense establishment and intelligence services, Askari had in recent years adhered to a moderate line when it came to relations with the West. After 9/11, a bitter conflict had broken out in the Iranian leadership, on the question of how the country should relate to al-Qaeda: Should it be seen as a movement with the same goals as the Islamic Revolution and therefore an ally? Or should Iran support the international coalition against it, led by the United States? Askari was on the moderate side in this debate. President Khatami heard from him that the Revolutionary Guards had given shelter to key figures in al-Qaeda, and he ordered that they be thrown out, immediately. There was a red line that should not be crossed, Askari maintained.

After Mahmoud Ahmadinejad was elected president in August 2005, however, Askari came under pressure. The two men had been rivals ever since they served together in Iranian intelligence during the Iran-Iraq War. The new president, much more hawkish than Askari, set about neutralizing the close associates of Khatami, and he nudged Askari out of his position of influence.

Finally, in February 2007, Askari defected to the CIA. A senior American official, speaking off the record, reports that Askari's defection was the culmination of a complex CIA operation. Askari has been debriefed in a secure facility outside Washington, D.C., and part of his family was also smuggled out of Iran. It is one of the most sensational defections in recent history.

In another achievement for the West, about a month before the Askari defection and apparently not connected to it, British intelligence was instrumental in securing the defection of the Iranian consul general in Dubai, Adel Asadiniyeh, who was actually an agent of the Revolutionary Guards. He gave a very detailed account of Iran's clandestine activities aimed at undermining the Gulf monarchies, complementing revelations from Askari.

Askari has shed light on many topics touching on the most intimate secrets of the Iranian regime with which he was directly or indirectly connected. On one issue, which was of great importance to Israel, the case of the missing navigator Ron Arad, Askari has said he does not know anything. However, on the nuclear issue, Askari apparently revealed three major hitherto unknown developments: First, Iran was trying to enrich uranium by means of laser treatment, a difficult process, expensive and not necessarily effective. The fact that the Iranians were prepared to invest resources in something that had caused other states mostly frustration showed that they were determined to enrich uranium and that they are continually searching for alternative methods, in case the Natanz site, where the centrifuge system is employed, is damaged or closed down.

Second, Iran had constructed an additional centrifuge enrichment plant near an existing facility at Natanz.

Finally, Iran was financing a joint nuclear venture launched by North Korea and Syria.

The Revolutionary Guards were responsible for both guarding the nuclear facilities and preventing information about the nuclear program from leaking out. Askari's deep involvement with the Revolutionary Guards over the years had given him intimate knowledge of the subject.

Unlike his extensive familiarity with the Iranian nuclear project, Askari's knowledge of the Syrian–Iranian–North Korean venture, all of which was being conducted outside Iran, was relatively limited. Nevertheless, the information about Syria came as a surprise to the Israelis. As far as had been known previously, Syria had not made any serious moves toward acquiring nuclear weapons. Damascus had taken some initial steps in the late 1970s, but American pressure on the countries that were selling it equipment—China, Russia, and Argentina—and the enormous costs involved, put a stop to this. Later, Syria received a tempting offer from the father of the Pakistani bomb, A. Q. Khan, to supply them with what he had already delivered to Libya and Iran, but the Syrians turned him down. Instead, Syria acquired chemical weapons, and an increasingly effective stable of solid fuel missiles, as a deterrent against Israel.

Syria has been producing chemical combat materials and weapons since the mid-1980s, and it has the capability to deliver them from airplanes or with its Scud missiles. Its arsenal includes several thousand bombs that contain sarin nerve gas, and another fifty to one hundred warheads for ballistic missiles. Most of the equipment for the manufacture of these items came from the Soviet Union and Czechoslovakia.

In the mid-1990s, the Syrians managed to produce the most lethal and sought-after chemical warfare agent, VX. General Anatoly Kuntsevitch, who served as Russian president Boris Yeltsin's adviser on chemical weapons disarmament, and was the top expert in Russia on the subject, began forming ties with Syria in 1995. He made a number of deals for the smuggling of VX components into the country. Some of the details became known to the Mossad in 1998, but the agency decided not to assassinate such a high-ranking official of a major power. In 1999, Prime Minister Ehud Barak warned President Vladimir Putin about Kuntsevitch's activities, to no avail. Finally, some Mossad operatives in Europe posing as freelance researchers for a documentary film on gas warfare contacted senior officials in the Kremlin and the Russian military, and told them that they had information that Kuntsevitch was selling chemical weapons to the Syrians. The idea was to create a chain reaction that would ultimately force the Russians to take action and put a stop to his activities.

Apparently, that didn't work either. He kept at it until April 3, 2002, when he died in mysterious circumstances on a flight from Damascus to Moscow. To this day, it is not clear exactly what happened.

Syria's interest in nuclear weapons changed when the presidency passed from Hafez Assad to his son, Bashar. Indeed, their attitudes diverged on several topics, with Bashar generally taking a more hawkish and dangerous position. For example, Assad Senior had seen Hizballah as, at most, an implement to be used in the struggle for hegemony in Lebanon and a card to be played against Israel to get it to withdraw from the Golan Heights. He saw Iran as an important ally, but always took care not to be drawn too closely into its embrace. Bashar, by contrast, saw Hizballah as a role model, and he never hesitated to do as many military deals with Iran as he could.

The Iranian connection, and his very ambitious desires and aspirations, led Bashar al-Assad to take a great leap forward in the arming of Syria with unconventional weapons. He encouraged a trilateral relationship with Iran and North Korea, for missiles and for nuclear weapons. Israel knew that Syria's missile acquisition is coordinated through a body known as the Scientific Studies and Research Center (SSRC), in Damascus. In May 2004, the United States issued a presidential order banning all exports to Syria, except for medicines and foodstuffs. In June 2005, the administration froze the assets of SSRC in the United States.

The intelligence efforts of the United States and Israel to understand what was going on inside Syria's and Iran's nuclear projects, and the operational moves that accompanied these efforts, have constantly been shadowed by the specter of two earlier grave intelligence blunders, both of them connected to Iraq.

The first such blunder occurred before the first Gulf War in 1991. From material obtained by the UN inspection team after the war, it emerged that by the eve of the war, Iraq had eliminated the delay in its nuclear program caused by Israel's bombing of the Osirak reactor in 1981. By applying other, secretly obtained methods of uranium enrichment, mainly centrifuges, the Iraqis had already acquired the ability to assemble a nuclear device. Indeed, the development of a nuclear warhead for Iraqi missiles was at a very advanced stage. If Saddam Hussein had not invaded Kuwait and thereby invited boycott and international inspection, Iraq would have become a nuclear power. Even the estimates of the best Western intelligence services never came anywhere near an accurate evaluation of the true dimensions of Iraq's military industry.

The second blunder happened in a similar way, but in reverse. Intelligence was again lacking, but this time Saddam's power and his weapons programs were exaggerated. When the UN weapons inspectors were thrown out of Iraq in November 1998, the Mossad and the CIA, who had relied on UNSCOM facilities and officials for their own intelligence in the country, were left in utter darkness.

Having been burned by their underestimation of Saddam's capabilities before the 1991 war, they filled in the gaps in their knowledge by inflating the value of whatever information they had and attributing more credibility to what they did manage to gather than it was actually worth. Information gathered by the CIA, the NSA, or the Defense Intelligence Agency was put through the Israeli channels, processed, amended, interpreted, inflated, and then sent back to the United States, as if it had come from a different, corroborating source and was cross-checked and credible.

A similar process occurred within the American system with Israeli information, and also in the use by both countries of questionable materials that came from other sources, such as France. So, for example, intelligence deemed to be "suspect" was transferred from Israel to the United States, from there to Germany and then to France, which sent it on to Israel without pointing out its provenance. The Israelis thought that what they had obtained from France was independent confirmation of their own intelligence, and so the "suspect" classification became "almost certain." Such transformation of originally low-quality, flimsy material ultimately led to the conclusion that Saddam Hussein had weapons of mass destruction and that the reason for his refusal to allow the inspectors to return was because he had something to hide, not merely a matter of his Middle Eastern pride.

With this failure in mind, the United States and Israel received later reports about nuclear developments in Syria with skepticism. Another reason for their doubts was the confidence of Israeli Military Intelligence that there was nothing happening in Syria that Israel didn't know about. The problem was that the Syrians too knew that the Israelis were paying very close attention to what was going on in their country. So President Assad ordered an exceptionally high level of field security for the nuclear project. He was so obsessed with keeping his expensive new toy a secret that he kept even his own military chief of staff, Ali Habib, out of the loop. But despite his efforts, the combined American-Israeli efforts did eventually solve the puzzle, albeit five years late.

American-Israeli research revealed that very soon after President Hafez Assad's death on June 10, 2000, and the installation of his son, Bashar, in his place, a number of secret meetings were held between high-ranking

Syrian and North Korean officials. The first took place on June 12, with members of the North Korean delegation who came to Syria for the funeral of the president. Discussed at that first meeting was the possibility that the North Koreans would supply Syria with a facility that would enable it to produce a nuclear bomb. Two weeks after that, Kim Jong Nam, eldest son of Kim Jong Il, and believed to be number two in the Pyongyang hierarchy, arrived in Damascus on a secret visit.

Changes on the ground were not long in coming: Syria froze a number of agreements it had signed with Russia for nuclear development for peaceful purposes, and set up several new institutions, including university departments to train nuclear scientists. Assad appointed some of his closest associates to head these institutions.

Alongside the Syrian Scientific Research Council (SSRC), the secret project is spearheaded by the Atomic Energy Commission of Syria (AECS). The joint U.S.-Israel investigations revealed that parallel with their official, overt titles and functions, the heads of that agency also wear other hats within the country's defense and intelligence systems. A detailed examination of the Syrian hierarchy shows that the AECS functions jointly with the Supreme Council of Science (SCOS), sometimes as a partner and sometimes as a subordinate. SCOS is the body that coordinates Syria's top-level military scientific research projects. Some of the senior officials in the AECS also hold positions in the SSRC, the most secretive organization in Syria. The SSRC is a huge octopus that operates under the cover of responsibility for higher education and scientific research, and uses a multitude of different names, with a very confusing flowchart. The one thing that these ostensibly academic organizations have in common is that they all have the same postal address in Damascus, identical to that of the SSRC.

At a summit conference in Damascus in July 2002, the details were worked out. Shortly thereafter, ships began arriving in Syria loaded with components for the project and carrying North Korean scientists and technicians. Satellite photographs taken a year later show a cubelike structure rising at Dir al-Zur.

On April 21, 2005, a dramatic event was played out on the high seas off the Syrian coast. At the very time that another meeting between top Syrian and North Korean officials was taking place in Damascus, a cargo ship flying the North Korean flag and bound for the Syrian port of Tartous started to sink. Manned by a crew of Syrians and Egyptians, according to its cargo manifest the vessel was carrying 1,400 tons of cement. "Cement" has for years been the cover used by North Korean intelligence to conceal the components for the al-Zur project. Fortunately for the crew, and by complete coincidence, an Israel navy missile boat was cruising nearby and helped rescue the Syrian and Egyptian seamen.

The Syrians also tried to obtain materials for construction of the al-Zur facility from other sources. In early 2004 a theft took place in Sweden of enriched uranium at a plant that recycles uranium from nuclear waste gathered from European reactors. The CIA received information linking Syrian research personnel to this event.

On April 22, 2005, there was an enormous explosion at a train station near a Pyongyang plant where materials to be shipped to Dir al-Zur were being loaded onto a train. Hundreds of people were killed by the blast, and great damage was caused to installations and buildings within a three-kilometer radius of destruction. Ten Syrian technicians, employees of the SSRC, were among the fatal casualties; their bodies were flown back home on May 1 in a Syrian plane that brought aid for the victims of the disaster.

During this period, some shipments of missile components and parts for the nuclear installations were seized. In September 2006, for example, a North Korean ship flying Panamanian colors, the *Gregorio 1*, was stopped in Cyprus en route to a Syrian port. The cargo documents said the vessel was carrying meteorological equipment, but inspection revealed military cargo, including eighteen mobile radar systems, made in North Korea, and tubing suitable for use in nuclear plants.

Meanwhile, images produced by Israel's Ofek spy satellite showed feverish activity underway at numerous facilities for the manufacture and storage of missiles and chemical weapons. Four plants were identified: one north of Damascus; another near the city of Homs; a third at Hama, apparently where VX, sarin, and tabun gases are produced; and the fourth and most important at al-Safir in the north. There, sarin and VX are produced, and Scud C and Scud D missiles, which can reach anywhere in Israel, are stored. As General Askari helped to confirm, Iran was aiding Syria by providing technical assistance and scientific personnel.

And what was Iran gaining from its alliance with Syria? An explanation of how it saw its ties with Syria on the one hand and Hizballah on the other appeared in January 2008, on the Iranian Web site Tabnak, which is affiliated with Expediency Council secretary and former Revolutionary Guards commander Mohsen Rezai:

> If the Iran-Syria Joint Strategic Defense Agreement is implemented, Iran need not launch long-range missiles from its territory, [but rather] will be able to face Israel with a wave of missile attacks from [missiles with] a maximum range of 500 kilometers, and with much higher explosive potential. At the same time, [even] if we leave out reciprocal attacks by the Islamic resistance in Lebanon [i.e., Hizballah], Iran and Syria know very well that an attack on Iran will bring in its wake an attack on Syria, and that an attack on Syria will bring in its wake an attack on Iran—and that in both situations, the third target or the parallel [target] are the Islamic Resistance [organizations] in Lebanon and Palestine.

But there were apparently other elements, for whom this harmony was disturbing and who sought to preempt at least part of the danger to Israel.

On July 25, 2007, at 11 a.m., some fifty Syrian and Iranian technicians were engaged in the final tests before fitting a warhead carrying VX nerve gas onto a Scud D missile at the al-Safir site. The production line was newly installed, built by the two countries. The tests indicated that all was in order and the assembly could move ahead. Everything appeared to be normal. From here, the loaded missile was to be transferred to its silo, deep underground, from which it would be aimed at a city in Israel, ready for firing if and when ordered.

As the warhead was being fitted onto the missile, a pipe feeding into the missile exploded. Some of the solid fuel inside the missile caught fire. In seconds, the entire assembly line became a hellish ball of flames and VX gas. The explosion blew the doors off the structure and the contaminated debris began spreading all over the al-Safir site.

Fifteen Syrians and ten Iranians were killed in the explosion. An unknown number of others were seriously affected by the gas and died later. American intelligence estimates put the total casualties at two hundred. The rescue and first aid forces posted at the site could not cope with the numbers, and the Syrians had to override security and secrecy considerations in order to bring in firefighters and rescue teams from the outside. Until the area was fully cleansed and the damage assessed, the entire al-Safir site had to be evacuated, apart from the smallest possible force required to guard the missiles and the materials stored there. All of the projects underway there were halted.

President Assad heard of the incident while on a visit to the city of Hama. Reports reaching the West said that he launched a special investigative team that believed the explosion was the result of sabotage. A senior Israeli minister, in an off-the-record conversation, would only say with a grin and a wink that it was a "wonderful mishap."

The information provided by Askari (and soon by other sources, in March 2007) as to the existence of the Iran–North Korea–Syria triangle was unsurprising on its face. What *was* surprising were his revelations as to one of the goals of the alliance: the development of nuclear weapons. Ultimately, in the wake of the revelations, analysts concluded that North Korea had agreed to provide Syria with a fast-track nuclear project, on the basis of the long years of research and experience that the North Koreans had accumulated. In order to accomplish this, it was necessary to do far more than just ship pipes disguised as "agricultural equipment" from one end of Asia to the other—scores, if not hundreds of technicians had to be sent. A certain degree of the concern caused by Askari's statements was expressed by Michael McConnell in his Annual Threat Assessment for the Senate Armed Services Committee on February 27, 2007:

> Iran and North Korea are the states of most concern to us. . . . We remain concerned it [North Korea] could proliferate these weapons abroad. Indeed, it has a long history of selling ballistic missiles, including to several Middle Eastern countries.

Iran promised aid to the tune of $1–$2 billion (sources vary). At a series of secret meetings between representatives of the three sides, held mainly in Tehran, it was decided that Syria would supply the territory, Iran the money, and North Korea the expertise, for the joint nuclear project.

To collect information on the project, the United States and Israel mobilized all the intelligence resources at their disposal. In Israel, the project was placed at the head of the list of priorities drawn up by Military Intelligence. The two countries cooperated closely, pooling all of their information. Together, they reached the conclusion that it was time for a bombing raid. The American national security adviser, Stephen J. Hadley, directed the intelligence-gathering and analysis operation from his office. He imposed the strictest possible security on the dissemination of what was learned. From the start, it seemed likely that a military operation would result.

One of the first questions that American intelligence tried to check: Had Syria deployed around the installation arising at Dir al-Zur advanced electronic equipment capable of disrupting guidance systems using GPS in order to divert missiles fired at the site? Fragments of information reaching the CIA indicated that the Syrians had acquired such instruments, but it could not determine if they had been positioned at the site.

Another point that emerged during the watch on the project was that the Syrians were acting on the assumption that there was no telephone, fax, or any other electronic data delivery system that either Israeli Military Intelligence's 8200 SIGINT unit, or the NSA, were not monitoring. The entire nuclear project was therefore conducted by the primitive means of couriers carrying sealed envelopes or short land lines.

Satellite surveillance showed that a great deal of construction was underway at a complex in the Dir al-Zur region in northern Syria. The builders were surrounding the complex with enormous concrete expanses. These were not fortification against bombings, the Israeli and American analysts decided, but merely a precaution to prevent any nosy inspectors who might poke around from being able to obtain tell-tale soil samples.

In May, American intelligence sources keeping a watch on North Korea reported that a group of scientists had left the country for Syria, and had taken up residence in a special area set up for them close to the sites that were under construction. Apparently, they weren't the only North Korean group in Syria. North Korea did not intend to hand over ready-made bombs, but rather to give Syria uranium rods from its reactor at Yongbyon. In Syria, the rods would undergo radiation in the Dir al-Zur reactor and then plutonium extraction. At a separate facility, the plutonium would be processed into the core to be used for nuclear warheads. The full warheads would be assembled at a third plant, similar to that constructed by the Iranians at their Parchin complex.

It also emerged from the surveillance that the Syrians had put a number of ships and their crews at the disposal of the North Koreans for the transfer of the necessary cargos. One of these vessels, the 1,700-ton *Al Ahmad*, made four voyages between Syria and North Korea during the six-month period in which it was being watched by the Americans and Israelis.

There were some in the intelligence communities of both countries, but mainly the United States, who were not satisfied with the intercepted communications and satellite photos. As a result, on a cloudy night in mid-August, twelve men from Israel's Sayeret Matkal commando unit were flown into Syria in two helicopters. They carried advanced measuring equipment supplied by the Israeli Atomic Energy Committee and travelled in vehicles identical to those used by the Syrian army. They did not penetrate the site itself, but took soil samples from beyond the vast concrete apron surrounding it. They brought a Geiger counter and a special kind of sponge that absorbs an air sample when exposed. This was a daring operation that was almost exposed when a Syrian patrol drove past the landing site where the helicopters were parked. The results provided clear-cut proof of the joint nuclear project.

Earlier, in July, the *Al Ahmad* had set sail from North Korea for Syria. In August, it anchored in a port in the Nile Delta, before moving to Tripoli in northern Lebanon. Finally, on September 3, it entered the port of Tartous in northern Syria. The vessel had made all of its voyages under the North Korean flag, and had been registered as such in the ports that it visited. (Later, after the bombing, Syrian intelligence changed the registration at the port of Tartous to "unknown flag.") The ship was carrying a cargo of uranium rods to Syria.

The Israelis and Americans decided to act—not because of the arrival of the *Al Ahmad* in Tartous so much as the fear that the details of the tripartite project would somehow leak out to the media, and that the Syrians and their allies would be able to take protective measures. In Israel and America, there was a feeling that too many people were already aware of it. There were some, like John Bolton, who spoke publicly of a Syrian–North Korean connection.

At 3 a.m. on the morning of Thursday, September 6, seven Israeli air force F-15Is took off and headed north over the Mediterranean. The crews knew the precise location of the targets that they had to destroy, but the exact nature of those targets, and the importance of their mission to the security of Israel, was divulged by their commander only just before takeoff. They flew very low along the Mediterranean coast and then over Turkey, before entering Syrian airspace. At a range of 50 kilometers, they launched twenty-two missiles at the three sites within the nuclear complex.

The Syrians were taken completely by surprise. Their air defense systems only detected the firing of the missiles, leaving no time for the sites to be evacuated. A few antiaircraft missiles were dispatched, but only after the planes were long gone. American and Israeli satellites hovering above Syria confirmed that the targets had been destroyed.

The Syrians were in a highly embarrassing situation. They feared that the Israelis would call a press conference and flaunt their victory with triumphant smiles, so they decided to publicize the incident first, in deliberately vague language. The official Syrian news agency announced that Israeli air force aircrafts had penetrated Syrian airspace and had been driven off by the Syrian air defense system. The Syrian military said that the planes had broken the sound barrier and caused a supersonic boom, and had dropped some undefined munitions. "Air defense units engaged the aircraft and forced them to depart without causing damage to people or property. Syria places the responsibility for this aggressive action on Israel and reserves the right to respond," the announcement continued. Residents of North Syria were quoted as saying they had heard five planes or more.

The Syrians had misjudged Israel's public relations strategy. In order to diminish the risk of war, the Israelis decided not to say anything about the raid. Or, as a top Israeli intelligence official put it, "Let's say I'm quarreling with a neighbor and I want to harm him. There's a big difference between beating him up in the middle of the street in broad daylight, with everyone watching, and putting his car out of action, at night, when only he and I know what happened."

Prime Minister Olmert and President Bush decided that both countries would maintain a policy of total non-reaction, without exceptions, and without winks or nods. If the Syrians had not been in a hurry to issue their own statements, the whole matter might not have been disclosed at all. The Syrians also sent a delegation to North Korea to explain what had happened. A number of North Koreans (fifteen, according to one report) had lost their lives.

President Bush received the report of the destruction of the targets both from U.S. intelligence officials and on the phone from Prime Minister Olmert, who warmly thanked the president for the American support from Israel "on this existential matter."

On April 25, 2008, the CIA dropped an intelligence atomic bombshell. During a congressional briefing on the North Korean nuclear project, the agency disclosed what both Israel and the United States had sworn to keep a secret: the intelligence information that had led to the bombing. Key to this information were photographs that had been taken inside the Dir al-Zur reactor.

Publicizing the photographs represented a highly unusual step in the annals of intelligence organizations, which as a rule keep the evidential basis for their assessments of the enemy to themselves, or pass it on secretly to the limited set of political leaders who must make the decisions about how to respond.

The CIA's move in divulging the photographs caused a great deal of resentment within Israeli intelligence, which did not want those specifics revealed. A senior source commented: "The American intelligence community was happy to show achievements, most of which were not its own. What it wants is to cleanse the terrible stain of having identified a nuclear arms development program of Saddam Hussein that never existed. That's the reason why the CIA pressed for the publication of the photos themselves. The U.S. intelligence chiefs knew that the world would not believe anything less. George Bush's White House is winding up its term in office with very few foreign policy achievements. The way that his hands were tied and an attack on Iran was prevented by the National Intelligence Estimates left him with few options in the few months remaining. In this situation, it's very nice for him to be able to bask in the glow of a successful operation to foil evil of whose existence there are no doubts."

Despite the resentment caused, the photos made their point. Experts in Israel and other countries who were asked to study them as part of the research for this book all said that there was no doubt that this was a nuclear reactor, that its purpose was the production of plutonium for the manufacture of atomic bombs, and that only in North Korea was there an identical reactor to the one destroyed in Syria.

Professor Uzi Even, who served in senior posts in the Israeli nuclear project, commented: "Judging from the diameter and the number of the tubes through which the fuel rods are inserted, it is possible to assert that what we are speaking about is a small reactor not capable of producing electricity, but only plutonium for atomic bombs. Furthermore, if the Syrians had wanted to produce electricity with this reactor, where are the high-tension cables to carry it to its destination? Such a reactor could produce enough plutonium for one bomb every year, or year and a half."

# CHAPTER 22

# The Second Lebanon War

The sensational disclosures about how Iran had hoodwinked the international community over the extent of its nuclear program, together with heavy pressure from the United States, as well as hints planted by Israel in the world media about the true nature of Iran's nuclear aims, seemed finally to rally the international community. Early in June 2006, the five permanent members of the UN Security Council, joined by Germany, served Iran with an ultimatum. They demanded that by July 12, when the G8 powers were due to meet in St. Petersburg, Iran reply to the requirement that it cease the enrichment of uranium forthwith. They also demanded that Iran reply to all IAEA inquiries, and open all of its installations to full inspection by IAEA agents. They were saying no more to cat-and-mouse games.

Iran attempted to postpone its reply until August 22, which was rejected. The international community's tough stance, and the falling into line of Russia and China, gave birth to a genuine hope for change; perhaps this time a country could be stopped by diplomatic action from going nuclear.

The Iranian response to the ultimatum came on July 12, a little after 9 a.m. The way in which they conveyed their reply was not, however, through diplomatic channels. Iran's proxy, Hizballah, set Israel's northern border alight, launching the Second Lebanon War.

On the face of things, what Israel calls the Second Lebanon War can be seen as a purely Middle Eastern affair. Yet the United States supported Israel's retaliation, Washington was kept fully informed of all developments, and the U.S. secretary of state ultimately brokered the signing of the cease-fire agreement.

The administration in Washington supported Israel's military strategy in the hope that Israel would inflict a knockout punch on Hizballah, and that the war would achieve five important U.S. objectives: strengthening Israel's status in the Middle East; achieving a victory in the global war against Islamic terror; demonstrating that the tactics and weaponry the United States had developed for fighting terror actually worked on the battlefield; weakening one of the forces operating against the U.S. forces in Iraq; and strengthening the international coalition against Iran. Israel's dismal failure in the war achieved the opposite on all five counts.

This failure has far-reaching implications for America's relations in the Middle East, and across the globe. Combined with what increasingly looks like an inevitable U.S. retreat from Iraq, Israel's near debacle is increasing radicalization and instability in the region.

The failures of the Second Lebanon War unfolded in several steps, and offer valuable lessons on a number of subjects.

## THE ABDUCTIONS

The kidnapping of Israel Defense Forces Sergeants Ehud Goldwasser and Eldad Regev on the morning of July 12 was Israel's casus belli. The abductions illustrate the lamentable state of the IDF's intelligence and combat readiness against Iran and its proxies on the northern front. Israel had reason to be more alert.

Every year since Israel withdrew from Lebanon in 2000, Hizballah had marked the anniversary, May 25, with a series of assemblies, processions, and speeches, as well as fireworks displays at Beaufort Castle in the south, built by the Crusaders and seen as the symbol of domination over the region. In 2006, at one such gathering, Hassan Nasrallah delivered a rousing speech in which he described Israel as a powerful country with a powerful economy, supported by the United States, but observed that it also had its weak points. One of these was the geographical advantage that Lebanese-based forces held over Israel. Northern Israel is full of vulnerable targets, both economic—ports, tourism facilities, industries, agriculture—and military—army bases and airfields.

Hizballah, Nasrallah continued, had the operational capability to help the weak Lebanese army and to create a deterrent against Israel: "The Resistance possesses over 12,000 missiles, if not 13,000, and I can state that the whole of the north of occupied Palestine is within the range of these missiles. Today, if I appear on television and I tell the residents of the colonies in occupied northern Palestine in the name of Hizballah,

'I advise you to go into your shelters in the next two hours,' they will all go to Tel Aviv."

A day after that speech, on May 26, at 10:30 a.m., Mahmoud al-Majzoub, the forty-one-year-old operations chief of the Islamic Jihad in Lebanon, and his brother Nidal, who was his bodyguard, left the offices of the organization in Sidon and walked to their silver Mercedes. As Nidal opened the driver's door, a huge explosion rent the air. A bomb hidden in the door had been detonated, apparently by remote control, killing the two men. Although they were from the Sunni Jihad and not the Sh'ite Hizballah, Iranian intelligence agents who arrived to investigate the incident brought members of the latter organization with them. Imad Moughniyeh, the Hizballah operations chief, said that any penetration of Lebanon by foreign intelligence elements, especially if it leads to the "killing of our brothers," was of interest to him. The investigation revealed that the bomb had been concealed inside the door in a way that had required dismantling and then reassembling it. Majzoub had received the car as a gift two weeks before, from someone who was apparently not a very good friend.

Israel made no comment on the incident, but Hizballah and the Islamic Jihad had no doubt who was responsible. Their response was to bombard the Israel air force's air control facility on Mount Meron, five kilometers from the border, that same day. They wanted to show the Israelis that Israeli strategic targets were within its range. Israeli jets immediately retaliated, bombing targets belonging to the Popular Front for the Liberation of Palestine, which had participated in the earlier attack. For two hours after that the front was quiet, but then Nasrallah chose to break the lull with another missile attack. In response the IDF this time let loose with a barrage along the entire front, including fourteen bombing sorties.

After the fighting died down in the late afternoon, the IDF claimed a great victory, declaring that all of Hizballah's forward emplacements had been destroyed. It was a blatant lie, but the Israeli media swallowed the military spokesman's statement whole. The claim created the impression, both within the Israeli army and among the public, that Hizballah could be defeated without sending in ground troops. The conflict seemed at a standstill, but in fact the drama continued.

On June 25, Hamas militiamen in Gaza dug a tunnel under the border fence. In a textbook commando operation, they raided an Israeli tank position, killing four men and taking Corporal Gilad Schalit prisoner. The Israeli Northern Command immediately placed its forces on high alert, fearing a copycat action by Hizballah. It had received several intelligence warnings of Hizballah's intention to snatch Israeli soldiers. Nasrallah had repeatedly declared that he saw such operations as a legitimate Hizballah objective, and in the two preceding years, there had been at least five abduction attempts.

The most notable one took place in the village of Rajar, which is divided by the Lebanon-Israel border, on November 22, 2005. Members of Hizballah's Special Forces unit, the reconnaissance section of the Nasser Brigade, infiltrated the Israeli sector under cover of morning mists in vehicles painted white, so as to resemble those used by the United Nations. Israeli Military Intelligence had been alerted to plans for an abduction in that sector, but they were unaware of a secret bunker used by the guerrillas. It was only thanks to the effective and resourceful response of a unit of paratroopers that the operation failed. Hizballah militiamen fired more than three hundred antitank missiles of various kinds at the Israeli forces, including the very latest Russian models, supplied by Syria. The Israeli paratroopers engaged the infiltrators, killing four of them with their first volley of fire. In the trouser pocket of one of the dead men the Israelis discovered IDF decoding keys, as well as a record written by the militiaman himself, in Hebrew, about the IDF's movements to and from Rajar. This should have been a wake-up call to Military Intelligence: Hizballah's intelligence had made a great leap forward.

On July 12, 2006, Hizballah would be much more successful. Israel's Yoav Battalion was on its penultimate day of a month of reserve duty. That evening, the men marked the end of their stint and the appointment of a new battalion commander with a celebration.

Nearby, on the back slope of the rocky hill which abuts point 105 on the Lebanese side, Hizballah militiamen had spent many weeks under cover of night constructing a spacious bunker and communication trenches, ready to shelter dozens of fighters and their weapons. These areas were thoroughly camouflaged and the bunker was connected by a fiberoptic cable network to Hizballah command headquarters in Beirut.

For two months, the guerrillas had quietly labored at strengthening their hideouts at spots that dominated the sole road on the Israeli side of the border, and stocking these points with weapons and ammunition. All of Hizballah's preparations for the kidnapping at point 105—the scouting activity, the positioning of weaponry and forces, the coordination of the operation, the communications procedures, the codes and the plans—had been entirely missed by Israeli intelligence.

In September 2006, as part of the research for this book, a reconstruction of the preparations and the actual abduction was held. A close look at the bunker revealed how it had been built literally under the nose of the Israelis, and perfectly camouflaged by the thick bushes that cover the rocky hill. So completely was the bunker hidden that it was not discovered throughout the entire war, although Israeli troops controlled the area from the first day. It was a miracle that Hizballah guerrillas never took advantage of it to strike at Israeli troops again after the abduction on July 12.

At about 3 a.m. on that day, in complete radio silence, a Hizballah special unit arrived and divided into two forces, one manning the camouflaged positions overlooking the road, and the other spreading out over the hill, waiting for an Israeli patrol, fingers on triggers. One word over the network would indicate the operation had begun; as soon as firing from point 105 was heard, everyone would join in.

At 03:05 a.m., shortly after the Yoav Battalion party ended, the electronic alarm system on the border fence signaled interference at "point 105." Lights flashed at divisional headquarters, but because of the fear of an abduction, soldiers were not sent out to investigate. This lack of initial response delayed but did not deter the kidnapping.

What happened next has been described in classified military investigation reports. The patrol that was ambushed later that same morning had not been scheduled. In contradiction of standing procedures, two armor-plated Humvees set out at 08:45 a.m. as one of the random patrols initiated by the commanders in the area. The lead Humvee was driven by a regular army NCO. In the seat next to him sat the patrol commander, Ehud Goldwasser. Behind them were Eldad Regev and another soldier, with a pile of equipment between them that included maps, aerial photographs, and communications codes. In the second vehicle were the driver, Wassim Nazal, and two other men. The men were in high spirits. The tapes of the battalion's communications that morning reveal a general laxity in discipline and preparedness. Some of the men in the patrol were not even wearing their bulletproof vests.

The vehicles were traveling east on the road between the farming communities of Zara'it and Shtula. The Hizballah units knew there were two vehicles in the patrol. They allowed the first one to pass a bend in the road and continue driving, coming up on their positions. They waited patiently until the second Humvee was also in their field of vision and had advanced a few meters, entirely exposed. At 09:03 a.m., a codeword was transmitted, and the whole sector erupted.

The last thing documented by a videocamera on the fence at Zara'it was an RPG rocket coming out of the bushes, straight at the camera. The camera then blacked out. At the same minute all the cameras in the sector were neutralized.

The guerrillas stationed at the high point of the hill rained RPG fire on the second Humvee. Nine rockets penetrated its armor. One man was killed on the spot; the others managed to escape from the burning vehicle, only to be cut down by a hail of fire from a Browning machine gun. That gun was later discovered to have been part of a shipment that Israel sold to Iran in the early 1980s. IDF investigators concluded that Hizballah never intended to reach the second vehicle. They only wanted to ensure that none of its crew escaped alive.

As soon as Goldwasser saw that the Humvee following him had been hit, he grabbed the radio handset and managed to shout, "They're firing." The signal was picked up only by chance by a soldier of the company, who informed his commanders by cellphone. The driver of Goldwasser's Humvee disobeyed standing orders, which call for driving on in the case of a missile attack. Instead, he stopped, jumped out, and hid in the bushes.

Hizballah fighters came out of their camouflaged positions and took aim at the lead vehicle. An RPG missile penetrated the passenger side door, starting a fire. Goldwasser and Regev were wounded. The man sitting next to Regev, Tomer Weinberg, managed to get out, but was hit and killed by the hail of fire before he could hide in the bushes.

The guerrillas nearest the road then blew open a gate in the border fence and charged at the burning vehicle. The wounded and bleeding Regev managed to get out of the Humvee, but the Hizballah men were already on top of him. He tried to lift his weapon and fire at them (and may even have succeeded), but he was hit again in the shoulder and thrown back toward the vehicle. The Hizballah fighters then opened the passenger-side door and pulled Goldwasser out. They dragged the two wounded men some 35 meters, leaving a trail of blood. After their flak jackets were removed, Goldwasser and Regev were put into a carrier made of sleeping bags, which was shouldered by two hefty Hizballah fighters, who moved as quickly as they could back into Lebanese territory. A few hundred meters across the border, an escape vehicle was waiting in the cover of an orchard. Once the Israeli abductees were loaded in, it tore away at top speed.

## BOMBARDMENT

As the abductions were investigated, war plans were agreed. The IDF had adopted a doctrine derived from combat tactics the United States had developed in the post–Cold War era: what the IDF called a "war of firepower"—fighting from a distance, with the fewest possible land forces. The air force would play the dominant role.

At a cabinet meeting on the evening of July 12, the top military brass presented the case for a massive air operation, both to teach Hizballah a lesson and, as Lieutenant General Dan Halutz stated, to bring about the implementation of Security Council Resolution 1559 of 2004. The goal of this UN resolution was the disarming of the militia and the posting of the Lebanese army units along the border with Israel. Halutz spoke of a weeklong operation, though he claimed afterward that he had not proposed any time limit.

The cabinet also approved land operations by certain elite units inside Lebanon, but the ministers understood from Halutz that the plan initially called for an aerial strike alone, and they endorsed the plan unanimously. Only Shimon Peres thought of asking, "Well, what happens after this operation?" Halutz replied, "We'll finish the first stage, and think about what to do next."

That night, the bombing operation code-named "Specific Gravity" began. Within thirty-four minutes, part of Hizballah's stockpile of long- and medium-range missiles was destroyed. This was an outstanding achievement, based upon painstaking intelligence work. In the six years since the Israeli withdrawal from Lebanon, Military Intelligence's sources had followed the shipments of missiles to Hizballah from Iran via Syria, and pinpointed the locations where they were positioned. A great deal of often frustrating but effective intelligence work was done, and Israel owes a huge debt to the U.S. National Security Agency, which provided much important information on shipping and air movements. Later in the war the Israeli intelligence work would prove far less helpful, but the information it provided on the first night of the aerial attack was vital to the strike's initial success.

The Israeli bombing of the missiles stunned Hizballah, which had no inkling of the degree to which Israel had zeroed in on its long-range missile sites. Yet the IDF were unprepared for what happened next.

Soon after the initial air bombardments, the northern Israeli home front took a beating from Hizballah, which still had all of its short-range and some of its medium-range missiles. The air force sent out more and more sorties of its best planes and pilots to try to hit the launch sites; it also used unmanned drones to attack enemy targets. But these efforts to destroy the launch sites had relatively little impact. The sites were so numerous and were replaced with such amazing rapidity that the air force simply could not handle them all. Only on rare occasions did the observation drones pick up Hizballah units setting up for a launch.

Undeterred, the air force continued to unleash a vast quantity of ordnance on Lebanon. Three weeks after the fighting broke out, the IDF informed the security cabinet that they had used the same tonnage of bombs as in the entire Yom Kippur War of October 1973. Soon the stockpiles began to run low, and a special airlift from the United States was necessary. Even though the Israeli air force dominated the skies, it could not win the war.

Over two years earlier, in February 2004, the Israeli Foreign Affairs and Defense Committee had sent a letter to the prime minister and to the defense ministers marked "Top secret, sensitive, for the addressees' eyes only." Anyone reading that letter today can only regret that it was not leaked to the media at the time. It contained a grave warning that the IDF was not ready for war against Hizballah and that there was no chance of victory from the air:

> Iran, through Hizballah and Syria, has placed Israel under a strategic threat that has no complete solution. The rockets deployed in South Lebanon have a quarter of the population of the state of Israel in their range. And this does not take into account the 220mm rockets, which are also to be found in Lebanon today. If they are fired, these missiles will disrupt life in the entire country for several weeks, and bring tens of thousands of refugees from the north to the center and paralyze vital economic and security installations. There is a critical gap in the intelligence neces-

sary to quickly and effectively suppress the firing of the rockets. Hence, the period during which northern Israel will be under rocket fire before it is suppressed could last several weeks, unless there is a land operation. Such an operation to root out the missile deployment would have extensive repercussions on the time that the campaign would take and its political results.

This situation, in which Hizballah represents a strategic threat to Israel, which has only limited responses, demands creative thinking about the diplomatic and military ways to change it. Parliamentary responsibility obligates us to warn you of the intolerable existing state of affairs.

The letter was a frighteningly accurate prophecy of disaster.

## INTELLIGENCE

In order to enhance the Israel air force's performance, special units were carrying out observation missions behind enemy lines. In addition to the support they provided for the air raids, they were also supposed to be gathering information to help close the gaps in the intelligence concerning Hizballah's fortification systems and its order of battle.

The gaps in the information provided by Military Intelligence were huge, and the initial success of mapping most of the medium- and long-range missile stockpiles was not repeated in any other sector. Back in 2000, Prime Minister Ehud Barak had forced the army to withdraw from Lebanon. After the withdrawal, Israel's intelligence sources dwindled. Attempts to find out details about the fortifications in the villages along the border had failed repeatedly, and even though the IDF had speculations about Hizballah's growing strength, there were many details that the military did not know. In truth, Israel had gone to war in almost total darkness.

## HIZBALLAH

On Friday night, July 15, 2006, Prime Minister Ehud Olmert arrived at the IDF's supreme command post, deep in the ground under the General Staff Headquarters in Tel Aviv, and met with the chief of staff, Lieutenant General Dan Halutz, who was managing the war from there. The two men walked quickly down the long corridor that leads to the air force command bunker. Here they watched a bombing raid on the Dahya, the Hizballah bastion in Beirut, at the heart of which is *al mraba al amniyya,* which translates to "the security square" and is the militia's headquarters. The IDF were hoping to destroy Hizballah's command-and-control center. This strategy was fundamentally flawed.

Hizballah had learned its lessons from previous encounters with the IDF in South Lebanon and knew that while the fighting was going on, it could not rely on help from the Palestinian militias based in the nearby refugee camps. It also could not depend on a steady supply of munitions from outside the combat arena, the region north of the Litani River. It had therefore placed large reserves of ordnance all over the region. Although Israel's aerial photography over the six years since the withdrawal had identified changes in various structures, and discovered some of the weapons, most of these stockpiles remained undetected.

Hizballah's strategic planning wasn't limited to weapons. Its leaders also developed and implemented a sophisticated intelligence system. During the war, militiamen who had learned Hebrew at the so-called Cultural Center of the Iranian Embassy in Beirut listened in to IDF radio networks, using advanced communications equipment and codes supplied to them by IDF members who were working with them in drug trafficking. Also intercepted were civilian beeper messages to officers engaged in the fighting. The IDF assumed that Hizballah was monitoring cell phone communications, but no evidence of this was uncovered. On top of all this, Hizballah maintained a close watch on Internet news sites and Israeli communications media, which often carried useful items about military operations. These intelligence capabilities, which were achieved thanks to Iran's aid in both equipment and expertise, were far beyond anything seen in most guerrilla organizations in history.

Hizballah's methods of fighting in built-up areas also came as a surprise to the Israelis. The militia had prepared certain houses for use as combat positions, with quantities of weapons and ammunition at the ready. Other houses were made to look as if they were used for combat, but were booby-trapped with tripwires connected to powerful explosive charges. In the urban environments entered by Israeli troops, there were generally no more than fifteen to twenty Hizballah fighters, who simply leapfrogged from house to house, using the prepositioned munitions, and creating the sense that far greater forces were in play.


## THE MID-EAST AXIS OF EVIL

On July 27, 2006, the sixty-first anniversary of the establishment of the Syrian armed forces, President Bashar al-Assad issued a belligerent message to the troops. As the Second Lebanon War raged nearby, he called on each unit to step up its training: "Despite our faith that martyrdom is the way to liberty and victory, we must believe that every effort and every drop of sweat now in training will save a drop of blood when the time comes. The battle continues as long as our land is occupied and our rights are plundered. Victory will come, with the help of Allah."

Bashar Assad's father had kept his distance from Iran, turning a blind eye to Iran's support of Hizballah. But ever since 2001, Bashar had embraced Hizballah, and crept closer to Tehran. His enthusiasm was boosted by the regular reports that he received from Iran and Hizballah about the blows that the American forces in Iraq were taking from Hizballah and Iranian Revolutionary Guards. Now, with the war raging, he could see the strength of the weapons, equipment, and intelligence information from Syria.

Assad was so pleased with the way the war was going that he ordered that Syria's links with Hizballah be strengthened. Approving of weapons shipments to Hizballah, he allowed the transfer of unidentifiable items such as light arms, explosives, or antitank missiles that were relatively easy to purchase on the world market. This gave the CIA the impression that Assad had given orders not to supply any arms from Syria itself. But it was later discovered that the Syrians also supplied Hizballah with weapons from their warehouses. In fact, 70–80 percent of Israeli casualties in the war were inflicted by weapons that came from Syria and not from Iran. Syria manufactured the 220mm and 302mm missiles that hit Israeli citizens and supplied the advanced Russian-made antitank weaponry that was used by Hizbollah to attack Israel's army.

Although they had withdrawn from Lebanon, the Syrians had left behind agents and observation equipment, and they were also able to convey large amounts of intelligence information and military advice to Hizballah. After the war, a European intelligence service reported to Israel that the Syrians were supplying Hizballah with up-to-date satellite photographs of Israel, and that Imad Moughniyeh's deputy went to the Iranian Embassy in Damascus to coordinate the flow of information. While the first Gulf War illustrated the way that Israel had learned to use the superiority of U.S. weapons and tactics, the Second Lebanon War revealed IDF weaknesses. As Major General Uri Saguy, the former head of Israeli Military Intelligence, explained: "The moderate Arab states, just like the United States, raised an eyebrow in disappointment over the IDF's capability. In Syria, they were happy about the performance. From their perspective, the war was another sign that they were closing the tactical and operational gaps between them and the IDF."

Despite the massive amount of effort that Israel put forth in this prolonged confrontation, it had failed to defeat a guerrilla army. The truth is that Israel lost the war in Lebanon. And unfortunately, because of that loss, the faults of the best army in the Middle East were made blatantly obvious.

## THE AFTERMATH

After the war, Hizballah began to analyze the conflict. These talks took place in two large and closely guarded buildings in Damascus and Tehran, and were held under the respective patronage of Syrian Military Intelligence and the two top Iranian intelligence organizations involved in Hizballah's activities, the intelligence units of the Revolutionary Guards and the Intelligence Ministry, VEVAK. There were also representatives of Hamas and the Palestinian Islamic Jihad, all of whom were eager to learn how Hizballah had succeeded and in what ways it had failed.

After attending these meetings, Hamas began applying the lessons of the war in Gaza and the West Bank. As part of this process, agents of the Revolutionary Guards have been stationed in Gaza to help with the establishment of an advanced intelligence apparatus for Hamas. The Palestinians are particularly interested in subterranean operations, advanced antitank missiles, various kinds of rockets, and especially the securing of information.

Qassam Sulimani, commander of the al-Quds force in the Iranian Revolutionary Guards, shared his thoughts on the meaning of the war's outcome to the Palestinian arena. In a speech marking "Jerusalem Day" in October 2006, he stated: "Following Hizballah's victory in Lebanon, a new Middle East has emerged, not an American Mideast, but an Islamic one. Parallel to the formation of Jihadist groups in Palestine, a Shi'ite organization called Hizballah has succeeded in exporting to Palestine the model for a believers' way of life. Hizballah has played a central role in turning the stones of the Palestinians into missiles."

In an interview on Al Manar, Hizballah's TV station, in August 2007, Hassan Nasrallah further expounded on what he saw as the failure of American policy in the Middle East: "There is an American plan . . . whose true essence is . . . hegemony over all the states of this region. . . . Hizballah is participating in the struggle against this American hegemony, together with all of the peoples of the Arab world and the Islamic world." Nasrallah predicted that the Americans would "pack their bags" within a few years and leave the Middle East and the Arabic and Islamic world, just as they had left Vietnam. He urged those who wager on getting U.S. assistance to learn from the Vietnam experience and to understand that when the Americans departed, those who had counted on them would be abandoned to their fate.

A tightening of ties between Iran, Hizballah, and Hamas has been underway. Prior to the assassination of Hamas founder Sheikh Ahmad Yassin in 2004 by Israel, Hamas had rejected Iranian offers of assistance for years, and the exiled leaders Khaled Mashal and Mussa Abu Marzook Yassin had been forced to take money from the country without Yassin's knowledge. However, after his death, and especially after the war, a rapprochement was accelerated.

On the public level, the process reached a peak when in December 2006 the Palestinian prime minister (and Hamas leader in Gaza) Ismail Haniyeh openly visited Tehran and returned literally with suitcases full of cash. Around the same time, increasing numbers of Hamas militiamen began attending training courses in Iran. More and more frequently, they were covertly crossing the border into Egypt and flying to Iran via Europe. A point of great concern for Israel intelligence is that Hamas will take its lead from Hizballah and evolve into an organization that has the intelligence and military capacities of entire governments at its disposal.

In July 2007, Mashir al-Masri, a Hamas representative in the Palestinian parliament, was asked if Hamas would ever accept assistance from Iran. He replied that the ideological differences between Iran and Hamas would not prevent the acceptance of any assistance offered, adding that assistance from Iran would be "a thousand times more preferable to casting in our lot with the Americans and the Zionists." Shortly after the war, Iranian assistance became apparent in the form of roadside bombs. During an incursion on September 12, 2006, the IDF discovered several of these devices close to the main thoroughfare in the Gaza Strip. What adds to fears surrounding the confirmation that Hamas and Iran are working together is that the devices that were found are more dangerous and have a higher penetration capability than those previously used by Palestinian terror organizations.

The Israeli weaknesses that were made apparent in the Second Lebanon War have built up a dangerous level of confidence within Hizballah. These failures have also contributed to frightening new relationships in the Middle East. As these ties between Syria, Hamas, and Hizballah strengthen, a number of critical issues must be addressed by the West.

Will Iran and Syria continue to draw closer together? Will Hamas become another Iranian proxy? These burgeoning relationships demand that we take the time to analyze and understand them, just as Hizballah has taken the time to study Israel. Without knowledge about the way these organizations operate, we cannot realistically expect to defeat them.

# EPILOGUE

Even in the secure, inner rooms, anyone who had stayed up late to work must have heard the blast on February 12, 2008. Like everyone else who lived and worked in the Susa neighborhood of Damascus, the people inside 17 Nisan Street must have hurried to their windows to see what had happened right in front of their home. They saw the flames shooting out of the Mitsubishi Pajero SUV that had been blown up in the middle of the street. Later, they and the world learned that inside the car was the charred corpse of the supreme military commander of Hizballah, the organization's brilliant operational brain and the favorite protégé of the Iranian Revolutionary Guards.

The assassination of Imad Moughniyeh in Damascus was a warning that eventually even the most elusive prey can be hunted down, given skill, determination, and patience on the part of the hunter. The blast that dispatched this arch terrorist, a top target for Israeli and American intelligence for most of three decades, was heard loud and clear by Khaled Mashal, the exiled head of Hamas, who was at a meeting with Syrian intelligence officers only few hundreds meters away at the time.

A European intelligence officer who until a few weeks before had been stationed in Damascus said the fear produced by this assassination, which was attributed to the Mossad, was afterwards visible in the eyes of members of radical Islamist groups like Hizballah, Hamas, and the Islamic Jihad in the Syrian capital. The fear was also evident in the embarrassed expressions of Syrian intelligence and security personnel, who realized that if Moughniyeh could be disposed of in the heart of the city's best-protected neighborhood, it was possible to reach anyone, including the people inside 17 Nisan Street.

That is the address of a group of buildings that houses the Atomic Energy Commission of Syria. Its hundreds of employees had already taken a severe blow when five months before, seven Israel air force jets had made a pile of rubble and a cloud of dust out of Syria's attempt to manufacture nuclear weapons with North Korean assistance.

Although Israel has denied responsibility for the assassination, the Moughniyeh hit was exactly the kind of thing needed to restore the country's faith in, and more importantly the enemy's fear of, Israel's intelligence services. Pinpointing the location of this evasive, supercautious quarry, placing the precise explosive charge in his SUV that would kill him and no one else ("Pity about that new Pajero," chuckled one intelligence official in Tel Aviv), and operating in the heart of an Arab capital saturated with secret police—these are the very stuff of the operations that gave the Mossad its famous reputation.

The Damascus assassination, the last in a series of attempts carried out over a quarter of a century to eliminate Moughniyeh, came far too late. His hands were stained with the blood of hundreds of victims of terror, and he conceived, perfected, and applied guerrilla warfare methods that caused severe damage to one of the world's best armies. What is more, despite his demise and because of it, fear of Iran and Hizballah was so great that Israelis and Americans were almost fatalistically certain that revenge, in the form of a terror attack bigger and more ambitious than anything they had done before, was only a matter of time.

I began researching this book in order to uncover and make sense of the history of the thirty years of secret war between the West—the United States and Israel in particular—and the Iran of Khomeini's Islamic revolution; to place the events, both those that are still classified and those that are already in the public domain, in their historical context; and to try to unravel the entangled threads that would help explain them. My intention was not to depict this history as a series of failures— but that is largely the way it has turned out.

Despite its substantial experience in dealing with Iran and Hizballah, until the Second Lebanese War in the summer of 2006, Israel simply never saw this confrontation for what it really is—a titanic struggle between an aggressive, ideology-driven Islamic revolutionary regime, assisted by a no less brutal ideological ally that is willing to do its bidding, and a complacent, satisfied society that thought it had put its existential fears behind it. The United States, too, lost its focus on Iran, worrying first about the Cold War and later about al-Qaeda and Iraq.

Many years will pass before historians are able to provide full and satisfying explanations for the failure of the mighty Israeli military machine in the Second Lebanon War, and for the broader failure thus far of the West in its war against Iran and its proxies. Nonetheless, it is already possible to draw four conclusions:

- The intelligence failures of the United States and Israel vis-à-vis Iran and Hizballah are symptomatic of the decline of the intelligence communities in both countries. At least in the case of Israel, this decline reflects a larger trend: an increasing lack of confidence in the institutions of government, as well as a rise in cynicism, materialism, and opportunism, which have taken the place of national solidarity. As a result, there is much less readiness to serve in demanding, dangerous governmental positions.
- The long years of confrontation have proved that Iran and Hizballah are more sophisticated, effective, and determined adversaries than Israel and the United States have previously encountered in the Middle East. These new enemies, the Shi'ites of Iran and Lebanon, have repeatedly outwitted Israel and the West, beating them across the board in politics, in intelligence gathering, and in war.
- The Second Lebanon War greatly strengthened Iran and Hizballah and resulted in the solidifying of an Iranian-Syrian alliance—undoubtedly one of Tehran's greatest political achievements to date. Evidence of this can be seen both in the U.S. readiness to talk directly to Iran after years of refusing to do so, and in the inability of the United States to impose an international regime of effective sanctions against Iran to pressure it to abort its nuclear program.
- In all other respects, the Lebanon War made little difference to either side. Hizballah still aspires to take control of Lebanon and to establish an Islamic puppet regime in Beirut, which would actually be controlled from Tehran. It took a step forward in May 2008, when it launched a successful armed campaign to counter the pro-Western Beirut government's attempt to curtail its attempts to build a state within a state, proving once again that Hizballah is the dominant military and political force in Lebanon.

Iran still aspires to export its revolution, still activates Palestinian terror against Israel, and is still bent on acquiring nuclear weapons. All this leaves Israel precisely where it was before the war. In fact, the Second Lebanon War may turn out to have been nothing more than a dress rehearsal for the seemingly inevitable confrontation between the two sides.

One can only hope that Western leaders, and those of the United States and Israel in particular, will learn from this war and the dismal chronicle of failures that preceded it, and finally grasp that their approach to Iran is fundamentally wrong. The many flaws displayed throughout the secret war against Iran may be repaired in time. Indeed, they must be.

The bottom line of this book also touches on the question that has been asked with increasing frequency in recent years in American public discourse. Simply phrased, it is: Was America right to support Israel over the years? or more bluntly: Have we backed the right horse? It seems to me that the story told here, a story of thirty years of a secret common struggle waged by the two countries against the menace of the Ayatollahs' regime in Iran, provides, in part at least, an affirmative answer. Radical Islam's perception of Israel and the United States as one common enemy has succeeded in uniting extremist Shi'ite and Sunni elements, usually united only in their hatred of each other. And indeed, Israel and the United States do have much in common that makes them anathema to those extremists. It is those shared values, and not just the fact that they have a common enemy, that lie behind the cooperation between the intelligence communities of the two countries. There have been failures and there have been successes, of each individually and of both acting together; but Israel's considerable contribution to America's endeavors to make the world a better place must be acknowledged.

During 2007 and the first half of 2008, there were glimmers of hope that the successes were at last outweighing the failures: The defection of General Askari, the "mishap" at the VX gas facility at al-Safir, Israel's stealth attack on the facility in northeast Syria, and the elimination of Imad Moughniyeh all suggest that we may be witnessing a change for the better in the functioning of the intelligence communities in the front line against Iran. The Mossad and the CIA, along with the signals and satellite intelligence units of both countries, managed to gather sufficient information to slow down the development of unconventional weaponry by Iran, Syria, and North Korea. Israel made it clear to the world that it still adheres to the "Begin Doctrine," first implemented in Israel's bombing of the Osirak nuclear installation near Baghdad in 1981: the Jewish state will not tolerate the development by its neighbors of weapons that may be used to destroy it. Sixty years after the end of World War II, the lessons of the Holocaust are still guiding Israel's leaders. Israel will do everything that has to be done in order to neutralize existential threats.

This point has important implications for the chances for stability in the Middle East in coming years. Iran, not Syria, is the state that is closest to developing nuclear weapons that may be aimed at Israel. Israel's move in northeast Syria signals that Israel may be seriously considering a military strike to resolve the Iranian threat. It thus also serves as a clear signal to Europe: If you sit on your hands or are otherwise unable to resolve this problem, we will be forced to send in our boys to do the job. Apparently, this message was also received in Arab capitals. The raid was condemned, as was to be expected, around the Middle East, but these condemnations were muted. Israel is not the only country in the region to be concerned about the prospect of Syrian nuclear weaponization and the spreading influence of Iran. Many Arab leaders also clearly relished the blow to Assad's prestige. And to the extent that the attack on Syria was a rehearsal for an operation against a nuclear Iran, the reactions to it around the world, and especially in the immediate neighborhood, were encouraging.

From Israel's point of view, however, the success of the attack also reflects, perhaps more than anything else, the dark side of the picture. The Supreme Leader of Iran, Ayatollah Khamenei, has succeeded more than his predecessor Khomeini in exporting the Islamist revolution. Hizballah is the central political and military force in Lebanon, and its leader Sheikh Hassan Nasrallah declared after the Moughniyeh assassination that the war against Israel would now be waged across the globe. Hamas, more than ever bound to Iran, rules in Gaza. The terrorist forces operating under the patronage of the Iranian Revolutionary Guards are dealing hard blows to the American forces in Iraq. Syrian president Bashar Assad, possessed by lust for revenge for the humiliations meted out to him by Israel, is tying himself up in a military alliance with and economic dependence upon Tehran, while loading Kim Jong Il onto the bandwagon.

In his briefing to the Senate Armed Services Committee in February 2007, the director of national intelligence Michael McConnell stated: "Iran's influence is rising in ways that go beyond the menace of its nuclear program. The fall of the Taliban and Saddam, increased oil revenues, Hamas's electoral victory, and Hezbollah's perceived recent success in fighting against Israel all extend Iran's shadow in the region. . . . Iranian President Ahmadinejad's administration . . . has stepped up the use of more assertive and offensive tactics to achieve Iran's longstanding goals. . . . At the center of Iran's terrorism strategy is Lebanese Hezbollah. . . . [Hezbollah has] contingency plans to conduct attacks against U.S. interests in the event it feels its survival—or that of Iran—is threatened."

Notwithstanding the peculiar National Intelligence Estimate that the National Intelligence Board issued not long after that, and even if we accept its conclusions, there's no doubt that Iran's nuclear program is reaching a critical stage. The West can only hope that its intelligence agencies are up to the enormous challenges that lie ahead. Will the thirty-year secret war with Iran end in a conflagration? Or can Iran be contained?

A spark could cause a conflagration in the region. When Israeli jets shot down six Syrian MiG fighters in April 1967, it was seen as a glorious feat by the Israel air force, but in retrospect it is seen as one of the reasons for the slide into a war that no one wanted two months later. The lessons of that incident must not be forgotten when studying the Israeli-American successes against Syria in the summer of 2007.

Israel, the United States, and the world community must be vigilant.

# ACKNOWLEDGMENTS

I am deeply indebted to the many people who kindly gave of their time to talk to me, verified and clarified facts on my behalf, and put relevant documents at my disposal, sometimes at considerable risk to themselves. For the members of many intelligence communities, past and present, who served as sources for much of the contents of this book, there was no personal gain; for many, there was only the danger of being caught and severely penalized. They did it out of sincere concern for the security of the citizens of their countries and the desire that these citizens get the intelligence services they deserve.

This is the third book on which we have worked together, but this time the task of Shachar Alterman, editor of *Point of No Return,* the Hebrew book on which this work is based, was particularly demanding. Without him, the project would not have reached fruition.

I owe a double debt of gratitude to Dov Alfon, who as editor of *Haaretz* magazine, encouraged me to investigate the issue of the Islamic Republic of Iran when it was still far from the top of the public agenda, and later, as editor in chief of the Kinneret, Zmora-Bitan, Dvir Publishing House (who published the Hebrew edition), showed his confidence in the book and patiently endured continual delays in its completion. My thanks go also to the others on his team who went to so much trouble in seeing the project through to the end.

I am deeply grateful to Bruce Nichols, executive editor of Free Press until October 2007, for his vote of confidence in acquiring the book and for his dedicated editing. Despite the difficulty of the task, the variety of subjects and their complexity, the constraints of time, and his struggles with the writer's graphomania, Bruce wielded his pen with the craftsmanship that made a real book out of the vast volume of raw material he was confronted with. Thanks also to Emily Loose, who took over from

Bruce in the final stages of preparing the book for publication. I am grateful for her professionalism, patience, and support.

This book would not have come about were it not for the professionalism, the friendship, and the wisdom of my agent, Deborah Harris, and the members of her staff, especially Ines Austern.

My special thanks are due to Ronnie Hope, for his diligent, professional, and intelligent translation work, which was far more than a literal rendition of the original Hebrew, but also included much judicious editing that saved me from the embarrassment of errors.

The unconditional and constant support and sage counsel of my journalistic mentor, Dan Margalit, have stood me in good stead.

I owe thanks also to several scholars and experts who have aided me over the years of research, and who also read sections of the manuscript: Professor David Menashri, Professor Yoram Meital, Dr. Avner Cohen, Reuven Merhav, and Ehud Eiran. My colleague Gil Meltzer was involved in the research for chapter 16, "Hizballah Prepares," and I am indebted to him for that as well as for years of enjoyable work together.

Thanks also to Shlomo Zabadi, who helped translate reports of German intelligence services; to William Royce from the Voice of America Persian station, who introduced me to the Iranian community in the United States, and contributed his remarkable expertise on the subject; to Professor Christopher Andrew, the greatest of all scholars of the history of intelligence and my mentor at Cambridge University, for his wise advice and valuable assistance; to Daniel Korski, Yakov Finzi, and Esad Hechamovic for their assistance in Bosnia; to Gabriel and Graciella Pasquini for the use of their excellent network of connections in Buenos Aires; to Dr. Stanley Bedlington of the CIA, who shared with me some of his assessments on terrorism; to Robert Baer, of the same agency, who shared some of his practical experiences in that same sphere; and to John Pike and Tim Brown for help in deciphering aerial photography.

I thank Nili Benjamin, Avshalom Suliman-Altschuler, and Anat Libin, who compiled the Bibliography and helped ready the book for publication.

Also deserving of my gratitude are all the editors under whom I have worked in the Israeli media and who gave me the freedom to undertake the prolonged research for this book. First and foremost, Moshe Vardi; but also Ehud Eil-Gil, Ehud Asheri, Ruth Yuval, Pninah Vellan, Yael

Admoni, Ital Katz, Nir Hefez, and Gadi Blum. Special thanks to Haim Rosenberg, who was always there when needed.

Finally, many thanks to the woman with the noble soul, Anat Harel, for her wise advice on the last draft, and for the great patience she showed on the innumerable occasions when I had to be at my computer rather than in her company.

All the good things about this book were achieved thanks to all of these wonderful people, and others I may have omitted, for which I am sorry. The errors are mine and mine alone.

Ronen Bergman
July 2008

# BIBLIOGRAPHY AND
# A NOTE ON SOURCES

This book is based upon thousands of documents—Israeli and others—mostly classified and gathered from various sources, as well as thousands of newspaper clippings, and hundreds of books and articles in academic journals. But most of all, it is based upon some three hundred interviews.

Oral history is a complex matter that demands various rules and precautions, mainly finding written or oral evidence to confirm the information it produces. Fortunately, such evidence, including personal diaries and documents written at the time of the relevant events, has frequently been found to exist. In some cases, this has led to the preference of one oral version over another.

For example, there has been a running argument for many years between Brigadier General Yitzhak Segev, Israel's last military attaché in Tehran, and the chief of the Mossad station there at the time, Eliezer Tsafrir, over details of the rescue of the thirty-four Israelis left stranded in Iran after Khomeini's return. Segev kept a diary that documented the events, which is held in the Defense Ministry archives. It jibes with his oral testimony, and I have therefore preferred his version. Often, I have been compelled to leave out excellent stories for lack of corroborating accounts. One such case was what I was told by a former Iranian intelligence official, who said that he met the missing Israeli navigator, Ron Arad, in the Evin prison in Tehran.

Particularly noteworthy are the sources that were used frequently in sections of the book dealing with historical, social, political, and theological background: All the works of Professor David Menashri, Israel's top expert on the subject of Iran; the extensive research by Dr. Efraim Kam of the INSS on Iran's military buildup; the outstanding doctoral dissertation on Hizballah by Shimon Shapira; the comprehensive doctoral dissertation by Ronen Cohen on the Mujahideen Khalq; Martin Kramer's book on Fadlallah; and Amir Taheri's biography of Khomeini. Also very helpful have been the excerpts from the Arab media gathered by MEMRI, which proved a qualitative and highly reliable source; the ongoing surveys published by Kenneth Timmerman in his newsletter *The Iran Brief*; and the material gathered by the Center for Information for Intelligence and Terrorism of the Center for Intelligence Heritage, compiled by Dr. Reuven Erlich, which includes unclassified information from the Arab states and Iran. In addition, there are the documents seized by Israeli Military Intelligence during raids inside the Palestinian Authority territories, to which I was given access in 2002–03.

Owing to lack of space, I am able to cite only the oral and academic sources here.

## INTERVIEWS
### (In alphabetical order)

Avi Aboulafia, Aharon Abramovitz, Shmuel Abuav, Udi Adam, Nathan Adams, Munir Alibavich, Kantajan Alibekov, Doron Almog, Yaakov Amidror, Meir Amit, Frank Anderson, Hugo Anzorreguy, David Arbel, Anna Aroch, Roger Auque, Pinhas Avivi, Ami Ayalon, Danny Ayalon, Dror Arad Ayalon, Avner Azulai, Ehud Barak, Amazia Baram, Uzi Baram, Jose Barbachia, Miki Barel, David Barkai, Stanley Bedlington, Yossi Beilin, Moshe (Mishka) Ben David, Benjamin Ben-Eliezer, Ilan Biran, Roy Blecher, Gabriella Blum, Naftali Blumenthal, Yossef Bodansky, Avraham Botzer, Avishay Braverman, Shlomo Brom, Jean-Louis Brugière, Ewan Buchanan, Yigal Carmon, Iftikhar Khan Chaudhry, Dvorah Chen, Uri Chen, Itamar Chizik, David Christan, Avner Cohen, Moshe Cohen, Ronen Cohen, Yitzhak Dar, Uzi Dayan, Puya Dayanim, Avi Dichter, Eli Dolgin, Dov Eichenwald, Giora Eiland, David Einhorn, Robert Einhorn, Yom Tov (Yomi) Eini, Ehud Eiran, Rolf Ekeus, Jean Pierre Elraz, Reuven Erlich, Shmuel Evyatar, Gideon Ezra, Meir Ezri, Raymonda Fisher, Manuchehr Ganji, Sadek Gardieh, Reuel Marc Gerecht, Amos Gilad, Yehiel Giloh, Karnit Goldwasser, Shlomo Goldwasser, Sarit Gomez, Ran Goren, Daniel Gorsky, Eran Guy, Eitan Haber, Aharon Halevi, Ephraim Halevy, Shaul Hamawi, Isser Harel, Akel al-Hashem, Mark Hasner, Robert Hatem, Robin Higgins, Gal Hirsch, Yaacov Hisdai, Yitzhak Hofi, Asad Homayoun, Lior Horev, Yehiel Horev, Dalia Itzik, Haim Karmon, Sami Katzav, Ya'akov Kedmi, Joy Kiddie, Motti Kidur, David Kimche, David Kolitz, Yossi Kostiner, David Kubi, Chen Kugel, Sergei Kurginian, Anat Kurtz, Raz Lerman, Carmel Levi, Gabriel Levinas, Alexander Libin, Avi Lichter, Rami Lieber, Alon Liel, Esther Limona, Amnon Lipkin-Shahak, Dror Livneh, Rebecca Lowenthal, Uri Lubrani, David Lubretzki, Salman Madah, Nahum Manbar, Victor Marchetti, Ismail Marakos Martivas, John McDermott, Ilan Meirson, David Menashri, Reuven Merhav, Dan Meridor, Shaul Mofaz, Yitzhak Mordechai, Hujat al-Islam Sayed Na'abi, Azar Nafisi, Hamid Nasrallah, Menahem Navot, Benjamin Netanyahu, Zilla Neumann, Frank Nickbecht, Yaakov Nimrodi, Alberto Nisman, Rafi Noy, Ehud Olmert, Eldad Pardo, Gabriel Pasquini, Yossi Peled, Gustavo D. Perednik, Shimon Peres, Yaakov Peri, Richard Perle, Yisrael Perlov, Amir Peretz, Antony Phillipson, Giandomenico Picco, Zvi Poleg, Jerrold Post, Masoud Rajavi, Hagai Ram, Haim Ramon, Beni Regev, Mohammad Reza Cyrus Pahlavi Shah . . . מאתל, Alexander Ritzmann, Yiftah Ron-Tal, Yehudit Ronen, Bill Royce, Rachel Sadan, Uri Saguy, Yom Tov Samia, Eli Sanderowitz, Uri Savir, Otniel Schneller, Yoram Schweitzer, Patrick Seale, Yitzhak Segev, Yossi Shahar, Yehoram Shai, Shimon Shapira, Yaacov Shapiro, Omri Sharon, David Shik, Zvi Shtauber, Florian Siwicki, Marion Sobel, Yuval Steinitz, Mahmoud Taichan, Avraham Tamir, Elchanan Tannenbaum, Keren Tannenbaum, Uri Tannenbaum, Binyamin, (Bini) Telem, Yitzhak Tidhar, Yona Tilma, Richard Tomlinson, Eliezer (Geizi) Tsafrir, Yehuda Unger, Matan Vilnai, Ali Waked, Anita Weinstein, Phillip Wilcox, James Woolsey, Yitzhak Ya'acov, Ami Yaar, Yoram Yair, Danny Yatom, Dov Zackheim, Bennie Zeevi, Dror Zeevi, Nadav Zeevi, Haim Zemach, Amnon Zichroni, and Eli Ziv.

In addition, there were 112 interviewees who asked to remain anonymous, as they were serving or had served in the intelligence, law enforcement, or diplomatic communities of Israel, the United States, the Palestinian Authority, Iran, Germany, Switzerland, France, Britain, Egypt, Argentina, Bosnia, Canada, and Jordan, or were members of Iranian opposition movements. Israeli military censorship barred the publication of the names of fourteen Israeli intelligence officials who were interviewed.

## BOOKS IN ENGLISH

Abrahamian, Ervand. *Khomeinism: Essays on the Islamic Republic.* London: University of California Press, 1993.

Adams, James. *The Unnatural Alliance.* London: Quartet Books, 1984.

Agee, Philip. *Inside the Company—CIA Journal.* Harmondsworth, UK: Penguin Books, 1975.

Andrew, Christopher. *For the President's Eyes Only.* London: HarperCollins, 1995.

———, and Vasili Mitrokhin. *The Sword and the Shield—The Mitrokhin Archive and the Secret History of the KGB.* New York: Basic Books, 1999.

———. *The Mitrokhim Archive II.* London: Penguin Books, 2005.

Asculai, Ephraim. *Rethinking the Nuclear Non-Proliferation Regime.* Tel Aviv: Jaffee Center for Strategic Studies, Tel Aviv University, 2004.

Avi-Ran, Reuven [Erlich]. *The Syrian Involvement in Lebanon Since 1975.* Boulder, CO: Westview Press, 1991.

Bakhash, Shaul. *The Reign of the Ayatollas in Iran and the Islamic Revolution.* London: Unwin Paperbacks, 1986.

Baram, Amatzia. *Building Towards Crisis: Saddam Husayn's Strategy for Survival.* Washington, DC: Washington Institute for Near East Policy, 1998.

Barnaby, Frank. *The Indivisible Bomb.* London: I. B. Tauris, 1989.

Ben-Menashe, Ari. *Profits of War—Inside the Secret U.S-Israeli Arms Network.* New York: Sheridan Square Press, 1992.

Bergen, Peter L. *Holy War Inc.—Inside the Secret World of Osama Bin Laden.* London: Weidenfeld & Nicolson, 2003.

Black, Ian, and Benny Morris. *Israel's Secret Wars: A History of Israel's Intelligence Services.* London: Hamish Hamilton, 1991.

Blum, Gabriella. *Islands of Agreement: Managing Enduring Rivalries.* Cambridge, MA: Harvard University Press, 2007.

Brecher, Michael. *Decisions in Israel's Foreign Policy.* London: Oxford University Press, 1974.

Calvocoressi, Peter. *World Politics 1945–2000* Harlow, UK: Pearson Education, 1968; 2001.

Carew, Tom. *Jihad: The Secret War in Afghanistan.* Edinburgh: Mainstream Publishing, 2000.

Cline, Ray, and Yonah Alexander. *Terrorism as State-Sponsored Covert Warfare.* Fairfax, VA: HERO Books, 1986.

Cobban, Helena. *The Palestinian Liberation Organization.* Cambridge: Cambridge University Press, 1984.

Cockburn, Andrew, and Leslie Cockburn. *Dangerous Liaisons. The Inside Story of the U.S.-Israeli Covert Relationship.* New York: HarperCollins, 1991.

Dekmejian, R. Hrain. *Islam in Revolution. Fundamentalism in the Arab World.* 2nd ed. Syracuse, NY: Syracuse University Press, 1994.

Eisenstadt, Michael. *Iranian Military Power: Capabilities and Intentions.* Washington, DC: Washington Institute for Near East Policy, 1996.

Eveland, W. C. *Ropes of Sand: America's Failure in the Middle East.* New York: W. W. Norton, 1980.

Freedman, Robert O. *World Politics and the Arab-Israeli Conflict.* New York: Pergamon Press, 1979.

Haeclerode, Peter. *Secret Soldiers. Special Forces in the War Against Terrorism.* London: Sterling Publishing, 2000.

Hala, Jaber. *Hezbolla.* New York: Columbia University Press, 1997.

Hatem, Robert M. *From Israel to Damascus: The Painful Road of Blood, Betrayal, and Deception.* La Mesa, CA: Pride International Publications, 1999.

Hersh, Seymour. *The Samson Option.* New York: Random House, 1991.

Hoffman, Bruce. *Recent Trends and Future Prospects of Iranian Sponsored International Terrorism.* Santa Monica, CA: RAND Corporation, 1990.

Hollis, Martin, and Stephan Smith. *Explaining and Understanding International Relations.* Oxford: Clarendon Press, 1990.

Juergensmeyer, Mark. *Terror in the Mind of God.* Berkeley: University of California Press, 2000.

Keddie, Nikki, ed. *Religion and Politics in Iran: Shi'ism from Quietism to Revolution.* New Haven and London: Yale University Press, 1983.

Kurginyan, Sergey. *The Weakness of Power: The Analytics of Closed Elite Games and Its Basic Concepts.* Moscow: ECC Publishing, 2007.

Kwintny, Jonathan. *Endless Enemies: The Making of an Unfriendly World.* New York: Penguin Books, 1984.

Laqueur, Walter. *The New Terrorism—Fanaticism and the Arms of Mass Destruction.* London: Phoenix Press, 1999.

Livingstone, Neil C., and David Halevy. *Inside the PLO.* New York: Quill/William Morrow, 1990.

Marchetti, Victor, and John D. Marks. *The CIA and the Cult of Intelligence.* New York: Dell Publishing, 1980.

Mearsheimer, John and Stephen Walt. *The Israeli Lobby and U.S. Foreign Policy.* New York: Farrar, Straus & Giroux, 2007.

Melman, Yossi. *The Master Terrorist: The True Story Behind Abu-Nidal.* London: Sedgwick & Jackson, 1987.

Menashri, David, ed. *Islamic Fundamentalism: A Challenge to Regional Stability.* Tel Aviv: Dayan Center, Tel Aviv University, 1993.

Mohadessin, Mohammad. *Islamic Fundamentalism: The New Global Threat.* Washington, DC: Seven Locks Press, 1993.

National Movement of the Iranian Resistance (Report), *Iran: In Defense of Human Rights.* Paris, 1983.

Norton, Augustus Richard. *Amal and the Shia: Struggle for the Soul of Lebanon.* Austin: University of Texas Press, 1987.

Oliphant, Laurence. *The Land of Gilead.* London: William Blackwood & Sons, 1870.

Parsi, Trita. *Treacherous Alliance: The Secret Dealings of Israel, Iran and the United States.* New Haven: Yale University Press, 2007.

Pipes, Daniel. *The Hidden Hand: Middle East Fears of Conspiracy.* New York: St. Martin's Press, 1998.

Posner, Steve. *Israel Undercover: Secret Warfare and Hidden Diplomacy in the Middle East.* Syracuse, NY: Syracuse University Press, 1987.

Ranelagh, John. *The Agency: The Rise and Decline of the CIA.* New York: Simon & Schuster, 1986.

Rimington, Stella. *Open Secret.* London: Hutchinson, 2002.

Rivlin, Paul. *The Russian Economy and Arms Exports to the Middle East.* Tel Aviv: Jaffee Center for Strategic Studies, Tel Aviv University, 2005.

Ruwayha, Walid Amin. *Terrorism and Hostage-Taking in the Middle East.* Paris: JCI, 1990.

Schiff, Ze'ev, and Ehud Ya'ari. *Israel's War in Lebanon.* London: Simon & Schuster, 1986.

Schulze, Kirsten E. *Israel's Covert Diplomacy in Lebanon.* Basingstoke, UK: Macmillan in assoc. with St. Antony's College, Oxford, 1998.

Shaul, Bakhash. *The Reign of the Ayatollas in Iran and the Islamic Revolution*. New York: Basic Books, 1984.

Shirley, Edward. *Know Thine Enemy*. New York: Farrar, Straus & Giroux, 1997.

Smith, Steven, Ken Booth, and Marysia Zalewski. *International Theory: Positivism and Beyond*. Cambridge: Cambridge University Press, 1996.

Taheri, Amir. *The Spirit of Allah*. London: Hutchinson, 1985.

Tenet, George, and Bill Harlow. *At the Center of the Storm: My Years at the CIA*. New York: HarperCollins, 2007.

Teveth, Shabtai. *Ben-Gurion's Spy. The Story of the Political Scandal That Shaped Modern Israel*. New York: Columbia University Press, 1996.

Theroux, Peter. *The Strange Disappearance of Imam Moussa Sadr*. London: Weidenfeld & Nicolson, 1987.

Transparency International, *Global Corruption Report, 2004*. London: Pluto Press, 2004.

Walsh, Lawrence E. *Firewall: The Iran-Contra Conspiracy and Cover-up*. New York: W.W. Norton, 1997.

Wardlaw, Grant. *Political Terrorism: Theory, Tactics and Counter-Measures*. Cambridge: Cambridge University Press, 1982.

Webman, Esther. *Anti-Semitic Motifs in the Ideology of Hizballah and Hamas*. The Project for the Study of Anti-Semitism. Tel Aviv, Tel Aviv University, 1994.

Weiner, Tim. *Legacy of Ashes: The History of the CIA*. New York: Doubleday, 2007.

Wright, Robin. *Sacred Rage: The Wrath of Militant Islam*. New York: Simon & Schuster, 1986.

Ya'ari, Ehud. *Strike Terror*. New York: Sabra Books, 1970.


## BOOKS IN HEBREW

Amidror, Yaacov. *The Art of Intelligence*. Tel Aviv: Ministry of Defense, 2006.

Amit, Meir. *Head On . . .* Or Yehuda: Hed Arzi, 1999.

Avi-Ran, Reuven. *The Lebanon War—Arab Documents and Sources. The Way to the War for the Peace of Galilee*. Vol. I. Tel Aviv: Ma'arachot, 1978.

———. *Syrian Involvement in Lebanon, 1975–1985*. Tel Aviv: Ministry of Defense, 1986.

Bergman, Ronen. *Authority Given*. Tel Aviv: Miskal-Yedioth Ahronoth, 2002.

———. *The Point of No Return: Israeli Intelligence Against Iran and Hizballah*. Or Yehuda: Kinneret, Zmora-Bitan, 2007.

———, and Gil Meltzer. *The Yom Kippur War—Moment of Truth*. Tel Aviv: Miskal-Yedioth Ahronoth, 2003.

Cohen, Avner. *The Last Taboo*. Or Yehuda: Kineret, Zmora-Bitan, 2005.

Edelist, Ran. *The Man Who Rode the Tiger*. Tel Aviv: Zmora-Bitan, 1995.

———, and Ilan Kfir. *Ron Arad—The Mystery*. Tel Aviv: Miskal-Yedioth Ahronoth, 2000.

Eiran, Ehud. *The Essence of Longing: General Erez Gerstein, and the War in Lebanon*. Tel Aviv: Miskal-Yedioth Ahronoth, 2007.

Elran, Meir, and Shlomo Brom. *The Second Lebanon War: Strategic Dimenions*. Tel Aviv: Miskal-Yedioth Ahronoth, 2007.

Eshed, Haggai. *One Man "Mossad": Reuven Shiloah: Father of Israeli Intelligence*. Tel Aviv: Edanim, 1988.

Farman Farmaian, Sattareh, with Munker Donna, *Daughter of Persia*. Rishon LeZion: Barkai Publishing, 2003.

Feldman, Shai. *Israeli Nuclear Deterrence: A Strategy for the 1980's.* Tel Aviv: Hakibbutz Hameuchad, 1983.

Fulvio, Martini. *Nome in Codice: Ulisse, Trent'anni di Storia Nelle Memorie di un Protagonista dei Servizi Segreti.* Jerusalem: Hed Artzi, 2001.

Gilon, Karmi. *Shin-Beth Between the Schisms.* Tel Aviv: Miskal-Yedioth Ahronoth, 2000.

Grau, Lester W., and Michel A. Gress. *The Soviet Afghan War: How The Superpower Fought and Lost.* Tel Aviv: Ma'arachot, 2005.

Horowitz, Eli. *Hizballah's Military Echelon: A Social Portrait.* Facts and Analysis Series. Tel Aviv: Dayan Center, Tel Aviv University, 1999.

Kam, Ephraim. *From Terror to Nuclear Bombs: The Significance of the Iranian Threat.* Tel Aviv: Ministry of Defense, 2004.

Kimche, David. *The Last Option: After Nasser, Arafat and Saddam Hussein: The Quest for Peace in the Middle East.* Tel Aviv: Edanim, 1992.

Klieman, Aharon. *Double-Edged Sword: Israel Defense Exports as an Instrument of Foreign Policy.* Tel Aviv: Am Oved, 1992.

Kramer, Martin. *Fadlallah: The Compass of Hizbullah.* Tel Aviv: Dayan Center, Tel Aviv University, 1998.

———, ed. *Protest and Revolution in Shi'I Isalm.* Tel Aviv: Dayan Center, Tel Aviv University, 1987.

Kupperman, Robert H., and Darell M. Trent. *Terrorism: Threat, Reality, Response.* Tel Aviv: Ministry of Defense, 1979.

Kurtz, Anat. *Islamic Terrorism and Israel: Hizballah, Palestinian Islamic Jihad and Hamas.* Tel Aviv: Papyrus, Tel Aviv University, 1993.

Lahad, Antoine. *In the Eye of the Storm: Fifty Years of Serving My Homeland Lebanon, an Autobiography.* Tel Aviv: Miskal-Yedioth Ahronoth, 2004.

Lewis, Bernard. *The Crisis of Islam: Holy War and Unholy Terror.* Or Yehuda: Kinnert, Zmora-Bitan, 2006.

Melman, Yossi, and Eitan Haber. *The Spies: Israel's Counter-Espionage Wars.* Tel Aviv; Miskal-Yedioth Ahronoth, 2002.

Melman, Yossi, and Dov Raviv. *The Imperfect Spies.* Tel Aviv: Ma'ariv, 1990.

Menashri, David. *Iran After Khomeini: Revolutionary Ideology versus National Interests.* Tel Aviv: Dayan Center, Tel Aviv University, 1999.

———. *Iran Between Islam and the West.* Tel Aviv: Ministry of Defense, 1996.

Merari, Ariel, and Shlomi Elad. *The International Dimension of Palestinian Terrorism.* Tel Aviv: Hakibbutz Hameuchad, 1986.

Nafisi, Azar. *Reading Lolita in Tehran.* Tel Aviv: Miskal-Yedioth Ahronoth, 2005.

Naveh, Dan. *Executive Secrets.* Tel Aviv: Miskal-Yedioth Ahronoth, 1999.

Perry, Yaakov. *Strike First.* Tel Aviv: Miskal-Yedioth Ahronoth, 1999.

Ram, Haggai. *Reading Iran in Israel: The Self and the Other, Religion, and Modernity.* Jerusalem: Van Leer Institute/Hakibbutz Hameuchad, 2006.

Ronen, Yehudit. *Sudan in a Civil War: Between Africanism, Arabism and Islam.* Tel Aviv: Tel Aviv University, 1995.

Saguy, Uri. *Lights Within the Fog.* Tel Aviv. Miskal-Yedioth Ahronoth, 1998.

Segev, Shmuel. *The Iranian Triangle.* Jerusalem: Domino Press, 1989.

———. *The Iranian Triangle: The Secret Relations Between Israel-Iran-U.S.A.* Tel Aviv: Ma'ariv, 1981.

Shapira, Shimon. *Hizbullah: Between Iran and Lebanon.* Tel Aviv: Hakibbutz Hameuchad, 2000.

Shay, Shaul. *The Axis of Evil: Iran, Hizballah, and Palestinian Terror.* Herzliya: Interdisciplinary Center, 2003.

———. *The Islamic Terror and the Balkans.* Herzliya: Interdisciplinary Center, 2006.

———. *The Never-ending Jihad.* Herzliya: Interdisciplinary Center, 2002.

———. *The Shahids: Islam and Suicide Attacks.* Herzliya: Interdisciplinary Center, 2003.

Shked, Ronni, and Aviva Shabi. *Hamas: Palestinian Islamic Fundamentalist Movement.* Jerusalem: Keter, 1994.

Sivan, Emmanuel. *The Fanatics of Islam.* Tel Aviv: Am Oved, 1986.

Sobelman, Daniel. *New Rules of the Game: Israel and Hizbollah After the Withdrawal from Lebanon.* Memorandum No. 65. Tel Aviv: Institute for National Security Studies (March 2003).

Tal, Nahman. *Confrontation at Home: Egypt and Jordan Against Radical Islam.* Tel Aviv: Papyrus, Tel Aviv University, 1999.

Tamir, Moshe. *Undeclared War.* Tel Aviv: Ministry of Defense, 2006.

Tsafrir, Eliezer (Geizi). *Big Satan, Small Satan: Revolution and Escape in Iran.* Or Yehuda: Ma'ariv, 2002.

———. *Labyrinth in Lebanon.* Tel Aviv: Miskal-Yedioth Ahronoth, 2006.

Weissbrod, Amir. *Turabi, Spokesman for Radical Islam.* Tel Aviv: Dayan Center, Tel Aviv University, 1999.

Wright, Lawrence. *The Looming Tower: Al-Qaeda and the Road to 9/11.* Or Yehuda: Kinnert, Zmora-Bitan, 2007.

## ARTICLES AND PAPERS IN ENGLISH

Abbas, William Sami. "The Shah's Lebanon Policy: The Role of Saval," *Middle Eastern Studies* (1997).

Alimov, Anatoly. "Iran: Are WMD Out of Reach?", *Yaderny Kontrol Digest (Moscow),* vol. 6, no. 2 (Spring 2001).

Amnesty International. "Sudan: Behind the Veil: Human Rights Abuses against Women," *AI Index: AFR* 54/53/94.

"Argentina Accuses Iran for Bombings," *The Iran Brief, Middle East Data Project, Washington, DC* (May 1998 and June 1999).

Avebury, Eric, and Robert Wilkinson. "Iran: State of Terror—An Account of Terrorist Assassination by Iranian Agents," Parliamentary Human Rights Group (London, June 1996).

Ben-Zvi, Abraham. "The Dynamics of Surprise: The Defender's Perspective," *Intelligence and National Security,* vol. 12, no. 4 (London, 1997).

———. "Hindsight and Foresight: A conceptual framework for the analyses of surprise attack," *World Politics,* vol. 28, no. 3 (April 1976).

"Bin Laden's Tripartite Pact," *Jane's Intelligence Review* (November 1998).

Burgin, Maskit, Ariel Merari, and Anat Kurz. "Foreign Hostages in Lebanon," Jaffee Center for Strategic Studies, *Memorandum No. 25* (April 1988).

Deutch, John. "Fighting Foreign Terrorism," Georgetown University, Washington, DC, 1995.

Drozdiak, William. "German Court: Iran Murdered Dissidents in Berlin," *Near East Report* (June 1997).

———. "Tehran Aid Key," *Australia Review,* vol. 22, no. 5 (April 24, 1997).

Dunn, Ross. "Death Turns the Cycle of Violence," *The Age,* Jan. 13, 1996.

Eisenstadt, Michael. "Iranian Military Power: Capabilities and Intentions," *Washington Institute for Near East Studies,* Policy Paper no. 42 (1996).

Emerson, Steve. "Iran and Irrational Rage," *Jerusalem Post,* Jan. 11, 1994.

————. "The Other Fundamentalists," *The New Republic,* Dec. 6, 1995.

Ayatollah Muhammed Hussyin Fadlallah. "Islam in Political Reality," *Middle East Insight* (November 1986).

Feiler, Gil. "The Globalization of Terror Funding," Begin-Sadat Center for Strategic Studies, Ramat Gan (September 2007).

Frisch, Hillel. "Motivation or Capabilities? Israeli Counterterrorism Against Palestinian Suicide Bombings and Violence," Begin-Sadat Center for Strategic Studies, Ramat Gan (December 2006).

Funding for Peace Coalition. "Managing European Taxpayers' Money: Supporting the Palestinian Arabs—A Study in Transparency" (August 2004).

Ganor, Boaz. "Defining Terrorism: Is One Man's Terrorist Another Man's Freedom Fighter?", *ICT Paper,* vol. 4 (August 1998).

"German Court Finds Iran Leaders Directed Assassinations." *International Enforcement Law Reporter* (May 1997).

Grinstein J. "Jihad and the Constitution: The First Amendment Implications of Combating Religiously Motivated Terrorism," *Yale Law Journal,* 105 (March 1996).

Gruenbaum, Ellen. "The Islamic State and Sudanese Women," *Middle East Report* (November–December 1992).

*Impeding Iran's Nuclearization—Deterring European and Japanese Investment: The Iran Foreign Oil Sanctions Act of 1995.* AIPAC, Iran Report No. 3, Nov. 28, 1995.

"International Terrorism: A Debate Between Richard N. Perle and Stansfield Turner," Jan. 21, 1997, School of Public Affairs, University of Maryland, *College Park,* 1997.

"The Iran Issue at The Halifax Summit: An Update on Sanctions Against Iran," *AIPAC, Washington, DC,* June 9, 1995.

"Iran's Phantom Bomb" (Report on Iran's nuclear profile), *The Risk,* vol. 1, no. 7 (September 1995).

Jones, Peter. "Iran's Threat Perceptions and Arms Control Politics," *The Nonproliferation Review* (Fall 1998).

Khashan, Hilal. "Do Lebanese Shi'is Hate the West?", *Orbis (Philadelphia),* vol. 33, no. 2 (Fall 1989), 587.

Kiernan, Sergio. "Still No Justice, Four Years After the AMIA Bombing," American Jewish Committee, *International Perspective,* No. 42 (1998).

Kramer, Martin. "The Moral Logic of Hizballah," *Occasional Papers,* No. 101 (August 1987).

Litvak, Meir. "The Islamization of Palestinian Identity: The Case of Hamas," Dayan Center, Tel Aviv University (1996).

Menashri, David. "Revolution at the Crossroads," Washington Institute for Near East Studies, Policy Paper No. 43 (1997).

————. "The Significance of Iran's Presidential Election," *Tel Aviv notes, an update on political and strategic developments in the Middle East, No. 138* (July 2005).

Michelle-Faraday, Tammy. "Iran: Perpetration of Terrorism Against Dissidents." Thesis submitted for Bachelor of Arts degree, Department of Politics, Monash University (November 1997).

Milward, W. M. "Containing Iran," Commentary, Canadian Security Intelligence Service, No. 63 (April 9, 1995).

Nader, George A. "Interview with President Ali Akbar Hashemi Rafsanjani," *Middle East Insight* (July–August 1995).

Neal, M. "Comprehensive U.S. Sanctions Against Iran: A Plan for Action," *AIPAC*, Washington, DC (1995).

Ottoway, David B. "Sheik with Iranian Ties Is Suspect in Bombings," *The Washington Post*, Oct. 10, 1983.

Ram, Haggay. "Mythology of Rage: Representation of the 'Self' and the 'Other' in Revolutionary Iran," Ben Gurion University of the Negev (1997).

Rubin, Uzi. "The Global Reach of Iran's Ballistic Missiles," Institute for National Security Studies, Tel Aviv (November 2006).

Schweitzer, Yoram, ed. "Female Suicide Bombers: Dying for Equality?", *Jaffee Center for Strategic Studies*, Memorandum No. 84 (August 2006).

Sidahmed, Awatif. "Women Under Sudan's Fundamentalist Regime," *Middle East Institute*, 3 (August 1990).

Sivan, Emmanuel. "The Mythologies of Religious Radicalism: Judaism and Islam," *Terrorism and Political Violence*, vol. III, no. 3 (Autumn 1991).

Venter, Al. "Iran Still Exporting Terrorism to Spread Its Islamic Vision," *Jane's Intelligence Review* (November 1997).

Walsh, James. "Iran's Smoking Gun," *Time* magazine, April 21, 1997.

Wehling, Fred. "Russian Nuclear and Missile Exports to Iran," *The Nonproliferation Review* (Winter 1999).

"Why Germany Has Befriended Iraq," *Foreign Report*, Jane's Information Group (August 1996).

Wolfson, Ze'ev. "Armenian 'Traces' in the Proliferation of Russian Weapons in Iran," Policy Paper No. 143, Ariel Center for Policy Research (December 2002).

Zubaida, Sami. "The Ideological Preconditions for Khomeini's Doctrine of Government," in *Islam, the People and the State. Economy and Society*, vol. 11, no. 2 (1982).

## ARTICLES AND PAPERS IN HEBREW

Arad, Uzi. *Surprise and Deterrence: Reservations About Empirical Research and Its Lessons for Israel.* Internal Paper (March 1999).

Asculai, Ephraim, and Emily B. Landau. "Developments on the North Korean Nuclear Axis: Parallels with Iran?", *Strategic Assessment, Jaffee Center for Strategic Studies*, vol. 9, no. 4 (March 2007).

Berkovich, Dani. "Can the Hydra Be Beheaded? The Campaign to Weaken Hizbollah," Memorandum No. 92, Tel Aviv, Institute for National Security Studies (December 2007).

———. "Doesn't Hizbollah Brake at Red Lights? The Crisis in Lebanon and Its Implications for Israel," *Strategic Assessment, Jaffee Center for Strategic Studies*, vol. 9, no. 4 (March 2007).

Evental, Udi. "The United States and the Challenge of the Iranian Nuclearization: A Choice Between Bad Options," *Strategic Assessment, Jaffee Center for Strategic Studies*, vol. 9, no. 1 (2006).

Feldman, Nizan. "How Powerful Is the Iranian 'Oil Weapon'?," *Strategic Assessment, Jaffee Center for Strategic Studies*, vol. 10, no. 2 (March 2007).

Gazit, Shlomo. "Between Deterrence and Surprise: On the Responsibility for the Formulation of a National Intelligence Estimate in Israel," *Jaffee Center for Strategic Studies*, Memorandum No. 66.

Hacham, David. "And the Land Was Full of Hamas." Lecture at Haifa University, 2006.

Hendel, Yoaz. "IDF Special Units: Their Purpose and Operational Concept," *Strategic Assessment, Jaffee Center for Strategic Studies*, vol. 10, no. 2 (March 2007).

Kam, Ephraim. "Changes in Iran's Strategic Posture," *Strategic Assessment, Jaffee Center for Strategic Studies*, vol. 9, no. 4 (March 2007).

———. "Iran Under Pressure," *Strategic Assessment, Jaffee Center for Strategic Studies*, vol. 6, no. 2 (September 2003).

———. "The Iranian Threat: A Cause for Concern, Not Panic," *Strategic Assessment, Jaffee Center for Strategic Studies*, vol. 1, no. 3 (November 1998).

Landau, Emily B. "Back to the Future on Iran: A Problematic Return to Negotiations," *Strategic Assessment, Jaffee Center for Strategic Studies*, vol. 10, no. 2 (March 2007).

Marcus, Ittamar. *Anti-Semitism in Schoolbooks in Jordan, the Palestinian Authority and Syria. A Comparative Study* (Mabat Lashalom, June 2000).

Moshe, Gilboa. "The Iranian Challenge: Background, Risks and Opportunities," *Nativ*, 2 (March 1998).

Paz, Reuven. "The Radical Islamic Movement's Position on Jews and Zionism in Our Day," in Ilan Pappe, ed., *Islam and Peace: Islamic Attitudes to Peace in the Contemporary Arab World*. Givat Haviva: Peace Research Institute, 1992.

———. *What Is the Islamic Movement?* International Institute for Counter-Terror Policy, Interdisciplinary Center, Herzliya, No. 1 (October 1998).

Rubin, Uzi. *The Iranian Satellite Launching Program and Its Implications. Israel in Space*. Begin-Sadat Center for Strategic Studies, Ramat Gan, National Security Discussions, No. 20 (July 2006).

Shafir, Yiftah. "Iran's Strategic Missiles," *Strategic Assessment, Jaffee Center for Strategic Studies*, vol. 9, no. 1 (March 2006).

Siboni, Gabriel. "Command and Authority in the IDF: The Winograd Challenge," *Strategic Assessment, Jaffee Center for Strategic Studies*, vol. 10, no. 2 (March 2007).

Tal, Nahman. "Israel and Suicide Terrorism," *Strategic Assessment, Jaffee Center for Strategic Studies*, vol. 5, no. 1 (June 2002).

Tira, Ron. "The Limitations of Standoff Firepower-Based Operations: On Standoff Warfare, Maneuvers and Decision," Tel Aviv, Institute for National Security Studies, Memorandum No. 89 (March 2007).

Yisraeli, Rafi. "Arab Islamic Terror Against Israel," *Nativ*, 5 (September 1996).

Ze'evi (Farkash), Aharon. "A Critical Look at Intelligence," *Strategic Assessment, Jaffee Center for Strategic Studies*, vol. 9, no. 4 (March 2007).

# INDEX

# ABOUT THE AUTHOR

RONEN BERGMAN is one of Israel's leading investigative reporters and the recipient of various awards. A former senior staff feature writer for Israel's daily newspaper *Haaretz*, he is currently the security and intelligence reporter and analyst for Israel's largest newspaper, *Yedioth Ahronoth*. He is also an anchor on a leading Israeli television news program, and a frequent guest on high-rating talk shows. He earned his PhD, the first about the Mossad, at Cambridge University, under Professor Christopher Andrew, the official historian of the British security service (MI5). Bergman is a lecturer in various forums worldwide and teaches investigative journalism at the Tel Aviv University. This is his third book.

**DATE DUE**

| | |
|---|---|
| JAN 03 2013 | |
| MAY 15 2013 | |
| JUN 12 2013 | |
| ▼ 0 8 2013 | |
| AUG 0 8 2013 | |
| APR 2 8 2016 | |
| | |
| | |
| | |
| | |
| | |
| | |

GAYLORD      #3523PI      Printed in USA